The Woman Client

The Woman Client

Providing Human Services in a Changing World

Edited by Dianne S. Burden
and Naomi Gottlieb

Tavistock Publications

New York and London

First published in 1987 by
Tavistock Publications
in association with Methuen, Inc.
29 West 35th Street, New York NY 10001

Published in the UK by
Tavistock Publications Ltd
11 New Fetter Lane, London EC4P 4EE

© 1987 Dianne S. Burden and Naomi Gottlieb

Typeset by Boldface Typesetters, London EC1, UK
Printed in the United States of America

Library of Congress Cataloging in Publication Data
The Woman client.
Includes index.
1. Social work with women – United States.
2. Social work with women.   3. Women – Services
for – United States.   I. Burden, Dianne S.
II. Gottlieb, Naomi, 1925 –
HV1445.W64   1986   362.8'353'0973   86-14392
ISBN 0-422-79770-7
ISBN 0-422-79780-4 (pbk.)

British Library Cataloguing in Publication Data
The Woman Client: providing human services
in a changing world.
1. Women – Services for – United States
I. Burden, Dianne S.   II. Gottlieb, Naomi
362.8'3'0973   HV1445
ISBN 0-422-79770-7
ISBN 0-422-79780-4 Pbk

Contents

List of contributors

Sharon Berlin, MSW, PhD, University of Washington, is an associate professor at the University of Chicago School of Social Service Administration. Her primary areas of interest are mental health of women, clinical research, and cognitive-behavioral intervention methods. Dr Berlin has published numerous articles relating to work with women clients. These include: (1984) The Effect of Relapse Prevention on the Durability of Self-Criticism Problem Change. *Social Work Research and Abstracts* 21 (Spring).

L. Diane Bernard, MSW, Tulane, PhD, Bryn Mawr, is the Interim Executive Director of the Council on Social Work Education (1985–86). Her major areas of interest are in administration and in the teaching of human behavior and the social environment, women's studies, and social policy. Dr Bernard is on the editorial board of the *Journal of Women in Social Work*.

Ruth A. Brandwein, MSW, University of Washington, PhD, Brandeis University, is the Dean of the School of Social Welfare at the State University of New York at Stony Brook. Her major areas of interest are family policy, female-headed families, women in administration, and the feminization of poverty. Her recent publications include: (1985) Feminist Thought Structure: An Alternative Paradigm of Social Change for Social Justice. In D. Gil and E. Gil (eds) *Toward Social and Economic Justice*. Waltham, Mass.: Schenkman; and (in press) Women in Macropractice. In *Encyclopedia of Social Work* (18th edn). New York: National Association of Social Work.

Katharine Hooper Briar, MSW, Columbia University, DSW, University of California at Berkeley, is an associate professor at the University of Washington School of Social Work in Seattle. Her current interests are in the areas of work and work problems, unemployment and underemployment, women as caregivers, and occupational social work. Dr Briar's recent publications include: (in press) Unemployment and Underemployment. In *Encyclopedia of Social Work* (18th edn). New York: NASW; (1986) The Anti-Institution Movement and Women Caregivers. *Women and Social Work* 1; (1984) Services to Battered Women. *Journal of Sociology and Social Welfare* 12(3).

Dianne S. Burden, MSW, University of Washington, PhD, Brandeis University, is an assistant professor of social policy and research at the Boston University School of Social Work. Her major areas of interest include work and family interactions, family policy, and single parent families. She is currently conducting two federally funded research projects on the effects of combined work and family stress both at home and at work. Publications include: (1986) Single Parents and the Work Setting: The Impact of Multiple Job and Homelife Responsibilities. *Family Relations* 35(1); and (1984) Teenage Parenthood: Factors Which Lessen Economic Dependence. *Social Work* 29(1): 11–16.

Eileen M. Corrigan, DSW, is a distinguished professor at Rutgers University. Her major area of interest is alcohol studies. Publications include: (1985) Gender Differences in Alcohol and Other Drug Use. *Addictive Behaviors* 10(3); (1985) Professional Roles – Collaboration between Clinicians and Researchers. In *Alcohol Related Health Issues for Women* (Monograph 17). Washington, DC: National Institute on Alcohol Abuse and Alcoholism; and, with Sandra C. Anderson (1985) Graduate Social Work Education in Alcohol Studies. In E. Freeman (ed.) *Social Work Practice with Clients Who Have Alcohol-Related Problems*. Springfield, Ill.: Charles C. Thomas.

Diane de Anda, MSW, PhD, is an associate professor at the University of California at Los Angeles School of Social Welfare. Her areas of particular interest are adolescent females, pregnant adolescents and adolescent mothers (especially Latino adolescents), and bicultural socialization. Recent publications include: (1984, with Rosina Becerra) Support Networks of Hispanic and White Adolescent Mothers. *Social Casework* 65(3); (1984, also with Rosina Becerra) Pregnancy and Motherhood among Mexican-American Adolescents. *Health and Social Work* 9(2); and (1984) Bicultural Socialization: Factors Affecting the Minority Experience. *Social Work* 29(2).

Addei Fuller, BA in sociology and social work, is the Manager of Direct Services at Seattle Rape Relief, Seattle, Washington. She has had extensive experience in work with women clients in the areas of sexual assault and domestic violence.

Naomi Gottlieb, MSW, DSW, is a professor of social work and Coordinator of the Concentration on Women at the University of Washington School of Social Work. Her current research interests are in the areas of work discontinuities in women's lives, feminist research, and the blossoming of the older woman. Recent publications include: (1985) Distinctive Attributes of Feminist Groups.

Social Work with Groups 6(3/4); (1982) Mental Health Services for Women. In M. Austin and W. Hershey (eds) *Handbook of Mental Health Administration*; and (1980) *Alternative Social Services for Women*. New York: Columbia University Press.

Marie D. Hoff, MSW, MPA, is a PhD candidate at the University of Washington School of Social Work in Seattle. Her doctoral dissertation is an investigation of values and leadership as foundations for social change. It is based on an assessment of the response to the American Catholic Bishops' recent statement on the ethical implications of the US economy.

Nancy R. Hooyman, MSW, PhD, is an associate dean of the University of Washington School of Social Work in Seattle. She is also an associate professor and Coordinator of the Concentration on Aging. Her areas of special interest are family caregivers of the elderly, older women, elderly abuse, and feminist practice models. Recent publications include: with W.Lustbader (1986) *Taking Care: Supporting Older People and Their Families*. New York: Free Press; with M. Bricker-Jenkins (1985) *Not for Women Only: Models of Feminist Practice*. New York: NASW; and (1985) The Impact of In-Home Service Termination on Family Caregivers. *The Gerontologist*, February.

Ginny NiCarthy, MSW, is a counselor and trainer at the Women's Counseling Group in Seattle, Washington. Ms NiCarthy is a renowned expert in work with abused women. She is a founding member of the International Network against Violence against Women (established in Nairobi, Kenya in 1985). She is the author of *Talking It Out: A Guide to Groups for Abused Women*. Her work in progress is entitled *The Ones Who Got Away: Stories of Women Who Left Abusive Men*.

Cheryl A. Richey, MSW, DSW, is an associate professor at the University of Washington School of Social Work in Seattle. Her current areas of work include women and mental health, interpersonal skill training, social support networks, and evaluation of clinical practice. Recent publications, both with E. Gambrill, are: (1983) Leader Issues Related to Group Social Skills Training. *Social Work with Groups* 6(3/4); (in press) Criteria Used to Define and Evaluate Socially Competent Behavior Among Women. *Psychology of Women Quarterly*; and (1985) *Taking Charge of your Social Life*. Belmont, CA: Wadsworth. Dr Richey is also the co-author with R. Levy of (in press) Measurement and Design Issues in Behavioral Medicine with Women. In E. Blechman and K. Brownell (eds) *Behavioral Medicine for Women*. New York: Pergamon Press.

Rosemary C. Sarri, MSW, PhD, is a professor of social work and faculty associate at the University of Michigan Institute of Social Research in Ann Arbor. She has done extensive work in juvenile and adult criminal justice, social policy and change, and gender and organizations, with particular concern about the relative ineffectiveness of service delivery for women. Dr Sarri has recently completed a cross-national comparative study of women, welfare, and the state. Publications include: (1984) Turning the Clock Back on Public Welfare. *Signs* 10(2); (1985) Federal Policy Change and the Feminization of Poverty. *Child Welfare* 64(3); and (1985) Juvenile Justice as Child Welfare. In J. Laird and A. Hartman (eds) *Handbook of Child Welfare*. New York: Free Press.

Essie Tramel Seck, MSW, PhD, University of Southern California, is a senior research associate at the Center for Health and Social Services Research, Pasadena, CA. Her areas of current interest include full employment and the quality of life; strategies for social work political intervention; minority youth unemployment; and work opportunities for older Americans. Publications include: (1986) *The Excluded Child: A Case for Child Advocacy*. Washington, DC: US Government Printing Office; and (1983) *The Magic Circle of Seniors and Kids: Enriching Pre-School Programs and Maximizing Resources*. Los Angeles: Andrus Gerontology Center, University of Southern California.

Nan Stoops, BA, is a legal coordinator and activist in the Battered Women's Movement in Seattle, Washington. She is a former counselor and administrator of the Shelter for Battered Women and Their Children in Seattle and former chair of the Women of Color Committee, Washington State Shelter Network.

Marie Weil, MSW, University of Pennsylvania, DSW, Hunter College, is an associate professor at the University of Southern California School of Social Work in Los Angeles. Her areas of current interest include services for families and children, connections between social work and the law, and services for vulnerable and refugee populations. She is currently teaching in the areas of community organization, administration, and family policy. Publications include: (1985) *Case Management in Human Service Practice*. San Francisco: Jossey-Bass; (1986) Women, Community and Organizing. In N. Van Den Berg and L. Cooper (eds) *Feminist Visions in Social Work Practice*. New York: NASW; and (1983) Preparing Women for Administration: A Self-Directed Learning Model. *Administration in Social Work* 7(3/4).

Ruth E. Zambrana, MSW, PhD, is an assistant professor at the University of California at Los Angeles School of Social Welfare. She is particularly interested in women and health; prenatal care use among low income racial/ethnic women; and racial/ethnic women and higher education. Dr Zambrana's publications include: (1985, with Rosina Becerra) Approaches to Latino Research: Methodological Considerations. *Social Work Research and Abstracts* 21(2); and (1982) *Work, Family and Health: Latino Women in Transition*. (Monograph no. 7) New York: Fordham University, Hispanic Research Center.

The Woman Client

1 Introduction

Dianne S. Burden and Naomi Gottlieb

Rationale and purpose

The social world of women has changed, and continues to change, and developments in empirical knowledge have reflected those changes. We believe the education of social workers and other mental health professionals needs to be grounded in this new knowledge. The first two phenomena – the dramatic shifts in women's personal and public lives, and the accompanying empirical findings about contemporary women – call for revisions and additions, based on empirical grounding, in how practitioners are trained to offer personal services to women. The book's major purpose is to present that grounding for review by educators.

Social changes in women's lives are everywhere apparent. Women have entered the workforce in unprecedented numbers. Laws and class-action suits challenge sex discrimination in the marketplace. Women are marrying later and having fewer children. The traditional family, i.e. the original couple and the wife at home with children, is in the minority. Demographic changes and greater longevity mean that women's caregiving responsibilities extend across several generations. Problems that had been defined only in individual terms – rape, domestic violence – or had no names previously – the displaced homemaker – are now recognized bases for community efforts and social study. Economics, personal and forced choices, demographics, politics, and social activism have each contributed to different circumstances and changing definitions of women's problems.

The scholarly work of social scientists has paralleled these developments. The value stance of these scholars has been that the maldistribution of power along gender lines, rigidly stereotyped sex roles and individual rather than social definitions of problems have been harmful to women. They also confirm the long-accepted stance that no social science is value-free and that much of the knowledge that has been used as a foundation for mental health and social services for women has been derived from a base of traditional values. The major difference between the traditional and newer social sciences is not the absence of values in either but the explicitness of the value stance of the non-sexist and feminist social scientists. Within this current framework, a considerable literature has accumulated based on carefully conducted studies about the condition of women.

That empirical literature comprises both the substance and justification of this book. We believe that the education of social workers and other mental health professionals is inadequate and not up-to-date unless recent grounded knowledge about women is considered by the educator. One may disagree with the value stance or the research findings but to ignore either is to fail to acknowledge major social changes and important intellectual developments.

The value stances of the contributors to the volume are congruent with those of the social scientists whose scholarly work forms the basis of this book's content. The writers represented here would all subscribe to the basic challenges to a traditional view of women, though they reflect a range of feminist viewpoints. As Maracek and Kravetz (1977) suggest, one's place on the continuum from a non-sexist perspective to a feminist one may be determined by the extent to which one subscribes to a sociopolitical analysis. The degree of adherence to that viewpoint may well vary among this book's authors. Although recognizing institutionalized sexism, the harms of power imbalance, and the different worlds of men and women, the contributors may still make varying interpretations of the consequences of these phenomena and propose varying solutions. This is an appropriate reflection of contemporary feminism.

Sexism in social work

One of the primary issues to be addressed in the book is sexism in social work. Since social work practice at its best is a process of client empowerment, attitudes towards women clients which prevent empowerment are particularly important to observe. Attitudes which stereotype women according to traditional sex-role biases are likely to maintain them in their dependent patient/client role and prevent them from achieving independent power.

Sexism is a non-functional system of sex-role stereotyping which tends to devalue and discriminate against women. It is not something that is done *to* women *by* men, but rather is a system which affects both men and women and is present everywhere – in the language, the media, the education system, the literature. Sexism is part of a cultural value system which perceives men as more valuable than women. Men's work is considered more important, and they are paid more than women for comparable jobs. Women in turn are socialized to be nurturing and supportive and to gain their primary sense of identity through men. The result leaves women financially and emotionally dependent and frequently leads to depression. Such dependency also leaves a woman vulnerable to poverty should she lose the man and to violence if she cannot afford to leave. The expectation of many women that they will be cared for all their lives by men simply does not fit with the reality of the last twenty-five years. Women are increasingly alone, whether before, between, or after marriage. As the population ages, declining sex ratios result in few men for the available women. The societal assumption that women should be provided for by men may no longer be a viable one.

Social work as part of society is just as likely to be affected by sexist attitudes and assumptions as the rest of the culture. If social work is to serve its clients adequately, it must focus on the sexism existing in the profession and endeavor to adopt non-sexist approaches to social work practice.

Sexism can be viewed as an important factor in social work from six different perspectives.

The effects of sexism on the lives of clients

Social work practitioners need to have sound knowledge about the multiple effects of sexism on the lives of clients. For example, evidence suggests that extreme socialization into traditional female roles leaves a woman at risk of learned helplessness and resultant depression. Sex-role socialization also has important consequences for clients' interpersonal relationships as well as for their intrapsychic dynamics. Relationships may be dysfunctional because of unrealistic expectations about male and female roles or because of extreme dependency which skews the power differential toward the male partner. Women may react to their powerlessness by inappropriate anger or with depressive symptomatology. Although women provide the nurturing in the family, they may be in dire need of nurturing themselves. They may fill the gap caused by insufficient nurturing by over-eating or by alcohol and drug abuse or by physical abuse of their children.

Women clients are also faced with serious environmental barriers due to sex-role socialization and outright sex discrimination. Low-paid, dead-end jobs, lack of child care, inadequate income maintenance, sex segregation in the labor force, and inequitable responsibility for combined job, homemaking, and child-rearing exert inordinate societal stress on women. Real life stress combined with the learned helplessness of sex-role socialization and media pressure to stay young and beautiful are vital elements in the lives of women clients that must be focused on clearly by social work practitioners.

Effects of sexism on the lives of practitioners

Practitioners, both male and female, are affected by the same issues of sex-role socialization and sex discrimination as clients. Practitioners need to examine their own situation and attitudes. Otherwise, their assumptions about appropriate sex-role behavior may be a serious barrier to providing empowering services to women clients. As the study of Broverman and colleagues pointed out some years ago (1972), both male and female therapists have sex-role stereotyped attitudes towards clients which tend to place women clients in an impossible double bind. Therapists view the attributes of healthy males and healthy adults as identical, while attributes of healthy females and healthy adults appear to be mutually exclusive. The view that women must somehow choose between being a healthy female and a healthy adult may reflect early culture-bound Freudian theory which has provided the traditional basis for much of social work education. Such views of female development must be re-examined if practitioners are to provide non-sexist social work intervention.

The effects of sexism on the lives of practitioners may become particularly important in the area of co-therapy. Male/female co-therapists can ideally provide an important opportunity for modeling functional interpersonal skills. However, they can also merely reinforce dysfunctional traditional sex-roles where the therapists themselves revert to those roles. Since males tend to be senior to females in social service agencies, the male may take on the dominant role in co-therapy, and the female, wanting to avoid conflict, may defer to him. This power imbalance may be especially evident where the male is the field instructor and the female the student. Similarly the sex of the client versus the sex of the therapist is an issue of particular importance to female clients. There may simply be times when the inherent power differential between males and females makes a male therapist antithetical to the progress of a female client.

The role of sexism in group dynamics
When people find themselves in stressful situations they tend to revert to familiar sex-role behaviors. This pattern needs to be clearly addressed as an element in group dynamics. When men and women are in groups together, whether a therapy group, a classroom situation, or a staff meeting, men tend to dominate and women tend to defer to them. Some studies suggest that group leaders (whether teachers or therapists) differentially perceive the participation of males and females and tend to reinforce male participation, but extinguish female participation. Men may be perceived as forceful when they are assertive, women may be perceived as 'strident.' Such dynamics are serious barriers to the empowerment of both women clients and staff and need to be addressed openly in non-sexist social work practice.

Organizational sexism
A key question in social work practice is whether a therapist in an agency can practice effective non-sexist counseling when the agency itself operates on a sexist model. What is the message to clients when the clerical and direct service staff are primarily female and the administrators and director primarily male?

While two-thirds of clients and direct practitioners are female, 70 per cent of administrators are male and only 30 per cent female. Even though social work is viewed as a women's profession, men are both paid more and have disproportionate power within the profession. The power differential in social work education is even more extreme where men predominate in senior tenured faculty and dean positions, while women are clustered into non-tenure track and junior faculty positions. What message does this polarization give to the 85 per cent of social work students who are now women? Barriers to women moving into management positions and to women advancing in the administrative hierarchy must receive serious attention in social work education.

Sexism as it relates to the mental health of men and women
Differential patterns of mental illness for men and women indicate that sex-role socialization plays an important part in determining appropriate behaviors for displaying emotional distress. While women are socialized to be helpless, passive, and depressed, men are socialized to be aggressive, violent, and to pursue and attack women. As a result women are seen more frequently for depression and anxiety-related problems at outpatient mental health centers. Women are far more likely than men to be sedated and medicated. The role of over-medication in maintaining women in passive, dependent positions is an area which requires exploration. Men, on the other hand, exhibit distress through the violent behavior of the extreme male sex role. They are consequently more likely to be channeled into the correctional system. Men are far more likely than women to be housed in state prisons and county jails. Acting out of extreme sex-role behaviors is closely linked with incidence of domestic violence. Although sexism could be viewed as a functional system which maintains women in a subordinate role, provides a low-paid labor pool, and preserves power for men in the culture, it can also be viewed as an extremely dysfunctional system in the negative impact it has on the mental health of both men and women.

Sexism as a political system
The final level where the impact of sexism becomes important for social work practice is the political system which provides the context in which clients lead their lives. Political awareness is important not only for social work's historic focus on social action, but for working with clients on an individual and group basis as well. Clients such as single parents may tend to internalize their problems and assume that they are having difficulty coping because they are inadequate or because they are 'crazy.' Developing an awareness about the political situation of women in the society becomes an important element of the empowerment process for women clients. Women clients need to be able to assess clearly the sources of their distress, whether internal or external, in order to develop effective strategies for dealing with their situation.

With the feminization of poverty in the last twenty-five years, inadequate income maintenance and support services are primarily issues for women and children. Single-parent families and older women, particularly if they are women of color, are at high risk for poverty. Child care is a woman's issue which has received little serious attention in our society. While the majority of women parents are now contributing large portions of the family income, they are also still expected to care for children for free. The result has been a growing pool of inadequately supervised latch-key children as child care is either not available or too expensive. The result has also been extreme stress for employed women parents as they try to balance their multiple roles with little assistance from the public or private sector. Historically child care has received federal assistance for one of two reasons: (a) during times of national crisis (i.e. in the Second World War to enable women to work in defense plants, or in the Depression of the 1930s to create jobs), or (b) to socialize minority groups into the majority culture (i.e. the Headstart program). Social work education must provide a clear focus on the impact that sexism in the political system has on the lives of individual clients. That knowledge is vital before clients can learn to manipulate that system to their greatest advantage.

In summary, the impact of sexism, through sex-role socialization, sex-role stereotyping, and sex discrimination, can be felt at all levels of social work. It is so pervasive that if special attention is not given in a curriculum, sexism runs the risk of disappearing into the background assumptions of everyone's lives. Effective social work practice requires the empowerment of clients to lead independent, productive, emotionally satisfying lives. For women clients in particular, this goal cannot be achieved without a purposeful, non-sexist approach to service provision in both direct and indirect services.

Format

The book's primary purpose, as stated, is to provide grounded content on women to inform the education of social workers and other mental health professionals. The subsidiary purpose is to suggest ways in which that content can be incorporated into curriculum sequences, and that secondary goal is sought in three ways.

First, the chronology and clusters of chapters are intended to parallel the major configurations in social work education. Core content mandated for all social work programs – social policy, social research, and human behavior in the social environment (general knowledge development in a social context) – is dealt with in the beginning chapters. The following section focuses on the specialized interventions of direct and indirect services, i.e. personal social services to individuals, families, and groups, as well as social welfare administration and community services. The theme of each of these sections is that all required content should incorporate gender variables and new grounded knowledge about women. The third cluster addresses specific population or problem areas which may appear as discrete courses or course components. Though clearly not an exhaustive list of subject areas in which gender is relevant, the eight fields represent either specialized subjects commonly represented in social work curricula or comprise suggestions of neglected areas. Any one of the total complement of chapters can be immediately applicable to some aspect of contemporary social work education.

The second aspect of the utility of the book's content and format extends beyond the social work classroom instructor. Although framed in the context of social work classroom courses, the content can easily be adapted to both the practicum component of social work education and to the class and internship settings in other disciplines, e.g. psychology, counseling, public policy. Discrete chapters are of interest to many other educators concerned with direct services or policy-planning for women. For example, sections on basic counseling skills, on domestic violence, or on the older woman are applicable to the work of other human service professionals. The grounded content is generic and usable in many contexts.

Third, we intend that the book's utility will be enhanced by the inclusion in most chapters of curriculum suggestions. These range from specific educational strategies and learning exercises to questions as to where to place specific content in the curriculum. Instructors make their own individual decisions about overall course construction, but we hope that the suggestions incorporated here in relation to gender-relevant content can usefully inform those decisions.

Finally, another format decision reflects an additional educational aim. Each of the chapters includes reference to distinctive issues for women of color and lesbians. The book's concern for the condition of women is not restricted to white, heterosexual women, and attention to all women makes clear that ethnicity and homosexual orientation can create special sets of issues. Considerations of ethnicity and sexual orientation are included throughout because we believe they are both integrated aspects of the knowledge base and because services to those women must address their particular concerns.

Summary

The book's rationale comes from the recognition of new knowledge about women's changing world and about sexism and sex discrimination. Empirical evidence about these factors and about the distinctive problems experienced by women clients needs to be part of the knowledge base of those being educated to serve women. It is hoped that the book's content will provide grounding for a changed, more empowering professional practice with women.

References

Broverman, I., Vogel, S., Broverman, D., Clarkson, F., and Rosenkrantz, P. (1972) Sex-role Stereotypes: A Current Appraisal. *Journal of Social Issues* 28(2): 59–78.
Maracek, J. and Kravetz, D. (1977) Women and Mental Health: A Review of Feminist Change Efforts. *Psychiatry* 40(4): 323–29.

PART I
The core curriculum

2 Overview

Naomi Gottlieb

All social work programs require content in the subject areas covered in this section: social welfare policy, human behavior in the social environment, and social research. The authors of these chapters argue that there are important gender issues to be addressed in each content area. The corollary argument is that the current basic curriculum needs to be altered if social workers are to be educated adequately to serve women clients. This content is not restricted to social work education alone. Other mental health professionals and women's studies scholars will find material presented in this section to be useful to their fields. Topics particularly relevant across disciplines include such information as gender issues in research design, the rationale used in policy development affecting women, and gender bias in theories of human development.

The section begins with a discussion of personal and institutional barriers to the incorporation in academia of gender-fair content on women. The context is social work education but the themes are applicable across disciplines. Diane Bernard and Naomi Gottlieb maintain that recognition and transcendance of these barriers are necessary before the content reflected in the remainder of the book can be utilized by educators.

In addressing social policy issues, Dianne Burden considers the values and belief systems inherent in past and present policies which have shaped our present social programs affecting women. She then applies this framework to four critical aspects of women's lives – their economic status, their work, their caregiving responsibilities, and their health. Burden's analysis of policy development includes the impact of the judicial system, an area often neglected in social policy content. Her discussions document the impact on women, particularly women of color and those in poverty, of society's gender-biased beliefs about women. This is important information both for future practitioners who will be working within the programs established by these policies and for social activists who will be trying to change the policies.

In the chapter on the knowledge base of practice, Dianne Burden and Naomi Gottlieb use the theme expounded by many in the women's movement that the 'personal is political' to make the point that theories of human development reflect the power differential between men and women but do not explicate that connection. Recognizing both internal and external factors leading to women's inequitable circumstances, their analysis screens several prominent theoretical orientations used as a basis for the treatment of women for the theories' undue emphasis on individual rather than social causation and their tendency to 'blame the woman.' Examples of restructuring of some theories are used to bolster the assertion that all theories of human development should be evaluated for their attention to the inequitable power position of women.

Power and politics are also evident in Naomi Gottlieb's chapter on research and women. Addressing the sociology of knowledge, she reflects on the political purposes of research and the role of power inequities between researcher and the researched. The focus of the chapter is not just one of reacting to the negatives of traditional gender-biased research. The intellectual debate among feminist researchers about the nature of research useful to women and the cautions expressed by many researchers about excessive measures reactive to traditional research, are both recognized for their value in fostering a vigorous and valid feminist research enterprise. The way knowledge about women is constructed is crucial to the manner in which services are provided to them. The education of future practitioners to be critical of the value base of empirical research procedures will enable practitioners to increase the scope and validity of their knowledge about women.

Since all students must study the general content areas covered in this section on the core curriculum, attention to the gender dynamic evident in these areas would go far toward moving the education of practitioners toward a more gender-sensitive approach.

3 Conditions for non-sexist education

L. Diane Bernard and Naomi Gottlieb

We believe that there are considerable barriers – both personal and institutional – which impede progress toward a non-sexist education. They have not been made explicit before, and they require discussion in an atmosphere that does not personalize issues nor place educators in a defensive posture. The recognition of those barriers may increase the utility of the content of the remaining chapters.

We first consider the special quality of the content of inequities based on sex. That content is complex, value- and emotion-laden, and its characteristics must be taken into account if it is to be considered seriously. Attention is then given to a set of barriers, both institutional and personal, which can form understandable resistance to curriculum change. We then look at conditions that may be necessary for individual educators to consider curriculum change: either because they have become convinced from personal experience about the need to do so or because they realize that change is necessary for their own self-interest. Surfacing these issues about the content, about barriers, and about conditions necessary for action is the main intent of this chapter.

We define non-sexist practice as the delivery of social services which do not reinforce stereotypes about women or men, and which recognize the power differentials between them. Non-sexist services for women specifically recognize that the range of problems women experience – interpersonal or family difficulties, poverty, depression – are rooted in and considerably influenced by societal expectations for women's behavior and in societal restrictions on their life possibilities. Non-sexist services recognize these roots (modified by individual determinants) and attempt to counteract them.

At the moment, there is a somewhat anomalous situation in social work education on the issue of non-sexist curricula. Since 1977, there has been a standard in effect (1234b) which requires that social work programs attend to inequities in areas of the status of women faculty and students, and in curriculum content on women. There is a growing body of literature on the condition of women and their distinctive social service needs (Brooks 1981; Gornick and Moran 1971; Gottlieb 1980; Hidalgo, Peterson, and Woodman 1985; Lopata 1973; Lowenstein 1983; Markson 1983; Norman and Mancuso 1980; Sedel 1978). There are important societal changes in family roles (Giele 1978; Lengermann and Wallace 1985; Rossi 1985; Sargent 1984; Skolnick and Skolnick 1983), in labor force participation of women (Foner 1980; Fox and Biber 1984; Lloyd and Niemi 1979; US Bureau of Census 1981), and in women's legal status (Kay 1983; Sachs and Wilson 1978; Thomas 1982). Recently developed programs have redefined social problems and have implemented new social work approaches in such areas as rape, sexual harassment, domestic abuse, and the displaced homemaker phenomenon. Yet these changing social conditions in the lives of women and in social work practice have had comparatively little effect on the way social work students are educated. Many programs are without specialized courses on women or leave such courses clearly out of the mainstream of the curriculum. Few, if any, programs have incorporated a general non-sexist perspective throughout the curriculum that challenges traditional sex roles.

In an important way central to the rationale of this chapter, the response to this content is clearly understandable. In comparison with other special population issues which social work education must address – ethnic minorities, disabled persons, sexual minorities – the issues of equity for women and of non-stereotyped social work practice affect almost everyone personally. We live in a society in which gender differences mark child-rearing more directly than other distinctions and in which sex-role determinants permeate adult relationships and social institutions. The expectation that social work educators view women's needs as distinctive from those of men or explore the effects of discrimination against women requires that both women and men educators question attitudes and behaviors of the most profound nature. Unquestionably there are individual barriers to doing so. This chapter attempts to give consideration to those barriers, and to suggest, nonetheless, that there may be ways for faculty to be open to both new content and a new perspective on this issue. Though the focus here is on content on women, it is hoped that the analysis offered will be useful in other arenas in which barriers exist, such as the special populations cited above.

The assumptions that underlie this discussion pertain to both the phenomenon of sexism and current needs in social work education. Sexism is defined here as the consequences of the sexual distinctions made throughout our society which are not inherently defined by gender and which tend to discriminate against women, and in which the power differential favors men. These distinctions result in stereotyped family roles, socially expected personal characteristics, as well as a series of sex-segregated phenomena – occupations, salary scales, and power positions in society – all of which devalue and restrict women.

Associated assumptions are that the problems which women present to social workers are clearly affected by their position in a society which stereotypes women to their detriment. The further assumption is that social work education must address the pervasiveness of sexism if services are to be responsive to women's needs and not constitute yet another example of society's stance. Finally, for the purposes here, the assumption is made that until some of the personal and institutional impediments to an open discussion of the issues are addressed, potentially useful curriculum models (Kravetz 1982; Lowenstein 1976) may not receive the attention they deserve and may stand little chance of implementation.

There is need for both dialogue and action. It is hoped tha the ideas presented here – and the further discussion they may stimulate – will enable social work and other human service educators to consider these issues with somewhat less of a sense of either guilt or ineffectiveness or annoyance. With some of the personal restrictions abated, it may then be possible to consider action alternatives.

Special quality of content

In several ways, challenges to sexism and attention to the distinctive needs of women provoke personal discomfort and intellectual argument, first because of the emotional and universal character of culture-bound sex differences, and then because the issues are complicated and sometimes paradoxical.

Academicians and other well-educated individuals take a certain pride in their ability to think clearly and dispassionately in most areas. It is awkward at best and disabling at worst to find oneself emotionally vulnerable and defensive with regard to such a pervasive and central concern as the differential treatment of men and women.

In the same way that it is impossible to be simultaneously of the human condition and independent of it, so it is with one's sexual identification. The same general inability to achieve perspective or distance in the social sciences plagues us specifically in relation to being objective about sexism. From the beginning of our entrance into life we are encased within a sexual identity which has been nurtured and developed in terms of particular characteristics even in anticipation of our individual birth. The prescriptions for femaleness and maleness are wholly culture-bound and while socialization provides for some differences from one culture to another, the roles, behaviors, expectations, and personality traits appropriate to each gender are prescribed by the society into which one is born.

All other special populations of interest to social work educators and practitioners, as well as to those concerned with human rights in a pluralistic society, can be perceived as essentially outside of 'self' in the sense of particular ethnic, religious, age, condition, or other qualifying characteristics which contribute to one's particular identification. While these features are not necessarily mutually exclusive (one may belong to more than one special population) and while everyone does not experience all of these differences, some being transitory, the one permanent difference experienced by all members of society relates to one's gender. It is therefore impossible to view women in any meaningful sense as a 'special' population. With the exception of child-bearing, the physical, social, and psychological traits associated with females and males are subject to cultural definition and are intrinsically bound to each other and the very fabric of a given social order. Sex differences, in short, affect everyone.

Because both men and women are profoundly and universally affected by a societal process which prescribes roles and behaviors based on gender, it is impossible either to place oneself apart or to be objective about sex-role content. This lack of objectivity is a difficult circumstance for academicians to face. An illustration of such emotional impact is the reaction to terms used to describe the situation of women in society. For example, the term 'patriarchal' appropriately defines a society in which power is largely invested in men. Many social science academicians, both women and men, quite accustomed to political explanations of societal positions, will be relatively unable to react to that definition dispassionately because their roles in such a society are deeply ingrained and so often less available for intellectual examination without the interference of personal interest.

Beyond these issues of universality and emotionality, paradoxes and complexities are also evident. A few examples will illustrate this.

Dependency

Individuals and groups with societal permission to occupy a dependent position can be viewed as fortunate and are, to some extent, envied. The pampered, indulged, contented 'little woman' is provided for by the benevolent caretaker and is protected from the demands and pressures of the world. The perception of the 'happy housewife' (or the advantages extolled for any protected group) frequently confuse the issue to the extent that protective behavior is glorified as gallant, responsible, and essentially virtuous. It is then difficult for all concerned to understand these arrangements as a cultural mandate rather than personal choice, to view the state of protection as oppression rather than as caring, or to see cloaking from responsibility as exclusion from autonomous behavior. As long as one person's protection is another person's privilege, consensus for change is difficult to achieve.

A further dimension may preclude both women and men from seeing clearly the negative consequences of these societal mandates. Where one has 'played by the rules' all through one's life, conformed to expectations, and modeled one's behavior in accord with society's prescriptions, irate cries that one has done it all wrong understandably do not sit well and, in fact, can block all possibility of re-examination of the issues. No individual, either the one assuming major responsibilities or the one in the role of the dependent adult, wants to hear that a socially approved way of life (of *all* one's life) has had harmful effects (Decter 1972; Lerner 1977).

Paradoxical results of female emancipation

Change in the direction of a non-sexist society can appear to make no difference or even to generate more negative results. As women move into certain positions within the hierarchy or into careers previously not open to them, the status, recognition, and financial rewards of these positions can actually decline in value because of women's presence. For example, when women moved into secretarial positions in the nineteenth and early twentieth centuries, those previously well-paid and high-status positions occupied by men on their way up became poorly paid and have remained dead-end occupations for women (Barker and Allen 1976; Epstein 1970).

The inverse relationship which occurs between role and status is highlighted by the current arbitrary and prejudicial reaction to participation in 'role reversal' responsibilities. As men become more involved in child care they receive the approbation and support of society, while women as single-parent heads of households suffer social stigma and inadequate remuneration. The life events creating the need for such cross-over of roles may affect men and women similarly but the differential responses of society reflect and reinforce the power of gender over circumstance. Participation and/or involvement by men automatically confers status while the reverse occurs when the activities become associated with women.

A more serious consideration is raised if one believes that human equality is truly a myth, an unattainable goal, and that the long-range results of any change in the social order – between females and males, blacks and whites – will only lead to a change in actors. The oppressed then become the oppressors. Keeping the upper hand then becomes more than a device for maintaining stability; it becomes the rationale for survival.

Social consensus/conformity

All of us participate in maintaining the social order by pretending that the myths are reality (Janeway 1971). Lifting the veil, revealing the facts, raising the questions, spilling the beans are considered impolite, hostile, or destructive. We are raised to save face, to maintain appearances, and to give lip-service to those social values which are to some extent believed in but never achieved. Individuals handle discrepancies when they cannot be denied as exceptions to the rule. This reaction works better and is more acceptable than challenging the rule and undermining the social structure.

One unfortunate consequence of supporting myths by maintaining the status quo and treating difference as deviance is that we engage in 'blaming the victim' explanations. Women are underpaid in the labor market because they are willing to work for less; women are sexually harassed because they trade sexual favors for advancement; women are emotional and ambivalent, making them erratic and undependable.

If one sees clearly the actual effects of sexism, one must acknowledge that society does not work for all its members. For many, maintaining society as it is becomes the highest priority. The irony is that though social work practitioners and educators deal with social problems every day, many need to believe that, essentially, society works.

Gender content does indeed have special qualities, with implications of profound change for everyone, and with a convoluted route to desired goals. The content does not make for easy, intellectual consideration.

Barriers to openness to a non-sexist perspective

As we have suggested, the issues associated with sexism are extremely complex, culturally embedded, in large measure paradoxical, and potentially disruptive of the social structure. Avoidance of the issues of sexism takes many forms but for the purpose of this chapter we will identify some possible barriers to inclusion of non-sexist content, seen first from an institutional and then from a personal perspective.

Institutional barriers

The institutional barriers we discuss range from the dilemmas of a value stance, to views about the urgent problems of the day, to the demands of the curriculum.

Within the ethics of both academic freedom and participatory democracy there is considerable reluctance to impose points of view. The dilemmas presented by the issues of sexism may be left unexplored in order to circumvent the greater paradox of maintaining a value-neutral stance within a value-laden profession. We only seem willing to take a clear stance and identify a social work position when consensus has been reached within the profession, as on racism. No such professional agreement has been acknowledged with respect to sexism.

Another argument is that the 'big,' 'real' problems facing social work – poverty, crime, health care – are both more important than and unrelated to non-sexist practice or women's distinctive needs. While the unequal status of males and females may be recognized as fundamental to society's differential treatment of individuals and groups, the issue is either avoided or treated as inconsequential. The negative effects of sexist inequities are neither perceived nor presented as significantly related to the pressing problems confronting social work and can therefore be reasonably ignored. Social policy courses, for example, can treat the issue of the Aid to Families with Dependent Children (AFDC) population as if that population does not consist almost wholly of women, socialized for dependence and trapped within low-paying jobs. Ignoring that connection, women's needs and a non-sexist perspective can readily be seen as unrelated to the consequential problem of public welfare.

A further barrier to a non-sexist perspective relates to the demands of the curriculum. There is constant pressure to include new content as the professional base expands. This pressure creates several kinds of problems directly related to the sexism issue and the curriculum. First, there is the question of whether this new knowledge concerning women and sexist inequities warrants definition as important, specialized content. Content identified as specialized receives attention in proportion to social visibility; affected individuals or groups need to be viewed as clearly disadvantaged by social conditions beyond their control. In this scheme, sexism claims limited priority. There is public, if not professional, disagreement about the extent to which conditions are truly negative; whether one role *is* actually advantaged over the other; and whether the problems are the result of the social structure or personal failure. If there is no clear indication that significant numbers are seriously disadvantaged, a rationale can be established for excluding or giving limited consideration to such 'specialized' content. Though social work is committed to alleviating negative conditions, the effect of sexism is not yet universally perceived as an example of a negative condition, nor, we would add, is it clear what consequences would ensue if faculty members did not address the issue.

Second, many faculty may be wary of content that claims to be important enough to be infused throughout the curriculum. Before undertaking the considerable effort of revising course content, faculty may be cautioned by previous examples of the shifting knowledge base in social work education and worry that this too may shift. Retooling might then quickly become obsolete.

A third curriculum issue is that the subject may be seen as one more distinctive area in social work education, requiring specialized knowledge, with faculty vying for turf and limited resources. Especially in an era of shrinking enrollments and dwindling funding sources, faculty may be understandably apprehensive about a new cadre of scholars and new curriculum space encroaching on their traditional territory. There may be particular apprehension if the norms about the importance of non-sexist practice shift in its favor and the advocates for this changed position gain more power and status within the organization.

This list of curricular issues and societal stances is clearly not exhaustive but suggests the nature of the obstacles to be overcome if social work schools are to attend to the empirical and theoretical knowledge now available as a base for a non-sexist academic perspective.

Personal barriers

The point was made earlier that content concerning sex roles, in contrast with much other content in social work education, can have a particular personal impact because everyone is affected by the pervasiveness of gender distinctions and sexist practices. For purposes of clarity, we comment first on how the issue may affect the social work educator interpersonally in his or her informal relationships with faculty colleagues and in classroom behavior, and then more intrapersonally in his or her individual reactions to challenges and conflicts prompted by this content.

Interpersonal considerations vis-à-vis faculty colleagues may make it difficult for individual faculty members to be honest about their position regarding sexist issues. In some instances, the official rhetoric may be a non-sexist one and faculty with reasonable objections to the ideas and strategies encompassed in that stance may feel constrained from open argument for fear of being perceived as sexist. In the same or other situations, despite official statements, the informal norm may remain traditional. A particular individual, who in fact may question sexist positions, will not wish to be considered different from her or his colleagues and will therefore remain silent or give lip-service to the prevailing informal norm. In this combination of circumstances, both faculty members with reasonable objections to a non-sexist perspective and those with reasonable openness to such proposals may stifle their own views for fear of endangering informal relationships. The unfortunate consequence of the silence is that both the objections and the openness, if expressed, could help move the field to a desired end. The informal pressures which lead to silence or to pretended compliance are a real and forceful aspect of organizational life.

Some of the same dynamics may be in operation in the classroom as well. What instructors sense about student opinions on the issue of sexism may influence their classroom behavior. The presence of militant feminists or, on the other hand, of traditionally oriented students can affect an instructor's public statements and actions. The feminists may push the instructor farther than she or he wishes to go; the traditionalists may place the instructor in an ethical dilemma if she/he wants to emphasize the negative consequences of a sexist society. Appropriate behavior for the educator is as prescribed by societal rules as are gender roles and faculty may not wish to be perceived as too far out of the mainstream in either direction.

In addition, both the emergent political stance and the recently developed knowledge about women may place the instructor in an uncomfortable and uncharacteristic position. Most instructors prefer to see themselves as both role models for students and as experts in their particular areas. The accusation that they may represent a sexist stance or that they are lacking in new knowledge about the implications of their area of expertise on the condition of women would be difficult for most instructors to accept with equanimity. The problem of credibility in the classroom may be particularly acute for the male instructor who may not be able to speak from personal awareness of women's experiences in society.

Beyond the dilemmas found in collegial and classroom interactions, there is an array of intrapersonal reactions a faculty member may experience in response to proposals about women's issues content or other challenges about sexism, and the following are illustrations of such consequences.

1. This curriculum issue is clearly a challenge to the person's belief system about relationships among people. We all hold strong belief systems and we are all reluctant to wrestle with the profound implications of change. In addition to the natural tendency to insulate ourselves from facing the prospect of upsetting our deepest beliefs, in this situation most of society supports traditional concepts about gender roles and so there is considerable resistance to change.

2. It is difficult to hear others say that what you have been teaching has serious flaws and omissions. This is analogous to the angry reaction of the traditional woman to the feminist challenge to her way of life. This is a serious affront to any academic's professional commitments and intellectual honesty, and in the case of social work to one's concern for the human condition.

3. Challenges to sexist content can create conflicts between one's personal and one's professional beliefs, and can highlight the discrepancy between them. For both male and female faculty members, academic content about the negative effects of stereotyped sex-roles and sexist inequities may conflict directly with the person's marital or other intimate relationships and with child-rearing practices. It would seem that no other academic area has this same impact. Because of the potential conflict prompted by a serious look at the implications of curriculum content about sexism, and the inherent challenge to one's personal life, there is a natural reluctance to deal with the issue.

4. The pressure to incorporate this content in one's teaching can lead to a sense of inadequacy. Any effort may seem both too little and too late and then one feels paralyzed in making further efforts. Faculty are expected to have comprehensive knowledge of their own subject area and feel beleaguered to keep up with the latest information. Now one is faced not only with additional content, but with content that is emotionally laden and potentially conflictual. Social work educators pride themselves in being 'right-thinking and socially concerned' individuals ready to incorporate valid new knowledge. It would be hard to admit that one is lacking in both these respects.

5. Male faculty in a predominantly women's profession and with a predominantly female student body may feel that the male presence in the profession needs to be reinforced in general and, more particularly, that their own

masculine identity needs to be clear. For some, this may be translated to mean a traditional masculine identity. Any challenge to that traditional definition may seem also to question their place as men in the profession.

6. The content may seem like a special topic to be taken up by whichever faculty might be interested. It is then easy to rationalize that this is not one's field – 'I'm not into this – let someone else do it' – and to continue to protect one's turf.

In sum, personal reactions which social work faculty may experience, are part of the way we all protect ourselves from conflict, from challenges to our belief systems, from feelings of inadequacies, and from working too hard.

The issue of becoming personally convinced

Even this brief discussion has suggested certain institutional and personal barriers of sufficient dimension that any faculty person must have compelling reasons to make the effort toward change. The barriers are considerable. Individuals need to be personally convinced of the necessity to proceed nonetheless. Faculty will invest both emotional and intellectual energy when they are excited by and convinced of the importance of a particular scholarly pursuit or practice question. All of us invest ourselves this way on certain issues. It is our contention that even in the face of barriers of various kinds, faculty can become convinced of the need for change.

Individuals can become convinced about a non-sexist stance through various routes, and can become convinced to varying degrees. Many women faculty have become committed to the issue through their raised consciousness about the effects of sexism on their own lives. They then can see the commonalities of socialization and inequities which all women share and can translate their own experiences to those of social work clients. In becoming aware of the pervasiveness of gender-based devaluation they have come to the conviction that the effects of sexism must be assumed in all client situations.

Personal circumstances can affect other individuals in different ways. Men whose wives have altered their roles and men who are concerned about a non-restrictive future for their daughters may see that the issue of devaluation of women comes quite close personally. Faculty – both men and women – may see competent women students in a non-stereotyped role, such as in administration, and may alter their views about the appropriateness of expanded roles for women. For these faculty the routes to being convinced may then be through seeing the effects of sexism on intimates or through being impressed with the capabilities of women who challenge stereotypes. This personal route may also include a male faculty member who has had a positive experience in a non-stereotyped intimate or professional relationship and sees the personal benefit to himself of altered expectations of both women and men.

Another route may be via the management of dissonance. Some faculty may recognize their own resistance to the issue but become aware nonetheless of the illogic of their long-held views. They may then wonder inwardly whether their present stance serves them well, whether it fits with their views of themselves as professional people, and whether their current values are ones they wish to continue to live with and display to other people.

In those schools in which non-sexist content has received some credibility, faculty may take a changed stance, albeit reluctantly at first, for fear of being viewed as behind the times, or because they feel their participation in the school will be limited if they ignore the issue. In a similar school situation, faculty may also engage in non-sexist behavior or use non-sexist language to avoid embarrassment, and the changed behavior may either lead directly to changed attitudes or to a dissonance requiring some resolution.

Whatever the routes to becoming convinced – either directly through raised consciousness, through various other personal experiences, or through self-protective mechanisms – and whatever the degree of conviction, altered perceptions can be achieved at least to some extent. We would conjecture that creating a non-sexist curriculum requires that a critical mass of faculty become convinced to some degree.

Summary

Our purpose has been to encourage further discussion of those circumstances – both institutional and personal – which seem to prevent social work education from moving ahead on its mandate to create a gender-equitable learning environment. We have also discussed those circumstances which result in a heightened conviction about needed progress. We believe the continuing dialogue must allow for reasonable questions and debate, and must decrease, rather than exacerbate, faculty frustration and defensiveness. Achievable action will follow, we believe, when more and more persons become convinced of the need for it and sufficiently committed to overcome the barriers.

References

Barker, D. and Allen, S. (eds) (1976) *Dependence and Exploitation in Work and Marriage.* London: Longman.
Brooks, V. (1981) *Minority Stress and Lesbian Women.* Lexington, MA: Lexington Books.
Decter, M. (1972) *The New Chastity and Other Arguments against Women's Liberation.* New York: Coward, McCann, and Geoghegan.

Epstein, C. (1970) *Women's Place: Options and Limits in Professional Careers*. Berkeley, CA: University of California Press.

Foner, P. (1980) *Women and the Labor Movement*. New York: Free Press.

Fox, M. and Biber, S. (1984) *Women at Work*. Palo Alto, CA: Mayfield Publishing.

Giele, J. (1978) *Women and the Future*. New York: Free Press.

Gornick, V. and Moran, B. (eds) (1971) *Women in Sexist Society*. New York: Basic Books.

Gottlieb, N. (ed.) (1980) *Alternative Social Services for Women*. New York: Columbia University Press.

Hidalgo, H., Peterson, T., and Woodman, N. (eds) (1985) *Lesbian and Gay Issues*. Silver Spring, MD: National Association of Social Workers.

Janeway, E. (1971) *Man's World, Woman's Place: A Study in Social Mythology*. New York: Dell Publishing.

Kay, H. (1983) *Cases and Materials in Sex-Based Discrimination*. St Paul, MN: West Publishing.

Kravetz, D. (1982) An Overview of Content on Women for the Social Work Curriculum. *Journal of Education for Social Work*, 18(2): 42–9.

Lengermann, P. and Wallace, R. (1985) *Gender in America*. Englewood Cliffs, NJ: Prentice-Hall.

Lerner, G. (1977) *The Female Experience: An American Documentary*. Indianapolis, IN: Bobbs-Merrill.

Lloyd, C. and Niemi, B. (1979) *The Economics of Sex Differentials*. New York: Columbia University Press.

Lopata, H. (1973) *Widowhood in an American City*. Cambridge, MA: Shenkman Publishing.

Lowenstein, S. (1976) Integrating Content on Feminism and Racism into the Social Work Curriculum. *Journal of Education for Social Work* 12(1): 91–6.

—— (1983) A Feminist Perspective. In A. Rosenblatt and D. Waldfogel (eds) *Handbook of Clinical Social Work*. San Francisco: Jossey-Bass.

Markson, E. (1983) *Older Women*. Lexington, MA: Lexington Books.

Norman, E. and Mancuso, A. (eds) (1980) *Women's Issues and Social Work Practice*. Itasca, IL: Peacock Publishers.

Rossi, A. (1985) *Gender and the Life Course*. New York: Aldine Publishing.

Sachs, A. and Wilson, J. (1978) *Sexism and the Law*. Oxford: Martin Robertson.

Sargent, A. (1984) *Beyond Sex Roles*. St Paul, MN: West Publishing.

Sedel, R. (1978) *Urban Survival: The World of Working Class Women*. Boston: Beacon Press.

Skolnick, A. and Skolnick, J. (1983) *Family in Transition*. Boston: Little, Brown.

Thomas, C. (1982) *Sex Discrimination*. St Paul, MN: West Publishing.

US Bureau of Census (1981) *Statistical Abstract of the United States, 102nd Edition*. Washington, DC: Bureau of the Census.

4 Women and social policy

Dianne S. Burden

Introduction

Social welfare policy is defined as strategies and plans that a society sets for itself to address social problems and meet social needs (Kahn 1979). Since numerous strategies and plans are available, policy-makers must choose from among alternatives. The key questions in any analysis of social policy thus become (a) what factors operate to provide the list of alternatives to be considered; and (b) what factors determine the selection of alternatives to be pursued. A society both shapes and is shaped by its social policy. Such policy decisions affect how resources will be allocated and how families will be supported. They also determine what lifestyles and life decisions will be rewarded and what segments of society will most benefit from the labor of the culture.

This chapter will focus on social welfare policy as it affects women in our society. It will address the question of why women in late twentieth-century America are disproportionately in poverty, relegated to low-paying dead-end jobs, increasingly living alone, and almost solely responsible for child-rearing. The chapter will focus specifically on factors which must be included in social policy curricula to increase understanding about the inequitable position of women in the culture and to develop awareness about why women are far more likely than men to be seen as clients in social service agencies. Three factors will be discussed to provide background for the current situation of women. These are (a) the social environment's impact on social policies affecting women, (b) underlying values and belief systems that determine what society defines as social problems, and (c) historical trends which have led to the current state of social policy. The chapter will then focus on specific current areas of concern for women and will discuss related policy issues. These areas include the feminization of poverty, the influx of women into the paid labor force, lack of adequate child care, health policy issues for women, and policy implications of changing roles of women. The chapter will finally focus on policy development, briefly discussing rational planning, the political process, the legislative process, and implementation issues, and in more detail discussing judicial policy-making as it affects women.

Social work curricula for non-sexist practice must focus on all three policy components addressed in this chapter – the social context, current problem areas, and the policy development process – if the inequitable situation of women in the society is to be clearly understood.

The social environment's impact on social policies affecting women

A key issue addressed in social policy courses is the interaction between the social environment and the policies which govern that environment. Social policies seek stability through the maintenance of the status quo (Horton 1968). As such they act to reinforce the sex-role socialization received by most men and women and to provide incentives for the maintenance of a sex-segregated world. The importance of sex-role socialization in determining the expectations that men and women have of themselves and of each other has been well established (Weitzman 1979). Both men and women are socialized to expect men to work their whole lives in the labor force and to be able to provide financial support for families. They are socialized to expect women to care for the home and children, to provide emotional sustenance for the male wage-earner, and to work in the paid labor force in a temporary, secondary capacity as family needs require. Such sex-role socialization tends to operate to make males more focused on gaining independence through the outside world of work and correspondingly to make females more focused on accepting dependence in the inside world of home and family (Guttentag, Salasin, and Belle 1980). The model depends heavily on the earning power of the male and as such has traditionally been functional primarily for white middle- and upper-middle-class families. While low-income and ethnic minority families have been socialized into the same model, it has not worked as effectively for them due to low male earning power or absence of the male earner (National Urban League 1984).

The importance of sex roles for social policy is evident in numerous policy outcomes. Men receive strong incentives to enter and stay in the workforce through disproportionately high salaries and status on the job compared with women. Women receive incentives to stay in the traditional roles through inadequate salaries, inadequate welfare benefits, non-existent or extremely expensive child care services, and tax and social security policies which reward traditional family forms (Lloyd and Niemi 1979).

The primary conflict in recent years has been that the social environment is changing faster than social policy can respond to it and is changing for a population that was socialized to expect traditional sex roles (Smith 1979). Economic necessity now makes two incomes a requirement for most families to maintain middle-class status. Increasing education and career aspirations for women, deferment of marriage and child-bearing, reduced family size, and changing expectations through the women's liberation movement all combine to exert major pressure on the traditional social environment and the policies which support it. Traditional male/female power differentials are being questioned, and the result is major conflict between the advocates of traditional and emerging roles and to an increasing extent between men and women. The status quo is being challenged by a conflict model of social change resulting for the most part from the economic necessity of women (Lloyd and Niemi 1979).

Increasing sex-role conflict is evident both within families and in the labor force. While women are taking a major share of the income-producing function of the family, they are still faced with the major share of homemaking and child-rearing as well (Burden 1986; Fox and Nickols 1983). The result is serious discretionary time inequity between men and women, drain on the energy and resources of women, and increase in family disruption through a divorce rate approaching 50 per cent (Bernard 1979). Growing sex-role conflict is also evident in the labor force where occupational sex segregation and major salary differentials between men and women are being addressed through growing unionization of women employees and support for comparable worth plans. The conflict in the social environment emerges in the policy arena through increased pressure by employed women for more equitable tax and social security policies, child care benefits, disability benefits for maternity, and family support benefits. The conflict also emerges in reduced political support for welfare programs which enable low-income women to stay home with children. With the majority of women parents now in the workforce, the pressure is likely to mount for work requirements for low-income women.

Underlying values and belief systems

Sexism in our society has traditionally been viewed as a functional system which reinforces the importance of the man as primary supporter and head of the family and rewards the role of woman as helpmate and keeper of the home. The system has been particularly well-suited to the needs of a capitalistic industrial society. The separation of work and home which occurred as a result of the industrial revolution enabled industrialists to maximize profits by centering production in large urban settings, thereby reducing overheads and taking advantage of economies of scale (Tebbetts 1981). Thus more output could be produced more efficiently. The traditional family form essentially provides employers with a two-person worker for the price of one. The male is able to devote himself to the job and to be available to his employer's will because his wife is at home managing the homemaking and child-rearing chores without additional pay.

In any analysis of women and social policy it is important to examine how the underlying values and belief systems of a society determine the view of women. In the United States, the prevailing values stem from eighteenth-century notions of individualism, liberty, the sanctity of property, and an abiding faith in the benefits of natural law (e.g. the free market system) unfettered by government constraint (Axinn and Levin 1982). These values were expanded in the nineteenth century to serve the needs of the burgeoning industrial revolution and the resultant separation of work and home. Social Darwinism provided an extreme justification of unbridled capitalist excesses (Fleming 1963). The glorification of motherhood which emerged in mid-century provided a rationale for maintaining women in dependent positions at home (Rich 1976). The recurring religious fervor of the nineteenth century further justified the secondary status of women in the power structure. From a social Darwinist perspective men were more 'fit' than women, as exemplified by their superior economic, political, and social power, and therefore were *deserving* of their rewards. The policy result of such a belief system was that married women lost their legal identity. Upon divorce, men received custody of the children since the children were viewed as the property of their father (Gersick 1979).

These values persisted into the twentieth century in attitudes about women's role as mothers. Mothers' pensions of the Progressive Era and Title IV, Aid to Dependent Children, of the Social Security Act (1935), were enacted upon the premise that mothers should stay at home to care for children. This underlying value has not resulted in adequate provision for women to care for their children, however, because of the competing values of individualism, family responsibility, and fear of fostering dependency which have mitigated effective assistance efforts. These competing values tend to place women in a double bind of being expected to care for children but being provided with inadequate resources to do so unless they are married. The combination has given women little choice but to be financially dependent on men. To understand the evolution of this dependency it is useful to trace historical trends of the status of women as well as of attitudes toward poor people.

Historical trends

The history of the status of women can be seen in the shift in women's economic power from an agrarian society to cottage industries to the factory system of the industrial revolution to the emergence of the post-industrial revolution service sector. The trend has been toward a decline in status of women's work. In a non-monetary, agrarian economy, women's work and men's work were viewed as equally necessary for the production of goods. In a cottage industry economy, women could be financially independent through weaving, sewing, knitting, and other handicrafts produced in the home and sold in the market (Tebbetts 1981). In both of these periods, work and family responsibilities could be carried out together. The industrial revolution resulted in a major increase in wealth and the subsequent development of a middle class. Because of the separation of work and family inherent in the new system, middle-class women lost their independent economic power and became primarily appendages of their husbands and unpaid caretakers of home and children. Low-income women, particularly immigrants and blacks, continued work for low wages in the factory system or as domestic workers.

Ironically the major social movements of the nineteenth century – women's suffrage, abolition, temperance, voluntary charity – developed largely from the impetus of those middle-class women who had been relegated to the home and denied a place in the paid labor force. The history of the status of women, therefore, not only includes women as subjects of social policy but women as makers and implementers of social policy as well. The beginning of social welfare policy, emerging in the Progressive Era from the activities of the Settlement House Movement and Charity Organization Societies, is the history of women activists such as Jane Addams, Florence Kelly, Sophinisba Breckenridge, and Lillian Wald (Brandwein, in press).

The history of the status of women, however, is not complete unless it is set in the context of the history of attitudes toward poverty. Poverty, sexism, and racism are intricately entwined. Negative attitudes toward poor people tend to become blurred with negative attitudes toward single women with children and toward blacks. A value system which stems from a Calvinist Protestant work ethic and equates wealth with virtue also tends to equate poverty with sin and worthlessness. In a society which values individual effort and claims the existence of equal opportunity for all, the personal defect rationale for poverty gains more credibility than the determinist rationale of the environmental impact explanation of poverty (Axinn and Levin 1982). The outcome therefore becomes the cause. The external sign of poverty becomes sufficient evidence of internal defect. From the Elizabethan Poor Laws to the Charity Organization Societies to the New Deal to the War on Poverty, the policy focus has always been on helping poor people help themselves through finding, creating, or being coerced into work. The first line of defense in the social welfare system has always been family responsibility financed by individual paid work efforts. By the nineteenth century, women in this system were either protected by men, or, if their men were poor, women were forced into the lowest levels of the paid labor force.

While liberal humanitarian trends have co-existed with conservative, social

Darwinist perspectives, the weight of opinion has remained with the individual-ist, family responsibility belief system. The notion of collective or communal responsibility for social problems such as inadequate child care, health care, income maintenance, and housing has found little support in a society which believes firmly in the power of the individual.

Current social problem areas and related policy implications

In the last twenty-five years the social environment and the roles of women have shifted to such a degree that policies providing incentives for traditional sex-role distinctions and family forms are becoming less responsive to the needs of women. Since currently less than 10 per cent of the population is living in the traditional family form of father at work and mother at home with children (Glick and Norton 1980), since more than half of married women with children and almost three-quarters of single women with children work outside the home (Hayghe 1981), and since one out of four children presently live in a single-parent family (NOW 1985), a value system which provides impetus for policies benefiting traditional roles is clearly inadequate.

Women are currently in a difficult transition period between old expectations that they will care for home and family and the new realities that they both choose to and must work outside the home (Giele 1978). If social welfare poli-cies are strategies and plans which aim to meet social needs, a new approach is required to meet the needs of women.

Key problem areas which need to be addressed in an adequate discussion of women and social policy include the following.

Women and poverty
Since only 7 per cent of male-headed families but almost half of female-headed families are in poverty (National Urban League 1984), the feminization of poverty has become the most compelling issue in social welfare policy today (Pearce 1979). The increase in the divorce rate, the high incidence of out-of-wedlock teenage pregnancy, the low earning power of women, and the absence of family support policies such as child care and children's allowances, have combined to create a large new class of low-income women and children (Child-ren's Defense Fund 1985; National Urban League 1984; Pearce 1979). Poverty for women and children has increased to such an extent in recent years that they are the fastest growing segment of the homeless population.

Low-income women appear to have three major alternatives. They can find a male to support them, they can apply for public assistance, or they can seek paid employment (Burden 1980). None of these alternatives is currently a viable solution to the problem. While acquiring a male family head does extricate a woman and her children from poverty (Ross and Sawhill 1975), sex ratios (particularly for black women) which indicate that there are simply more available women than men preclude this option for many women (Guttentag and Secord 1983). The dependency engendered by such financial reliance on men may also leave a woman at high risk of physical and emotional abuse. The second option, public assistance, does little to raise a woman out of poverty as the principle of lesser eligibility dictates in most states that assistance levels remain well below the federal poverty level. While public assistance may provide a short-term solution for women, the political climate, rather than recognizing the social utility of providing income maintenance for all children, is turning away from a willingness to provide support for low-income women (Palmer and Sawhill 1982). With the large majority of women parents currently in the workforce, low-income women are finding less support for cash assistance and greater emphasis on job training and placing women in the first available jobs. The third option, employment, is the most viable long-term solution for the disproportionate poverty of women. However, employment is currently unlikely to raise low-income women very far out of poverty. Occupational sex segregation, sex discrimination in hiring, promotion, and salary levels, and lack of support for family responsibilities make the employment option far less rewarding for women than it is for men (Smith 1979). Women and social policy courses need to examine carefully the impact on women of income maintenance policies, job training and placement policies, and housing policies to address the needs of the growing number of poor and even homeless women and children.

Some policy analysts have suggested that the problem of female poverty can be solved by coercing absent fathers into supporting their families. While divorce has been economically devastating for women it has been beneficial to men. After divorce, a woman's standard of living declines on average by 73 per cent while a man's increases by 42 per cent (NOW 1985). This inequity in financial status after divorce appears largely related to fathers' failure to meet child support responsibilities. Of those women who headed families in 1984, only 58 per cent had been awarded child support, and only 23 per cent were actually receiving any support. While the average court-ordered yearly support in 1983 was $2,290, the average received was $1,330 (NOW 1985). Low-income and non-white women are less likely to be granted child support awards, thus exacerbating the poverty situation for those in greatest need of support. Even middle-class, white, employed women, however, frequently receive little support from their child's father. A recent study of employed single mothers revealed that half received no support at all, and those who did received only $1,800 per year (Burden 1986).

In an attempt to remedy this inequitable financial situation, Congress has enacted the Child Support Enforcement Amendments to Title IV of the Social

Security Act (effective October 1985). These require states to use vigorous means to collect child support, including wage withholding, expedited legal processes, tax refund offsets, liens against property, and reports to credit bureaus (NOW 1985). Requiring equal support of children by both parents may be instrumental in moving women out of poverty. The price, however, may be major governmental intrusion into the economic lives of single parents.

Women and work

Employment is a key factor in extricating low-income women from poverty. Of those single-parent families where the female head does *not* work, 51 per cent are in poverty; of those where she works part-time, 19 per cent are in poverty; and of those where she works full-time, only 8 per cent are in poverty (Smith 1979). While employment does tend to raise single mothers out of poverty, as has been noted it does not raise them very far. The median income for employed single mothers in 1980 was $11,900 for white and $8,900 for black mothers. For single mothers not in the labor force, the median income was $5,000 for white and $4,400 for black women (Grossman 1982). Employment is also a major factor for married women, however, in enabling dual-earner families to maintain middle-class lifestyles. In 1980 the median income for dual-earner families was $26,500, while for two-parent families where the mother did not work it was $21,300. Working wives now earn 26–38 per cent of their families' incomes (Grossman 1982).

Work in the paid labor force is not only an important factor in the economic well-being of women and their families. Employed women also tend to be physically healthier, have less emotional disturbance, have greater life satisfaction, and live longer than women in traditional homemaker roles (Belle 1982; Guttentag, Salasin, and Belle 1980).

Because employment is such a vital element in the lives of the women clients whom social workers serve, a careful analysis of factors affecting employment policy is particularly important in social work education. Occupational sex segregation has relegated 80 per cent of employed women to low-paying traditional female occupations such as clerical, service, and domestic work. As a result the median annual earnings of women working full-time year-round are only 60 per cent of men's earnings (Rytina 1982; Smith 1979). Title VII of the 1964 Civil Rights Act has guaranteed equal pay for equal work regardless of gender. The primary factor depressing wages for women, however, is that women receive lower pay for *different* jobs. Thus a multi-sided approach is required if policy options are to be adopted which will effectively address the inequitable financial situation of women in the workplace. Policy options focus on employer discrimination in hiring, pay, and promotion of women. They include (a) affirmative action and equal employment opportunity programs which give incentives to employers to improve the numbers and status of women and minorities in the present workforce; (b) on-the-job training for women to increase their job mobility – such training would be intended to give women access to the informal network of training, support, and mentorship which enables male employees to advance in their careers; and (c) comparable worth legislation to increase salaries in traditional female occupations by rewarding equally jobs which require comparable skills and responsibility (Burden 1983).

Changing roles of women – who will care for the children?

While women have assumed a major share of the income-producing function in families, they have had to continue to bear the major responsibilities for child-rearing, homemaking, and emotional support activities in the family. Employed women spend twice as many hours per week on homechores and child-rearing as either their spouses or their male colleagues (Burden 1985). Married men show no difference in the amount of housework they do whether their wife works outside of the home or not (Bernard 1979; Burden 1985, 1986; Fox and Nickols 1983; Nickols and Metzen 1982). Single women parents receive little support or assistance with child-rearing from their children's father (Burden 1986). The result is serious inequity in the amount of discretionary time available to employed women parents. The result of such role overload has been increased stress and decreased physical and emotional well-being (Burden 1983, 1986).

Inequity in discretionary time for employed women appears to be a symptom of a difficult transition period that society is undergoing between a traditional middle-class view of women's role at home and the contemporary reality of women's increasing role in the paid labor force. The transition is characterized by few policies at either the corporate or government level which provide support for employed women parents. Current policy has been based on traditional assumptions about women's role in the family and about occupational sex segregation in the workplace. The result has often been discrimination against women employees by providing incentives to maintain traditional roles. For example, the tax system taxes employed wives' earnings at the higher rate that is usually determined by their husbands' incomes. As a result, the tax rate on employed wives of upper-income men is so high that there is a strong disincentive for them to work outside of the home (Lloyd and Niemi 1979). Another example of government incentives to traditional roles is the social security system, which penalizes employed wives (who are the majority) by providing for non-employed wives of working men without additional contributions. Since wives who do not work tend to be married to higher-salaried men, the social security subsidy is essentially a redistribution of income from lower- and middle-income to upper-income groups (Gordon 1979; Ozawa 1982).

Tax and income transfer programs, therefore, tend to reduce the advantage of market work for married women. Two-earner families pay more taxes and receive lower benefits than one-earner families where the wife stays home. Low-income female heads of household, however, are increasingly expected to work, the incentive being that women should be dependent on husbands, not directly on the government. At the same time, pressure from working women has pushed the enactment of anti-discrimination legislation and the enforcement of affirmative action and equal employment opportunity programs. This policy line emphasizes the equality of all individuals in the workplace. Since large numbers of dependent wives and mothers remain at home, government programs still tend to discriminate against working women and in favor of non-working women.

Another crucial area where the assumption of traditional female dependency has resulted in barriers to women's economic advancement is in the development of child care policy. The assumption behind the lack of government support for child care is that families should care for their own children and that women should stay home to do that (Friedman 1983). The further assumption is that if a female parent joins the labor market she does so in a secondary and supplemental role to her responsibilities at home. The primary dilemma for government policy-makers is to find ways to support the needs of employed women while at the same time supporting the continued functions of homemaking and child-rearing. To continue simply to rely on women to do both does not seem to be a realistic long-term policy.

Policy options need to be assessed in all of these areas to determine which choices support equity for employed women and parents.

Women and health

The impact on women's physical and emotional well-being of increasing roles and responsibilities makes health care policy a major women's issue in social welfare policy courses. Women are the most frequent users of the health care system due primarily to the medicalization of women's reproductive function and to the greater frequency of chronic health problems among old people, most of whom are women (Rothman 1984). Both service provision and funding policies therefore are of particular significance to women since they are more likely than men to be low-income and less likely to be covered by private health insurance. Medicaid and Medicare need to be thoroughly examined in policy courses to determine their impact on women. Examples of recent health care policy issues which are of primary concern to women are: abortion, teenage pregnancy, and over-medication of women patients. The impact on women of policies addressing these and other health-related issues is a vital component of training for non-sexist social work practice.

Policy development

In addition to analyzing factors which influence policy development and current social problems and their policy implications, social welfare policy courses need to assess the policy development process itself as it affects women. A thorough overview of policy development includes discussion of (a) rational planning, (b) the political process, (c) the legislative process, (d) implementation issues, and (e) judicial policy-making. Knowledge of each stage of policy development is required before effective strategies can be formulated aimed at developing and implementing social policies to meet the needs of women in the contemporary world.

To gain skills in analyzing policy development, students may conduct an in-depth policy analysis of a piece of legislation of particular concern to women. The purpose of the analysis is to conduct a rational planning procedure through a careful analysis of the problem addressed by the legislation along with a discussion of policy options available. Problem and policy analysis models utilizing a social context framework are most useful in the rational planning stage (see for example Gil 1976; Morris 1979). This exercise underlines the importance of basic values and belief systems as starting points in problem and policy analysis. For instance, diametrically opposed outcomes concerning child care policy can be arrived at with equally sound logic if underlying value systems differ concerning the role of women in society.

Analysis of political and legislative processes examine such factors as interest groups affected, lobbying strategies developed, and legislators involved. For legislation which has been passed and implemented, an implementation analysis examines policy-making at the service provider's level to determine whether the intent of the legislature is being carried out (see Pressman and Wildavsky 1979). Obstacles to implementation must be identified to develop more succesful implementation strategies. An implementation analysis identifies both anticipated and unanticipated consequences of the legislation. For example, does requiring parental notification of contraceptive prescription actually increase family communication or merely serve to limit access to reproductive choice to teenage women?

Judicial policy-making: women and the law

A policy making arena which is frequently overlooked in social policy courses is the impact of the judicial system on policy development. Knowledge of major judicial decisions is particularly important for women and policy curricula as the courts have determined public policy regarding AFDC eligibility, reproductive freedom, and family law (i.e. divorce law and child custody), all areas of major concern to women.

It was the judicial system, for example, not the legislative or administrative branch, which made AFDC more accessible and less punitive to many low-income women. The US Supreme Court outlawed durational residence requirements for public assistance and affirmed the fundamental right of interstate travel in *Shapiro v. Thompson*, 394 US 618 (1969). The Court then affirmed AFDC recipients' due process rights to an administrative hearing before termination of aid in *Goldberg v. Kelly*, 397 US 254 (1970). Finally the Court responded to the infamous 'midnight raids' being conducted against welfare recipients in California by holding that home visits could not be required as a condition of receiving aid in *Wyman v. James*, 400 US 309 (1971). In recent years, however, the Court has taken a more conservative turn toward welfare recipients by allowing states to deny benefits to pregnant women for their unborn children even though they would qualify for aid after the children were born (*Burns v. Alcala*, 420 US 575 (1975)).

Reproductive freedom is another area primarily affecting women where the prevailing social policy has been developed by the judiciary. State legislatures were not prevented from outlawing contraceptives (even information about contraceptives to married people) until *Griswold v. Connecticut*, 381 US 479 (1965) held that such laws infringed on married persons' fundamental right to privacy. The landmark *Roe v. Wade* decision, 410 US 113 (1973), cited the same right to privacy argument to declare abortion a private matter between a woman and her doctor. The judicial trend toward empowerment of women over their own bodies continued with *Planned Parenthood of Mississippi v. Danforth*, 428 US 52 (1976), where spousal consent requirements for abortion were declared to be an unconstitutional infringement on a married woman's right to privacy.

This trend has slowed considerably in recent years, however, with the upholding of a series of laws restricting funding of abortions and requiring parental notification for minors' abortions. In 1977, the Court upheld a state's refusal to fund medically unnecessary abortions under Medicaid (*Maher v. Roe*, 432 US 464). Three years later the Court went even further and sustained the federal Hyde Amendment banning public funding even of medically necessary abortions (*Harris v. McRae*, 448 US 297 (1980)). The Court reasoned that the right to abortion does not include the right to public funding, thus potentially denying abortion to low-income women in states which refuse to pay for it. Similarly, while parental consent requirements for minors' abortions were overturned (*Bellotti v. Baird (Bellotti II)*, 443 US 622 (1979)), parental notice requirements were upheld (*H.L. v. Matheson*, 450 US 398 (1981)), and judicial alternatives to a parental consent requirement were upheld (*Planned Parenthood of Kansas City v. Ashcroft*, 462 US 476 (1983)). The result of recent decisions puts major obstacles to abortion in the way of the most vulnerable groups of women, low-income women and pregnant teenagers.

Judicial policy-making, like other forms of policy development, reflects the underlying values and belief systems of a society along with the political realities of the current social environment. When it comes to public assistance and abortion these beliefs and current political realities have tended to operate against women in recent years. The belief system underlying traditional family values has had more influence in the last ten years than the belief system advocating equal rights for women and gender-free policy development. Ironically, where gender-free principles have been upheld in recent years they have frequently operated more in favor of men than of women. Alimony is now gender-free, based on need and ability to pay (*Orr v. Orr*, 440 US 268 (1979)). The trend has been to limit alimony to specific short-term periods primarily for rehabilitative purposes. In 1983, only 13.9 per cent of women were awarded alimony, down from 14.9 per cent in 1981 (NOW 1985). Both parents are now considered equally responsible for child support, and child custody decisions are theoretically gender-free. Repeal of mother preference state statutes in custody awards began in the 1970s. In 1973, California repealed mother preference and replaced it with custody awarded according to the best interests of the child. A joint custody alternative has been gaining credence in many courts in recent years.

This shift in judicial policy toward child custody awards holds potential concerns for women. Before the twentieth century fathers were normally awarded custody of children because the children were considered their property, and fathers were considered better able to care for children and to prepare them to enter society (Gersick 1979; Mnookin 1978). With the separation of work and family engendered by the industrial revolution and with pressure from the nineteenth-century women's movement, a judicial turn toward mother preference enabled women to obtain legal custody of their children after divorce. The current award standard of the best interests of the child combined with weakened maternal preference could mean a return to awarding of custody to fathers under the rationale that they are more financially able to provide for the child. Men not only have substantially higher incomes than women after divorce, but are more likely to keep the family home and to remarry earlier (Weiss 1979). If the value bias of the court is toward a higher-income two-parent family as the preferred lifestyle for a child, women seeking custody may be at a distinct disadvantage in an ostensibly gender-neutral approach. This disadvantage may be particularly strong for lesbian mothers who face serious obstacles to receiving custody of their children.

Judicial decisions may thus serve to modify the intentions of rational planners, legislators, and policy implementers by developing public policy under constitutional scrutiny tempered by the values and beliefs of the justices and by the social environment of the time. Social workers need a clear understanding of how the judicial system operates to effect policy which impacts the daily lives of clients.

Conclusion

This chapter has identified three major domains which need to be addressed in social welfare policy curricula focusing on the needs of women. The first, the context of social policy, includes underlying values and belief systems along with the social and historical context. This context determines policy-makers' views of proper roles for women and men. It also determines the role of government in meeting identified social needs. The second domain focuses on current social problems concerning women and assesses the interaction of policy options with the contemporary social context. It aims to increase awareness about the etiology of current problem areas and about cultural barriers which exist to solving those problems. The third domain addresses the process of policy development itself. In addition to acquiring knowledge about the background of social welfare policy and the current problem areas and policy implications which result from that background, students need to be equipped with an understanding of how social policy change can be effected to enhance the lives of women clients. Policy changes may be effected through rational planning, the political and legislative processes, implementation, or the judicial system.

Introductory social policy courses can provide a broad overview of the impact of the social, political, and historical contexts on policies toward women. They can also assess a broad range of current social problem areas primarily affecting women such as poverty, teenage pregnancy and parenthood, the stress of single-parent families, lack of adequate child care, and inequitable responsibility for combined job and home demands. More in-depth, advanced policy courses can then focus narrowly on specific policy issues, pieces of legislation, programs being implemented, or judicial decisions. In these courses students gain more practical, detailed understanding of how societal values and the sociopolitical context come to bear on the development of policy which affects the lives of women. Such an approach will empower students to view the lives of their clients in a social, economic, political, and historical context and to bring understanding to women clients about the policy factors infringing on their lives. Knowledge of action which can be taken to change policy toward women can be the final step in empowering women clients to take control over their social environment and thus gain a sense of personal political power.

References

Axinn, J. and Levin, H. (1982) *Social Welfare: A History of the American Response to Need*, 2nd edn, NY: Dodd, Mead.
Belle, D. (ed.) (1982) *Lives in Stress: Women and Depression*. Beverly Hills: Sage Publications.
Bernard, J. (1979) Policy and Women's Time. In J. Lipman-Blumen and J. Bernard (eds) *Sex Roles and Social Policy*. Beverly Hills: Sage Publications.
Brandwein, R. (in press) Women in Macropractice. In A. Minahan (ed.) *Encyclopedia of Social Work*. NY: National Association of Social Workers.
Burden, D. (1980) Women as Single Parents: Alternative Services for a Neglected

Population. In N. Gottlieb (ed.) *Alternative Social Services for Women*. NY: Columbia University Press.

—— (1983) The Interaction of Job and Homelife Responsibilities: A Comparison of Married and Single Parent Employees. Doctoral dissertation, Waltham, MA: Heller School, Brandeis University.

—— (1985) Managing Job and Homelife Roles and Responsibilities in Corporations. Progress report no. 3 to DHHS, Office of Human Development Services, October.

—— (1986) Single Parents and Employment. *Family Relations* 35: 1.

Children's Defense Fund (1985) *A Children's Defense Fund Budget*. Washington, DC: CDF.

Fleming, D. (1963) Social Darwinism. In A. Schlesinger (ed.) *Paths of American Thought*. Boston: Houghton Mifflin.

Fox, K. and Nickols, S. (1983) The Time Crunch: Wife's Employment and Family Work. *Journal of Family Issues* 4: 61–82.

Friedman, D. (1983) *Encouraging Employer Support to Working Parents. Community Strategies for Change*. A report of the Working Parents Project, NY: Carnegie Corporation.

Gersick, K. (1979) Fathers by Choice: Divorced Men Who Receive Custody of Their Children. In G. Levinger and O. Moles (eds) *Divorce and Separation: Context, Causes, and Consequences*. NY: Basic Books.

Giele, J. (1978) *Women and the Future: Changing Sex Roles in Modern America*. NY: Free Press.

Gil, D. (1976) *Unravelling Social Policy*. Cambridge, MA: Schenkman Publications.

Glick, P. and Norton, A. (1980) New Lifestyles Change Family Statistics. *American Demographics* 2: 20–3.

Gordon, N. (1979) Institutional Responses: The Social Security System. In R. Smith (ed.) *The Subtle Revolution: Women at Work*. Washington, DC: Urban Institute.

Grossman, A. (1982) More Than Half of All Children Have Working Mothers. *Monthly Labor Review* 105(2): 41–3.

Guttentag, M. and Secord, P. (1983) *Too Many Women: The Sex Ratio Question*. Beverly Hills: Sage Publications.

Guttentag, M., Salasin, S., and Belle, D. (1980) *The Mental Health of Women*. NY: Academic Press.

Hayghe, H. (1981) Husbands and Wives as Earners: An Analysis of Family Data. *Monthly Labor Review* 104: 46–52.

Horton, J. (1968) Order and Conflict Theories of Social Change as Competing Ideologies. *American Journal of Education for Social Work* 4: 1.

Kahn, A. (1979) *Social Policy and Social Services*. New York: Random House.

Lloyd, C. and Niemi, B. (1979) *The Economics of Sex Differentials*. NY: Columbia University Press.

Mnookin, R. (1978) *Child, Family and State: Problems and Materials on Children and the Law*. Boston: Little, Brown.

Morris, R. (1979) Social Policy of the American Welfare State: An Introduction to Policy Analysis. NY: Harper and Row.

National Urban League (1984) *The State of Black America, 1983*. NY: National Urban League.

NOW (1985) Child Support Enforcement Watch Launched by Women's Rights Groups. *National NOW Times*, October/November, 3–5.

Nickols, S. and Metzen, E. (1982) Impact of Wife's Employment upon Husband's Housework. *Journal of Family Issues* 3: 199–216.

Ozawa, M. (1982) Who Receives Subsidies through Social Security and How Much? *Social Work* 27: 2.

Palmer, J. and Sawhill, I. (1982) *The Reagan Experiment*. Washington, DC: Urban Institute.

Pearce, D. (1979) Women, Work and Welfare. In K. Feinstein (ed.) *Working Women and Families*. Beverly Hills: Sage Publications.

Pressman, J. and Wildavsky, A. (1979) *Implementation*, 2nd edn. Berkeley: University of California Press.

Rich, A. (1976) *Of Woman Born: Motherhood as Experience and Institution*. NY: Norton.

Ross, H. and Sawhill, I. (1975) *Time of Transition: The Growth of Families Headed by Women*. Washington, DC: Urban Institute.

Rothman, B. (1984) Women, Health, and Medicine. In J. Freeman (ed.) *Women: A Feminist Perspective*, 3rd edn. Palo Alto: Mayfield.

Rytina, N. (1982) Earnings of Men and Women: A Look at Specific Occupations. *Monthly Labor Review* 105: 25–31.

Smith, R. (ed.) (1979) *The Subtle Revolution: Women at Work*. Washington, DC: Urban Institute.

Tebbetts, R. (1981) Work, Family, and Depression in the Lives of Low-Income Mothers. Doctoral dissertation, Harvard University, Cambridge, MA.

Weiss, R. (1979) Going It Alone: The Family Life and Social Situation of the Single Parent. NY: Basic Books.

Weitzman, L. (1979) Sex-Role Socialization. In J. Freeman (ed.) *Women: A Feminist Perspective*, 2nd edn. Palo Alto: Mayfield.

5 Human behavior in the social environment: the knowledge base for practice

Dianne S. Burden and Naomi Gottlieb

Human behavior in the social environment (HBSE) curricula have traditionally emphasized theories about individual variations in human behavior or theories about group and organizational dynamics. These theories have provided inadequate explanations about political factors which determine gender differences in this culture. Both internal factors such as psychological differences between men and women and external factors such as social policies which reinforce traditional female roles need to be addressed. This chapter will elaborate the theme that the 'personal is political' for work with women clients and will argue that theories of human development that ignore the social and political realities for women provide inadequate grounding for practice. The chapter first outlines the major internal and external factors to be included in human behavior and the social environment courses to increase awareness about the political power imbalance between men and women in our society. The assumption is that since a primary goal of social work intervention is to empower clients to achieve optimum functioning, major attention must be paid to factors which place women in a particularly powerless, at-risk position. The chapter will next focus on some theories that have been developed to explain differential human behavior. The discussion will examine the rationales they offer for the power imbalance. A key issue to be addressed is whether the theories themselves may contribute to the political subjugation of women clients. It is hoped that the ideas raised in this chapter will be useful as a screening device in critically evaluating theoretical bases and substantive background material utilized in HBSE courses. Since the large majority of clients are women, it is essential that social work education provides basic knowledge which explains the dynamics of their vulnerable situation.

Factors contributing to the political power imbalance of women in society

Both internal and external factors play major roles in determining the inequitable position of women in the late twentieth century. An internal factor is one which stems from basic individual differences or family interaction patterns. These include biological and psychological differences, sex-role socialization patterns, power differentials within families, and the impact of multiple responsibilities for job, homemaking, and child-rearing. These factors combine to reduce the sense of personal power that women have and to reduce their overt power within families. External factors are those which stem from outside the individual and family and over which the individual has little control. These include occupational sex segregation which relegates women to low-paying dead-end jobs and sex discrimination in organizations which effectively limits women's access to upper-level decision-making positions whether in corporations, educational institutions, governmental agencies, or social service organizations. External factors also include sexual harassment and exploitation which act to maintain women in a passive, powerless position; social policies at the federal and state levels which reinforce traditional sex roles; and exclusion from the political power structure where those policies and other external barriers could be changed.

To state that the factors, both internal and external, which prevent women from achieving full equality are political implies a functional perspective of human behavior. Sex discrimination and the inequitable position of women are not random events. They serve an important function in the social system and need to be recognized as such. As a result of the political power imbalance, women provide important labor for little or no reimbursement. Along with earning over a third of the family income, they provide free child care, homemaking services, health care, emotional support, care for aging parents, and care for deinstitutionalized family members. All of these functions save the public sector considerable amounts of money, funds which are available for redistribution elsewhere (e.g. through reduced taxes or increased defense spending). Women also enable the private sector to maintain high profits through the provision of a low-paid labor pool. The resistance to change is likely to be high as the consequences for men of making the system more equitable may include greater responsibility for homechores, higher taxes, and lower salaries. Factors which maintain women in their vulnerable position thus have serious political implications which need to be understood clearly by social work practitioners in order to appreciate fully the intransigence of the status quo.

Internal factors

Two biological factors are frequently mentioned to explain women's vulnerable position. These are the lesser body strength and size of women compared with men and the impact of women's reproductive systems on their lives. The facts that women are smaller and spend portions of their lives bearing and raising children have been used to justify the need to provide protection for women within families. Hormonal differences related to women's reproductive systems have also been used to suggest that women are not fit for leadership due to emotional instability during menstruation, pregnancy, and menopause. Similar attention is not paid to male hormonal cycles which may be biological determinants of levels of aggression. Differential biological factors, however, and their impact on cognitions and behavior are important areas for concern for a non-sexist approach to HBSE. Evidence suggests, however, that environmental, not biological, factors are most significant in determining sex roles (Weitzman 1979). Therefore, to understand their true impact, male/female biological differences should be examined in the light of the demands of the modern world. The importance of physical size and strength, for example, has little relationship to the higher income of males. Highest-paid occupations tend to be professional, technical, and managerial occupations which require high levels of education but not physical strength. The average woman now has one or two children and a life expectancy of seventy-six years. She is likely to be pregnant, therefore, for about one and a half years and an active parent for less than twenty years of her life. The importance of biological differences in the overall life-cycle of women therefore need to be examined.

Beliefs about female psychological development have until recently been based on theories and information about male psychological development. As a result, what has been perceived to be healthy male development has also been assumed to be healthy adult development. Women have fallen short by comparison (Broverman *et al.* 1970). Two issues are of particular importance in assessing the differential impact of psychological development for men and women: (a) what are the actual gender-related psychological differences, and (b) do men and women have the same psychological perceptions of the world? The first issue has been addressed extensively by researchers such as Maccoby and Jacklin (1976). Their findings indicate greater variation within genders than between them. They also find that social class and ethnic variations may outweigh the impact of gender on psychological development. Evidence supports gender differences in psychological development as regards anxiety levels, level of activity, competitiveness, dominance, compliance, nurturance, verbal versus spatial ability, and aggressiveness (Maccoby and Jacklin 1976). Evidence does not support assumptions that females are more social, suggestible, have lower self-esteem, or are less achievement-motivated. This last finding particularly raises questions about women's supposed fear of success (Horner 1972).

Sex-role socialization is an internal factor which shapes the behavior and cognitions of both women and men from infancy (Weitzman 1979). Girls are touched more frequently by their parents, encouraged not to separate from parents, and encouraged to gain support from parental approval. Such interactions appear to foster both dependency and fear of rejection in girls. Conversely, boys are encouraged to move outside the parental sphere, to experiment, and to gain support from external stimuli. They receive more physical punishment and are constantly warned not to engage in female behavior. This last factor in particular may be the beginning of the misogyny expressed by many males (Weitzman 1979).

Girls are also socialized at the outset to perform a series of household behaviors that are held in low esteem (Weitzman 1979). This pattern leads to lifelong inequity between males and females in responsibility for home and child care chores. Even a woman's strong economic status has little impact on the amount of housework she can expect from her male partner. She can expect on average to do about twice as much as he regardless of whether she is employed or not and regardless of how much income she contributes to the family (Burden 1983, 1985; Condran and Bode 1982). The stress caused to women and to relationships by such imbalance is a key issue of concern in any analysis of human development or family dynamics. Similarly, the political power differential in families evidenced by women's inequitable levels of discretionary time and decreased levels of physical and emotional well-being is a vital dynamic of family systems which must be addressed fully in social work education (Bernard 1979; Burden 1985). Political powerlessness of women is thus fostered through sex-role socialization and reinforced through inequitable family dynamics. It has been referred to as learned helplessness, and is a major element in reducing women's sense of internal locus of control and making them vulnerable to depression and anxiety (Guttentag *et al*, 1980; Seligman 1975).

The second issue to be considered in an analysis of the psychology of women is whether men and women have distinct value systems and world views and if so, what the implications may be for social work practice. Sociologists have long held views of men as aggressive, active, instrumental, and of women as passive, dependent, emotional (Parsons and Bales 1955; Weitzman 1979). Men are perceived to be task-centered and linear in their thinking; women, process-centered and circular (Crow 1978). Recent thought on women's moral development suggests critical differences from that of men, largely based on the social pressure for women to be more other-oriented and to develop a sense of self through caring for others (Gilligan 1982). A key issue for feminist theoreticians in recent years has been the desire to assess and value women's particular characteristics, rather than to use male characteristics as the standard by which women are measured. Differences in world views are important factors relating to how women perceive and cope with their powerlessness.

This review of internal factors has illustrated the close tie between individual and family dynamics, and women's place in the larger society, but societal forces per se require separate attention.

External factors
External factors complete the pattern of limitation of political power for women. Occupational sex segregation insures that a woman will be limited in her career choices and income-generating capabilities. Since evidence from income maintenance studies suggests that high income for women is associated with increased likelihood of leaving marriages, maintaining low wages acts to stabilize the status quo of the traditional family (Steiner 1981). Similarly, sexual harassment at the workplace and restriction of access to the decision-making structure of organizations (the 'old boy network') function to reduce the potential power of women and maintain men in their positions of control. The result is again to diminish women's sense of internal locus of control and, because of inadequate financial resources, to reduce further their instrumental power.

The larger social environment through its public policy-making function also acts to reduce the political power of individual women by providing policy incentives for them to stay in their traditional roles. The social security and income tax systems provide disproportionately higher benefits to families where wives stay at home in the traditional homemaker role. The result is redistribution of income from employed women largely to wives of middle- and upper-middle-class men. The income maintenance system, by keeping assistance levels low, also provides a disincentive for women to leave their husbands. The goal of income maintenance is not financial emancipation of low-income women, but maintenance of traditional family forms. Indeed, the only factor which significantly extricates female-headed families from poverty is the acquisition of a male family head (Ross and Sawhill 1975). With increasing divorce and declining sex ratios, the likelihood that a woman will be alone and in poverty is a crucial factor of her social environment. The lack of child care policy is another example of policy's impact on the powerlessness of individual women. Insufficient child care makes it extremely difficult for women to be financially independent and essentially acts to force her into dependent roles. Women as individuals or as a constituency have had little power to overcome these barriers through legislative action since the political process is firmly entrenched in the hands of male leaders. The role of these external factors on increasing stress levels for individual women clients is an essential factor in understanding the psychological status of women.

HBSE courses have traditionally focused on the topic of human development across the life-cycle and have examined such theoreticians as Freud, Erickson, Piaget, and Levinson. Differences in development between males and females have received inadequate attention. Men and women think and behave differently because they have been socialized into different worlds and because they function in essentially different social environments. As a result men and women have, in general, vastly divergent levels of political power available to them. These critical differences must be examined closely if the at-risk position of women in our society is to be adequately comprehended.

Theoretical orientations and the 'personal is political' perspective

This chapter's thesis that sociopolitical factors are major determinants of women's personal lives calls for an examination of the theoretical frameworks used to educate social workers and other mental health professionals. When practitioners are offered theoretical knowledge to explain the development and behaviors of women, to what extent do these theories clarify the external/internal connections described above or, on the other hand, reinforce traditional beliefs?

The examples to be presented address some major theoretical orientations and will demonstrate the kind of analysis recommended for any explanatory system used to guide practice with women. The arguments of this chapter and the empirical content of the remaining chapters provide evidence that the understanding of women requires an orientation which recognizes the social, economic, and political consequences of women's lives. Challenges need to be made to existing theories in view of this political stance and of new empirical evidence about women and men in a changing world.

The emphasis on the individual

Theoretical orientations as widely disparate as the psychoanalytic and the cognitive-behavioral share similar emphases on the individual although through very different lenses. The question for both schools of thought concerns the rationale for the focus on the individual woman to the exclusion of a focus on the political impact of power imbalance between men and women.

Freudian psychoanalysis has a long history of criticism both from within and outside the ranks concerning Freud's conception of women. Horney challenged Freud's thinking by asserting that the traits he described as natural to women – dependency, passivity, submissiveness, and masochism – were in fact harmful to them (Horney 1967; Wetzel 1984). Similar criticisms have come from other psychoanalysts (Marmor 1974; Salzman 1974) including the questions raised by Mitchell (1974). An advocate for the psychoanalytic framework, Mitchell nonetheless acknowledges that psychoanalytic practice 'has done much to readapt discontented women to a conservative feminine status quo, to an inferiorized psychology and to a contentment with serving and servicing men and children' (Mitchell 1974: 299). The criticisms by feminists outside the psychoanalytic tradition have been stronger in their assertions about Freud's blatant misogyny and his unexamined reflection of the androcentric culture of his times (Greer 1971; Firestone 1971; Millet 1970).

Though there has been a considerable evolution of Freud's initial conceptualization, encompassing ego psychology and object-relations theory (Wetzel 1984), certain basic concepts remain which are critical to the present analysis. The emphasis continues to be on internally generated pathology and on the individual's intraspychic structure which is then imposed on outside social situations (Chodorow 1978). It is the individual's idiosyncratic history, not social situational factors, that are implicated in the etiology of personal problems (Kaplan and Yasinski 1980). Within that emphasis on the individual, the desirability of traditional roles is fostered, with heterosexuality and motherhood considered 'the universal requirement for fulfillment' (Maracek and Kravetz 1977).

Some psychoanalytic voices have questioned that individual and traditional focus. Chodorow (1978) argues that, given society's values, the usual sexual division of family roles inherently breeds inequality. Marmor (1974) and Salzman (1974) challenge Freud's basic assumptions about women's development, stressing the importance of social forces. Gelb (1974) asserts that the most meaningful therapeutic work with women is to identify the impact of social inequalities and to engage them in the struggle for social change.

In spite of the modifications of early Freudian formulations and the questions raised by some contemporary adherents, the original issue remains: to what extent does the educator's use of psychodynamic theory cloud the impact of sociopolitical factors by placing the emphasis of analysis on the individual psyche as the primary causal factor of personal problems? This question does not deny the importance of individual responses to social forces, but it does support the etiological primacy of the gender-based power imbalance in our society, the related inferior status assigned to women, and the therapeutic value of the appropriate analyses of their problems.

There is a marked contrast from psychoanalytic theory to be found in the explanatory analysis of the cognitive-behavioral approach, but the same question about individual focus can be posed. Berlin acknowledges that:

'the cognitive-behavioral literature contains remarkably little discussion of the influence of social factors (interpersonal relationships, friendship support, access to natural resources and opportunity) in enhancing or obstructing coping efforts . . . there is the implication that social circumstances are fixed – too big, too overwhelming – and thus attention is most fruitfully directed toward more modifiable psychological factors.'

(Berlin 1983: 1109–120)

Ironically, the empirical validation which has grounded cognitive-behavioral theory has only strengthened the individual focus. Kagle and Cowger (1984) argue that evaluation methodology has reinforced the propensity toward a person-centered perspective and away from the more difficult-to-measure environmental factors.

The focus on the individual woman in the cognitive-behavioral approach raises other gender-linked concerns. The selection of target behaviors or cognitions may be influenced by the client's sex, as illustrated in Blechman's (1980) review of studies in which differential choices were made across gender, e.g. comparable behaviors judged as appropriately assertive in men but aggressive in women. The reinforcement paradigm itself may also contain obstacles for women. Because 'female socialization is so inundated with aspersions concerning their goodness and badness' (Wetzel 1984: 186), women may interpret even positive feedback in terms of moral judgment.

The enlargement in recent years of the behavioral orientation to include both cognition and affect has added to the scope of the explanatory theory. Even with that enhancement, the perspective still leaves etiology and treatment targets at the individual woman's doorstep. Blechman hopes the discipline will be guided 'away from the technological fix and toward social system change' (Blechman 1980: 217). A first step toward that change would be the client's awareness of the larger scope of the problem.

Women and self-blame

Compounding overemphasis on the individual woman to the exclusion of societal influences is the tendency for women to blame themselves for their problems (Brewin and Shapiro 1984). Women have not only been defined primarily for their family roles, but have been held responsible for maintaining family harmony (Gurman and Klein 1980). The example of the social systems approach to the problem of domestic violence demonstrates the potential for theory to exacerbate individual self-blame.

In many respects, social systems theory is congruent with this chapter's thesis. The importance of context for the understanding of behavior, the interconnectedness of all events, and the primacy of interactions between people (Anderson and Carter 1984) would match a view which stresses sociopolitical etiology.

Even though in the main this framework should permit a useful sociopolitical analysis, problems emerge in its application to women. The use of systems theory to explain family violence illustrates its inappropriateness, particularly as to attribution of blame. The interactional perspective results in the definition of domestic violence as a systemic product and not as the individual behavioral pathology of the perpetrator (Straus 1973). The systemic and dynamic interpersonal transactions are fully developed to explain the behavior of individual family members. In this view, the victim is presented as an active agent, not a passive object (Gulotta and Neuberger 1983). In Straus's interpretation of a systems approach, the wife who flinches or crouches during an argument may be 'responsible' in provoking her husband's violent behavior (Straus 1973).

Lost in these explanations and descriptions is the responsibility of the perpetrator (the man in most instances) for a criminal act, and lost also is the analysis of power differentials and tolerance of violence in a male-dominated society (Dobash and Dobash 1979; Lowenstein 1983). The woman is left not only with the traumas, physical and emotional, of the violence itself, and with the blame for not assuring family harmony, but is additionally burdened with the stigma of the agreement of 'experts' that family interaction, not individual criminal behavior, is the explanation for the violence.

Some systems theorists acknowledge that structural patterns of the larger social system are not sufficiently dealt with in the theory's formulations, but also assert that the paradigm is intended to explain *how* events happen and not *why* (Giles-Sims 1983). The fuzzy distinction between 'why' and 'how' and the blurred assignment of responsibility raises questions about the utility of systems theory as grounding for service to women in these problem situations.

Even in less serious family circumstances, social systems theory has been criticized for its distortion of women's participation in family systems. The analysis of communication patterns, a critical component of the systems orientation, may not be sensitive to women's conditioned need to maintain family peace and therefore to communicate only positive feelings (Gurman and Klein 1980). Some exponents make little mention of gender issues (Anderson and Carter 1984). Others are criticized for viewing the family as a closed system and the wife's outside activities as disruptive (Gurman and Klein 1980).

Theoretical reorientation

These examples suggest revisions in theoretical formulations necessary to respond to the accumulating empirical evidence of the personal effects of political realities on women's lives. The harmful consequence of reinforcing women in traditional roles without attention to power imbalances have been well documented (Maracek and Kravetz 1977). Myths have been negated about the 'positives' (e.g. blissful motherhood) and 'negatives' (e.g. the empty nest) of women's lives (Lowenstein 1983). Theories of development based only on the study of men are being challenged (Gilligan 1982; Gurman and Klein 1980). Most important, the outside world and its political and economic ramifications are being analyzed for their effects on individual therapeutic approaches (Dobash and Dobash 1979; Gelb 1974).

Possibilities for theoretical reorientations have appeared in the literature. Following a thoroughly developed argument within a psychoanalytic framework about the consequences for both girls and boys of the mothering done by women, Chodorow (1978) acknowledges that these psychological consequences are not immutable. Should men do more parenting and should there be more equality in roles, Chodorow predicts a very different set of psychological results. Sons might develop more affiliative characteristics and daughters might become more autonomous. More relevant to this chapter's analysis, Chodorow recognizes that traditional ideas about masculinity and parenting roles are tied to the devaluation of women. The different social organization of gender and more equitable power relationships can lead to different internal psychological structures.

As noted above, Blechman (1980) calls for a revision of the cognitive-behavioral paradigm to include attention to the breadth of environmental contexts. Kagle and Cowger's (1984) recommendation for research methodology to study environmental variables would help to test these theoretical reorientations.

Theories about women can also be developed or altered on the basis of new empirical evidence. In one example, women's increased labor force participation appears to have wide-ranging psychosocial effects. Numerous studies indicate that working women are healthier and have more self-acceptance, greater satisfaction with life, greater freedom from emotional disturbance, fewer physical symptoms, greater longevity, increased marital satisfaction, and tend to have adolescent daughters with higher achievement patterns (Belle 1982; Guttentag *et al.* 1980; Hofferth and Moore 1979; Hoffman and Nye 1974; Kanter 1977).

A screening paradigm

The major theme of this chapter is reflected in Gurman and Klein's statement that 'imbalances in power, status and social-economic resources have contributed to women's status and to their personalities, self-images and characteristic pathology' (1980: 163). In light of the empirical evidence grounding this assertion, the theoretical base for any human development paradigm requires screening for its appropriateness for women. The question is not whether this stance is political while others are not; all theorists of human behavior are influenced by their culture and take a 'political' stand, either supporting or challenging the status quo. 'The question is rather "whose politics?"' (Lowenstein 1983: 539). Also the question is not whether this analysis pays adequate attention to the individual. The question is whether one starts with the premise of individual deficiencies or the impact of societal inequities. We believe the emphasis on the former has not served women well.

References

Anderson, R. and Carter, I. (1984) *Human Behavior in the Social Environment: A Systems Approach.* New York: Aldine.

Belle, D. (ed.) (1982) *Lives in Stress: Women and Depression.* Beverly Hills: Sage Publications.

Berlin, S. (1983) Cognitive Behavioral Approaches. In Aaron Rosenblatt and Diane Waldfogel (eds) *Handbook of Clinical Social Work.* San Francisco: Jossey-Bass.

Bernard, J. (1979) Policy and Women's Time. In Jean Lipmen-Blumen and Jessie Bernard (eds). *Sex-roles and Social Policy.* Beverly Hills: Sage Publications.

Blechman, E. (1980) Behavior Therapies. In Annette Brodsky and Rachel Hare-Mustin (eds) *Women and Psychotherapy.* New York: Guilford Press.

Brewin, C. and Shapiro, D. (1984) Beyond Locus of Control: Attribution of Responsibility for Positive and Negative Outcomes. *British Journal of Psychology* 75: 43–9.

Broverman, I., Broverman D., Clarkson, F., Rosenkrantz, P. and Vogel, S. (1970) Sex-Role Stereotypes and Clinical Judgments of Mental Health. *Journal of Consulting Psychology* 34(1): 1–7.

Burden, D. (1983) The Interaction of Job and Homelife Responsibilities: A Comparison of Married and Single Parent Employees. Unpublished doctoral dissertation, Brandeis University, Waltham, MA.

—— (1985) Preliminary Report on the Managing Job and Homelife Demands in Corporations Study. Progress report to USDHHS Office of Human Development Services.

Chodorow, N. (1978) *The Reproduction of Mothering.* Berkeley: University of California Press.

Condran, J. G. and Bode, J. G. (1982) Rashomon, Working Wives and Middletown. *Journal of Marriage and the Family* 44: 421–26.

Crow, G. (1978) The Process/Product Split. *Quest* 4(4): 15–23.

Dobash, R. E. and Dobash, R. (1979) *Violence against Wives: A Case against the Patriarchy.* New York: Free Press.

Firestone, S. (1971) *The Dialectic of Sex.* New York: Bantam Books.

Gelb, L. (1974) Masculinity-Femininity: A Study in Imposed Inequality. In Jean Baker Miller, *Psychoanalysis and Women.* New York: Penguin Books.

Giles-Sims, J. (1983) *Wife Battering: A Systems Theory Approach.* New York: Guilford Press.

Gilligan, C. (1982) *In a Different Voice.* Cambridge, Mass: Harvard University Press.

Greer, G. (1971) *The Female Eunuch.* New York: McGraw-Hill.

Gulotta, G. and Neuberger, L. (1983) A Systemic and Attributional Approach to Victimology. *Victimology* 8 (1–2): 5–16.

Gurman, A. and Klein, M. (1980) Marital and Family Conflict. In Annette Brodsky and Rachel Hare-Mustin, *Women and Psychotherapy.* New York: Guilford Press.

Guttentag, M., Salasin, S., and Belle, D. (1980) *The Mental Health of Women.* New York: Academic Press.

Hofferth, S. L. and Moore, K. A. (1979) Women's Employment and Marriage. In Ralph Smith (ed.) *The Subtle Revolution: Women at Work.* Washington, DC: Urban Institute.

Hoffman, L. N. and Nye, F. I. (1974) *Working Mothers.* San Francisco: Jossey-Bass.

Horner, M. (1972) Toward an Understanding of Achievement-Related Conflicts in Women. *Journal of Social Issues* 28(2): 157–76.

Horney, K. (1967) *Feminine Psychology.* New York: W. W. Morton.

Kagle, J. and Cowger, C. (1984) Blaming the Client: Implicit Agenda in Practice Research. *Social Work* 29(4): 347–51.

Kanter, R. M. (1977) *Work and Family in the United States.* New York: Russell Sage.

Kaplan, A. and Yasinski, L. (1980) Psychodynamic Perspectives. In Annette Brodsky and Rachel Hare-Mustin, *Women and Psychotherapy.* New York: Guilford Press.

Lowenstein, S. (1983) A Feminist Perspective. In Aaron Rosenblatt and Diane Waldfogel (eds) *Handbook of Clinical Social Work.* San Francisco: Jossey-Bass.

Maccoby, E. E. and Jacklin, C. N. (1976) Summary and Commentary from *The Psychology of Sex Differences* (1974). In Sue Cox (ed.) *Female Psychology: The Emerging Self.* Chicago: Science Research Associates.

Maracek, J. and Kravetz, D. (1977) Women and Mental Health: A Review of Feminist Change Efforts. *Psychiatry* 40 (4): 323–29.

Marmor, J. (1974) Changing Patterns of Femininity. In Jean Baker Miller (ed.) *Psychoanalysis and Women.* New York: Penguin Books.

Millet, K. (1970) *Sexual Politics.* Garden City, NY: Doubleday.

Mitchell, J. (1974) *Psychoanalysis and Feminism.* New York: Pantheon Books.

Parsons, T. and Bales, R. F. (1955) *Family, Socialization and Interaction Process.* New York: Free Press.

Ross, H. L. and Sawhill, I. V. (1975) *Time of Transition: The Growth of Families Headed by Women.* Washington, DC: Urban Institute.

Salzman, L. (1974) Psychology of the Female: A New Look. In Jean Baker Miller (ed.) *Psychoanalysis and Women.* New York: Penguin Books.

Seligman, M. E. P. (1975) *Helplessness.* San Francisco: W. H. Freeman.

Steiner, G. Y. (1981) *The Futility of Family Policy.* Washington, DC: Brookings Institute.

Straus, M. (1973) A General Systems Theory Approach to a Theory of Violence among Family Members. *Social Science Information* 12(3): 105–25.

Weitzman, L. J. (1979) Sex Role Socialization. In Jo Freeman (ed.) *Women: A Feminist Perspective.* Palo Alto, CA: Mayfield Publishing.

Wetzel, J. (1984) *Clinical Handbook of Depression.* New York: Gardner Press.

6 Dilemmas and strategies in research on women

Naomi Gottlieb

Researchers concerned with sound knowledge about women have raised issues that should be incorporated into the social work curriculum for several reasons. First, the burgeoning literature in feminist research has a healthy quality of vigorous intellectual debate. Scholars have raised serious questions about the basis of social science knowledge, and they disagree among themselves about the philosophical and methodological base for research activities. That debate reflects the diversity among academic feminists and demonstrates to students that research is an alive subject and a social process. Second, this intellectual ferment poses serious challenges to specific procedures in mainstream research. Some of these challenges are not new, and have been raised by other groups. They alert researchers and consumers of research to deficiencies in current procedures, and to the potential for a better knowledge base. Third, taken as a whole, the challenges and proposed remedies illustrate the socially determined nature of knowledge development.

This chapter is organized around these three utilitarian aspects of the current debate: (a) major questions and dilemmas surfaced by feminist researchers, (b) the specific corrections proposed for the research process, and (c) issues in the organization of research activities and the sociology of knowledge. The chapter's rationale is that social work research training is incomplete without attention to these issues. The challenges pertain to both current, and needed, knowledge about more than half of the population, and an even greater majority of social service clients. In fact, the perspective highlighted in gender-relevant research has the promise of a sounder knowledge base for all persons.

Issues in feminist research

The quantitative-qualitative debate

The debate about the ascendancy of quantitative methods in social science is a long-term one (Glaser and Straus 1967), and is raised again by feminist scholars for some old and some new reasons. Similar to anthropologists, ethnographers, and grounded theorists before them, feminist proponents of qualitative methodology maintain that understanding the lives of women must be done from women's own perspective, and requires an open, empathic interaction (Reinharz 1983). Additionally, they raise Bakan's (1966) framework of 'agency' (associated with masculine traits) and 'communion' (reflective of feminine characteristics), to argue that the favored quantitative methods reflect a 'masculine' approach to knowledge development. In Bakan's terms, agentic methods are mastering, controlling, separating, and quantifying; communal methods are naturalistic, co-operating, participatory, and qualitative (Bakan 1966; Carlson 1972). Thus, the preference for agentic, quantitative procedures may be less a question of appropriate choices for particular questions than the operation of a male world view which values control, mastery, and linear thinking (Carlson 1972; Wallston 1981).

Proponents of qualitative methodology for the study of women believe that the world of women has been made invisible by traditional research, and that only through studies of women's own experience and language will distortions be corrected. DuBois (1983) terms this the 'central agenda' of feminist scholarship. Experiential analysis as developed by Reinharz (1983) is illustrative of such qualitative approaches, and is characterized by self-reflective activities by the researcher (an explicit awareness of values and role), a collaborative, non-authoritarian involvement with subjects (inclusion of the women under study in the formation and implementation of the research), and analysis and interpretation grounded in subjects' experiences. The central argument of such approaches is that so much of women's reality has been distorted by male-dominated research that studies 'de novo' from women's perspectives must be done as necessary correctives.

Other scholars argue that positivism and quantitative methods are not inherently sexist (Morgan 1981), nor is there a specific feminist research methodology (Kelly (1978). Jayaratne (1983) has addressed specific claims that quantitative research is not useful to the understanding of women. For example, she responds to the challenge that traditional research does not make an impact on social problems of women by asserting that well-grounded statistical data documenting the condition of women can be very useful to activists. To the question that quantitative data cannot convey in-depth understanding of women, Jayaratne argues that quantitative methods make possible the analysis of complex research designs.

There are conciliatory positions as well. Kelly (1978) calls for a wide range of methodologies, not replacement of some by others. Jayaratne (1983) suggests reworking those elements of quantitative research that are antithetical to feminist ideas. Echoing Kaplan's (1964) earlier plea, Wallston (1981) argues that the choice of method must depend on the research question. Advocates for a more open research approach maintain that qualitative procedures can often increase the soundness of quantitative data. Qualitative procedures can enhance structured ones in several ways. Responses to direct, structured questions can often be contradicted later by indirect techniques, calling for analyses encompassing both (Armstrong and Armstrong 1983). Vague concepts are made more explicit (Hornstein 1979), and initial answers made clearer by fuller subject-oriented inquiry (Acker, Barry, and Esseveld 1983). Keller (1980) cites the work of McClintock in the physical sciences to illustrate the creative articulation of contrasting methodologies. In scientific work on plant genetics, McClintock includes intense periods of open observation, achieving a 'feeling for the organism.' This intuition is then 'secured by empirical and logical demonstrations of utmost rigor' (Keller 1980: 345).

A paradigm shift

Following Kuhn's (1970) analysis of the history of science, the development of knowledge about women and about gender differences may spark a paradigm shift. Kuhn cites the prevalence of anomalies which do not fit into current theories as forerunners of such a shift. Feminist scholars have accumulated an array of such challenges to major social science theories.

Because most social science research has been conducted by men, studies of women have naturally been influenced by male views of women in society and by male definitions of problems. Distortions about the condition of women have resulted. Women's perspectives and experiences have been trivialized or ignored (Hornstein 1979) and their contributions to society devalued (Westkott 1979). Men have been conceptualized as the norm, and women as deviant (Patai 1983). As Gould (1980: 164) comments, social science has been guided by 'androcentric assumptions about who is what and which is better.' Empirical findings about women's experiences now bring into question the validity of much of current knowledge, and, equally important, challenge the assumptions underlying the development of that knowledge.

Feminist scholars question that the categories of masculine and feminine are natural categories accompanied by natural roles, and assert that they are socially derived historical constructs (Keller 1980). Some scholars insist on a move from predominantly psychological explanations for personal differences to the social context of gender-related expectations (Giele 1972; Grady 1981; McGuigan 1974). With the recognition that women's place in society is a function of power relationships and male definitions, the scientific paradigm shift necessary to understand women and include them in human understanding suggests a revolutionary turn. Patai (1983: 177) asserts that the question being raised may 'challenge and ultimately overturn traditional views of men, women and human society along with the social structures that both legitimize and perpetuate these views.'

Researchers and educators are thus faced with the issue of modifying current knowledge and research procedures. The choices range from redefining certain accepted concepts (e.g. women's achievement motivation) through a challenge to general theoretical orientations (e.g. psychoanalytic interpretations) to a revolutionary stance as posed by Patai. The teaching of research is enhanced through student understanding of changing paradigms and related options in the research process.

Political purposes of research

A major characteristic of current scholarship concerning women is the clear statement that there must be social science *for* women, not just about women (Acker, Barry, and Esseveld 1983). Reflecting the general judgment of the women's movement that the 'personal is political', the condition of women is explained by the socioeconomic structure, and scholarship on women's lives is expected to have an impact on that structure (Duelli-Klein 1983; Mies 1983). Research findings then become a strategy for documenting the social conditions of women so that change can occur (Roberts 1981), and facts are sought as a route to seeking alternatives to oppressive conditions (Westkott 1979). People of color have similarly called for humaneness and utility of research activities (Friedlander 1970).

The term 'passionate scholarship' (DuBois 1983) is used to make clear that scholars of women's lives are asking new questions for new reasons (Kelly 1978), knowing that such work may be devalued as 'political rather than scientific' (Wallston 1981). The response to this charge is twofold: first, the recognition that such scholarship demands 'rigor, precision and responsiblity' (DuBois 1983: 112), and second, the assertion that such an overtly political position is different from other social science research only in making political motivations clearly open and public.

'Value-free' science has long been questioned, both in academic (Kaplan 1964) and political terms (Becker 1967; Gouldner 1968). The stance of feminist scholars makes overt the fact that all social science research has a political context (Oakley 1981), and that traditional research also has political objectives (Cummerton 1983). 'Social scientists, if they are any good,' Hochschild (1970: 13) argues, 'write about what interests them and interests are socially conditioned.' Even supposedly detached research can mask 'a strong commitment to the status quo' (Jayaratne 1983: 157).

The consequence for research education of this explicit stand about motivations is to force critics to look for the effects of biases and value bases in all research. In this way, it becomes less possible for scholars to screen the political context of their work. Consumers can then judge the soundness of the findings in full awareness of the researcher's motivations.

Power and research subjects

Feminist scholars have also raised questions about the power balance between researcher and researched. They recognize that in social inquiry, the power differential is in favor of the investigator who defines both the question and the process of answering it (Acker, Barry, and Esseveld 1983). Researchers may reinforce women's usual devalued role by treating women primarily as data-generating objects, not collaborators, thereby reinforcing the power inequity (Westkott 1979).

Scholars have raised the question of the power imbalance between researcher and researched in part because they are concerned that flawed data might result from this circumstance. In unequal power relationships, the data are likely to reflect the behavior or attitudes subjects believe are expected of them, and not their real actions or feelings (Mies 1983). In addition to the generally acknowledged factors of response set and experimenter bias in research (Kerlinger 1964; Orne 1962), such insights as those derived from the power relationships between colonialists and their subjects enlarge awareness of the behaviors and statements of persons on the lower end of the power imbalance (Seiden 1976).

The greater issue is that the unequal research process itself does not contribute to changing women's condition. Wallston (1981) and others recommend that women subjects participate in the research process by such activities as assisting in the formulation of the problem, and in the dissemination of the results. By recognizing the common condition of researched and researchers as women, the power imbalance can be diluted (Acker, Barry, and Esseveld 1983). Mies (1983) recommends a process of 'conscientization' which, in her definition, enables women to formulate their own problem, provides them with the research tools to understand and appropriate their problem (i.e. take it as their own), and leads to their collective action to ameliorate the problem.

Acker and her associates (1983) recognize the tension inherent in such approaches. If consciousness-raising is part of research subjects' participation, then scholars will only come to study like-minded individuals. The resolution is not easy, since as already has been argued, political processes are present in any research situation and data can be in question whether or not one tries deliberately to change the power imbalance. Further, if research subjects become active participants, the researcher still has the obligation to analyze and generalize (Acker, Barry, and Esseveld 1983).

Procedural corrections

The preceding discussions imply many adjustments to research procedures. The next section specifies some of these recommended changes or cautions, placing emphasis on the all-important problem formulation stage, but commenting on subsequent aspects of the research process as well.

Problem selection and formulation

The major argument about what research problems are pursued and how they are defined is that there has been a 'non-conscious ideology' (Frieze *et al.* 1978) that has assumed male behavior as normative, and that has not taken gender differences into account (Morgan 1981), with the result that the understanding of both men and women has suffered. Since the researcher's own experiences are the major source of questions for study, and since most research scholars have been male, white, and heterosexual, it is not surprising that the questions they have pursued have by and large excluded women, ethnic minorities, and homosexuals. In Grady's (1981) terms, a 'habit of mind' has led to the assumption that men (usually white, heterosexual men) are representative, and masculine behavior has been equated with human behavior (McGuigan 1974). Women have been seen primarily in their relationship to men and within a 'marriage script' (Laws and Schwartz 1977) that leaves those that fall outside – e.g. single mothers, lesbians, and career women – unstudied. Corrections lie in three areas: the study of both men and women, using gender as an explanatory variable; the study of men in previously ignored aspects of their lives; and the raising of wholly new and neglected research areas about women.

Examples of uncharted or newly researched areas suggest the potential for knowledge development. Taking gender differences seriously, one might learn more about decision-making by not exclusively valuing the male world arena, and, for example, studying secretaries' decision-making processes as well as those of executives (Lofland 1975). In the same vein, Barnett and Baruch (1978) believe that the study of men's life patterns, as exemplified by Erikson (1963) and Levinson (1978), fail to take into account a very different life course for women. Gilligan's (1982) work on gender differences in moral development suggests that other well-accepted theories about human beings based on the study of men may be slanted and flawed. Other theories ignore the social context, so that role theory does not include a political analysis of *why* roles are so defined (Roberts 1981). The understanding of men, too, has been handicapped by severely restricting the areas of their lives under study. Comparatively little has been learned about men's roles in families or about the domain of their feelings, thus alienating men from whole aspects of their existence (Daniels 1975; Steinmetz 1974).

The array of comparatively unstudied areas of women's lives, beyond the confines of reproductive and family roles in the majority culture, indicate the gap in knowledge. A partial list includes: work in women's lives, both paid and unsalaried; the private lives of women and children; friendship; gay women; the life-span from a woman's perspective; economic inequities; women as victims of violence; and complexities of sexism experienced by women of color.

Variable selection and definition

Beyond the decision on the research question, the choice of variables influences gender-related outcomes. For example, in social stratification studies, an emphasis on educational attainment, rather than occupational distribution, may lead to different outcomes in view of the sex segregation of women's employment (Blau 1981). Focusing primarily on the husband's occupation ignores the wife's possible higher class consciousness or even her actual higher occupational level. This choice of the husband's occupation as pivotal also ignores the status of the adult, unmarried daughter living at home (Steinmetz 1974). In family research, studies of the mother—son relationship and not the father— or mother—daughter tie assume that the daughter's development is less important than the son's (Scott 1982). In studies of contraceptive decision-making or fertility, the man's role is frequently down-played or omitted (McGuigan 1974; Scales 1977). Smith and Stewart (1983: 4) assert that 'the stereotype literature is filled with studies of how subjects see "blacks" or "women", without specifying gender in the first case or race in the second.'

The example of women's work demonstrates potential bias in the step following the choice of variables – their operational definitions. The definition of work usually excludes women's unpaid work at home, and the classification 'housewife' ignores the fact that women frequently are in and out of the workforce. Armstrong and Armstrong's (1983) critique of the Canadian government census highlights other definitional distortions about work and economics. Their list includes the criterion of 'family maintainer' defined as the provider of shelter and energy (usually the husband), even though many women wage-earners pay for other essential family needs such as food, clothing, and services. Comparing the hours of part-time work (usually done by women) with full-time work ignores the absence of vacation and holidays for the part-time worker. The care-giving role (usually carried by women) is defined only by children's care, and not that given to other relatives, which is also often a large part of women's responsibilities.

Sampling

The influence of sampling decisions is the source of the major critique that women have not been included appropriately in the development of theory. Gender differences and the special concerns and attributes of women are concealed when all-male samples are used, as they are frequently, or when sex differences in mixed samples are ignored. When gender analysis is done on data from mixed-sex samples, sex differences are found in most instances (Carlson and Carlson 1960). In this connection, Roberts (1981: 15) comments that the all-male sample is seen as 'unproblematical,' while the all-female sample is termed 'odd, inadequate or perverse.' Interestingly, Reardon and Prescott (1977) report that there has been a recent tendency to overgeneralize from all-women samples, as has been traditionally done with all-male samples.

The reasons offered for the exclusion of women are instructive. Working wives are excluded from a retirement study because the husband's retirement is considered more important. Working women are not included in a menopause study because they are 'deviant' (Barnett and Baruch 1978), and women schizophrenic patients are excluded because they are less tractable than men (Wahl 1977). In entire areas of study, e.g. criminality and chemical dependencies, women have only recently been studied (Gottlieb 1980; Leonard 1982).

Scholars have critiqued other sampling decisions. Morgan (1981) argues that wives selected on the basis of a random sample of husbands should not be considered representative of women, even of those with partners, and clearly not of unattached women. Smith and Stewart (1983) maintain that much knowledge of black women is skewed by the selection of samples of 'special' black women.

Issues in gender-fair and woman-oriented research go beyond these critical decisions about the research question, the definitions of the variables under study, and the choice of the persons to be the sources of information. Data gathering and the interpretation of findings have also been the object of scrutiny and challenge.

Data collection, analysis, and interpretation

Though there is literature about control for experimenter bias (Orne 1962), gender as a stimulus variable in the data collection context is usually ignored (Grady 1981; Parlee 1981). In 'blind' experiments the sex of the researcher is known, even though the hypothesis may only be guessed at (Frieze *et al.* 1978).

Gender-relevant issues surface in specific measurement decisions. In achievement inventories devised for educational counseling, though women perform better on items derived from their own experiences, such test items are rare (Donlon, Ekstrom, and Lockheed 1979). In studies of aggression, men's reactions are studied behaviorally and women's through paper and pencil tests (Grady 1981). Woodward and Chisholm (1981) report the difficulty in avoiding sex-differentiated assumptions in asking wives and husbands about their respective work. Whatever the subject, gender-free language in data collection is an issue (Diamond 1975).

The power imbalance was referred to earlier as an influence on the validity of data. Westkott (1979) and Duelli-Klein (1983) also consider that since women have had to mask their feelings in adjusting to societal demands, 'faking' may be part of their natural repertoire and will thus influence the data collection process.

Problems in data analysis and interpretation reflect both the anomalies in knowledge development (Kuhn 1970) and the procedures that do not take gender fully into account. Researchers have eliminated information on women when it did not fit well with male data, or when theories could not predict female behavior (McGuigan 1974). An illustrative result is a 'literature on schizophrenia that does not apply equally well to both sexes' (Wahl 1977: 198). Data analysis in studies of both racism and sexism does not sufficiently separate the effect of sexism experienced differentially by minority and majority women, and racism experienced differentially by minority men and women (Smith and Stewart 1983).

Report writing, discussion sections, and even titles can distort findings. In studies of sexuality, a more assertive sexual stance by women is labelled 'deviant' (Grady 1981); if male subjects are studied, the report is apt to conclude 'individuals are ...', while if a female sample is studied, then 'women/girls/females are ...' (Grady 1981); specific findings on aggression in boys and girls have been reported incorrectly to emphasize verbal aggression in girls (Maccoby and Jacklin 1974). Patai (1983) suggests that Montagu's (1976) book has been inappropriately titled *The Nature of Human Aggression*, since the conclusions are based on the study of men only.

Conclusions

Each of the previous discussions supports an analysis of knowledge development as a societally influenced enterprise (DuBois 1983; Gould 1980). In traditional research, the problems which have been selected, the definitions used for concepts, decisions about data analysis, and interpretations offered have all been influenced by the dominant value systems of society, as reflected in the investigators' activities. Social change brings a different set of social values. The current women's movement spurs academics to question the former 'sociological mode of production' (Morgan 1981: 87), and to see research and knowledge development as a social process.

The obligation of feminist researchers is not just to name traditional research as subject to societal forces, but to recognize the vulnerability of their own research efforts as well. Those cautions have already begun to appear in the literature. These include the risks of romanticizing feminist culture (Keller 1980), including feminist processes in research production (Acker, Barry, and Esseveld 1983); the tendency to latch onto findings which make intuitive sense, and to have 'nonreplicated positive findings sweep through the literature' (Maccoby and Jacklin 1974: 5); the phenomenon that once widely heralded feminist conclusions have come under serious criticism, e.g. androgyny and fear of success

(Deux 1985; Tresemer 1975). Westkott (1979) warns of a cycle of heyday and decline, as in black scholarship. The challenge is to recognize the tension between truth-seeking and social reform, the place for polemic and commitment, the danger of over-empathy (Acker, Barry, and Esseveld 1983; Kelly 1978), the fact that women are not homogeneous (Matthews 1982), and that much work needs to be done to develop viable, empirically tested theories (Jayaratne 1983).

However, it is not a question of potentially biased movement-directed feminist research as against 'objective' research (Blau 1981; Bleier 1978; Keller 1978). Current researchers on women's concerns do not accept the interpretation that men's scholarship concerning men and women has been unbiased whereas when women study women, skewed findings result (Frieze *et al.* 1978; Acker, Barry, and Esseveld 1983). Beyond the long-term debate about 'value-free' scholarship, feminist scholarship has now made gender bias explicit for all research. The terms 'conscious partiality' (Mies 1983) or 'conscious subjectivity' (Duelli-Klein 1983) do not imply an uncritical acceptance of methodology, but a recognition of both values and reform objectives along with procedural protections against the effects of bias.

In addition to methodological issues, the sociology of knowledge development about women's lives is being made explicit in other ways. Illustrations are found in Reinharz's (1981) typology of feminist researchers as categorized according to their acceptance of traditional paradigms, the several analyses of gender-biased publication processes (Grady 1981; Spender 1981), and the cautions just referred to about the swift acceptance of unreplicated findings.

As important, scholars have set out agendas for the work ahead. Lists of unfinished business include new knowledge about women with different sexual orientations (Morin 1977) and ethnicities (Smith 1980; Smith and Stewart 1983), and more research on men, done through non-linear, more communal approaches (Wallston 1981). More fundamentally, a reinterpretation of existing knowledge is called for because of the gender bias of previous work (Kelly 1978). Hochschild (1970: 14) terms this 'getting science straight.'

Curriculum issues

The format of this chapter suggests ways of incorporating the material into research courses. The major issues discussed first can be interwoven with initial content on purposes of research, values, and problem formulation. The procedural corrections fall naturally into the chronology of steps in the research process. Beyond mainstream courses, a specialized course in feminist research can utilize more extensively the bibliography cited here. The extent of empirical research and analyses on the condition of women provides ample grounding for specialized study (Reinharz and Bombyk 1983). For either course, the chapter's content can be a resource for a useful analysis of the sociology of knowledge.

References

Acker, J., Barry, K., and Esseveld, J. (1983) Objectivity and Truth: Problems in Doing Feminist Research. *Women's Studies International Forum* 6(4): 423–35.

Armstrong, P. and Armstrong, P. (1983). Beyond Numbers: Problems with Quantitative Data. In Mary Kinnear and Greg Mason (eds) *Women and Work*. Winnipeg: University of Manitoba Institute for Social and Economic Research for the Social Sciences and Humanities Research Council of Canada.

Bakan, P. (1966) *The Duality of Human Existence*. Chicago: Rand McNally.

Barnett, R. and Baruch, G. (1978) Women in the Middle Years: A Critique of Research and Theory. *Psychology of Women Quarterly* 3(2): 187–97.

Becker, H. (1967) Whose Side Are You On? *Social Problems* 14: 239–47.

Blau, F. (1981) On the Role of Values in Feminist Scholarship. *Signs: Journal of Women in Culture and Society* 6(3): 538–40.

Bleier, R. (1978). Bias in Biological and Human Sciences: Some Comments. *Signs: Journal of Women in Culture and Society* 4(1): 159–62.

Carlson, R. (1972). Understanding Women: Implications for Personality Theory and Research. *Journal of Social Issues* 28(2): 17–32.

Carlson, E. and Carlson, R. (1960) Male and Female Subjects in Personality Research. *Journal of Abnormal and Social Psychology* 61(3): 482–83.

Cummerton, J. (1983) A Feminist Perspective on Research: What Does It Help Us to See? Paper presented at the annual meeting of the Council on Social Work Education.

Daniels, A. (1975) Feminist Perspective in Sociological Research. In Marcia Millman and Rosabeth M. Kanter (eds) *Another Voice*. New York: Doubleday.

Deaux, K. (1985) Sex and Gender. *Annual Review of Psychology* 36.

Diamond, E. (1975) Guidelines for the Assessment of Sex Bias and Sex Fairness in Career Interest Inventories. *Measurement and Evaluation in Guidance* 8(1): 7–11.

Donlon, T., Ekstrom, R. and Lockheed, M. (1979) The Consequences of Sex Bias in the Content of Major Achievement Test Batteries. *Measurement and Evaluation in Guidance* 11(4): 202–14.

DuBois, B. (1983) Passionate Scholarship: Notes on Values, Knowing and Method in Feminist Social Science. In Gloria Bowles and Renata Duelli-Klein (eds), *Theories of Women's Studies*. London: Routledge and Kegan Paul.

Duelli-Klein, R. (1983) How to Do What We Want to Do: Thoughts about Feminist Methodology. In Gloria Bowles and Renata Duelli-Klein (eds) *Theories of Women's Studies*. London: Routledge and Kegan Paul.

Erikson, E. (1963) *Childhood and Society*. New York: Norton.

Friedlander, F. (1970) Emerging Blackness in a White Research World. *Human Organization* 29(4): 239–50.

Frieze, I., Parsons, J., Johnson, P., Ruble, D., and Zellman, G. (1978) *Women and Sex Roles*. New York: W.W. Norton.

Giele, J. (1972) New Developments in Research on Women. In Viola Klein (ed.) *The Feminine Character*. Urbana, IL: University of Illinois.

Gilligan, C. (1982) Why Should a Woman Be More Like a Man? *Psychology Today* 16(6): 68–75.

Glaser, B. and Strauss, A. (1967) *The Discovery of Grounded Theory*. Chicago: Aldine.

Gottlieb, N. (1980) Women and Chemical Dependency. In N. Gottlieb (ed.) *Alternative Social Services for Women*. New York: Columbia University Press.

Gould, M. (1980) The New Sociology. *Signs: Journal of Women in Culture and Society* 5(3): 459–67.

Gouldner, A. (1968) The Sociologist as Partisan: Sociology and the Welfare State. *American Sociologist* 3: 103–16.

Grady, K. (1981) Sex Bias in Research Design. *Psychology of Women Quarterly* 5(4): 628–36.

Hochschild, A. (1970) The American Woman: Another Idol of Social Science. *Transacton* 8(11–12): 13–14.

Hornstein, G. (1979) New Approaches to the Study of Female Friendship and Communication. Paper presented at the annual meeting of the Association for Women in Psychology.

Jayaratne, T. (1983) The Value of Quantitative Research for Methodology in Feminist Research. In Gloria Bowles and Renata Duelli-Klein (eds) *Theories of Women's Studies*. London: Routledge and Kegan Paul.

Kaplan, A. (1964) *The Conduct of Inquiry*. San Francisco: Chandler Publishing.

Keller, E. (1978) Gender and Science. *Psychoanalysis and Contemporary Thought* 1: 409–33.

—— (1980) Feminist Critique of Sciences: A Forward or Backward Move. *Fundamenta Scientiae* 1: 341–49.

Kelly, A. (1978) Feminism and Research. *Women's Studies International Quarterly* 1: 225–32.

Kerlinger, F. (1964) *Foundation of Behavioral Research*. New York: Holt, Rinehart, and Winston.

Kuhn, T. (1970) *The Structure of Scientific Revolutions*. Chicago: University of Chicago Press.

Laws, J. and Schwartz, P. (1977) *Sexual Scripts*. Hinsdale, IL: Dryden Press.

Leonard, E. B. (1982) *Women, Crime and Society*. New York: Longman.

Levinson, D. (1978) *The Seasons of a Man's Life*. New York: A. A. Knopf.

Lofland, L. (1975) The 'Thereness' of Women: A Selective Review of Urban Sociology. In Marcia Millman and Rosabeth M. Kanter (eds) *Another Voice*. New York: Doubleday.

Maccoby, E. and Jacklin, C. (1974) *The Psychology of Sex Differences*. Palo Alto, CA: Stanford University Press.

Matthews, S. (1982) Rethinking Sociology Through a Feminist Perspective. *The American Sociologist* 17 (February): 29–35.

McGuigan, D. (1974) *New Research on Women*. Ann Arbor: University of Michigan.

Mies, M. (1983) Toward a Methodology for Feminist Research. In G. Bowles and R. Duelli-Klein (eds) *Theories of Women's Studies*. London: Routledge and Kegan Paul.

Montagu, A. (1976) The Nature of Human Aggression. New York: Oxford University Press.

Morgan, D. (1981) Men, Masculinity and the Process of Sociological Enquiry. In Helen
Roberts (ed.) *Doing Feminist Research*. London: Routledge and Kegan Paul.

Morin. S. (1977). Heterosexual Bias in Psychological Research on Lesbianism and Male
Homosexuality. *American Psychologist* 32(3): 629–37.

Oakley, A. (1981) Interviewing Women: A Contradiction in Terms. In Helen Roberts
(ed.) *Doing Feminist Research*. London: Routledge and Kegan Paul.

Orne, M. (1962) On the Social Psychology of the Psychological Experiment: With Particular Reference to Demand Characteristics and Their Implications. *American Psychologist* 17 (November): 776–83.

Parlee, M. (1981) Appropriate Control Group in Feminist Research. *Psychology of
Women Quarterly* 5(4): 637–44.

Patai, D. (1983) Beyond Defensiveness: Feminist Research Strategies. *Women's Studies
International Forum* 6(2): 177–89.

Reardon, P. and Prescott, S. (1977) Sex as Reported in a Recent Sample of Psychological
Research. *Psychology of Women Quarterly* 2(2): 157–61.

Reinharz, S. (1981) Dimensions of the Feminist Research Methodology Debate: Impetus,
Definitions, Dilemmas and Stances. Paper presented at the American Psychological
Association Division 35 Symposium.

—— (1983) Experiential Analyses: A Contribution to Feminist Research. In G. Bowles
and R. Duelli-Klein (eds) *Theories of Women's Studies*. London: Routledge and Kegan
Paul.

Reinharz, S. and Bombyk, M. (1983) Methodological Issues in Feminist Research. A Bibliography of Literature in Women's Studies, Sociology and Psychology. *Women's
Studies International Forum* 6(4): 437–54.

Roberts, H. (ed.) (1981) *Doing Feminist Research*. London: Routledge and Kegan Paul.

Scales, P. (1977) Males and Morals: Teenage Contraceptive Behavior Amid the Double
Standard. *The Family Coordinator* 26(3): 211–22.

Scott, P. (1982) Debunking Sapphire: Towards a Non-Racist and Non-Sexist Social
Science. In G. T. Hull, P. Scott, and B. Smith (eds) *But Some of Us Are Brave*. Old
Westbury, NY: Feminist Press.

Seiden, A. (1976) Research on the Psychology of Women, II. *American Journal of Psychiatry* 133: 1111–123.

Smith, A. and Stewart, A. (1983) Approaches to Studying Racism and Sexism in Black
Women's Lives. *Journal of Social Issues* 3: 1–15.

Smith, B. (1980) Racism and Women's Studies. *Frontiers* 5(1): 48–9.

Spender, D. (1981) The Gatekeepers: A Feminist Critique of Academic Publishing. In
Helen Roberts (ed.) *Doing Feminist Research*. London: Routledge and Kegan Paul.

Steinmetz, S. (1974) The Sexual Context of Social Research. *The American Sociologist* 9
(August): 111–16.

Tresemer, D. (1975) Assumptions Made About Gender Roles. In Marcia Millman and
Rosabeth M. Kanter (eds), *Another Voice*. New York: Doubleday.

Wahl, V. (1977) Sex Bias in Schizophrenic Research: A Short Report. *Journal of Abnormal Psychology* 86(2): 195–98.

Wallston, B. (1981) What Are the Questions in Psychology of Women? A Feminist
Approach to Research. *Psychology of Women Quarterly* 5(4): 597–617.

Westkott, M. (1979) Feminist Criticism of the Social Sciences. *Harvard Educational
Review* 49(4): 422–30.

Woodward, D. and Chisholm, L. (1981) The Expert's View? The Sociological Analysis of Graduates' Occupational and Domestic Roles. In Helen Roberts (ed.) *Doing Feminist Research*. London: Routledge and Kegan Paul.

PART II
Specialization by intervention

7 Overview

Dianne S. Burden

This section focuses on the impact of gender on social work intervention strategies at both the direct and indirect service levels. The heart of social work practice is direct services with individuals, couples, families, and groups. Most social work practitioners will spend some significant portion of their careers in an agency providing direct services. Others will provide service through community organization – assisting clients to change their lives by impacting the political environment through social action. Since the great majority of social service providers, as well as clients, are women, gender issues which affect provision of services take on particular importance for social work education. While women are concentrated in the profession as clients and service providers, men are found primarily as higher-status, higher-paid administrators and directors. This power imbalance between men and women in social services acts to reinforce the low-status, powerless position of women clients and thus provides a serious obstacle to empowering them.

The three chapters in this section focus on this dysfunctional power differential between men and women in social work at the interpersonal, organizational, and societal levels. The chapters assert that the primary objective of intervention at all three levels – direct services, administration, and community organizing – should be to empower women, both clients and practitioners, to gain a fair share of control over their environments. The section reprises the theme that for women in social work, the personal is political. That is, women's personal problems stem to a considerable degree from inequitable power distribution in the political and economic systems. This lack of power deprives women of a sense of internal locus of control which in turn may contribute to dysfunctional intrapsychic and interpersonal dynamics.

Cheryl Richey in her chapter on 'Incorporating Gender Content in Direct Practice Curricula' finds little evidence of gender content in current social work practice literature. The goal of her chapter is to incorporate interdisciplinary scholarship on women into both classroom and field instruction. She reviews theoretical and applied literature on direct practice with women and assesses recent social science literature on women in psychology, sociology, and political science. The chapter focuses on increasing practitioner awareness of gender as a major variable in all human interactions and institutions. It then provides material to increase skills in unbiased behavior with clients. Unbiased clinician behavior is developed not only by facilitating non-sexist attitudes, but by increasing awareness about the role of gender throughout the intervention process. Richey discusses gender as it affects the relationship-building, assessment, and intervention components of direct service. Her goal is to inform human service providers of ways gender biases, sex-role stereotypes, and sexist attitudes affect practitioner and client behavior. Throughout the chapter Richey suggests strategies to recognize and counter gender-related bias which may impede the direct service process.

Marie Weil's chapter on 'Women in Administration: Curriculum and Strategies,' focuses on the inequity women face in human service management positions despite the fact that they were the founders of the profession. Weil discusses causes of the inequity and recommends strategies to assist women to move into administration. She identifies barriers to entry into management as well as barriers to advancement in human services administration. These barriers include structural, interpersonal, and personal factors which prevent or inhibit women from achieving positions of authority. Structural barriers, for example, include the male/female power differential within organizations which acts to exclude women from gaining significant power in the hierarchy. Tokenism gives an impression of admitting women into the power structure. However, exclusion of women from informal networks where major decisions are made offsets the impact of allowing a few women into management positions. Women are further restricted from advancing in administration by an opportunity structure which excludes them from career ladder positions and relegates them to dead-end direct service jobs where they have little opportunity to demonstrate their administrative capacity. Sex-role stereotyping assigns the care-giving role to women and equates it with weakness. This stereotype reinforces the view of social work as a women's field, except for administration which is male-dominated. The dichotomy leads to continued occupational sex segregation within the field, wage discrimination, discounting of women, and sexual harassment. Weil asserts that women are at further disadvantage because of the lack of emphasis on career development in their lives, and because of the conflict they face as private caregivers. They must find a way to balance multiple roles of job and home with inadequate support from family or the workplace. The chapter concludes with curriculum implications to increase awareness about and develop strategies to overcome barriers to women achieving full partnership in social service administration.

Ruth Brandwein in her chapter on 'Women and Community Organization' continues the examination of perceptions of micropractice as appropriate for women and macropractice as appropriate for men as she assesses the role and contribution of women in community organizing. She identifies two models of community organizing descending from the Charity Organization Society and Settlement House Movements. The thread of practice coming from the Charity Organization Society Movement focuses on co-ordination of services, reduction of fraud and duplication, and efficiency of fund-raising and service delivery. Its locus is in formal organizations in work, primarily with agency directors and boards. The second thread, emanating from the Settlement House Movement, focuses on social reform, legislative advocacy, and community organizing of constituencies to self-help. Its locus is in the neighborhoods, particularly with a social action approach. Women have tended to be involved in the second trend and not in the first. Men have traditionally dominated in higher-status, more conservative, establishment-oriented formal organizations. Women have pre-dominated in neighborhood agencies, organizing volunteers, and as unpaid advocates for legislative and political change. Brandwein identifies a recurring cycle of activist periods in community organizing dominated by women, alter-nating with conservative periods dominated by men. The activist periods focus on locality development and are characterized by volunteer work and social action. Conservative periods by contrast are dominated by male community organizers with an image as tough-minded business managers. Brandwein proposes a feminist approach to community organizing which would avoid the polarization of previous decades. She then discusses the policy and curriculum implications of this feminist approach to community organizing.

The primary mission of social work practice is to provide interventions which will change clients' lives for the better. To be effective, change strategies in both direct and indirect services must consider the impact of gender bias, sex-role socialization, and stereotyping on the lives of clients as well as on the dynamic of the intervention itself. The chapters in this section address particular areas of social work intervention in direct practice, administration, and community organizing and identify major issues of gender-related content that should be included in social work curriculum content if practitioners are to be trained to serve the needs of women clients.

8 Incorporating gender content in direct practice curricula

Cheryl A. Richey

While human service professionals continue to diversify in the roles they per-form, the social problems they address, and the population groups they serve, it is nevertheless recognized that a central mission of social work remains direct practice with individuals, families, and groups. Moreover, despite evidence that a sizable percentage of clinicians find themselves in management and adminis-tration at some point in their careers, most entry level positions are still in the direct services. Thus, since most practitioners will likely perform in a clinical capacity for some part of their careers, it is critical that issues relevant to non-sexist practice be included in course content which will reach the greatest number of people in the most comprehensive way. This chapter will focus on integrating gender-relevant content into beginning and intermediate level practice courses. Not only is competence at these levels critical for anyone preparing to work with clients, but training in basic and intermediate practice skills is frequently required, meaning that content in these offerings will likely reach the greatest number of student-practitioners. These 'centerstage' offerings provide an ideal platform for addressing issues pertaining to gender-fair and culturally sensitive practice.

Evidence of gender content in current practice literature

Despite arguments for incorporating gender-relevant content into direct practice training, little evidence of this integration was found in a subject index survey of five texts appropriate for introductory methods courses. While certainly not a representative sample, nor an exhaustive survey, the tally did prove informative. Two volumes contained no subject references to 'gender,' 'sex-roles,' or 'women/men' (Gambrill 1983; Shulman 1984). The books by Cormier and Cormier

(1985) and Hepworth and Larsen (1982) included several pages on sex-role stereotyping. Ivey and Authier (1978) use five pages to discuss women's issues in microcounseling and include a detailed transcript of two interviews in which a male 'helper' exhibits sexist and non-sexist responses with a female 'helpee.' While more gender-relevant content may well be contained in these volumes, it does not appear to be a major subject or topic in direct practice skills training.

Incorporating interdisciplinary scholarship on women

This chapter provides the classroom and field instructor with practical guidelines for integrating two relatively distinct bodies of literature. One includes the theoretical and applied literature on direct practice which contains specific suggestions for developing counseling skills. The second knowledge base emanates largely from other social science disciplines, including psychology, sociology, anthropology, political science, and women's studies. This growing interdisciplinary literature, much of it data-based, suggests that gender is a variable to be reckoned with in all human interactions and social institutions. Gender influences the development and expression of attitudes and expectations about self and others, and affects the development and display of words and actions in daily interpersonal exchanges. For example, survey data document the existence among clinicians of sex-role stereotypes of mental health standards and conservative or traditional attitudes toward women (cf. Sherman 1980). While study outcomes are not always consistent, several relevant patterns have been noted: (a) male therapists tend to express more stereotypic and conservative views of women (especially working mothers) (Sherman 1980); (b) strong correlations have been found between traditional sex-role attitudes or sexist beliefs and homophobia (Weitz 1984); and (c) therapist attitudes toward women appear to become more liberal or less stereotyped over time (Sherman 1980).

Ostensibly, the existence of stereotypic attitudes about women and men (not to mention biased views of clients diverse in socioeconomic class, cultural background, and/or sexual orientation) could jeopardize many aspects of the practitioner–client relationship and their work together. Certainly, providing student-practitioners with opportunities to examine and challenge their own attitudes and assumptions about women and men can enhance self-awareness (Kravetz 1982). To this end, the reader is referred to several texts which include introductory material and learning activities on clarifying values (Hepworth and Larsen 1982) and identifying sex-role stereotypes and biases (Cormier and Cormier 1985).

Expecting more than attitude change

Since facilitating non-sexist or liberal attitudes may not be a guarantee against unbiased behavior with clients (Miller 1983; Sherman 1980), this chapter will attempt to go beyond attitude exploration and attitude change. More specifically, the focus will be on overt or concrete manifestations of, and safeguards against, gender bias in work with clients during three phases or components of practice – relationship-building, assessment, and intervention. It is postulated that student-practitioners might be more willing and able to acknowledge and respond to specific feedback on what they *do* or fail to do than they might be to general admonitions to 'correct' their attitudes, values, and world views. Throughout, the emphasis will be on ways to introduce material so that practitioners regardless of theoretical orientation will be more likely to acknowledge the importance of gender issues in practice, explore their overt and covert responses to various clients and their situations, and alter behaviors which may interfere with non-sexist clinical practice.

Relationship-building

Social science research strongly suggests that gender can influence the pattern, style, and outcome of interaction. This information is especially pertinent to practitioner training given the importance placed on building rapport or a 'therapeutic alliance' by virtually all clinical treatment approaches. For example, anecdotal, analogue, and field data of same and mixed-sex interactions suggest that the following verbal and non-verbal behaviors can communicate and maintain gender-role stereotypes and power differences between women and men: greeting rituals including forms of address, touching, amount of talk, frequency of interruptions, extent of affective communication, awareness of non-verbal cues, and displays of active listening responses. Henley (1977) suggests that gender and power gestures are related. When interacting with men, women appear to display, rather consistently, behaviors that are associated with subordinate status. Usually interactions between social equals are symmetrical, whereas relationships between people of unequal status are characterized by asymmetry. For example, higher-status individuals touch lower-status persons, and men touch women (Henley 1977). Even a seemingly innocuous interaction, such as greeting someone, can reflect subtle status and power differences which may in turn reinforce an individual's subordination based on gender, ethnicity, or other factors. Again, the rules of status equity and symmetry apply. When asymmetry occurs, the individual who uses a more familiar form of address (calls someone by her first name) may be communicating status superiority.

Practitioners can refer to findings from social science research when examining their own and others' initial behaviors with clients and colleagues for possible bias. For instance, are female clients more likely to be touched and called by their first names than male clients, thus 'reminding' women of their inferior social status? Of course, the cultural norms of those interacting must also be considered when assessing the appropriateness of specific worker behaviors. For example, when working with Latinos, Valdez and Gallegos (1982) stress the importance of respecting *personalismo* by greeting Hispanic clients informally and exchanging first names. Alternatively, work with Pacific-Asian clients will likely be facilitated if the practitioner accepts the client's definition of the counselor as an authority figure, and maintains attention to the elaborate social etiquette governing most relationships (Ishisaka and Takagi 1982).

Asymmetry also characterizes the conversational interaction between men and women and mirrors the speech asymmetries of high- and low-status individuals (Crosby, Jose, and Wong-McCarthy 1981). Numerous studies report that when men are in all-male and mixed-sex groups they display an interactional 'dominance' pattern by doing more talking (cf. Argyle and Dean 1968) and interrupting (cf. Zimmerman and West 1975). The practice implications of these findings appear extensive, including the ramifications for facilitating equitable participation among co-therapists, and among male and female group and family members in counseling.

Practitioner attentiveness and emotional responsivity

Gender has also been found to influence attentive listening and affective expression. For instance, studies of gazing behavior have repeatedly found that women engage in more eye contact with their partners in dyads than do men (cf. Exline, Gray, and Schuette 1965). Since women look more, it is understandable that they also consistently demonstrate greater sensitivity to non-verbal or paralinguistic cues, such as facial expressions, gestures, and voice inflections (Rosenthal *et al.* 1979). In addition to more looking in conversations and greater perceptiveness of social signals, women also evidence more active listening responses like 'right' or 'um-hmm' during same and mixed-sex conversations (Adams and Ware 1984). Encouraging clients to express themselves fully in counseling is critical given that clients who reported more successful outcomes in both psychodynamically oriented and behaviorally oriented treatment also spoke for longer periods of time in their sessions (Sloane *et al.* 1975). In light of these findings, possible gender differences in practitioner attentiveness to or reinforcement of clients would be an important issue to pursue in training.

After reviewing the research literature, Maracek and Johnson (1980) conclude that gender appears to be a strong determinant of affective expression in therapy. For example, one study found that client–therapist pairs containing either a female client or a female therapist expressed more feelings (Fuller 1963). In another study, female clients with female therapists perceived the treatment process as more comfortable and supportive, whereas women with male counselors reported feeling more tense and self-critical (Orlinsky and Howard 1976).

These findings underscore the importance of practitioner self-surveillance. For instance, does a male clinician find that clients, especially women, are more reticent in sessions than is helpful? In what ways might his own verbal and non-verbal behavior be influencing or supporting low client involvement (does he fail to respond adequately when a client elaborates, or does he fail to reflect the client's emotional message when this would be appropriate)? Do practitioners over-compensate for observed or expected gender differences in clients' conversational behavior? For example, in marital counseling, does the worker unwittingly place more value and emphasis on the male partner discovering and expressing his emotions, thus limiting the woman's arena for self-expression (Robbins 1983)?

The observations presented above reaffirm the importance of drawing on the social science literature when attempting to pinpoint and alter practitioner behaviors which may facilitate or impede unbiased, growth-promoting interactions with clients. Of particular interest is the possibility that men and women entering careers as professional helpers bring with them certain interpersonal strengths and limitations which result from their gender-role socialization experiences. Male counselors may benefit from more specific feedback on and 'remedial' training in attentive, empathic listening skills. Female counselors, on the other hand, may require additional training in verbal 'assertiveness' with some clients or with some treatment modalities (e.g. with groups and families). To facilitate practitioner self-awareness, self-observation, and self-modification of specific interpersonal behaviors which may be gender-biased, sample learning activities, including exercises and assignments appropriate for class and field application, are presented below.

Learning activities for enhancing competence in relationship-building

Increasing descriptive reporting An important generic skill which provides the foundation for many additional competencies to be discussed in this and later sections is the ability to describe or operationalize observations about behavior. Beginning practitioners may be more likely to 'hear' and respond to a descriptive or objective account of some aspect of their interview behavior, e.g. 'I observed five interruptions during your fifteen-minute interview,' than they would if the feedback was vague and inferential, e.g. 'You were very controlling and domineering in that interview.' Descriptive accounts of practitioner (and client) behavior focus on what the person actually says and does (or fails to say and do) rather than on (or certainly in addition to) the observer's subjective interpretation of the person's intent, emotions, or morality.

A useful exercise, which has been employed with students and practitioners, involves showing videotaped vignettes and requesting participants to write descriptions of what they observed after each segment. 'Simple' vignettes can be shown first (one person engaging in an action, no talking), followed by more complex interactions (a couple discussing a problem, a worker–client interview). After each segment respondents share their descriptive reports, pointing out inferences (many of which are gender-biased, e.g. 'She was seductive') and replacing these with more behaviorally specific terms. Once the description/inference distinction is clear, skills in behavioral specification can be elicited and refined in subsequent practice training activities.

Identifying gender bias in other practitioners Activities that engage practitioners in observing and describing helpful and unhelpful responses of others in the counselor role can prepare them to observe and specify their own interviewing behaviors. Observation of discrete interviewer behaviors can be facilitated by employing checklists or rating forms. For example, Gambrill (1983) includes checklists for reviewing listening, self-expression, and demonstrating respect. Ivey and Authier (1978) present scales for rating verbal and non-verbal attending behavior and provide guidelines for taking specific behavioral counts.

For a number of years in introductory practice courses, the author has shown a videotape which demonstrates the effects of clinician bias on the process and outcome of treatment. A Caucasian female counselor interviews an ethnically-mixed couple in conflict. The wife, who is also Caucasian, wants to go back to school and pursue a career; the Asian-American husband is uncertain how these changes will affect traditional marriage and family roles. In sharp contrast to what students expect, i.e. a clear anti-feminist or traditional gender-role bias, the worker demonstrates unilateral and unequivocal support for the woman's position and perceptions. The clinician through her verbal and nonverbal responses clearly 'sides with' the wife, alienates the husband, and all but severs whatever therapeutic relationship may have been developing. The tape is powerful because it is a real – not staged – exemplar of clinician bias demonstrated by a worker who is an experienced, highly regarded feminist therapist thus illustrating that biased responding is not limited to men, sexists, or neophytes. Because students frequently identify with the clinician's pro-feminist stance they become more personally involved with and touched by the awkward, insensitive, and reckless advocacy of a particular value orientation, even one with which they agree and believe to be 'politically correct'. During discussion, students acknowledge the ubiquitous threat of biased responding and the importance of ongoing surveillance of how one's biases may influence such fundamental treatment activities as building a relationship, developing a service agreement or contract, and encouraging clients to consider alternative viewpoints and options.

Identifying one's own biases   Self-observation is a valuable activity for recognizing one's own biases and how socialization influences behaviors in obvious and subtle ways. Self-observation can be facilitated in beginning and intermediate practice courses by having trainees videotape simulated interviews with peers who enact various client characteristics and problem situations. Ideas for diverse client vignettes can be drawn from the direct practice literature (cf. Green 1982; Hall 1978; Hepworth and Larsen 1982). While the validity of analogue interviews must be cautiously interpreted (Maracek and Johnson 1980), the author's experience with such simulations and the resultant feedback from students suggests that generous amounts of the 'practitioner's' pattern and style of interacting with 'clients,' including emotional reactions, are evoked by role-playing.

The thoroughness and objectivity with which trainees observe and evaluate their recorded interviews can be enhanced with a structured review procedure. For example, 'workers' use a form introduced in training for rating their verbal and non-verbal behavior. They also receive feedback from the instructor, peers, and 'client.' Client feedback is essential in determining whether the goal of developing a beginning rapport with the client was achieved. Multi-source information on the same interview can result in a powerful learning experience.

Self-observation of gender-role patterns and gender biases can also take place in the real world. Class sessions and agency staff meetings often provide good 'laboratories' for monitoring behavior. For example, female students have reported the impact of observing in an agency case staffing the patterns of verbal and spatial dominance of male participants, and their own constricted interaction by comparison.

Changing specific behaviors   Self-awareness of stereotypic and gender-biased behavior is an important but not sufficient ingredient for behavior change. Given years of conditioning and the institutionalization of sexism, racism, and other prejudices, meaningful change will require practice, monitoring progress, and more practice. Many specific skill-building exercises can be readily incorporated into class and field training, including activities for improving listening and empathic responding (cf. Cormier and Cormier 1985; Hepworth and Larsen 1982).

Trainees can also pursue self-modification by contracting with an instructor or supervisor to pinpoint, monitor, and alter relevant behaviors, feelings, and thoughts which may interfere with non-sexist practice (cf. Barth 1984). Examples of practice behaviors 'targeted' by students include reducing interruptions of individual clients and families; increasing responsivity to examples of client independence and assertiveness; breaking into the discussion sooner (without interrupting, if possible) when the client's husband verbally abuses her during sessions.

Assessment

Assessment activities, including gathering information and selecting goals and progress indicators, can also be adversely affected by ignorance of gender differences, gender-role stereotypes, and sexist attitudes. With the first client contact, gender biases can begin influencing the focus and accuracy of assessment. For example, practitioners may inquire about some areas and not others, develop hypotheses about 'causation,' form judgments about client ability and motivation to change, and identify 'reasonable' and 'socially appropriate' treatment goals. This section discusses activities which can enhance unbiased or gender-fair assessment, including using descriptive language, gathering multidimensional information, identifying client assets and resources, and involving clients in selecting meaningful goals and progress indicators.

Attending to language usage

'Linguistic sexism' (Adams and Ware 1984) among clients and counselors can contribute to inaccurate and incomplete assessment. Adams and Ware argue that women and men have developed distinctive speech habits which not only reflect but also reinforce institutional sexist attitudes. For example, women clients may over-use terms which trivialize their concerns and define themselves primarily in relationship to men. Given the possibility that women's language may reflect a 'subculture' or at least a reality different from that of men (Gilligan 1982), it is important that practitioners do not assume they understand the words used by clients. The interplay of additional cultural factors, including ethnic minority and sexual minority affiliations, multiply the error factor in interpreting client communications.

The anthropological literature on ethnographic interviewing (Spradley 1979) can provide practitioners with useful tools for clarifying the meaning women clients attach to particular words and phrases. Ethnographic interviewing encourages the descriptive accounting of specific 'cover terms' or linguistic cues used by the respondent who is perceived as the guide to her 'insider's' perspective (Green 1982). For instance, if a client says, 'My partner doesn't love me any more,' the practitioner would ask her to describe and exemplify the terms 'partner' and 'love,' and not assume, a priori, a convergence in understanding.

Practitioners' use of descriptive language is equally critical in reducing gender biases in case reports and the clinical judgments they inspire. Diagnostic terminology is especially vulnerable to subjective interpretation and biased labeling practices (Kaplan 1983). In a review of clinical judgments in counseling analogue studies, Sherman (1980) found considerable evidence of sex-role stereotyping. For example, women and men who deviated from traditional gender role expectations were frequently rated as less adjusted and more in need of counseling. To counter biased inferences, beginning clinicians must be repeatedly urged to use descriptive, client-specific language, and to question the reasons or behavioral evidence for their conclusions and recommendations.

Exploring multidimensional factors

Gender bias in assessment can be further reduced if information gathering is multidimensional, including examination of clients' behavioral, physiological, and cognitive responses in their environmental or systemic contexts. Further, clarifying the sequence or chain of events in situations can provide additional depth or complexity. Systematic use of a multidimensional approach to assessment allows clinicians to identify and correct gender biases and sex-role stereotypes. For instance, are the physiological or affective features of a problem more thoroughly identified for female than male clients? Since there is evidence that women (Seiden 1976) and some ethnic minority populations (Valdez and Gallegos 1982) somaticize psychological distress, it is important that the physiological aspects of client complaints be fully explored. However, a narrow unidimensional focus can limit exploration of other related response domains.

A multidimensional assessment procedure can also assist identification of the external or environmental concomitants of women's concerns. Often the situational antecedents to and consequences of women's difficulties are not adequately explored. For example, MacDonald (1982) postulates that women may not be less assertive than men, but rather that they may be presented with more situations that infringe upon or challenge their rights. Some research suggests that women may experience more acute and chronic stressors than men (Radloff and Rae 1979).

Environmental sources of stress for women which may be overlooked in assessment are inadequate income (Almquist 1984) and inadequate time to fulfill multiple roles. Black women may experience multiple role strain more keenly than other women (Almquist 1984). An examination of the amount of time a client devotes to 'shoulds' and 'wants' (Marlatt and Gordon 1985) may help clarify the extent to which excessive role and time demands and inadequate resources contribute to feelings of helplessness, hopelessness, anger, and low self-esteem.

Identifying client assets and resources

In addition to using descriptive language and multidimensional information sources, identifying clients' assets and environmental resources can also facilitate gender-sensitive assessment. Focusing on women's strengths, coping abilities, and supports is especially important since gender-role stereotypes tend to devalue and label as less 'healthy' traditional 'feminine' characteristics (e.g. Broverman *et al.* 1972).

Identifying client assets and resources can include finding out about the circumstances surrounding the non-occurrence as well as the occurrence of a problem. For example, under what circumstances is the client more likely to handle interpersonal conflict satisfactorily, report more self-confidence, or feel less jittery? What does she do personally and collectively to overcome depression (Rippere 1977)? Exploring how women cope with less traditional lifestyles, for example lesbianism, can also provide evidence of existing survival skills and resources (Weitz 1984).

Effective coping strategies can be emotion-focused, where feeling better is the main objective, and/or problem-focused where the goal is changing the personal and environmental sources of stress (Lazarus and Folkman 1984). Gender-role socialization and expectations may influence the types of coping skills clients develop and the configuration of skills that are mobilized for particular types of stressors, e.g. health, family, or employment concerns. For example, are women trained and encouraged to regulate their emotional reactions in situations more than they are to manage or alter the source of stress?

Some forms of coping function to regulate emotions as well as solve problems. For instance, while talking to others about one's feelings can be a form of emotional coping, it can also bolster problem-solving efforts by generating different solutions and increasing reinforcement for actions taken. Many people seek informal help for problems before requesting professional assistance (Gottlieb 1980).

Even though a woman client may possess and be able to mobilize an interpersonally supportive structure of kith and kin, assessment of these resources could be restricted by traditional gender-role assumptions and biases. For instance, limiting inquiry about sources of support to a woman's husband and immediate family ignores other possible caregivers in her environment, including cohabiting non-family members (Lipman-Blumen 1984), and friends or compadres (Padilla, Ruiz, and Alvarez 1975).

Selecting and measuring target goals
Determining the goal of intervention and selecting indicators of progress can be influenced in numerous ways by gender bias. For example, of all the concerns presented by a client, does the targeted area reflect the client's priorities or the clinician's stereotypic perceptions of what is 'appropriate,' or 'possible'? Goal conflicts can be compounded by lack of practitioner knowledge of and sensitivity to clients' cultural values or sexual preferences. For example, a Native American woman may reject the clinician's emphasis on assertive self-expression because she views this as antagonistic to her values (Almquist 1984). Likewise, practitioners may make faulty assumptions about client goals because they fail to recognize or encourage disclosure of alternative lifestyles.

Even when the practitioner's target focus is gender-fair, the client's own sex-role expectations can limit the types of goals selected. For instance, women clients may be especially prone to select treatment goals that reflect their view of personal responsibility for family problems (Gurman and Klein 1984). Moreover, because some women accept certain role prescriptions as inevitable, they may not recognize available alternatives. These situations present the practitioner with opportunities to suggest or demonstrate options that may be broader than those originally anticipated by the client.

Goals which balance self-understanding, self-change, and environmental change are also more likely to promote gender-fair practice. While it is important to help women understand their behavior in situational contexts, feel better, and think more 'rationally,' it is also imperative that service providers enable women to achieve real as well as perceived control in their lives (Rodin and Langer 1980). Thus, goals should include a focus on the attainment of overt, observable outcomes in real-life situations.

Exclusive emphasis on client behavior change, however, can also be problematic. For instance, time management and cognitive coping skills may help a single parent feel less tense, but her role demands may remain unaltered.In addition to helping her manage her 'shoulds' more efficiently, another equally suitable goal might be to modify external demands to a less oppressive level, thereby increasing the actual amount of time she has for 'wants.' Thus, looking from the person to her context may suggest socioenvironmental change targets which in turn hold promise for influencing specific client reactions.

Finally, it is important that treatment goals for women be specified so that progress or lack of progress can be measured and thus clearly determined by clients and practitioners. Vaguely defined goals allow gender biases to remain undetected by consumers and thus may allow women to be deluded that the situation is improving when it may not be (Gambrill and Richey, in press). Even when goals are specified clearly enough to be measured, clinicians must continue to look out for potential gender bias in observational procedures, standardized questionnaires, rating scales, and physiologic measures (Levy and Richey, in press).

Learning activities for enhancing gender-fair assessment

Exploring gender biases in assessment and target goal selection   Structured learning activities which replicate the numerous analogue studies on gender and therapist judgments can create powerful self-awareness experiences for participants. Virtually any case presentation can be modified to explore differential practitioner reactions. For example, case vignettes can be distributed with some students receiving a female client and some a male client. With all other case information identical, and students remaining uninformed of the gender manipulation, trainees can be asked to determine diagnosis, prioritize target areas, offer a prognosis, determine need for psychotropic medication, and comment on their attitude toward and desire to work with the client. The exercise can be completed individually or in small groups, each group having the same gender client. After the exercise, the gender manipulation is disclosed and participants present their decisions and reactions for discussion.

Identifying women's strengths Providing practitioners with guidelines for and practice in locating personal and environmental resources will increase their thoroughness, diligence, and creativity in pinpointing client assets. Gambrill (1983: Appendix D) provides a Resource Checklist which can facilitate assessment of individual, family, and community resources. Lazarus and Folkman (1984) present a revised sixty-seven-item 'Ways of Coping' checklist which asks respondents to indicate what they thought, felt, or did to cope in a recent personally stressful situation. Finally, a recent review of several available social support measures may help practitioners select appropriate instruments for assessing clients' interpersonal networks (Tardy 1985).

Intervention

While research on gender bias and sex-role stereotyping in human change technologies is less abundant and concrete than in other areas of the treatment enterprise, extrapolations from the literature can nevertheless alert practitioners to possible oversights, missed opportunities, and constricted approaches that may ultimately result in less effective work with women clients. Gender issues may influence the intervention roles assumed by the practitioner, the balance of procedures to enhance client self-understanding and/or change, and the modality of intervention selected. Intervention specification and planning for maintenance of treatment gains are additional activities important to gender-fair practice.

Re-examining practitioner intervention roles
Human service practitioners can assume numerous roles in their work with different clients or with the same client over time. These roles, including 'therapist,' 'advocate,' 'trainer,' 'consultant,' 'educator,' 'mediator,' and 'expeditor,' are influenced by such factors as the organizational features and service mandates of the employing agency, the nature of clients' presenting problems and client resources for problem solution, and practitioner training and proclivities. It is also likely that gender-related variables affect intervention role selection. For example, stereotypic assumptions that women are dependent, passive, and emotional may result in practitioners assuming a more active, advice-giving role, or a more nurturing, caregiving role with female clients. Further, practitioner sex-role socialization may contribute to differential selection of intervention roles. Are female clinicians more comfortable with and more skilled in the roles of 'therapist,' 'consultant,' or 'trainer'? Conversely, do male practitioners select more often the roles of 'advocate,' 'mediator,' and 'expeditor'? Some male

clinicians may experience discomfort and uncertainty with the 'nurturing' functions of the therapist role, whereas women may have difficulty exercising the authority of an expeditor or handling the conflict inherent in the advocate role (cf. Weissman, Epstein, and Savage 1983). Research is needed to determine the extent to which client and practitioner gender influence the selection or delegation of intervention roles and the impact these roles have on client outcomes.

Selecting modalities of change
Gender composition may also influence the modality of intervention selected from individual, couple, family, or group treatment options. Working with women in groups can be especially powerful in helping members understand their common experiences and reduce isolation, view their concerns in a sociopolitical context, and achieve realistic changes (Gottlieb *et al.* 1983).

Individual treatment may be preferable to group treatment if a woman evidences extremely high interpersonal anxiety. Being with others in a group may be so anxiety-provoking as to be counterproductive. There is evidence that female clients diagnosed with anxiety reactions and given individual treatment improve more with female than with male therapists (Orlinsky and Howard 1980). Thus, attending to the interaction among gender, client problem, and intervention modality may also be important with respect to treatment outcome.

Selecting couple or family interventions for women must be done with the awareness that such treatment modalities may reinforce stereotypic gender roles (cf. Gurman and Klein 1980). As some would suggest, the marital relationship per se may be antagonistic to women's mental health given its institutionalized inequities (Steil 1984). However, since most women have been, are, or will be in marital-type relationships with others, and given the importance of perceiving individuals in person–situation transactions, the technology of relationship counseling will likely continue to offer women ways of improving communication and negotiating conflicts. Moreover, family-focused interventions, especially those which include extended kinship members, are often the treatment of choice for certain ethnic minority clients (cf. Ishisaka and Takagi 1982; Valdez and Gallegos 1982).

Specifying intervention components
Describing specific intervention components is important in clinical work with women because it enables clients to assume a more active role in their own treatment and thus helps reduce the power inequities in the helping relationship. Clients will likely be more invested and involved in treatment and be more capable of using these therapeutic procedures in a self-care capacity to manage future problems, if interventions and their rationale are made explicit. 'Therapy' can be demystified by actively engaging the client as a partner in change rather than treating her as a patient to be cured. This partnership can be enhanced by describing

in precise terms all relevant intervention steps, encouraging clients to select the intervention of choice from several alternatives presented, providing clients with handouts describing procedures, and giving clients reading material related to their problems and the techniques selected.

Intervention specification also allows clients to exercise their informed consent regarding participation in any procedure. Because females may be more vulnerable than males to pressures to be 'good clients' and to respond in socially desirable ways (Levy and Richey, in press), women's rights in clinical settings must be a fundamental consideration for practitioners as well as for researchers. Human subjects guidelines should be followed in practice settings including protection from negative effects, access to appropriate and effective treatment, and the right to refuse participation in or withdraw from an intervention procedure without penalty.

Finally, describing the intervention or independent variable allows the practitioner and others to evaluate treatment effectiveness, which can result in improved services for women. If progress indicators suggest client improvement, it would be important to specify the 'recipe' for intervention so that this can be replicated with similar cases in the future. In this way, a knowledge base of non-sexist and effective interventions with women is developed from which practitioners can draw case-by-case. Identifying intervention ingredients also makes possible experimental manipulation – reordering, adding, or withdrawing components and observing treatment effects (cf. Bloom and Fischer 1982). Intervention specification thus allows for flexible and creative 'packaging' of treatment variables which in turn encourages responsive and client-oriented service.

Maintaining treatment gains

If stress is viewed as a permanent feature of women's lives, including, for many, daily reminders of inequality and oppression, and if problems are perceived as person–environment transactions rather than as symptoms of pathology, then the ultimate goal of treatment is more logically 'coping' not 'cure.' A coping skills perspective in direct practice intervention emphasizes providing clients with the resources and tools for handling their own future life problems (Berlin 1983). A client's coping repertoire can be expanded by helping her develop and practice techniques for handling problem reoccurrence, locate and mobilize social support networks, and access bibliotherapy resources and other self-help aides.

Introducing clients to a relapse-prevention model for dealing with particular stresses can help them cope with post-treatment setbacks (Marlatt and Gordon 1985). The relapse-prevention model emphasizes the perspective that slip-ups are expected. It helps clients pinpoint high-risk antecedents to relapse and their initial reactions to these which become cues to cope. The model then helps clients develop and enact coping responses in stressful situations, thus reducing the likelihood of problem re-emergence.

A client's coping repertoire can also be fortified by locating, mobilizing, or developing supportive networks or mutual aid resources. The client may have resources available but may use them inconsistently because of competing demands or 'shoulds,' or she may find that size or gender composition of a support group influences her participation (Martin and Shanahan 1983). Alternatively, the client may lack the comfort and skills to request help from or give assistance to others, or she may not know how to locate or cultivate new resources. Anticipating the important maintenance function of mutual support, treatment can include information on community resources and how to access these (cf. Whittaker and Garbarino 1983). Attention can also be devoted to helping clients start their own mutual help groups (cf. NiCarthy, Merriam, and Coffman 1984).

Bibliotherapy resources can provide an additional boost to client coping efforts. While the production of self-help aides has increased at a faster pace than supporting evidence of their utility, many readable and useful guides are available to help individuals, for example, to improve their interpersonal skills and make friends (e.g. Gambrill and Richey 1985).

At this point, little is known about possible gender issues in the mutual-help and self-help movements. While women clients may be quite willing to seek out help and engage in self-improvement activities, perhaps even more than men, the extent to which they follow through with suggestions and advice, and the value of these experiences in terms of problem reduction and enhanced coping, are still largely unknown.

Learning activities for enhancing gender-relevant intervention

Exploring practitioner preferences for skills in diverse intervention roles Student-practitioners can be encouraged to examine and expand the intervention roles they assume with real clients and case vignettes. Within the case presentation format, participants discuss current intervention functions and creatively explore adding to or changing these. An exercise involving the same case but with an undisclosed client gender manipulation could also be useful in facilitating examination of gender factors in the selection of intervention roles. Practitioners may also benefit from rehearsing specific components of certain intervention tasks with which they feel uncomfortable or unskilled, for example, conflict resolution skills needed for the 'mediator' role or assertiveness for the 'advocate' role.

Increasing practitioner skill in non-sexist group and family interventions Given the potential therapeutic value and cultural relevance of group and family treatment modalities, practitioners may benefit from specific training in working with people in groups in ways that do not reinforce sex-role stereotypes nor limit options for women. For instance, trainees could improve their skills for facilitating interactional equity between female and male co-therapists, and among group and family members (cf. Martin and Shanahan 1983). Practitioners can also expand their treatment repertoire by experimenting with structured exercises and games with couples and families which can help reduce the influence of gender-role prescriptions and patterns in communication and problem resolution (cf. Blechman and Rabin 1982).

Evaluating intervention effectiveness Numerous learning activities can be introduced in classroom and field settings which familiarize trainees with the components of practice evaluation so that these procedures are routinely integrated with ongoing practice activities (cf. Bloom and Fischer 1982). For example, with standard vignettes or real case examples, students individually or in small groups can specify or operationalize the independent variable or intervention; and specify and suggest measures for the dependent variable or treatment outcome. Valuable learning can occur when practitioners carry out self-improvement projects in which all evaluation components are employed to bring about personal and/or environmental change (cf. Watson and Tharp 1981). These component activities include identifying and specifying a meaningful target concern (e.g. smoking/drinking, interpersonal relationships, time management, stress reactions, or depression), collecting data on the target problem or goal over time, specifying the intervention(s), selecting and introducing an appropriate single-case research design, graphing data and interpreting results, and altering procedures based on observed outcomes. This personal involvement with evaluation frequently convinces practitioners of the empowering or enabling function of these activities for clients, above and beyond their accountability function.

Summary and conclusions

This chapter has drawn upon the social science literature in an effort to inform human service providers of the many ways in which gender biases, sex-role stereotypes, and sexist attitudes can affect practitioner and client behaviors in concrete ways from greeting to goodbye. Exposing clinician-trainees to literature outside of their immediate professional domain may encourage them to continue to explore alternative perspectives and to challenge favorite interpretations once in practice.

It is hoped that the evidence and speculations offered in this chapter concerning gender biases underscore the ubiquitous nature of these and related culture-bound beliefs and behavioral patterns. No one is exempt or safe from their potential influence. Thus, the importance of developing in beginning practitioners a well-developed habit of self-surveillance becomes a very important goal indeed, given the inevitable waning of external observation and evaluation by educators and supervisors.

The maintenance of clinician self-surveillance will be enhanced if client feedback on therapeutic process and outcome is routinely and systematically solicited, summarized, and referred to. Consumer feedback on relationship factors, intervention effectiveness, and goal attainment can help practitioners develop the helpful and modify the less helpful aspects of their style and approach, case-by-case. In this way, clients can become more active participants in building and refining better services for women.

Acknowledgements

The author is grateful to Hideki A. Ishisaka, Judy Kopp, and Paula S. Nurius for their helpful comments on an earlier version of this chapter.

References

Adams, K. L. and Ware, N.C. (1984) Sexism and the English Language: The Linguistic Implications of Being a Woman. In J. Freeman (ed.) *Women: A Feminist Perspective*. Palo Alto, CA: Mayfield.

Almquist, E. M. (1984) Race and Ethnicity in the Lives of Minority Women. In J. Freeman (ed.) *Women: A Feminist Perspective*. Palo Alto, CA: Mayfield.

Argyle, M. and Dean, J. (1968) The Effects of Visibility on Interaction in a Dyad. *Human Relations* 21: 3–17.

Barth, R. P. (1984) Professional Self-Change Projects: Bridging the Clinical-Research and Classroom-Agency Gaps. *Journal of Education for Social Work* 20(3): 13–19.

Berlin, S. (1983) Cognitive-Behavioral Approaches. In A. Rosenblatt and D. Waldfogel (eds) *Handbook of Clinical Social Work*. San Francisco, CA: Jossey-Bass.

Blechman, E. A. and Rabin, C. (1982) Concepts and Methods of Explicit Marital Negotiating Training with the Marriage Contract Game. *American Journal of Family Therapy* 10(4): 47–55.

Bloom, M. and Fischer J. (1982) *Evaluating Practice: Guidelines for the Accountable Professional*. Englewood Cliffs, NJ: Prentice-Hall.

Broverman, I. K., Vogel, S. R., Broverman, D. M., Clarkson, F. E., and Rosenkrantz, P. S. (1972) Sex-Role Stereotypes: A Current Appraisal. *Journal of Social Issues* 28(2): 59–78.

Cormier, W. H. and Cormier, L. S. (1985) *Interviewing Strategies for Helpers: Fundamental Skills and Cognitive Behavioral Interventions*. Monterey, CA: Brooks/Cole.

Crosby, R., Jose, P., and Wong-McCarthy, W. (1981) Gender, Androgyny, and Conversational Assertiveness. In C. Mayo and N. M. Henley (eds) *Gender and Nonverbal Behavior*. New York: Springer-Verlag.

Exline, R., Gray, D., and Schuette, D. (1965) Visual Behavior in a Dyad as Affected by Interview Control and Sex of Respondent. *Journal of Personality and Social Psychology* 1: 201–09.

Fuller, F. (1963) Influence of Sex of Counselor and of Client on Client Expressions of Feeling. *Journal of Counseling Psychology* 10: 34–40.

Gambrill, E. D. (1983) *Casework: A Competency-Based Approach*. Englewood Cliffs, NJ: Prentice-Hall.

Gambrill, E. D. and Richey, C. A. (1985) *Taking Charge of Your Social Life*. Belmont, CA: Wadsworth.

Gambrill, E. D. and Richey, C. A. (in press) Criteria Used to Define and Evaluate Socially Competent Behavior Among Women. *Psychology of Women Quarterly*.

Gilligan, C. (1982) *In a Different Voice: Psychological Theory and Women's Development*. Cambridge, MA: Harvard University Press.

Gottlieb, B. H. (1980) The Role of Individual and Social Support in Preventing Child Maltreatment. In J. Garbarino, H. Stocking, and Associates (eds) *Protecting Children from Abuse and Neglect*. San Francisco: Jossey-Bass.

Gottlieb, N., Burden, D., McCormick, R., and NiCarthy, G. (1983) The Distinctive Attributes of Feminist Groups. *Social Work with Groups* 6(3/4): 81–93.

Green, J. W. (1982) *Cultural Awareness in the Human Services*. Englewood Cliffs, NJ: Prentice-Hall.

Gurman, A. S. and Klein, M. H. (1980) Marital and Family Conflicts. In A. M. Brodsky and R. T. Hare-Mustin (eds) *Women and Psychotherapy: An Assessment of Research and Practice*. New York: Guilford Press.

—— (1984) Marriage and the Family: An Unconscious Male Bias in Behavioral Treatment? In E. A. Blechman (ed.) *Behavior Modification with Women*. New York: Guilford Press.

Hall, M. (1978) Lesbian Families: Cultural and Clinical Issues. *Social Work* 23(5): 380–85.

Henley, N. M. (1977) *Body Politics: Power, Sex, and Nonverbal Communication*. Englewood Cliffs, NJ: Prentice-Hall.

Hepworth, D. H. and Larsen, J. A. (1982) *Direct Social Work Practice: Theory and Skills*. Homewood, IL: Dorsey Press.

Ishisaka, H. A. and Takagi, C. Y. (1982) Social Work with Asian- and Pacific-Americans. In J. W. Green (ed.) *Cultural Awareness in the Human Services*. Englewood Cliffs, NJ: Prentice-Hall.

Ivey, A. E. and Authier, J. (1978) *Microcounseling: Innovations in Interviewing, Counseling, Psychotherapy, and Psychoeducation*. Springfield, IL: Charles C. Thomas.

Kaplan, M. (1983) A Woman's View of DSM-III. *American Psychologist* 38: 786–92.

Kravetz, D. (1982) An Overview of Content on Women for the Social Work Curriculum. *Journal of Education for Social Work* 18(2): 42–9.

Lazarus, R. S. and Folkman, S. (1984) *Stress, Appraisal, and Coping*. New York: Springer.

Levy, R. L., and Richey, C. A. (in press) Measurement and Design Issues in Behavioral Medicine with Women. In E. A. Blechman and K. Brownell (eds) *Behavioral Medicine for Women*. New York: Pergamon Press.

Lipman-Blumen, J. (1984) *Gender Roles and Power*. Englewood Cliffs, NJ: Prentice-Hall.

MacDonald, M. L. (1982) Assertion Training for Women. In J. P. Curran and P. M. Monti (eds) *Social Skills Training: A Practical Handbook for Assessment and Treatment*. New York: Guilford Press.

Maracek, J. and Johnson, M. (1980) Gender and the Process of Therapy. In A. M. Brodsky and R. T. Hare-Mustin (eds) *Women and Psychotherapy: An Assessment of Research and Practice*. New York: Guilford Press.

Marlatt, G. A. and Gordon, J. R. (eds) (1985) *Relapse Prevention: Maintenance Strategies in the Treatment of Addictive Behaviors.* New York: Guilford Press.

Martin, P. Y. and Shanahan, K. A. (1983) Transcending the Effects of Sex Composition in Small Groups. *Social Work with Groups* 6(3/4): 19–32.

Miller, S. O. (1983) Practice in Cross-Cultural Settings. In A. Rosenblatt and D. Wald-Fogel (eds) *Handbook of Clinical Social Work.* San Francisco: Jossey-Bass.

NiCarthy, G., Merriam, K., and Coffman, S. (1984) *Talking It Out: A Guide to Groups for Abused Women.* Seattle, WA: Seal Press.

Orlinsky, D. E. and Howard, K. I. (1976) The Effects of Sex of Therapist on the Therapeutic Experiences of Women. *Psychotherapy: Theory, Research, and Practice* 13: 82–8.

—— (1980) Gender and Psychotherapeutic Outcome. In A. M. Brodsky and R. T. Hare-Mustin (eds) *Women and Psychotherapy.* New York: Guilford Press.

Padilla, A. M., Ruiz, R. A., and Alvarez, A. (1975) Community Mental Health Services for the Spanish Speaking/Surnamed Population. *American Psychologist* 30: 892–905.

Radloff, L. S. and Rae, D. S. (1979) Susceptibility and Precipitating Factors in Depression: Sex Differences and Similarities. *Journal of Abnormal Psychology* 88: 174–81.

Rippere, V. (1977) What's the Thing To Do When You're Depressed? – A Pilot Study. *Behaviour Research and Therapy* 15: 185–91.

Robbins, J. H. (1983) Complex Triangles: Uncovering Sexist Bias in Relationship Counseling. In J. H. Robbins and R. J. Siegel (eds) *Women Changing Therapy: New Assessments, Values and Strategies in Feminist Therapy.* New York: Haworth Press.

Rodin, J. and Langer, E. (1980) Aging Labels: The Decline of Control and the Fall of Self-Esteem. *Journal of Social Issues* 36: 12–29.

Rosenthal, R., Hall, J. A., DiMatteo, M. R., Rogers, P. L., and Archer, D. (1979) *Sensitivity to Nonverbal Communication: The PONS Test.* Baltimore: Johns Hopkins University Press.

Seiden, A. (1976) Overview: Research on the Psychology of Women. II. Women in Families, Work, and Psychotherapy. *American Journal of Psychiatry* 133: 1111–123.

Sherman, J. A. (1980) Therapist Attitudes and Sex-Role Stereotyping. In A. M. Brodsky and R. T. Hare-Mustin (eds) *Women and Psychotherapy: An Assessment of Research and Practice.* New York: Guilford Press.

Shulman, L. (1984) *The Skills of Helping Individuals and Groups.* Itasca, IL: F. E. Peacock.

Sloane, R. B., Staples, F. R., Cristol, A. H., Yorkston, N. J., and Whipple, K. (1975) *Psychotherapy Versus Behavior Therapy.* Cambridge, MA: Harvard University Press.

Spradley, J. P. (1979) *The Ethnographic Interview.* New York: Holt, Rinehart, and Winston.

Steil, J. M. (1984) Marital Relationships and Mental Health: The Psychic Costs of Inequality. In J. Freeman (ed.) *Women: A Feminist Perspective.* Palo Alto, CA: Mayfield.

Tardy, C. H. (1985) Social Support Measurement. *American Journal of Community Psychology* 13(2): 187–202.

Valdez, T. A. and Gallegos, J. (1982) The Chicano Familia in Social Work. In J. W. Green (ed.) *Cultural Awareness in the Human Services.* Englewood Cliffs, NJ: Prentice-Hall.

Watson, D. L. and Tharp, R. G. (1981) *Self-Directed Behavior: Self-Modification for Personal Adjustment.* Monterey, CA: Brooks/Cole.

Weissman, H., Epstein, I., and Savage, A. (1983) *Agency-Based Social Work: Neglected Aspects of Clinical Practice.* Philadelphia: Temple University Press.

Weitz, R. (1984) What Price Independence? Social Reactions to Lesbians, Spinsters, Widows, and Nuns. In J. Freeman (ed.) *Women: A Feminist Perspective*, Palo Alto, CA: Mayfield.

Whittaker, J. K. and Garbarino, J. (eds) (1983) *Social Support Networks: Informal Helping in the Human Services.* New York: Aldine.

Zimmerman, D. and West, C. (1975) Sex Roles, Interruptions and Silences in Conversation. In B. Thorne and N. Henley (eds) *Language and Sex.* Rowley, MA: Newbury House.

9 Women in administration: curriculum and strategies

Marie Weil

Introduction

From the period of social work's emergence as a profession, women have been involved in program development and administration. Mary Parker Follett has been recognized as an originator of administrative theory and procedures. Many of the heroines of early social work were deeply involved with designing and administering social work programs in settlements, health settings, mental health settings, Ys and Centers, and agencies providing services for families and children (Vandiver 1980). Historically social work has been identified as a women's field largely because of the caring function embedded in many social programs. The ranks of social work have been filled by women. However, despite the traditional identification of social work as a woman's profession, research indicates that women currently experience significant barriers at entry and in advancement in social administration (Belon and Gould, 1977; Fanshel 1976; Gould and Kim 1976; Scotch 1971; and Szakacs 1977).

This chapter explores the causes of this inequity and recommends strategies and a curriculum designed to assist women social workers to move into administration with competence and confidence. Structural, interpersonal and/or personal barriers may discourage women from entering administration (Chernesky 1980a; Pierson 1982; Weil 1983). The under-representation of women in administration, teaching, and research in social work provides a partial explanation for the ways in which the profession has been unresponsive to the particular needs of women as clients at all stages of the life-cycle. Overt and covert sexism in agency organization and in theoretical and practice models has contributed to the undervaluing of women as clients, and as managers and administrators. The absence in social agencies of women and men trained to examine the particular problems of women clients and the stresses of women's societal role as caregivers and as wage-earners has resulted in service systems which have frequently overlooked or ignored specific needs and problems of women clients.

The rapid development of special services for women who have experienced family violence or sexual assault has occurred following the second wave of the women's movement and the establishment of feminist-oriented alternative service programs (Hooyman *et al.* 1986; Masi 1981; Weil 1986). As is documented in other chapters of this book, particular needs of women clients such as older women, women with chemical dependencies, or women involved in caregiving roles for which there are no policy and programmatic supports have only recently gained recognition and concerted response in social service planning.

Preparing more women for administration and equipping women and men with knowledge of the particular needs of women clients can increase the likelihood that programs will consider and respond to women's experiences. For women to be effective in administration, however, they must be equipped to deal with the barriers to entry and performance that currently confront women administrators. Women need preparation to deal with organizational barriers and they need skills to engage in organizational change to promote gender equity.

Building supportive curricula is one means of furthering the movement of women into administrative practice. While educational strategies cannot eradicate societal and institutional sexism and inequity, they can produce women graduates who are better equipped to change current organizational realities.

All students of administration must be prepared for leadership in interpersonal, technical, organizational and task environment change processes (Argyris and Schon 1975; Hassenfeld 1983; Schein 1972, 1985). But for women, there are additional areas of preparation which need to be built into administrative curricula. Women must learn not only the process and task skills for administrative and community practice, they must learn how to deal with sexism and institutional barriers, and how to develop support networks for their own survival and the support of other women. They also need the opportunity to learn (a) multiple models of organizational structure and administrative practice which can enable them to analyze existing organizations and programs with regard to gender equity, and (b) organizational change strategies to prepare them to alter organizational structure and processes so that human service work settings can be more equitable, more humane, more feminist in orientation, and more supportive of women as clients, workers, and administrators.

This chapter analyzes the types of barriers women face in entering and advancing in administration. It offers curriculum strategies for dealing with these barriers, notes the need for inclusion of feminist orientations, and provides specific content on women for administrative curricula.

Issues for women in administration

A growing body of research literature provides evidence of discrimination against women in social work (Chafetz 1972; Fanshel 1976; Kravetz 1976; Kravetz and Austin 1984; Szakacs 1977; Williams and Felder 1974; Zeitz and Erlich 1976). While the profession is preponderantly female – over two-thirds of social workers are women – numerous studies document male dominance in administration and management. In a 1977 study Szakacs found that in two decades men have replaced women in administrative positions at a rate of two per cent per year.

Within the membership of the National Association of Social Workers (NASW), similar trends have also been documented. A membership study (Stamm 1969) found that women were disproportionately placed in the lowest levels of administration. By 1972 a sharper polarization was evident in membership: 37 per cent of men and only 18 per cent of women members identified administration as their primary responsibility.

The same problems appear in local studies. A study of public welfare administrators in Minnesota documents the decline of women in administration between 1935 and 1969 (Kruzich 1978). While total aggregates of all administrative positions show an increase of women between 1970 and 1977, when first-line supervisors and lowest-level administrators are removed from the sample the percentage of women in administration drops from 51 per cent to 26 per cent between 1975 and 1977. These findings document that while affirmative action may increase the numbers of women entering administration, it has not substantially affected their opportunity to advance in organizations. A Michigan survey of twenty agencies serving families and children also found that women advanced into administration only after considerably longer periods of time in direct service positions than their male colleagues (Knapman 1977).

Despite a history of remarkable women leaders (Brandwein 1982; Vandiver 1980) most positions of influence and leadership in social work have been held by men (Chernesky 1980a; Meyer 1982). Brandwein (1982) presents a useful history of the multi-causal ascendance of men in administration and community practice related to (a) adoption of business models of efficiency in the 1920s (and male board members' greater comfort in dealing with male social welfare executives), (b) the availability of veterans' benefits in the 1950s, accompanied by (c) intentional recruitment of men into schools of social work in an effort to increase the relative prestige of the profession in the 1950s and 1960s, and (d) the popularization of anti-female (i.e. anti-Momism) perspectives grounded in psychological theories which devalue women and women's experience. Two national studies document not only the prevalence of men in leadership positions in administration, research, and teaching but a sharp decrease in recent years in numbers of women in major administrative positions in the profession (Fanshel 1976; Szakacs 1977).

Kravetz and Austin (1984) critique the literature that views male domination in administration as 'natural' because of the focus on rational planning and task orientation. Men's over-representation in upper administrative ranks has been justified also as a means to help men feel comfortable with their choice of a 'woman's' field (Kadushin 1976).

In contrast to earlier assumptions justifying a natural ascendency for men in social work, more recent research and literature on women in social administration documents the structural and interpersonal barriers of sexism which women experience in pursuing and maintaining administrative careers (Chernesky 1980a, 1980b, 1983; Kravetz and Austin 1984; Terborg 1977).

Barriers to women in social administration

In analyzing the under-representation of women in social administration it is important to be aware of theoretical positions which in effect blame the victim. Brandwein (1984) has presented an analysis of the theoretical perspectives on causation: (a) the 'biology is destiny' argument which argues that physiological differences between women and men dictate that women should be involved exclusively with domestic concerns; (b) the psychological argument which uses psychodynamic theory regarding gender-based differential ways of resolving oedipal conflicts to indicate that women are not sufficiently achievement-oriented to carry administrative functions (the fear of success concept of loss of femininity as a result of achievement illustrates this argument); (c) the sociocultural explanation which focuses on differential sex-role socialization for girls and boys as the cause of women's under-representation; and (d) the structural/situational approach which analyzes the informal and formal structure of the workplace. Brandwein refutes the first two causal theories, indicates the flexibility inherent in the third, and gives credence to the fourth perspective which analyzes the interaction between women and their work environments.

Structural perspective on women in organizations
Most of the research on women in social administration followed the ground-breaking work of Kanter. In her study, *Men and Women of the Corporation* (1977), Kanter identified three major structural barriers to the advancement of women in management: power, structure of opportunity, and numbers or proportions of members of stigmatized groups. These critical factors in combination have prevented women from advancing in organizations based on their performance.

Power Kanter defines power in formal organizations as the ability to influence the behavior of others, the ability to obtain and mobilize resources, and the ability to accomplish goals and tasks. In the structure of traditional organizations, the ability to get things done depends on rank in the hierarchy. If women are excluded from formal leadership positions, they cannot be viewed as being powerful or being leaders within the organization. While women are placed in positions that preclude leadership behavior and the opportunity to produce change, they will continue to be viewed as lacking power in organizations, and more importantly they will be perceived as lacking the potential for leadership.

Chernesky (1980a) comments that women in social administration take on many jobs such as co-ordinator or technical assistant that may appear to be administrative but do not lead to increasing responsibility and advancement. Obstacles to advancement from these positions occur because (a) there is no career ladder, (b) the tasks do not allow demonstration of abilities which would be taken as indicating capacity for advancement, and (c) high performance in such jobs can itself be viewed as evidence of inability to perform at higher levels (Chernesky 1980a).

Numbers or proportions   Kanter (1977) discusses the destructive power of tokenism as a factor which can preclude the advancement of women and minorities. Tokens are placed in double jeopardy. Initially they are perceived as just like all women or all blacks, and that perception typically involves negative stereotypes. If they are successful, they are then seen as dramatically different from their reference group. The lone woman or lone minority group member is always highly visible and the object of critical observation. The entrance of someone viewed as different into an established group often heightens the sense of commonality within the group and accentuates exclusion of the token. This visibility creates undue pressure to perform, and the individual seeks to excell and takes on the burden of changing negative stereotypes. Kanter found that women were either excluded from informal networks, or, if they were included, discovered that the price was participating in the belief that they were suitable for management only because they were unlike other women. The roles available to women in such situations, Kanter found, were reduced to sex stereotypes – mother, seductress, pet, or iron maiden. While many women attain managerial levels despite the operation of such stereotypes, their success is not without psychological costs including isolation and the negative adaptation to view oneself as different from other women.

Opportunity structure   The structure of opportunity in an organization relates to the possibilities for advancement and professional growth from particular positions. Where one senses no opportunity for growth, a typical coping response is to curtail aspirations. Such adaptation can induce outside perceptions that one is not sufficiently motivated to merit advancement. The over-representation of women in lower levels of social work practice where there is little opportunity for mobility or advancement makes it likely that they will be viewed as less committed to career goals. The negative impact of being closed out of the organizational opportunity structure may also drive women into private practice or to the view that only in alternative service structures can women impact service design and delivery. These structural barriers to administrative entry and advancement are experienced by women differently, based on their own personality and the organizational environments in which they work. However, considerable research documents common problems for women administrators in the social services.

Specific issues for women in social work and human service organizations

A number of gender inequity issues have a heightened and particular impact in social agencies because of social work's historical status as a woman's profession and the contradictions between professional mission and sex discrimination. The following discussion summarizes major factors.

Sex stereotyping in the profession   Sex stereotyping has a negative effect in social work in two ways: (a) the profession is often cast as a handmaiden to other professions which negates professional power and advocacy functions, and (b) within the profession the leadership positions in administration, teaching, and research remain predominantly a male preserve. Unfortunately the caring role which has typically been assigned to women by society is all too often equated with weakness. From a feminist perspective, it becomes essential to emphasize the societal value of caring and nurturing, to eliminate the logically faulty connection of caring and weakness, and to teach and enable men as well as women to enact nurturing and caring functions for vulnerable populations. In its mission social work embodies the humanitarian tradition in Judeo-Christian culture. The values of preserving individual dignity and social responsibility represent strength rather than weakness in human evolution.

As Brandwein (1984) has noted, the efforts to recruit men into social work were intended to strengthen the profession. The view taken was that if social work remained a woman's field, it would never be considered a full-fledged profession. This stance may indeed have influenced the men who entered the field supported by the GI Bill following the Second World War to masculinize the profession and model its administrative practices more closely after profit-motivated corporate management styles. Chernesky (1980a) comments that:

'the qualities needed for excellence in social work practice are generally considered by society to be feminine qualities. The professional tasks of helping, protecting, and fostering the growth of others continue to be labeled women's functions, requiring feminine or expressive attributes such as warmth, patience, understanding and sensitivity.'   (p. 243)

This set of attributes and values are indeed required for competency in direct service; however, they should also inform and direct administrative and policy-making functions in social welfare. Social workers, female and male alike, should be engaged in illustrating and documenting the strength required to nurture and enable growth in others.

Within the field, the sex segregation of jobs perpetuates negative societal attitudes – men are assumed to be needed to legitimate the profession and to handle the rational tasks of planning, budgeting, and administering social programs, while women are relegated to expressive functions related to direct service. This sexual division of labor denies the intellectual and rational capacities of women and denigrates and undercuts the sensitivities and nurturing abilities of men. Support is needed in social work education and practice for men who wish to be engaged primarily in direct service and for women who wish to be primarily engaged in administration.

As the profession was intentionally opened up to encourage men to enter it, so the field now needs consciously and conscientiously to strive to equalize opportunity for women and to provide the supports needed for entry into and advancement in management.

Wage and job discrimination   One of the central manifestations of sexism in the profession is the exclusion of women from higher administrative positions and from the job pools and career ladders which lead to administrative responsibility. As Kravetz and Austin (1984) reported from their study of women administrators, the issue in civil service controlled salary systems was not that men were paid more but that men got the jobs that paid more. Inequitable promotion systems inevitably enforce wage discrimination along with job discrimination.

Social work as a whole is an underpaid profession, and when women fill only the lower echelons, sex-based wage discrimination is perpetuated. Belon and Gould (1977) have carefully documented salary inequities between women and men in social work, and Kravetz (1976) has illustrated the operation of sexism in wage and job discrimination in this field. National and local studies have documented discrimination against women seeking to move into and up in administration (Fanshel 1976; Kravetz and Jones 1982; Kruzich 1978; Szakacs 1977; Scotch 1971).

Structural, affirmative action approaches need to be utilized to enable women to participate in the opportunity structure of agencies. Policies and procedures which make it possible to complain about inequitable decisions need to be formulated and enforced. In addition, the low wages which women administering alternative service programs receive need to be raised so that they are commensurate with the program and administrative responsibilities involved.

Sexual harassment   The demands from men for sexual favors from women they work with, particularly women who are organizationally subordinate, has begun to receive serious consideration only in the last few years. While demands for sexual interactions are the most problematic, harassment may also take the form of unwanted touching or verbal harassment from propositions to innuendoes, and frequently direct or implied threats of retaliation if requested favors are denied (Kravetz and Austin 1984). The prevalence of sexual harassment has been documented in large-scale government agencies such as the federal Department of Housing and Urban Development and in moderate and small-scale agencies. Kravetz and Austin (1984: 34) report that 44 per cent of their sample of fifty-seven women administrators stated that they had been subjected to sexual harassment by agency superiors, board members, co-workers, and members of funding sources. Sexual harassment victimizes women, often puts them in the position of feeling that they have to choose between honor and continued employment, and produces serious stresses in professional and personal life. Sexual harassment, indeed, operates to keep women in their place (that is, subservient to men) and contributes to preventing upward mobility in employment (MacKinnon 1979; Maypole and Skaine 1983).

A variety of personal, organizational, and legal strategies can be used to fight sexual harassment. As the prevalence of this problem is revealed it should become more possible for women to talk about harassment openly, document its occurrence, and form support and action groups to combat it. A major reason that it is important to act against sexual harassment is that it can divert much of a woman's energy from performance of her job to the need to protect herself. Not acting assertively in the face of sexual harassment can lead to a sense of personal devaluation, to feelings of depression, and to viewing oneself as a victim.

Career development Career development for women has received relatively little attention in the management literature. Most studies and typologies of career development are based on men (Hansen and Rapoza 1978). Women typically have more complex career patterns and need to balance more complex role conflicts than men (Collins 1981; Hansen and Rapoza 1978; Hunt 1978; Weil 1983). Women most frequently bear the central responsibility in juggling education, career development, child care and nurturing, and family responsibilities. Pressures on single women raising children and on women in dual career families have been insufficiently studied, but all too frequently there is little support for the multiple roles which women carry. For lesbians with and without children there are still frequent problems of discrimination which affect lifestyle and career advancement.

It can take extraordinary personal resources for women to pursue administrative careers; because female children, adolescents, and adults are still more likely than males to receive ambivalent, contradictory, or negative messages about investing in career development. Insufficient research has been done on women's developmental patterns over the life-span. In some studies, however, women are seen as insecure or overly dependent because they seem to place greater emphasis on intimacy and relationships than male adolescents and adults do. Interestingly, material on male post-midlife development now documents greater concern with nurturing and often a sense of loss related to insufficient investment in relationships earlier in life. It seems, therefore, sexist and inappropriate to denigrate women for an emphasis on relationships and intimacy when that need is a basic factor of all human life and development.

Most of the research on career patterns has examined the work of men. Separate studies by Hall and Nougaim (1968), Miller and Form (1951), and Super and Bohn (1970) delineate career stages for men proceeding from exploration to establishment, advancement, maintenance, and retirement. This model, however, does not smoothly fit women's development and life choices (Weil 1983). If women choose to bear children in their twenties, their thirties, or increasingly in their forties, difficult choices have to be made regarding relative emphasis on career development and child development. These are issues which still tend to have less impact on the career patterns of men. More research is needed on the stages of life as experienced by women and their career patterns, options, and choices. Hunt (1978) and Weil (1983) have developed basic typologies to examine women's life stages and career development. Such content should be included in professional education to assist women in planning and developing their careers.

Women as private caregivers   In addition to greater responsibilities for child care, women are disproportionally more likely to have major responsibility for caring for aged parents or other relatives. For women in direct or indirect social work services, much emotional energy is demanded in the care of targeted vulnerable populations. Where women engaged in such work are also providing intensive personal care for children or aged relatives, the possibilities for emotional and physical overloads are apparent. Neither the full burdens nor the joys of participation in child development should be reserved for women. Men also need to be involved in the care of the vulnerable. The need for adequate child care programs for young children and for day care or respite care for aged or infirm elders is well documented. The absence of such service systems further penalizes women as they seek to fulfill personal responsibilities and life goals.

Lack of support networks   One means of developing individual and collective power for women is through support networks. Kravetz and Austin (1984) state that for the women administrators they surveyed, women's support networks had become a critical survival strategy. Sixty-five per cent of their sample reported that being a woman excluded them from the important informal networks in their agencies and professional communities. While informal networks are routinely open to men, for women those networks typically are exclusionary. When women form their own support groups for administrative survival, the lower numbers of women in administration render these networks rather different from those of men. Support groups for women tend to be composed of people outside the woman's agency. Frequently, such networks include women employed across a broad range of administrative roles (Kravetz and Austin 1984). In men's informal support groups, similarity of position seems to shape networks, but for women, the issues related to being a woman in management form the common ground. The scarcity of women in administration renders mutual support and encouragement all the more important.

There are relatively few older women who are available to mentor women entering administrative careers. Not having a mentor can mean that a woman has to take much more time and energy to come to understand the functioning and mobility patterns in an organization. Mentors can be valuable assets in career development (Collins 1981). Mentors or support groups can be valuable to women in examining and avoiding the double bind described by the Brovermans and their colleagues (1970). Traditional, subservient female role behavior will not be effective in administration. However, assertiveness and competence – qualities needed by all administrators – are likely to be resented, negated, and criticized in women (Weil 1982a).

Women's support groups and mentors can assist women in examining and discarding assumptions that women must be just like men to be successful. The plethora of books, manuals, and articles advising women to adopt male managerial styles and dress standards indicate that women should copy the macho model and yet be as inconspicuous as possible. Bennis (1980) states that expectation of the formalistic macho management style prevents men as well as women from examining organizational cultures and developing appropriate managerial styles.

Exclusion of feminist orientations Exclusion of feminist literature and research in curricula prevents female and male students from fully examining the expectations, assumptions, and ideologies embedded in administrative behavior and practice courses. Analysis of feminist perspectives and inclusion of feminist program development, administrative, and planning models can open possibilities and alternatives for women and men alike. Feminism, as a philosophical orientation which supports democratic structuring, reconceptualizing power as shared, values of synthesis, wholeness, and process, and orientation towards structural change to promote justice and equality, has much to offer curricula for administration and direct service in social work (Bricker-Jenkins 1982; Hooyman *et al* 1986).

Barriers and curriculum strategies

The growing literature on women in administration documents three essential types of barriers to women's entry and advancement: (a) personal or psychological barriers; (b) interpersonal barriers; and (c) structural barriers (Chernesky 1980a; Flanagan 1977; Pierson 1982). The following discussion illustrates the nature of these barriers and presents curriculum strategies to assist students confronting and dealing with them.

Personal/psychological barriers

Much of the literature on women in administration over-emphasizes women's internal psychological barriers to achievement and gives insufficient consideration to structural barriers. Brandwein (1984) and Chernesky (1980a) note that emphasis on this perspective results in blaming the victims (women) for societal constraints.

It is of course important for social work curricula to assist women in analyzing internal barriers which result from early socialization, but it is critical to go beyond psychological and personal characteristics to structural and interpersonal causes. Citing the psychological barrier literature, Chernesky notes that characteristics such as 'low self-esteem, lack of self confidence, low-achievement motivation, role conflict or fear of success' are typically employed to 'explain' lack of advancement. However, empirical studies of these psychological factors 'do not necessarily support the hypotheses and are generally inconclusive' (Chernesky 1980a: 245).

Despite conflicting research results, Matina Horner's (1972) concept of 'fear of success' is still used in the popular literature to account for ambivalence in women regarding administrative careers. Popular literature tends to reinforce the prejudice that women are not as 'career-oriented' as men. Unfortunately, much of the 'games mother never taught you' type of literature focuses nearly exclusively on gamesmanship, macho-power politics, and manipulation. If one considers seriously Carol Gilligan's investigations of female development and values, it becomes clear that this 'gamesmanship' approach goes against the grain of much that is positive in female development (Gilligan 1982). Feminist analysis stresses development of collaborative and mediative strategies (Bricker-Jenkins 1985). Indeed much of the current organizational literature now eschews leadership based on domination and documents the effectiveness and power of collaborative styles (Bennis and Nanus 1985; Ouchi 1981; Sargent 1983; Schein 1985; Walton 1985).

As Pierson (1982) notes, personal or internal barriers, such as 'attitudes, behaviors and aspirations,' within women which derive from the socialization of women into subservient roles are to say the least not useful in administrative functioning. Internalization of negative sex-role socialization can result in women having problems related to 'diminished self-confidence, unwillingness to take risks, avoidance of competitive or assertive behavior, an over-riding desire to please, dependent behavior, fear of success, absence of career orientation and failure to understand the politics of organizational advancement' (Pierson 1982: 7). It is important for women to understand how and why they may have internalized negative stereotypes of women and why qualities such as nurturance and co-operation have been devalued in earlier management literature. However, more humanistically oriented management philosophies are emerging which value nurturing and co-operative behavior as well as androgynous qualities such as flexibility, resilience, visibility, objectivity, self-confidence, decisiveness, trust, and assertiveness (Bennis and Nanus 1985; Public Management Institute 1980; Schein 1985). Social work curricula can assist all administrative students in developing these leadership and administrative qualities and can give special attention to preparing women for new roles and for career development and advancement (Pierson 1982; Schein 1985; Weil 1983).

The following strategies can be incorporated into curricula to deal with personal/psychological barriers.

Curriculum strategies to deal with personal/psychological barriers

1. Clarify the impact of negative familial/societal sex-role socialization. Use group discussion and presentations to define and analyze these issues (Pierson 1982).
2. Utilize written assignments or class discussion to define desired characteristics for administrative roles such as assertiveness, flexibility, and co-operation. Analyze organization settings for the appropriate use of collaborative/co-operative strategies.
3. Incorporate career planning issues into curricula. Highlight particular pressures and needs of women in clarifying career goals and direction (Pierson 1982; Weil 1983).
4. Provide role models for women students of competent and confident women administrators (faculty and guest lecturers).
5. Analyze issues of career ladders and career advancement. Present literature and practice strategies related to networks, mentoring, and location of resource people (Chernesky 1980a; Pierson 1982; Weil 1983).
6. Provide curriculum structure learning projects, and exercises to assist in preparing women for new roles in administration (Weil 1983).
7. Include feminist organizational literature in curricula. Consider special issues women face in adult development and structure learning projects which teach methods and skills for developing competence and confidence in administrative roles (Weil 1983).

Interpersonal barriers

Interpersonal barriers result from negative sex stereotyping and 'non supportive or hostile patterns of behavior in family, friends, co-workers and superiors' (Pierson 1982: 8). The socio-cultural perspective on women described by Brandwein (1984) highlights these issues. Overt or covert prejudices may undermine women by assuming that they are less capable than men, irrational, unstable, or not dedicated to career development. Extreme forms of this perspective hold that women are not biologically equipped for leadership and support a gender division of labor which relegates women to the private world of the home and men to the public world of politics and economics. The presence in organizations of this perspective indicates that women students need to be able to analyze and deal with these barriers.

Curriculum strategies to deal with interpersonal barriers of sexism

1. Analyze familial, social, and organizational sexist attitudes which devalue women.
2. Provide workshops for field instructors and field agency directors to deal with issues of career development for women and with affirmative action issues.
3. Use administrative classes to promote a safe forum for women and men students to analyze and explore issues of sexism and racism in organizational behavior. Discuss the goals and implications of affirmative action policies in social agencies.
4. Encourage support groups among women students entering administrative field placements and employment.
5. Build analysis and rehearsal of various leadership and decision-making styles into class projects. Analyze the relationships between organizational culture and leadership styles.
6. Include curriculum content on effective communication methods and assertiveness, including role-plays. Assist students in the use of administrative authority and assertiveness. Discuss methods of conflict resolution and mediation as management skills.
7. Locate faculty and field supervisors who are committed to mentoring women students for leadership development.
8. Assist women students in analyzing and developing strategies to balance their multiple role demands.
9. Provide information on networking, creation of women's networks, and gaining access to existing networks.

Structural barriers

Structural barriers are those obstacles built into organization policy, structure, and behavior which disadvantage women. Chernesky (1980a), Kanter (1977), and Pierson (1982) analyze structural barriers women face such as entering administrative positions that do not offer career ladders, overt discrimination, lack of affirmative action policies, or lack of commitment to policies designed to control racism and sexism in the opportunity structure. Other less formal structural barriers relate to insensitivity to workers' and administrators' family roles – for example even agencies which provide services to children typically do not offer child care services to their own staff. Lack of effective maternity and paternity leave options for new parents and inflexible work hours also constitute structural barriers.

Pierson (1982) notes the subtle barriers related to entry position options and tendencies in organizations not to perceive women as leaders or as having leadership potential. Other analyses indicate that structural barriers are the most powerful causes and explanations for the low percentages of women in upper-level decision-making positions in social welfare programs. The following curriculum approaches can serve as enabling factors assisting women students in being prepared to confront and surmount structural barriers to entry and advancement in organizations.

Curriculum strategies for structural barriers

1. Structure courses to encourage analysis of agency policies and present formats for analyzing organizational patterns which intentionally or unintentionally disadvantage women and minority group members (Pierson 1982; Weil 1982b).
2. Include in the curriculum analytic tools and strategies for dealing with sex discrimination in agencies, including personal actions, class actions, collective bargaining, and negotiation/mediation.
3. Provide a forum for discussion and identification of structural barriers students have already encountered which may have been felt by them, or interpreted to them, as personal problems.
4. Provide a forum for discussion of sexual harassment and prepare students not only to recognize subtle as well as overt forms of this but to develop tactics to confront and deal with such situations so that they can protect themselves.
5. Include anlaysis of career ladders in course material on organizations. Prepare students with means to analyze opportunity structures in agencies.
6. Teach models of administration, including feminist models which seek structural change toward democratic structuring and humanizing the workplace (Hooyman *et al.* 1986; Pierson 1982; Weil 1983).
7. Include analysis of strategies for organizational change from below (Resnick and Patti 1980) and models of management which empower staff.

8. Include models for administering feminist workplaces and women's pro-
    grams such as shelters, rape crisis hotlines, women's centers, and support
    and employment programs.
9. Encourage students to form support groups following graduation to assist in
    analysis and strategy development to cope with structural barriers encoun-
    tered in job-seeking and employment.

Curriculum design and implications

With regard to curriculum structure, there is divergence of opinion regarding
whether there should be separate courses for women in administration. Whatever one's ideological view on this issue, it seems unlikely that many schools can
allocate faculty resources on a continuous basis to provide separate courses for
women. However, classes can function for female and male students as relatively
safe areas to test out varieties of managerial theories and styles. Additionally,
combined courses provide opportunities for men to learn about issues of sexism
and the professional responsibility to fight against institutionalized sexism as
well as racism. However, if there are opportunities for some single-sex labora-
tory sessions, it can be useful for women to have an opportunity to focus on skill
development in areas such as risk-taking, decision-making, collaborative working processes, and shared leadership as well as feminist analysis of organizational issues.

Curriculum model for women in administration

A curriculum model should be used for women in administration which fosters
autonomy. The model should be grounded in content on women as learners,
women's career directions, women's developmental tasks, and feminist-oriented
knowledge (Weil 1983). Professional education should be a process of empowerment designed to assist students in moving toward independence and competence
in practice. Research on adult development and learning supports the conclusion
that self-direction is a major factor in adult learning (Bruner 1961; Knowles 1972).
Women need to learn methods and skills for administrative practice through an
andragogical adult learning process which stresses self-directed learning[1] (Weil
1983). Women need to emerge from administrative education with (a) competencies in the process and task skills needed for managing people and information; (b) knowledge of and abilities to handle sexism and discrimination in the
workplace; (c) knowledge of various models of organizational structures and

---

1. The term *andragogy* was coined by Malcolm Knowles to denote the needed process for the
    teaching of adults (from the Greek *andros* – 'man' – and *gogy* – 'teaching'). The concept is based
    on the developmental interests and self-concept of adults, as expressed in active, self-directive
    learning styles.

cultures; (d) knowledge of how to develop a managerial style appropriate to the organizational setting and culture; and (e) knowledge of and skills in organizational change processes in order to build programs and organizations more supportive of women as clients, workers, and administrators. The goal of preparing women for competent administration and leadership throughout the range of human service organizations, though valuable, is not an end in itself; it must be borne in mind and in curricula that the ultimate goal of sound human service administration is the benefit of clients and vulnerable populations.

References

Argyris, C. and Schon, D. A. (1975) *Theory in Practice: Increasing Professional Effectiveness*. San Francisco: Jossey-Bass.

Belon, C. J. and Gould, K. (1977) Not Even Equals: Sex Related Salary Inequities, *Social Work* 22: 466–71.

Bennis, W. G. (1980) False Grit: The Myth that Says You've Got to Be Macho to Get Ahead. *Savvy*, June: 43–7.

Bennis, W. G. and Nanus, B. (1985) *Leaders: The Strategies for Taking Charge*. New York: Harper and Row.

Brandwein, R. A. (1982) Toward Androgyny in Community Organizational Practice. In A. Weick and S. T. Vandiver (eds) *Women, Power and Change*. Washington, DC: National Association of Social Workers, pp. 158–70.

—— (1984) Where Are the Women and Why: An Analysis of Women Administrators in Jewish Community Services. *Journal of Jewish Communal Services* 60 (Spring, 3): 204–13.

Bricker-Jenkins, M. (1982) Feminist Ideology and Organizations. Paper presented at Council on Social Work Education, Annual Program Meeting, New York.

Bricker-Jenkins, M. (1985) Of, By and For the People: Feminist Perspectives on Organizations and Leadership. Presentation at the Council on Social Work Education, Annual Program Meeting, Washington, DC, February.

Bricker-Jenkins, M. and Hooyman, N. (1983) Feminist Ideology. A discussion paper prepared for the Feminist Practice Project, National Association of Social Workers, Washington, DC.

Broverman, I. K., Broverman, D. M., Clarkson, R. E., Rosenkrantz, P. and Vogel, S. R. (1970) Sex-Role Stereotypes and Clinical Judgements of Mental Health Professionals. *Journal of Consulting and Clinical Psychology* 34 (February): 1–7.

Bruner, J. (1961) The Act of Discovery. *Harvard Educational Review* 31 (Winter).

Chafetz, J. S. (1972) Women in Social Work. *Social Work* 17 (September): 12–18.

Chernesky, R. H. (1980a) Women Administrators in Social Work. In E. Norman and A. Mancuso (eds) *Women's Issues and Social Work Practice*. Itasca, IL: F. E. Peacock, pp. 241–61.

—— (1980b) Preparing Women for Management in Social Welfare: Issues and Curriculum Needs. *Social Work Reporter* (newsletter of the Council on Social Work Education), January.

—— (1983) The Sex Dimension of Organizational Process: Its Impact on Women Managers. *Administration in Social Work* 7(3/4): 133–43.

Collins, S. (1981) *Career Development of Women Administrators: Implications for Social Work Education.* Paper presented at the Education Innovation Exchange on Achieving Equity for Women, Council on Social Work Education, Annual Program Meeting Louisville, KY, March.

Fanshel, D. (1976) Status Differentials: Men and Women in Social Work. *Social Work* 21 (November): 448–54.

Flanagan, M. (1977) Women in Social Work: Perceptions of Barriers to Administrative Advancement. *Womanpower*, December: 2–4.

Gilligan, C. (1982) *In a Different Voice: Psychological Theory and Women's Development.* Cambridge, MA: Harvard University Press.

Gould, K. and Kim, B. L. (1976) Salary Inequities between Men and Women in Schools of Social Work: Myth or Reality? *Journal of Education for Social Work* 12 (Winter); 50–5.

Hall, D. T., and Nougaim, K. (1968) An Examination of Maslow's Needs Hierarchy in an Organizational Setting. *Organizational Behavior and Human Performance* 3: 12–35.

Hansen, L. S. and Rapoza, R. S. (eds) (1978) *Career Development and Counseling of Women.* Springfield, IL: Charles C. Thomas.

Hasenfeld, Y. (1983) *Human Service Organizations.* Englewood Cliffs, NJ: Prentice-Hall.

Hooyman, N. R., Cunningham, R., Ellsworth, C., Ruff, R. A., and Tucker, J. (1986) An Alternative Administrative Style. In N. J. Van Den Berg and L. Cooper (eds) *Feminist Visions for Social Work.* New York: National Association of Social Workers.

Horner, M. S. (1972) Toward an Understanding of Achievement Related Conflicts in Women. *Journal of Social Issues* 28(2): 157–76.

Hunt, M. L. (1978) Women and Career Development. In M. Vandervelde and R. J. Patti (eds) *Management Preparation for Women*, report of the Social Welfare Management Curriculum Development Project. Seattle, WA: University of Washington.

Kadushin, A. (1976) Men in a Women's Profession. *Social Work* 21: 440–47.

Kanter, R. M. (1977) *Men and Women of the Corporation.* New York: Basic Books/Harper Colophon Books.

Knapman, S. K. (1977) Sex Discrimination in Family Agencies. *Social Work* 22 (6, November): 462–69.

Knowles, M. S. (1972) Innovations in Teaching Styles and Approaches Based upon Adult Learning. *Journal of Education for Social Work* 8(2).

Kravetz, D. (1976) Sexism in a Woman's Profession. *Social Work* 21 (November): 421–26.

Kravetz, D. and Austin, C. D. (1984) Women's Issues in Social Service Administration: The Views and Experiences of Women Administrators. *Administration in Social Work* 84 (4, Winter): 25–38.

Kravetz, D. and Jones, L. (1982) Career Orientations of Female Social Work Students: An Examination of Sex Differences. *Journal of Education for Social Work* 18, 77–84.

Kruzich, J. M. (1978) Women and Public Administration in Minnesota: Past, Present and Future Perspectives. In E. Wattenberg (ed.) *Room at the Top: Moving Women into Administrative Positions in Social Welfare*. Minneapolis: University of Minnesota.

MacKinnon, C. (1979) *Sexual Harassment of Working Women*. New Haven: Yale University Press.

Masi, D. A. (1981) *Organizing for Women: Issues, Strategies, and Services*. Lexington, MA: Lexington Books.

Maypole, D. and Skaine, R. (1983) Sexual Harassment in the Workplace. *Social Work* 28: 385–90.

Meyer, C. H. (1982) Issues for Women in a 'Women's Profession.' In A. Weick and S. T. Vendiver (eds) *Women, Power, and Change*. Washington, DC: National Association of Social Workers, pp. 197–205.

Miller, D. C. and Form, W. H. (1951) *Industrial Sociology*. New York: Harper and Row.

Ouchi, W. (1981) *Theory Z: How American Business Can Meet the Japanese Challenge*. Reading, MA: Addison-Wesley.

Pierson, J. (1982) *Moving Women Up: A Manual for Breaking Down Barriers*. Silver Spring, MD: National Association of Social Workers.

Public Management Institute (1980) *Nonprofit Management Skills for Women Managers*. San Francisco: Public Management Institute.

Resnick, H. and Patti, R. (1980) *Change from Within*. Philadelphia: Temple University Press.

Sargent, A. G. (1983) *The Androgynous Manager*. New York: AMACOM.

Schein, E. H. (1972) *Professional Education: Some New Directions*. Sponsored by the Carnegie Commission on Higher Education, New York: McGraw-Hill.

Schein, E. H. (1985) *Organizational Culture and Leadership*. San Francisco: Jossey-Bass.

Scotch, B. C. (1971) Sex Status in Social Work: Grist for Women's Liberation. *Social Work* 16(7): 5–11.

Stamm, A. M. (1969) NASW Membership: Characteristics, Development and Salaries. *Personnel Information* 12(5): 34–45.

Super, D. E. and Bohn, M. J. Jr (1970) *Occupational Psychology*. Belmont, CA: Wadsworth.

Szakacs, J. (1977) Survey Indicates Social Work Women Losing Ground in Leadership. *NASW News* 22(4): 12.

Terborg, J. R. (1977) Women in Management: A Research Review. *Journal of Applied Psychology* 562(12): 647–64.

Vandiver, S. T. (1980) 'A Herstory of Women in Social Work.' In E. Norman and A. Mancuso (eds) *Women's Issues in Social Work Practice*, Itasca, IL: F. E. Peacock, pp. 21–38.

Walton, R. E. (1985) Establishing and Maintaining High Commitment Work Systems. In J. R. Kimberly and R. H. Miles (eds) *The Organizational Life Cycle*. San Francisco: Jossey-Bass.

Weil, M. (1982a) Building Curriculum for Women in Administration: Issues, Options and Directions. Administration Symposium Council on Social Work Education, Annual Program Meeting, New York, March.

—— (1982b) Racism: Institutional, Group and Individual Analysis of a Typology and Social Work Response Strategies. National Association of Social Workers, National Minority Issues Conference, Los Angeles, June.

—— (1983) Preparing Women for Administration: A Self Directed Learning Model. *Administration in Social Work* 7: 3–4.

—— (1986) Women, Community and Organizing: Feminist Visions and Issues. In N. J. Van Den Berg and L. Cooper (eds) *Feminist Visions for Social Work*. New York: National Association of Social Workers.

Williams, M. and Felder, L. (1974) Career Patterns: More Grist for Women's Liberation. *Social Work* 19(7): 463–66.

Zeitz, D. and Erlich, J. L., (1976) Sexism in Social Agencies: Practitioners' Perspectives. *Social Work* 21: 434–39.

10 Women and community organization

Ruth A. Brandwein

Community organization is, along with casework and groupwork, one of three major methods of social work practice. It is a form of macropractice intervention that comprises locality (neighbourhood or community) development, advocacy, social action, and social planning (Gurin 1971; Rothman 1970).

While the majority of social work practitioners have been women, a gender-specific functional differentiation has prevailed in the profession. Micropractice – casework and groupwork (work with individuals, families, small groups) – has been seen as appropriate for women, and women are overwhelmingly represented in this area of practice. Conversely, the macropractice level – policy development and analysis, administration and management, social research, social planning, and community organizing – has attracted higher proportions of men. This was true even in the early periods of social work (Giovannoni and Purvine 1973) but was exacerbated in the 1950s when men were encouraged to enter social work and in the 1960s when a social science-based macropractice was developing (for a more thorough discussion of this phenomenon and its historical fluctuations see Brandwein 1981; Brandwein, in press).

This chapter examines the role and contribution of women in community organization practice. It first sets forth the thesis that within community organization two different and often contrasting models have developed. These are described with particular reference to the differential roles women have played in each model. These models are briefly reviewed historically, highlighting the contributions of a few outstanding women in the field. The chapter then moves beyond the historical to the conceptual, presenting and explicating a feminist approach to community organization. Practice and policy implications are discussed in relation to the salience of gender and a feminist approach. Finally, the chapter concludes with specific suggestions for incorporating this material into the social work curriculum.

Two models of community organizing

Historically, there have been two branches of community organization practice. One branch emerged from the Charity Organization Society (COS) and the community chests and councils. Its concerns have been co-ordination of services, reduction of fraud and duplication, and efficiency of fund-raising and service delivery. Its locus is within formal organizations and in the interorganizational field. Practitioners of this branch of community organization tend to work with agency directors and boards rather than directly with clients. For that reason, this type of social work practice is considered as 'indirect' service.

The second branch of community organization emerged out of the Settlement House Movement. It has been concerned with social reform, legislative advocacy, and the organizing of constituencies in self-help groups to advocate on their own behalf. Citizen participation, involvement of clients in decisions affecting them, and empowerment of oppressed groups have been central concerns of this branch of community organization. The locus of this branch of community organization is in the neighborhood in informal settings. Its practitioners work with community residents as well as with agency directors and public officials. This kind of practice may encompass both locality development and social action (Rothman 1970). These community organizers are involved in direct service (though not of a clinical nature) with a client system.

Community organizers in the more conservative, formal organization-based model tend to have a higher status and a recognzied professional role, whereas practitioners of the second model tend to have a lower status, and the distinction between professional and volunteer/community activist is often unclear. In Lubove's (1965) dichotomy of 'cause' and 'function' in social work, the first model (or branch) of community organization emphasizes 'function' (that is, professionalization, technical skills) while the second emphasizes 'cause' (that is, social work values, social reform, social movements).

Rein has created a matrix for understanding this dichotomy by classifying the first model of community organization as conservative and the second as radical (Rein 1970). Another way of explicating the difference is that the first is concerned with organizations in the community and the second is concerned with organizing the community.

It is important to understand the differences between these two models of community organization since the historical tendency has been for women to be involved in the second to a greater degree than the first. Simultaneously with the overall trend for women to be concentrated in micropractice and men in macropractice, this second, less recognized differentiation has prevailed. Within macropractice men have occupied the higher-status, more conservative, more establishment-oriented positions in formal organizations. Women have tended to work in small neighborhood agencies, organizing volunteers and community

Table 10.1 *Two models of community organization*

I *Organizations in the community*		II *Organizing the community*
Historical source	Charity Organization Society, community chests	Settlement Houses, Progressive movement
Locus	Formal organizations, interorganizational settings	Informal groups, neighborhoods
Approach to social work	'function'	'cause'
Constituencies	Agency directors and boards, government officials, businesspeople	Neighborhood residents, clients of services, oppressed groups
Purpose	Co-ordination and efficiency of fund-raising and service provision	Involvement and organizing citizens to identify problems and meet needs
Professional roles	Enabler, facilitator, expert	Enabler, facilitator, advocate
Activities	Social planning, administration	Locality development, social action
Status	High	Low
Orientation	Conservative	Radical

groups in informal settings, and have been advocates for legislative and policy changes. While this is, of course, not an absolute pattern – there have been male reformers and advocates and female administrators – the overall trend is clear. To what extent this differentiation has occurred by choice and to what extent women have been excluded from the higher-status, high-paid positions is not a subject that can be explored here (see Brandwein 1984 for a thorough discussion of obstacles to women in social work administration).

Historical background

Historically, one need only examine the activities of the major figures in the early social welfare movement to find strong female role models for the social reform branch of community organization in social work. Jane Addams founded Hull House, the American prototype of the settlement house in which the workers lived in the community with the residents. Her activities included political organizing in Chicago, but later expanded into broader national and international social policy issues. She was first president of the Women's International League for Peace and Freedom and president of the International Congress of

Women at the Hague. She was the first woman to win the Nobel Peace Prize for her anti-war activities before and during the First World War (James 1971; Morris 1977).

Julia Lathrop, Sophonisba Breckenridge, and Florence Kelly also lived at Hull House. Lathrop was active in the social reform of poor-houses, mental institutions, and the care of delinquents. She was also active in the women's suffrage movement. Breckenridge was active in women's employment issues and the women's trade union movement. She was also involved with the NAACP, the Progressive Party, and the Women's Peace Party, in addition to being dean of the Chicago School of Civics and Philanthropy (which later became the University of Chicago School of Social Service Administration). Florence Kelly, as secretary of the National Consumers' League, organized sixty state leagues and two international conferences, and was involved in research and legislative advocacy in the areas of women and child labor. She was instrumental in gaining minimum wage legislation in nine states. She had also lived at the Henry Street Settlement in New York City before coming to live at Hull House in Chicago (James 1971; Morris 1977).

Lillian Wald, the founder of the Henry Street Settlement, was a tireless worker in civic campaigns for parks, playgrounds, housing, and vocational education. She also worked for legislation outlawing child labor and with Jane Addams founded the National Child Labor Committee. Mary Follett lived and worked at the Roxbury Neighborhood House in Boston. Before her later work as a theorist in social groupwork, conflict resolution, and social administration she worked for legislation for the Boston School Centers which opened schools for neighborhood recreation. The Goldmark sisters were not as active in local organizing but both made important contributions in legislative advocacy. Josephine Goldmark was a member of the investigatory committee of the Triangle Shirtwaist Factory fire and drafted legislation for Senator LaFollette to protect working women. Pauline Goldmark was executive secretary of the New York Consumers' League, a powerful advocacy organization, and was active in child labor legislation (James 1971; Morris 1977).

These are but the most famous of a generation of women,[1] and the forebears of many others who have been involved in fighting for 'causes' – in social movements – to improve the lives of oppressed groups. They did not make distinctions between their professional and personal lives, living as well as working in their communities, involving themselves in issues of labor organizing, minority rights, and peace as inherently part of their social welfare concerns.

With the Flexner speech in 1915 challenging social work to become a profession, the end of the Progressive Era and the broader conservative trends of post-First

---

1.   Grace and Edith Abbott have been omitted as their activities were mainly in administration, research, and education rather than community organizing.

World War society, social work also took a turn toward conservatism. It became overly concerned with 'professionalism' which led to an emphasis on technique and narrowly defined areas of expertise. At the microlevel, Freudian theory ushered in the dominance of the psychiatric social worker. At the macrolevel, agency executives were adopting business management techniques. The profession in general seemed somewhat embarrassed by settlement house and locality development organizing activities. These were seen as volunteer, non-professional work which muddied the image of social work as a profession requiring a specific body of knowledge and training.

This cycle repeated itself in the 1950s and 1970s, in contrast to the 1930s and 1960s when social workers participated as community organizers in social action with the unemployed, with tenant groups, and with residents of ghetto communities. In the conservative periods male community organizers were more acceptable as fulfilling the image of tough-minded business managers, whereas women evoked the low-status image of volunteers.

Interestingly, in the 1960s, while neighborhood-based community organizing again became popular, the adoption of adversarial social action strategies was tinged with a definite anti-female cast. The idea of toughness and the acceptance of conflict as a valid strategy was more consonant with stereotypical 'masculinity.' Moreover, the infusion of a social science theory base in community organization and planning introduced male-dominated disciplines such as economics, political science, and sociology. The men who had been recruited into social work in the 1950s became leaders of the conflict-oriented, social science-based community organization of the 1960s and recruited more men into the profession (Brandwein 1981).

Of Rothman's three models of community organization (1970), two fit the male gender stereotypes – social action as tough, 'macho,' and conflict-oriented, and social planning as scientifically based, rational, and logical. Only his third model, locality development, with its emphasis on enabling and participation, could fit into the female gender stereotype. Not surprisingly, this model was generally unpopular and came under increasing criticism during the height of interest in community organizing in the late 1960s and early 1970s.

The literature of the period as well as the skewed proportion of male students in community organization reflect the predominance of men in community organization. In the 1950s the National Conference of Social Welfare published annual collections of papers on community organization. In the early 1950s half of these papers were authored by women but by the late 1950s their numbers had dramatically decreased (National Conference of Social Welfare 1951, 1955, 1958, 1961). This trend is further reflected in the 1960s. One widely adopted book of community organization readings published in 1969 included only two women authors among a total of forty-two (Kramer and Specht 1969; also see Brandwein, in press, for a fuller discussion of this subject). In the 1971 edition of the *Encyclopedia of Social Work* not one of nineteen articles specifically about community organization was authored by a woman (Morris 1977).

By the mid-1970s, reflecting the conservative turn of the nation, all forms of community organization were again at their nadir, as they had been in the other conservative periods of the 1920s and 1950s. In the latter part of the decade macropractice was again being represented by the administrators, managers, and researchers who had joined the bandwagon of cost-efficiency, management information systems and other accountability techniques designed to keep down the cost of social services.

Feminist approaches to community organization

Beyond an understanding of historical cycles and proportionate representation of men and women in community organization, the concept of a feminist approach contributes a new prism through which to view community organization practice. It is understood that not all women are feminists and that some men may be. Nevertheless, because of their differential socialization and relation to power, women have often approached community organization differently than men. By now, feminist literature has begun to codify certain behaviors and attitudes that can be considered feminist. Among these are androgyny, wholism, synergy, a win–win orientation to power, and the centrality of relationships (Brandwein 1981, 1985, in press; Hooyman 1980; Van Den Bergh and Cooper 1986). What is the feminist approach and how does it apply to community organization practice?

Androgyny
First it may be well to clarify what feminism is not. It is not the same as 'feminine.' Traditional stereotypes consider masculine traits to be aggressiveness, rationality, logic, 'tough-mindedness,' decisiveness, and task orientation. Conversely, stereotypically feminine traits are passivity, irrationality, emotionalism, warmth, nurturance, and process orientation. A feminist approach is androgynous, that is, it accepts both sets of characteristics as being essentially human, and not limited to nor denied from the behavioral repertoire of either males or females. It considers it an erroneous artifice to tie such behaviors and attitudes to gender.

Wholism
Compatible with an androgynous view of human behavior is the concept of wholism. Wholism is an inclusionary rather than an exclusionary approach. Therefore, while a 'masculine' approach to community organization may be product-oriented, a feminist approach is not simply process-oriented. Rather it

acknowledges the necessity of both/and rather than either/or. The community organization literature of the 1960s was sharply critical of earlier process-oriented community organization while a feminist analysis is critical of the uni-dimensional task orientation promoted in the 1960s. Using a Hegelian dialectic one can consider process orientation as *thesis*, product orientation as *antithesis*, and the wholistic both/and feminist approach as *synthesis*.

Synergy

A feminist approach is also synergistic. Thus it is not based on a simple linear logic of addition. Consistent with wholism, synergy can be most simply under-stood as the concept that 'the whole is greater than the sum of its parts.' For example, a feminist approach incorporates the concept of participation and involvement in decision-making, not simply because it makes people feel 'good' or is nurturing, but in the belief that better decisions will emerge. The mascu-line approach, in contrast, considers participatory decision-making as inefficient and time-consuming at best and resulting in poor decisions at worst. One emi-nent social scientist, in opposition to maximum participation of the poor, is pur-ported to have said that if poor people could make such good decisions, they wouldn't be poor! In contrast, a feminist approach posits that better decisions can emerge through a group process than from one individual. The whole is greater than the sum of its parts – the group is more than the additive ideas of each individual. Through the interactive process new ideas are created and a better product is achieved than could result from individual effort.

Win – win power orientation

The adversarial strategies of the 1960s social action approach were based on a 'win–lose' power game. This assumes power is a finite zero-sum equation in which if you win I lose. It would be naive to deny that this is sometimes the case, particularly in situations of limited resources or limited options. Femin-ism, however, embraces a 'win–win' approach to power. In many cases – in more than we often assume – power is infinite: we may play a 'win–win' rather than a 'win–lose' game. In such a case I do not lose power if you are also empowered. To convert a situation into a 'win–win' game one must not avoid conflict but rather master the creative resolution of conflict. For example, in a situation of a community group fighting a highway it seems a clear 'win–lose' game. Either the highway is built and the community loses or the highway is not built and the Highway Department, suburbanites, and 'downtown interests' lose. However, if the parties can focus on the overarching goal of enhanced suburban commuter flow into downtown rather than the short-term objective of a highway, then a mass transit system may redefine the issue into a win–win situation. It is an alternate objective to achieve the same broad goal. The community is not bisected by a highway but suburbanites can get downtown to work and shop.

Web of relationships

Gilligan (1982) used this term in her important work on moral development in women. In it she demonstrated how women tend to see events as part of a chain over time rather than as isolated occurrences and to see individuals in relationship to each other over time rather than as unitary, ahistorical beings. This perspective again is related to the concepts of wholism and synergy. Tactics and strategies, individuals and activities are seen in a broader context. For example, while a confrontational tactic might result in a short-term gain, the longer-term effect might be to reduce the organization's credibility. In the context of time that tactic might hurt the overall strategy of building credibility. In another context, however, confrontation might be appropriate if the target of the confrontation were not needed to confer credibility. In yet another situation the confrontation itself might create a more dynamic image for an organization with low credibility because of its inability to take forceful positions.

Egalitarian relationships

The concepts of win—win power orientation, the web of relationships, and synergy all lend themselves to egalitarian rather than hierarchical relationships. Hierarchy assumes a win—lose power relationship. The one at the top of the hierarchy has more power; if he or she 'gives in' to a subordinate, power is lost. Conversely, in an egalitarian relationship there are no permanent dominants and subordinates. Relationships shift situationally, depending on who has more expertise in different areas. Decisions are made communally, not because equalizing power is an end in itself, but because better decisions come about in a synergistic relationship. Egalitarian relationships also lend themselves to conflict resolution, whereas in unequal power relationships subordinates may resort to subversion and manipulation since honest conflict would be dangerous (Miller 1976).

Practice and policy implications

Both the salience of gender and feminist approaches to community organization have direct implications for both practice and policy considerations. Since community organization practice is practice often designed to affect or change social or agency policies, the discussion of practice cannot be separated from that of policy implications.

The previous section included some examples to illustrate how feminist approaches are applied in practice. The implications of such practice can be briefly summarized. It is simply good social work to utilize that strategy which is appropriate to a particular situation. Yet some community organization practitioners lock themselves into a particular strategy they believe in ideologically (for example, a Marxist belief in conflict as the only way to produce change) or with which they are comfortable (for example, a collaboration because they are uncomfortable in taking unpopular stands). Both wholism and the valuing of context help the practitioner to consider an array of strategies and then select the one that may be appropriate to the particular context. Moreover, seeing oneself in the context of a web of relationships, rather than as an individual practitioner, encourages the community organizer to work collectively with others. If organizers no longer cast themselves into the role of the sole change agent, they may call upon others who have more expertise or are more comfortable employing that strategic approach most appropriate for the particular situation.

The concepts of synergy and win–win power orientation lead logically to the value of empowering the client system in the decision-making process. In systems terms this would mean that wherever possible the client system – for example, hospital patients or mothers on welfare – would also become part of the action system, that is, participants in the change process. When a consensus or collaborative approach is appropriate, the target system would also be part of the action system (Pincus and Minahan 1973). In other terminology, participation by those to be affected by the change effort – the 'output constituency' – also become part of the 'input constituency' – that is, the decision-makers. For example, the board of United Way is the input constituency making policy decisions affecting an output constituency – social agencies and their clients. Putting agency workers and clients on the board brings the output constituency into the input constituency.

Finally, by acknowledging a win–win orientation to power, the feminist community organizer seeks to redefine the issue in such a way that all can win. While this may not be possible in cases of two groups with clearly competing interests and limited resources, the feminist approach encourages creative conflict resolution which may identify other resources, may expand the interest groups, or may identify a superordinate goal that all may endorse. The earlier example of converting a highway versus anti-highway conflict into a shared objective of mass transit illustrates such a resolution. The advantage of a win–win solution is that one does not face the inevitable backlash phenomenon that occurs over time as the losers re-enter the fray. Because the feminist approach acknowledges relationships over time, it becomes clear that in a win–lose confrontation, a win at one point of time is not the end of the situation. As is tragically clear from national events, the radical 1960s which seemed to usher in a new order of politics and culture was followed by the backlash of the 'silent majority' which finally recouped enough power to reintroduce conservative politics, religion, and lifestyles.

In addition to a feminist approach to community organization we discussed earlier the distribution of women in community organization. Because women are generally more likely to have had exposure to the feminist approach, the presence of more women community organizers will make it more likely that a feminist approach will be employed. The opposite can occur, however, if women who overcame obstacles to become community organizers over-identify with the prevailing value system. Where only small numbers of women enter an overwhelmingly male system as tokens, the pressure is for them to adapt to the prevailing values and behaviors. On the other hand, if enough women enter the system it is more likely that the system, rather than they, will change (Kanter 1977).

Moreover, women practitioners are important in community organization because of the areas of organizing which they can address. In such sensitive areas as child sexual abuse, wife battering, and teenage pregnancy it is obvious that the client system may be more open to developing relationships with women workers. Moreover, women workers are more likely to have experience from the clients' viewpoints which gives them greater credibility in organizing the client system to advocate for new policies or services. In other less obvious areas, the gender of the worker may also be a key. Neighborhood organizing often begins around issues pertaining to children – safe street crossings, recreation and day care facilities, after-school activities, and toxic wastes in the community. Because of both the increase in single-parent families and the unfortunate continuation of traditional roles in two-parent families, mothers have primary responsibility for children. Women workers therefore can often play a key role in such organizing. Not only can women workers identify the issues but they are more likely to organize mothers without a power and status differential which frequently occurs with a male organizer of a women's group. Moreover, the heterosexual tensions and game-playing which often occurred in the 1960s welfare organizing movement ceases to be a dynamic. (This phenomenon is discussed in Brandwein 1982.)

Simultaneous to women reasserting their position in locality development, social action, and neighborhood organizing, they must actively seek (and must be actively encouraged to assume) positions in the higher-status arenas of community organization, social planning, and policy analysis. Our forebears provide examples of the major contributions women can make in these areas. In a feminist approach to community organizing, practice and policy are not separate. Direct community organizing practice at the neighborhood level should contribute to discussions of policies rather than the traditional male model of central planning divorced from local input (for an example of this male model see Mayer, Moroney, and Morris 1974). It is likely that Addams, Kelly, and the others were so effective at the national level because they lived with the problems and people at the local level on a daily basis.

Curriculum issues

In order to prepare more women for community organization practice, to address issues of concern to women and to introduce a feminist approach into community organization practice, one must address the curriculum in schools of social work. The following are specific suggestions for introducing such content on women in four aspects of the curriculum: core courses, community organization practice courses, field of practice courses, and field curriculum (see also Brandwein 1981).

Core courses

1. In core practice courses a wholistic approach to practice, which is consistent with general practice, should be introduced and identified as part of a feminist approach. This can be contrasted with the traditional model of practice, especially at the graduate level, which emphasizes specializations.
2. Emphasize androgynous roles for social workers and avoid stereotypes in presenting micropractice and macropractice. Where possible employ female faculty in macropractice positions to provide positive role models. Students often choose specializations based on their ability to identify with people and their anticipated roles and functions.
3. In core policy courses, include historical content about women social workers who were involved in policy-making, policy analysis, and development of social programs. (For example, Addams 1910, 1922, 1930, 1935; Conway 1964, 1971; Goldmark 1925, 1953; Kelly 1909; Lasch 1965; Lenroot 1949; *Social Service Review* 1948; Wald 1915, 1934; Wright 1954. In addition there are a number of other primary source articles and monographs by Kelly and Goldmark.)
4. Include policy readings by women authors (for example, Burns 1936, 1949, 1956, 1970, 1973, 1977; Kamerman 1980, 1983; Kamerman and Kahn 1975, 1978, 1981; Ozawa 1980, 1982a, 1982b, 1983, 1984).
5. Emphasize the connection between policy development and the need for community organizing to gain acceptance of desired policies and to insure their implementation.

Community organization courses

1. Address neighborhood organizing and locality development as well as higher-status macropractice roles.
2. Include the feminist approach to community organization in course content.
3. Present a balance between the facilitator/enabler and the advocate/adversary role.
4. Present a balance between process and task orientation; to operationalize the latter include skills in group process and collective decision-making.

5. Explicitly address issues of power and control; to operationalize win–win power orientation include skills in conflict resolution (see Follett 1924).
6. Utilize the contextual theme of practice; introduce the concept of 'web of relationships' in a community, utilizing extensive interorganizational literature; include the concept of time as a factor in community change (see Brandwein 1977; Gilligan 1982; Warren 1971).

Field of practice courses

In courses covering such practice areas as health, family and children, criminal justice, and aging include the issue of organizing the clients of these services. Organizing clients around policies and service delivery contributes to their empowerment and helps break down the power differential between the worker as 'helper' and the client as passive recipient of services. Specific issues to be covered may be differential organizing tactics with different client groups, resistance from supervisors, and the changing relationship between worker and client.

Field curriculum

1. Develop placements in women's agencies, both traditional and alternative, such as YWCAs, offices of women legislators, state chapters of the National Organization for Women, rape crisis centers, and battered women's shelters.
2. Increase numbers of women placed in high-status, traditionally male placements such as United Way, Governor's office, planning councils, and offices of welfare commissioner and hospital directors.
3. Consciously identify and use field instructors who are feminist role models for both male and female students.
4. Encourage women students to seek out female mentors. In field seminars explicitly address relationships and differential roles and behaviors of female and male students, supervisors, and clients, especially in organizing and planning activities.

This list is not comprehensive but can be a start in adding content on women to the community organization curriculum in schools of social work.

Conclusion

Community organization, like other forms of social work practice, is not gender-neutral. What problems are identified, how they are defined, and what kinds of organizing strategies are employed, are all affected by both the gender of the practitioner and the overall approach used. As in other activities, women have historically played an important but largely overlooked and ignored role. As social work educators it is incumbent upon us consciously to educate women to become community organizers and consciously to educate both men and women to incorporate a feminist approach in their community organization practice. The benefits are twofold: the result will increase opportunities for qualified women to engage in this practice, but even more importantly it will improve practice for the recipients of our services.

References

Addams, J. (1910) *Twenty Years at Hull House.* NY: Macmillan.
—— (1922) *Peace and Bread in Time of War.* NY: Macmillan.
—— (1930) *Second Twenty Years at Hull House (1909–1929).* NY: Macmillan.
—— (1935) *My Friend, Julia Lathrop.* NY: Macmillan.
Brandwein, R. (1977) *A Working Framework for Approaching Organizational Change.* Doctoral dissertation, Florence Heller School, Brandeis University, Waltham, MA.
—— (1981) Toward the Feminization of Community and Organizational Practice. In A. Lauffer and E. Newman (eds) *Community Organization for the 1980s,* special issue of *Social Development Issues* 5(2–3): 180–93.
—— (1982) Toward Androgyny in Community and Organizational Practice. In A. Weick and S. Vandiver (eds) *Women, Power and Change.* Washington, DC: National Association of Social Workers, pp. 158–70.
—— (1984) Where Are the Women and Why: An Analysis of Women Administrators in Jewish Communal Services. *Journal of Jewish Communal Service* 60(3): 204–13.
—— (1985) Feminist Thought-Structure: An Alternative Paradigm of Social Change. In D. Gil and E. Gil (eds) *Toward Social and Economic Justice.* Cambridge, MA: Schenkman.
—— (in press) Women in Macropractice. In A. Minahan (ed.) *Encyclopedia of Social Work.* NY: National Association of Social Workers.
Burns, E. (1936) *Toward Social Security: An Explanation of the Social Security Act and a Survey of the Larger Issues.* NY/London: Whittlesey House/McGraw-Hill.
—— (1949) *The American Social Security System.* Boston: Houghton Mifflin.
—— (1956) *Social Security and Public Policy.* NY: McGraw-Hill.
—— (1970) *Social Economics for the 1970's: Programs for Social Security, Health and Manpower.* NY: Dunellen.
—— (1973) *Health Services for Tomorrow: Trends and Issues.* NY: Dunellen.
—— (1977) *Social Welfare in the 1980's and Beyond.* Berkeley, CA: Institute of Governmental Studies.
Conway, J. (1964) Jane Addams, An American Heroine. *Daedalus* 93(2): 761–81.
—— (1971) Women Reformers and American Culture: 1870–1930. *Journal of Social History* 5(2): 165–77.
Follett, M. (1924) *Creative Experience.* NY: Longman, Green.
Gilligan, C. (1982) *In a Different Voice: Psychological Theory and Women's Development.* Cambridge, MA: Harvard University Press.
Giovannoni, J. and Purvine, M. (1973) The Myth of the Social Work Matriarchy. In National Conference of Social Welfare, *Social Welfare Forum.* NY: Columbia University Press.

Goldmark, J. (1925) Labor Laws for Women. *Survey* 29 (January): 552–55.

—— (1953) *Impatient Crusader* (biography of Florence Kelly). Urbana, IL: University of Illinois Press.

Gurin, A. (1971) Social Planning and Community Organization. *Encyclopedia of Social Work*. NY: National Association of Social Workers, pp. 1324–37.

Hooyman, N. (1980) Toward a Feminist Administrative Style. Paper presented at the National Association of Social Workers First National Conference on Social Work with Women, Washington, DC, September.

James, E. (ed.) (1971) *Notable American Women: 1607–1950*. Cambridge, MA: Belknap Press of Harvard University.

Kamerman, S. (1980) *Parenting in an Unresponsive Society: Managing Work and Family Life*. NY/London: Free Press/Collier Macmillan.

—— (1983) *Meeting Family Needs: The Corporate Response*. NY: Pergamon Press.

Kamerman, S. and Kahn, A. (1975) *Social Services in the U.S.: Policy and Programs*. Philadelphia: Temple University Press.

—— (1978) *Family Policy: Government and Families in Fourteen Countries*. NY: Columbia University Press.

—— (1981) *Child Care, Family Benefits and Working Parents*. NY: Columbia University Press.

Kanter, R. (1977) *Men and Women of the Corporation*. NY: Basic Books.

Kelly, F. (1909) Invasion of Family Life by Industry. *Annals of the American Academy of Political and Social Sciences* 34 (July): 90–6.

Kramer, R. and Specht, H. (eds) (1969) *Readings in Community Organization Practice*. Englewood Cliffs, NJ: Prentice-Hall.

Lasch, C. (1965) *The Social Thought of Jane Addams*. NY: Bobbs-Merrill.

Lenroot, K. (1949) Sophonisba Preston Breckenridge, Social Pioneer. *Social Service Review* 23(1).

Lubove, R. (1965) *The Professional Altruist*. Cambridge, MA: Harvard University Press.

Mayer, R., Moroney, R., and Morris, R. (eds) (1974) *Centrally Planned Change*. Urbana, IL: University of Illinois Press.

Miller, J. B. (1976) *Toward a New Psychology of Women*. Boston: Beacon Press.

Morris, R. (ed.) (1977) *Encyclopedia of Social Work*, sixteenth issue (2nd edn) NY: National Association of Social Workers.

National Conference of Social Welfare (1951) *Group Work and Community Organization*. NY: Heath Publ.

—— (1955) *Group Work and Community Organization*. NY: Columbia University Press.

—— (1958, 1961) *Community Organization*. NY: Columbia University Press.

Ozawa, M. (1980) Development of Social Services as an Industry: Why and How. *Social Work* 25(6): 464–70.

—— (1982a) *Income Maintenance and Work Incentives: Toward a Synthesis*. NY: Praeger.

—— (1982b) Who Receives Subsidies Through Social Security and How Much. *Social Work* 27(2): 129–34.

—— (1983) Income Security: The Case for Non-White Children. *Social Work* 28(5): 347–53.

—— (1984) The 1983 Amendments to the Social Security Act: The Issues of Intergenerational Equity. *Social Work* 29(2): 131–37.

Pincus, A. and Minahan, A. (1973) *Social Work Practice: Model and Method*. Itaska, IL: Peacock Publishing.

Rein, M. (1970) Social Work in Search of a Radical Profession. *Social Work* 15(2): 13–28.

Rothman, J. (1970) Three Models of Community Organization Practice. In F. Cox, J. Erlich, J. Rothman, and J. Tropman (eds) *Strategies of Community Organization.* Itaska, IL: Peacock Publishing, pp. 20–36.

Social Service Review (1948) Memorial issue to Sophonisba Breckenridge, 22(4).

Specht, H. (1969) Disruptive Tactics. In R. Kramer and H. Specht (eds) *Readings in Community Organization Practice*, pp. 372–86.

Van Den Bergh, N. and Cooper, L. (eds) (1986) *Feminist Visions of Social Work.* NY: National Association of Social Workers.

Wald, L. (1915) *House on Henry Street.* NY: Henry Holt.

—— (1934) *Windows on Henry Street.* Boston: Little, Brown.

Warren, R. (1971) *Truth, Love and Social Change and Other Essays on Community Change.* Chicago: Rand McNally.

Wright, H. (1954) Three Against Time: Edith and Grace Abbott and Sophonisba Breckenridge. *Social Service Review* 28(1).

PART III
Specialization by problem or service context

11 Overview

Naomi Gottlieb

Women use the services of social workers and other mental health practitioners to address a variety of problems, some of which are represented in the chapters of this section. Although the problems may differ, certain themes recur. The authors in this section describe and analyze the nature of the difficulties women face in a series of problem areas. They go further to identify the programs and policies which address those areas.

The first theme which emerges is the comparative newness of the attention given to distinctive issues for women. The reader will be aware that attention has only recently been given to a whole range of aspects of women's lives. This newness is evident in Eileen Corrigan's discussion of women and chemical dependencies, in Rosemary Sarri's treatment of women and the criminal justice system, in the description of the world of women's paid work presented by Katharine Briar, Marie Hoff, and Essie Seck, and in the listing of yet unclear areas surrounding the abuse of women by men included in the discussions of Ginny NiCarthy, Addei Fuller, and Nan Stoops. Until recently, many problems experienced by women were either ignored completely or distorted by undue attention to the experiences of men, particularly white, heterosexual men.

A second theme throughout these chapters is the pervasiveness and consequences of stereotyped views of women. Naomi Gottlieb's discussion of the intrusiveness of traditional views on the physician's treatment of reproductive health care of women is a case in point. Sharon Berlin's analysis of how women's mental health may be enhanced by a synthesis of the needs for both affiliation and autonomy suggests the potential benefit of moving away from stereotyping women into the relationship-centered pole of behavior. The elevation of women's role in the paid workforce to a legitimate concern for social workers, a central purpose of the section by Briar and her associates, illustrates how women have been perceived almost exclusively in the context of their family roles. Corrigan demonstrates how society's negative attitude toward the alcoholic or drug-dependent woman has determined the comparative lack of knowledge about chemically dependent women as well as the nature of the treatment offered.

Third, issues of power and control are evident throughout the chapters in this section. The abuse of women by intimate partners illustrates the powerless position of women on a personal level, as demonstrated by NiCarthy and her colleagues. Gottlieb's analysis of the hierarchical medical model and its effects on female health care providers and female patients presents a clear example of how power held by men in the health care system determines how women fare in giving and receiving services. Similarly, Sarri describes the influence of powerlessness on the experiences of women as both perpetrators and victims of crime.

A fourth theme is the determining influence of institutional sexism on problems faced by women. Attitudes toward women in large-scale systems reflect the sexism found throughout society. This influence is demonstrated in health care, in women's place in the paid workforce, and in the workings of the criminal justice system as related to the woman criminal and victim.

Finally, the discussions document the compounding effects in each of these problem areas when the women concerned are lesbians or women of color. Homophobia and racism place women in double and triple jeopardy.

Although the problems described in these chapters are important and are representative of content areas stressed in many educational programs, they are not the only problems faced by women. It is hoped that the analysis presented in the chapters of this section will be applied to an exploration of the problems women must deal with in other spheres as well.

12 Women's health and health care

Naomi Gottlieb

Women's place in the health care system, both as providers and consumers, provides a clear illustration of the effect of gender on a major social institution. Definitions of women and their illnesses and issues of power and control influence women as patients and as health workers. How women fare in that system, where they are present in overwhelming numbers but do not have power or control, is the subject of this chapter. The rationale for this focus is that social workers and other helping professionals who are assisting women in their negotiation with the health care system need to understand the important gender dynamic in order to provide high-quality service to women clients.

The examples which support the need for this analysis range from 'the tendency to diagnose women's physical ills as psychogenic ... [to] the difficulties faced by female providers in nursing ... and medicine ... through dehumanizing aspects of pregnancy and delivery' (Lewin and Olesen 1985: 2–3). Women health care providers are no more immune to the effects of devalued views of women than are their women patients. The services that social workers offer or plan for will be enhanced through an awareness of these factors.

This chapter will document the demographics of providers of health care, will briefly review a history of the emergence of the predominant medical model of care and will present gender differences in the use of care. The experiences of special groups of women will demonstrate variations on this central theme of the influence of gender. The implications of recent technological and policy changes and the case of the reproductive life of women will provide particular examples of how the view of women's role determines the health care they receive. Feminist health care programs and social action will illustrate alternatives to mainstream care. Finally, suggestions will be made for curriculum development to include this perspective.

It is important at the outset to emphasize that all health care services are influenced by class, race, and economic status and that these issues affect men as well as women. The poor and people of color do not receive the same care as that of the majority population. In fact, Berger and Hawley (1984) suggest that poverty and racism are themselves major causes of ill health. The health care system does not provide equitable treatment for all, and attitudes toward the poor and ethnic minorities result in different service delivery (Salk *et al.* 1984). Blacks' greater use of public health facilities rather than private providers may relate only partly to economics and may result as much from their intent to avoid more personalized relationships with white providers (Weaver and Garrett 1983).

The emphasis on women and the gender factor in this discussion does not deny the importance of race and class. Rather, this chapter illustrates that, within these societal distinctions, as well as throughout social relations, women are treated differently from men. Further, this different treatment tends to operate to the disadvantage of women, both as providers and recipients of care.

Health care providers

Women comprise the considerable majority of health care providers, both formal and informal. Seventy-five per cent of all health care workers are women. In hospitals, that proportion is 85 per cent (Salk *et al.* 1984). There is little relationship, however, between these numbers, and power and control.

> 'We carry out most doctors' orders – treatment regimens like special diets, medications, and bed rest, etc. – either as unpaid workers at home or as paid workers. We teach about health in the home and in the system – what is "good" and what is "not good" for you. At home we are usually the first person to be told when someone doesn't feel well, and we help decide what to do next.... Most "patient" communication for and about family members flows through women: we report signs and changes, symptoms, responses to treatment and medications. The system also depends on women: our direct reporting forms the basis of much of what medicine calls "scientific results"....
>
> Yet despite our overwhelming numbers and the tremendous responsibility we carry for people's health, we have almost no power to influence the medical system.'
>
> (Salk *et al.* 1984: 556)

Whether women health workers are professionalized or natural providers, they are rarely recognized, acknowledged, or paid in accordance with the services or functions they perform. Males represent a large majority of directors or administrators (Brown 1983; Ruzek 1978). Women are on the lower rungs of the power and influence ladder, and this includes many women social workers.

There are two major reasons for this imbalance. First, the medical profession and many of its subsidiary services are directed for the most part by upper-class white men. These demographics are true for both medical schools and the American Medical Association. In addition, the Association and its 'affiliate medical societies have the right to set the curriculum, direct the training program, control professional certification and sit on the state licensing boards of (at last count) 16 other occupations' (Brown 1983: 108). Nursing has maintained its independence as a profession but still does not have the control in health care delivery commensurate with its numbers and the nature and extent of services its members offer. The way health care is offered derives from the perspective of doctors who are generally high-income white men and whose personal values affect their medical decisions (Gottlieb 1980: 66). Because physicians have defined their domain of expertise broadly and because the public, by and large, accepts physicians' status as directors of health care delivery, physicians' moral positions and views of society are permitted to intrude on their professional activities (Freidson 1970). As Sedgewick comments (1973: 29), 'The medical enterprise is from its inception value-loaded; it is not simply an applied biology, but a biology applied in accordance with the dictates of social interest.'

Second, the actual work done by the respective groups which make up health care professions reflect society's ideas about which of these occupations are important. The care provided by most women health workers, including social workers, is devalued in our society relative to the technical services doctors offer. This situation replicates the general view that men do the important work in society and that women are the 'maintenance crews.' The considerable influx of women into the medical profession – estimated to rise to 25 per cent in the United States by the year 2000 (Salk *et al.* 1984: 570) – may constitute a constructive change toward greater sharing of power. However, this may happen only if women physicians can respect women's socialized traits of caring, combine these with technical competence, and not be smothered by the training they receive or co-opted by the male physician's world (Salk *et al.* 1984). Brown (1983) maintains that the determining factor in the power issues is not primarily the hierarchy of occupations but the gender of the participants.

'Much of the "natural" behaviors between occupations turn out to be based on the sex of the incumbent rather than the status of the occupation. Male doctors do not treat male subordinates the same way they treat female subordinates. . . . When an intern is coached on how to handle nurses to get what he wants, he is simply relearning at a higher level his teenage lessons on how to handle girls.'

(Brown 1983: 109)

Similarly women also view professional interaction in terms of traditional relationships. Not only do women health care workers generally accept the status differentials, but they tend to evaluate difficulties in professional encounters with doctors in terms of their own behavior rather than the physician's. 'Often we believe that the doctor's superior education, training, experience, sex and (sometimes) age automatically produce infallible judgment' (Salk *et al.* 1984: 562). Women then attribute to themselves the cause of any interpersonal problems with physicians. In view of the predominance of women among social workers in health care, their vulnerability to the same gender-biased behaviors is critical to their professional roles vis-à-vis male health workers, particularly physicians.

The professional relationships between nurses and doctors illustrate the pervasive effects of gender-related issues. That relationship is easily compared with family roles, the nurse assuming the role of mother and the doctor that of father. The doctor's 'curing' competence comes from an active learning process in the outside world and the nurse's 'caring' function is considered a passive, naturally derived one (Passau-Buck 1982). In comparison with the high-status male who has had to learn sophisticated technology, the nurse (and other female health workers including social workers) are perceived first as women, less educated, lower in class, more likely to be women of color and to be passively performing their 'natural functions.' These differentials not only influence the professional lives of participants but, as Passau-Buck (1982) indicates, may directly and negatively affect patient care. Both quantity and quality of direct communication between nurses and doctors are unduly limited, have a caste-like quality and result in dysfunctional consequences for patients. In order to gain physician approval, nurses follow directions of questionable validity or cushion their own worthwhile suggestions so as not to appear assertive (Kalisch and Kalisch 1982).

The roles of health care providers appear to mirror many other gender-related social interactions. An historical review is instructive since, earlier, women played a different role.

Historical development of the medical model

Over the centuries, participation of women in health care had been considerable. Women had been the traditional midwives and healers for society (Ehrenreich and English 1973; Marieskind 1980). Women who performed in these traditional health care roles are viewed as ancestors of both nursing and medicine (Leeson and Gray 1978).

The concept of health and well-being that is, to a large extent, being recycled and expanded within society, was an integral part of the earlier role of midwives. For example, midwives were involved in the total birthing process of women. They taught women about their roles and functions as the processes were occurring. As a result, women were able to experience fully – emotionally, physically, spiritually, psychologically – the event of giving birth (Rothman

1984). The role of midwives was not only important in the birthing process but also because midwives were viewed as the informal doctors of the community.

The role of midwives was usurped by the advent of 'professionalism' and the creation of the scientific bio-medical model. Medical professionalism gained momentum through the development of specializations and processes which would determine exclusion or inclusion of individuals to practice medicine (Leeson and Gray 1978).

The late nineteenth and early twentieth centuries witnessed a significant change in the status of the physician. To establish medicine as a respected profession, physicians had to convince the public that they had the right to control health care and to be paid commensurately for their services. Among a series of activities toward that end, several focused directly on women. Upper-class women were defined as frail and delicate, to be protected and treated medically and in need of the services of the newly professionalized physician (Ehrenreich and English 1973). Thus physicians gained respectability among the influential. Significantly, this 'cult of invalidism' was not seen as applicable to the millions of working-class women expected to work in the fields and factories whatever their health (Rothman 1984: 71).

Parallel with this effort toward acceptance among the upper classes, physicians worked at the exclusion of midwives from the important (and potentially lucrative) area of pregnancy and childbirth. By the early twentieth century, childbirth was no longer defined essentially as a family and religious event but as a medical one. By the 1920s, physicians had successfully ousted midwives from the ranks of accepted healers, even though the midwives' safety record remained better than the physicians' (Rothman 1984). America was one of the last industrialized countries to replace the autonomous healers with a medical profession dominated by white men. 'For the first time in the history of the world, women were forbidden by law to be responsible for other women's childbirth and were replaced almost exclusively by male physicians' (Salk *et al.* 1984: 561). A most important consequence is that, by and large, women do not now see other women as role models for healing and for the integration into ongoing life of normal physical processes, such as childbirth.

In addition, physicians controlled membership in the medical profession by reducing the number of medical schools and by placing barriers to women's entrance into medical careers (Ehrenreich and English 1973). Women began to enter the medical profession in the latter part of the nineteenth century after the establishment of the first medical schools for women, but between 1910 and 1940, there was a reduction in the proportion of female doctors (Leeson and Gray 1978). Only since the early 1970s have the number of female medical students risen appreciably in the United States. As of 1981, however, the proportion of women among all active physicians was still only 12 per cent (USDHHS 1984).

In sum, women who use health care services face a profession dominated by white men and staffed in large part by women who play subservient roles vis-à-vis the physician. The medical knowledge and strategies used to treat them has been developed essentially by men whose ideologies may devalue or ignore women's own needs and interests (Doyal 1985; Evers 1985).

Gender, illness, and the use of health care

Studies consistently indicate that women, compared with men, have higher morbidity rates, use health care facilities more frequently, and live longer (Anderson, Lion, and Anderson 1976; Erhardt and Berlin 1974; Salk *et al.* 1984). Morbidity and mortality rates, for all adults and children, are higher among minority populations. For example in 1983, for black females, the life expectancy was 73.8 years, and for white females, 78.8 years. Black children were twice as likely to die in early infancy as their white counterparts, and the maternal mortality rate for black women was four times higher than for white women. When mortality and morbidity rates for both men and women are considered, gender differences within minority groups are similar to the majority population, i.e. minority women compared to minority men are ill and use medical facilities more frequently but live longer (USDHHS 1984).

Over recent decades as more and more women have entered the workforce, occupational health issues have become important for their health care. On the positive side, employed women have fewer chronic illnesses and fewer days of restricted activities, fewer physical symptoms, and better general health than women at home. Some of these findings may be influenced by differences between the two groups as to tendencies to report illness (women at home being more likely to do so) than actual differences in physical illness (Waldron 1983).

Negative conesquences of occupational changes may not yet have received necessary attention. Generally, women's occupations are considered less dangerous than those of men and only recently have questions been raised about occupational risk factors for women. Questions about women's health in the workplace had earlier focused on the hazards of certain substances to women's reproductive capacities. More recently, concerns have widened to include the dangers of new electronic technology to the considerable population of women office workers and the stress experienced by women in high-level jobs. As to the latter, social supports and other strategies women use are seen as mediating and reducing the effects of such psychological stress (Lewin and Olesen 1985; Waldron 1983).

Social expectations and sex-stereotyped behavior may influence both reported morbidity rates and use of health care. Men tend to use health services only in crises (Salk *et al.* 1984), possibly because they are socialized to ignore symptoms of illness and not to admit weakness (Verbrugge 1976). Women not only have social permission to admit failings and to seek help, but may also be more likely to be labeled as ill by professionals. As Rothman (1984) suggests, since women are seen as the less important and active contributors to society, they are more easily diagnosed as ill and needing care and attention. Ironically, this greater frequency in use of services by women, implying readier attention to illnesses in their early stages, may be part of the reason for women's greater longevity (Spiegelman and Erhardt 1974). Men's higher mortality rate is related to their greater likelihood of having dangerous jobs and their socialization to hard-driving, competitive behavior leading to stress-related conditions (Waldron 1983). Graham (1985) adds another piece of understanding about women and their health by describing how women caregivers may jeopardize their own health through protecting the health of other family members. Men's and women's illnesses and deaths seem as much related to gender-based expectations as their everyday interpersonal interactions.

Both men and women may be negatively affected by general issues of accessibility to health care, although additional barriers may play a role for women. Deterrents to appropriate use of health care services include cost of care, delays in appointments for service, inability to communicate due to language or cultural differences, and office hours inconvenient to the lifestyles of the community or the working schedules of its members (Marieskind 1980). In addition to these general issues of ease of accessibility, women face particular deterrents. The lack of child care coupled with long periods in waiting rooms are examples of practical problems. Women also face gender-biased services. 'Many different studies have shown that medical care providers treat male patients with more respect than women and offer fewer tranquilizers and less moral advice' (Salk *et al.* 1984: 556).

The factors of race and sexual orientation may further influence the reaction of health care providers and the resultant service to women. Discrimination on the basis of race in society as a whole has been thoroughly documented and is as prevalent in the health care system as in other social institutions (Weaver and Garrett 1983). The non-white woman patient faces double jeopardy in her encounters with the health care system.

Only recently have the experiences of lesbians with the health care system been described. Ryan (1985) comments on the number of ways homophobia interferes with effective health services to lesbians and, in fact, asserts that homophobia itself is a major social disease. Lesbians who are reluctant to reveal their sexual orientation may receive inappropriate treatment, particularly related to gynecological issues. When lesbians are open about their sexual preferences, they may find that their sexual identity, rather than the problem for which they sought help (e.g. alcoholism or drug addition), is considered the 'illness' to be treated.

'During medical emergencies (without a predesigned medical power of attorney which some gay couples are now initiating) lesbian and gay lovers/partners have *no power* to sign the legal consent forms that routinely afford heterosexual spouses legal guardianship for their partners' lives.... Lesbian and gay patients, when so identified in emergency rooms and hospitals, are known to receive inferior, painful and needlessly delayed medication and services.'

(Ryan 1985: 60)

In general, then, there are significant gender differences in illness and illness behavior and in accessibility to health care, especially for women of color and lesbians. The instance of services for reproductive problems illustrates special concerns for the woman patient.

Reproductive health care

'Particularly in those areas of medical care that more directly impinge on women's lives as women – gynecological examinations, birth control and abortions, sexuality, childbirth and psychotherapy – feminists have been articulate critics of the nature and quality of medical treatment.'

(Fee 1983: 17)

Much of that criticism focuses on the moral nature of the health care system's position regarding reproduction, particularly that of the physician, and the stereotyped views of women reflected in attitudes toward women and their reproductive systems. The intent of this section is to highlight a few aspects of this issue to demonstrate how women are affected as they seek services for gynecological and obstetrical purposes.

First, a major determinant of physicians' attitudes toward and treatment of women's reproductive problems is their traditional view of women as essentially family-oriented. Because women are seen by society primarily as bearers and rearers of children, many physicians reflect societal constraints in their attitudes toward reproductive freedom and abortion. As Luker (1984) suggests in her study of the views of women about abortion, the underlying issue in the abortion debate is whether women will have the choice to break away from traditional norms of family life. Luker found that anti-abortion activists placed primary value on the traditional role of women as mothers and homemakers. Pro-abortion activists advocated for the equal importance of other roles for women, particularly in the paid workforce. Physicians can be on either side of that debate, but women consulting traditionally oriented physicians about reproductive choice may find that their stereotyped attitudes interfere with appropriate medical care. The question of power and control is also evident here since the demands of feminists that women control their own bodies (Petchesky 1985) can be in direct conflict with the physician's psychological need to control not only the medical treatment, but the women – both patients and providers – related to that treatment.

The physician's approach to menopause constitutes another example of the influence of stereotyped ideas about women. Since women are defined by their childbearing functions, the end of that possibility has been described by physicians as a 'living decay' (Wilson 1966) and the menopausal woman as 'not really a man, but no longer a functional woman' (Reuben 1969). In the treatment of menopause, physicians have tried to keep women youthful, often with estrogen replacement therapy, and to respond to the complaints of husbands and other family members about the mood swings or irritability of the woman experiencing menopausal symptoms (Doress 1984). There are situations when physical symptoms need attention or when intervention is appropriate, for example in the use of estrogen replacement therapy for osteoporosis prevention. However, the consequences of stereotyped attitudes of physicians are that by and large menopause has been treated as a disease and an unfortunate aspect of aging, rather than as a normal process.

A second theme in this reproductive system area is the lack of valid empirical knowledge about women's reproductive cycle. This lack of knowledge is partly the result of diagnosing normal processes as diseases requiring intervention. This is evident in inappropriate interventions in childbirth and in menopause, as just described. In fact, the disease view of menopause has hampered a balanced approach which would include women who do not experience difficulties. The lack of knowledge is also related to the tendency to diagnose women's reproduction-related conditions as psychological rather than physical. Lennane and Lennane (1973) cite evidence that clearly suggests organic etiology for four problems related to reproductive functions – dysmenorrhea, nausea in pregnancy, pain in labor, and infantile behavioral disturbances – to which most physicians attach labels of psychological origin. Since, in the traditional view, women are expected to accept easily their child-bearing and child-rearing roles, only psychological causation can explain something going awry in that process. As these two instances illustrate, if medical scientists were open to other than stereotyped views of women, scientific knowledge would include the symptom-free menopausal woman and the organic bases for 'psychological' reproductive problems.

A third theme is the illogic and contradiction often evident as physicians rationalize medical treatment based on moral values. For example, physicians opposed to abortion (along with like-minded persons in the general public) contend that teenagers are too young or immature to 'understand the implications of abortion but mature enough to bear a child' (Petchesky 1985: 164). Petchesky suggests that this view reflects 'the ancient patriarchal idea of childbearing as woman's "natural" biological function, whatever her age or situation, and abortion as a violation of her "nature"' (Petchesky 1985: 164). A similar illogic is seen in the 'medical' argument that abortion carries more risk to a young woman's health than child-bearing – a conclusion in direct contradiction to medical fact (Petchesky 1985: 164).

Earlier discussions in this chapter have focused on how gender bias affects women as patients or providers. This section concerning reproductive issues has demonstrated how these same distortions affect a domain of distinctive importance to women. We turn now to important societal changes, in technology and policy, and consider how they affect women as users of the health care system.

Technological and policy changes

Three current issues in health care – developments in sophisticated technology, the impact of DRGs (diagnostic related groups) on hospital practice, and the increasing emphasis on prevention – will be examined briefly in the light of this chapter's central issue of effects on women.

The use of advanced technology, especially in reproductive system care, has had mixed results for women, mainly related to the intrusion of gender-biased and moral stances taken by physicians. Doyal contends that obstetricians 'whose job satisfaction often lies in high technology intervention have been able to appropriate much of the satisfaction of childbirth from the woman concerned' (Doyal 1985: 250). Hubbard (1984) lists several factors which make her wary of the benefit to women of sophisticated technology, as follows:

'[the] degree of invasiveness and medical manipulation; the white, professional, affluent men [who] make up the overwhelming number of the scientists who research these technologies, the physicians who apply them, the legislators who approve and fund the research and the drug company directors who translate them into products to be advertised, sold, and profited from. Despite claims that these technologies are to "serve" women, our experience with the use of other technologies has taught us to be suspicious; physicians and hospitals now virtually force birthing technologies on us, and sterilization has been outrageously misused against women of color.'

(Hubbard 1984: 317)

In other newly developed procedures, the physician's moral stance interferes. For example, Hubbard (1984) advocates for the self-application of donor insemination, a feasible and safe procedure, as particularly useful to persons in nontraditional relationships such as lesbians, since doctors restrict the technology (similarly for *in vitro* fertilization) to married women.

The primary purpose of the federal government's recent system of diagnostic related groups (DRGs) is to place severe constraints on reimbursement for inpatient care depending on expectations of length of hospital stay for specific conditions. The consequence for hospital service is that patients are being discharged much more readily than previously. The consequences for women in the community are considerable. Since patients are often discharged home, women as the primary caregivers in the family become the caregivers to discharged patients as well. The fact that 'family care' means care by women is currently being brought to light by feminist writers (Briar and Ryan 1986). While health care providers stress the impact of the DRG system on hospital staff and on quality of medical treatment, the long-term effects on women caregivers also require attention.

Medicine has begun to enter the field of health and wellness in the form of preventive strategies. Implications for women illustrate sensitivity to their social condition. Changes in lifestyles are essential ingredients in disease prevention, and healthful nutrition is a key element. Food provision is usually the woman's realm in the family, and two issues are readily apparent. As Mitchell (1985) comments, proper nutrition requires sufficient funds. Considering the proportion of women who are poor, a large minority of the population would appear to have difficulty affording proper nutrition. Also, women's socialized habits of placing the needs of other family members before their own may result, if funds are limited, in better nutrition for other family members than for themselves.

Another issue in health promotion raised by Doyal (1985), in the British context, is the effect of home conditions on women's health. Dampness in deteriorating houses, home accidents, domestic violence, and depression – the last 'the most common occupational disease of domestic labor' – are presented as preventable occupational hazards, particularly relevant to women at home (Doyal 1985: 258). The exposure of these issues only recently demonstrates that women's distinctive needs are hidden from the mainstream health care system.

Finally, effective preventive medicine, particularly for women, requires empowering them with sufficient knowledge and skills to maintain health. Such an approach would recognize and reinforce the need for women to care for themselves through such means as self-help groups to enable them to make informed choices. This strategy has the positive potential to create in women a greater sense of autonomy and control. While group support is a needed strategy, it may be met with resistance from traditional health care providers fearful of losing control over the health care system.

This discussion of a few selected issues of current trends demonstrates how, in each instance, there are special implications for women, some of which challenge the health care system. We turn now to some strategies and programs that groups have already organized to counter the established system.

Health care alternatives and social action

Common to both alternative programs and social action are the challenges to traditionally organized health care and the empowerment of women consumers and providers. A basic theme of activities in both arenas is mirrored in this chapter, i.e. the recognition that both women consumers and women providers are affected by sexism and discrimination within the system.

The women's health movement parallels the general women's movement in both the United States and Britain. Stacey (1985) comments on the special circumstances in Britain where feminists need to defend the National Health Service against attacks and, at the same time, continue criticism of its shortcomings with regard to women. In the United States, the women's health movement developed alternate health care services mainly focused on reproductive issues (Gottlieb 1980; Ruzek 1978), produced important self-help literature (Boston Women's Health Book Collective 1984) and challenged medical myths (Salk *et al.* 1984). The intent has been to enable women to reclaim health service areas in which they had previously played a major role (e.g. midwifery), to demystify medical information, and to place more control and autonomy directly in women's hands. Alternative therapies were offered to parallel mainstream medical care (Berger and Hawley 1984).

Self-help groups and self-healing are important characteristics of the women's health movement, particularly to give women support as they challenge the main system and to offer alternate approaches. Olesen and Lewin (1985) recognize that much scholarly work on the impact of self-help groups remains to be done. Ironically, the knowledge being acquired by women in such groups about the health care process may serve physicians' preventive medicine purposes. Physicians concerned about iatrogenic outcomes and possible malpractice suits may feel 'it was becoming wiser to have a patient actively involved in the treatment decision' (Kaufert and McKinlay 1985: 132). For the most part, however, alternative feminist programs represent a challenge unwelcome to mainstream medicine.

Nurses' activism has been a primary example of organized attempts by groups of providers to protest against the system's inequities. Organizing and strikes by nurses and other hospital workers have the aim of improving not only their own work conditions but patient care as well (Reaves 1984; Salk *et al.* 1984). Nursing organizations now frequently lobby at the state and national level. In some states, nurses have successfully established a licensed nurse-practitioner role which permits increased professional autonomy. Heide (1982) presents a useful review of a series of protests and organizing activities engaged in by nurses and nursing organizations over the past several decades.

These activities by feminists and others concerned with health care for women and the status of female providers of care are paralleled by other consumer challenges about accessibility and quality of health care. For example, the development of health maintenance organizations and the greater choice consumers have among them places more control into consumer hands. Enrollments in or defections from health maintenance organizations may reflect degrees of consumer satisfaction.

Curriculum development

The primary recommendation for curriculum development is the use of the analytic framework proposed in this chapter, i.e. to screen all aspects of health care for the influence of the gender dynamic and to consider the impact of sexism on both consumer and provider. Although the role of the social worker in health care teams with other professionals has been given scholarly attention, the special issues for the woman social worker or other mental health professional in relation to men above her in the medical model hierarchy still needs adequate analysis and action.

The analysis proposed in the chapter would be usefully accomplished in mainstream courses, as an added understanding to other general subjects. For example, social policy courses which include health care issues can study health care programs for the extent to which they reinforce or counteract gender-biased services. Methods courses focused on direct services in health care can investigate gender bias in interactions with clients and with professionals in other disciplines. Courses in administration and program planning which employ health care setting examples can consider to what extent service programs are influenced by stereotyped views of both consumers and providers. Human development and family treatment courses which include health issues and the interaction of individuals with the health care system would provide greater understanding about women's circumstances through this chapter's perspective. Courses in health care concentrations need to consider this analysis, not only for the benefit of the clients that students will serve but for the future practitioners themselves, particularly women, who will have to negotiate the interdisciplinary team system. The references for this chapter would provide a beginning resource list for curriculum development.

References

Anderson, R., Lion, J., and Anderson, O. (1976) *Two Decades of Health Services: Social Survey Trends in Uses and Expenditures.* Cambridge, MA: Ballinger.
Berger, P. and Hawley, N. (1984) Health and Healing: Alternatives to Medical Care. In Boston Women's Health Book Collective (eds) *The New Our Bodies, Ourselves.* New York: Simon and Schuster.
Boston Women's Health Book Collective (1984) *The New Our Bodies, Ourselves,* New York: Simon and Schuster.
Briar, K. and Ryan, R. (1986) The Anti-Institution Movement and Women Caregivers. *Affilia: Journal of Women and Social Work* 1: 1.
Brown, C. (1983) Women Workers in the Health Service Industry. In Elizabeth Fee (ed.) *Women and Health: The Politics of Sex in Medicine.* Farmingdale, NY: Baywood Publishing.
Doress, P. (1984) Women Growing Older. In the Boston Women's Health Book Collective (eds) *The New Our Bodies, Ourselves.* New York: Simon and Schuster.

Doyal, L. (1985) Women and the National Health Services: The Carers and the Careless. In Ellen Lewin and Virginia Olesen (eds) *Women, Health and Healing*. London: Tavistock Publications.

Ehrenreich, B. and English, D. (1973) *Complaints and Disorders*. Old Westbury, NY: Feminist Press.

Erhardt, C. and Berlin, J. (1974) *Mortality and Morbidity in the United States*. Cambridge, MA: Harvard University Press.

Evers, H. (1985) The Frail Elderly Woman: Emergent Questions in Aging and Women's Health. In Ellen Lewin and Virginia Olesen (eds) *Women, Health and Healing*. London: Tavistock Publications.

Fee, E. (1983) Women and Health Care: A Comparison of Theories. In Elizabeth Fee (ed.) *Women and Health: The Politics of Sex in Medicine*. Farmingdale, NY: Baywood Publishing.

Freidson, E. (1970) *Profession of Medicine*. New York: Donald Mead.

Gottlieb, N. (1980) Women and Health Care. In Naomi Gottlieb (ed.) *Alternative Social Services for Women*. New York: Columbia University Press.

Graham, H. (1985) Providers, Negotiators, and Mediators: Women as the Hidden Carers. In Ellen Lewin and Virginia Olesen (eds) *Women, Health and Healing*. London: Tavistock Publications.

Heide, W. (1982) Feminist Activism in Nursing and Health Care. In Janet Muff (ed.) *Socialization, Sexism and Stereotyping*. St Louis: C.V. Mosby.

Hubbard, R. (1984) New Reproductive Technologies. In Boston Women's Health Book Collective (eds) *The New Our Bodies, Ourselves*. New York: Simon and Schuster.

Kalisch, B. and Kalisch, P. (1982) An Analysis of the Sources of Physician-Nurse Conflict. In Janet Muff (ed.) *Socialization, Sexism and Stereotyping*. St Louis: C.V. Mosby.

Kaufert, P. and McKinlay, S. (1985) Estrogen-Replacement Therapy: The Production of Medical Knowledge and the Emergence of Policy. In Ellen Lewin and Virginia Olesen (eds) *Women, Health and Healing*. London: Tavistock Publications.

Leeson, J. and Gray, J. (1978) *Women and Medicine*. London: Tavistock.

Lennane, K. and Lennane, R. (1973) Alleged Psychogenic Disorders in Women: A Possible Manifestation of Sexual Prejudice. *New England Journal of Medicine* 288: 288–92.

Lewin, E. and Olesen, V. (1985) *Women, Health and Healing*. New York/London: Tavistock Publications.

Luker, K. (1984) *Abortion and the Politics of Motherhood*. Berkeley, CA: University of California Press.

Marieskind, H. (1980) *Women in the Health System: Patients, Providers and Programs*. St Louis: C.V. Mosby.

Mitchell, C. (1985) Nutrition as Prevention and Treatment in the Elderly. In Marie Haug, Amasha Ford, and Marian Sheafer (eds) *The Physical and Mental Health of Aged Women*. New York: Springer Publishing.

Olesen, V. and Lewin, E. (1985) Women, Health, and Healing: A Theoretical Introduction. In Ellen Lewin and Virginia Olesen (eds) *Women, Health and Healing*. New York/London: Tavistock Publications.

Passau-Buck, S. (1982) Caring vs. Curing: The Politics of Health Care. In Janet Muff (ed.) *Socialization, Sexism and Stereotyping*. St Louis: C. V. Mosby.

Petchesky, R. (1985) Abortion in the 1980s: Feminist Morality and Women's Health.

In Ellen Lewin and Virginia Olesen (eds) *Women, Health and Healing*. London: Tavistock Publications.

Reaves, J. (1984) Nurses Strike a Symptom of New Style of Medicine. *Chicago Tribune*, 10 July.

Reuben, D. (1969) *Everything You Always Wanted to Know About Sex*. New York: David McKay.

Rothman, B. (1984) Women, Health, and Medicine. In Jo Freeman (ed.) *Women: A Feminist Perspective*. California: Mayfield Publishing.

Ruzek, S. (1978) *The Women's Health Movement*. New York: Praeger.

Ryan, C. (1985) Gay Health Issues: Oppression Is a Health Hazard. In Hilda Hidalgo, Travis Peterson, and Natalie Woodman (eds) *Lesbian and Gay Issues: A Resource Manual for Social Workers*. Silver Spring, MD: National Association of Social Workers.

Salk, H., Sanford, W., Swenson, N., and Luce, J. (1984) The Politics of Women and Medical Care. In Boston Women's Health Book Collective (eds) *The New Our Bodies, Ourselves*. New York: Simon and Schuster.

Sedgewick, P. (1973) Illness – Mental and Otherwise. *Hastings Center Studies* 1(3): 30–1.

Spiegelman, M. and Erhardt, C. (1974) Mortality and Longevity in the United States. In Carl Erhardt and Joyce Berlin (eds) *Mortality and Morbidity in the United States*. Cambridge, MA: Harvard University Press.

Stacey, M. (1985) Women and Health: The United States and the United Kingdom Compared. In Ellen Lewin and Virginia Olesen (eds) *Women, Health and Healing*. London: Tavistock Publications.

US Department of Health and Human Services (1984) *Minorities and Women in the Health Fields*. Washington, DC: US Government Printing Office.

Verbrugge, L. (1976) Females and Illness: Recent Trends in Sex Differences in the United States. *Journal of Health and Social Behavior* 17: 387–403.

Waldron, I. (1983) Employment and Women's Health: An Analysis of Causal Relationships. In Elizabeth Fee (ed.) *Women and Health: The Politics of Sex in Medicine*. Farmingdale, NY: Baywood Publishing.

Weaver, J. and Garrett, S. (1983) Sexism and Racism in the American Health Industry: A Comparative Analysis. In Elizabeth Fee (ed.) *Women and Health: The Politics of Sex in Medicine*. Farmingdale, NY: Baywood Publishing.

Wilson, R. (1966) *Feminine Forever*. New York: M. Evans.

13 Women and mental health: anger, anxiety, dependency, and control

Sharon Berlin

'The relationship between women and the experts was not unlike conventional relationships between women and men. The experts wooed their female constituency, promising the "right" and scientific way to live, and women responded – more eagerly in the upper and middle classes, more slowly among the poor – with dependency and trust. It was never an equal relationship, for the experts' authority rested on the denial or destruction of women's autonomous sources of knowledge.... But it was a relationship that lasted right up to our own time, when women began to discover that the experts' answer to the Woman Question was not science after all, but only the ideology of a masculinist society, dressed up as objective truth.'

(Ehrenreich and English 1979: 5)

The relationship between women and experts which Ehrenreich and English point to as an historical fact existed for more than the 150 years encompassed in their analysis. Although women today are much more likely to cast a cynical eye on expert advice, the experts (including social workers) are still out there attempting to discern and/or prescribe women's nature. Notwithstanding all of this ongoing advice, the terms 'dependent,' 'passive,' and 'compliant' remain among the most frequently used adjectives for describing women's problems, or, more accurately, for describing women with problems. Idealized during an earlier era, scorned as pathological products of bad socialization during more recent times, and now romanticized again as 'feminine virtues,' these ubiquitous traits are still at the core of accounts of women's identity – either as aspects of what is wrong with them or what is 'special' about them.

It is not that women's concerns are inappropriate foci for study and intervention by experts. Indeed, the very fact that the preponderance of people seeking psychological help are women presses for careful analysis of women's mental health problems (President's Commission on Mental Health, 1978). The issue is the extent to which we are able to teach our students, our up-and-coming experts, to base their understanding and advice on women's own sources of knowledge. If we begin with the premise that our most fundamental assumptions and mental constructs are a product of male thinking (Stimpson 1981) it becomes clear that taking a woman-centered perspective on mental health – or any other area of concern – is an ongoing process of discovery. Embarking on that process does not mean we have to throw out everything that traditional theorists have told us; instead we need to critique and recast our assumptions about mental health for women from a frame that elevates women's experience.

It is in this spirit of approximation and building that the issue of women's mental health is addressed here. What follows is an elaboration of one version of a woman-centered perspective that can be used to guide curriculum planning for mental health courses. It is a perspective that values women's tendencies toward affiliation, emotional openness, and nurturing but does not idealize them, and would hope to build upon them so that women do not continue to play out the same old limited 'solutions' to complex life problems – for example, single-mindedly depending on relationships as the sole means for achieving wants. At the same time, the negatively connoted aspects of 'female traits' (dependency, passivity, resentment, manipulation) are seen as the maladaptive sequelae of consistently relying on others to provide for the needs of the self – as attempts to get one's needs met without ever standing separate as a self-respecting, responsible, autonomous individual.

After a brief review of the bipolar nature of historical and current resolutions to questions about women's nature, the work of Gilligan (1982) and Benjamin (1984) are relied upon to suggest the importance of women finding a balance between the extremes of self-definition, between autonomy (consideration of oneself) and connection (consideration of others). The mental health problems of excessive dependency, anxiety, and anger are then explored as the consequences of narrow social and self-definitions. Finally, the chapter takes up specific curriculum considerations. Several other important mental health issues are omitted from this chapter (e.g. mental health policy; poverty and mental health; service delivery systems; the nature of feminist therapy; helping underserved groups), but should not be omitted from mental health curricula. These dimensions of mental health services for women are addressed elsewhere (e.g. Belle 1982; Brodsky and Hare-Mustin 1980; Carmen, Russo and Miller 1981; Kaplan 1983; Walker 1984). The main reason for using the limited space available here to explore what might constitute a healthy intrapersonal/interpersonal stance for women is that this question seems both basic and timely.

Cultural information and conceptions of the self

Romantic versus rational views of women's place

By some accounts (Ehrenreich and English 1979), serious questions regarding the nature and role of women first arose as a side-effect of the industrial revolution. While women's place and nature in regard to religion and social issues had been subjects of intense discussion in medieval and Renaissance times, the question of women's economic position became particularly open to discussion during the industrial revolution. Prior to that time, women were viewed as subordinate but as essential to the survival of the home-based economic unit. It was only when production was taken out of the home and men claimed the world of commerce and industry as their own that the issue of women's place and nature in relation to economic activity emerged. According to Ehrenreich and English, two basic and masculinist responses have been offered. The romanticist solution, which held ascendancy from the late nineteenth to the mid-twentieth century, proclaimed that women's natural function was to be the goddess of the home who found fulfillment in bringing ease and comfort to her spouse and children. Compliance, dependence, and nurturing were useful behaviors in the new order and they were characterized as intrinsic to femaleness. The second solution which emerged during the 1950s and 1960s sought to undo women's 'bad' socialization and turn the 'romantic woman' into a female version of 'economic man' so that she too could participate in a new market based on self-indulgence. This new rationalist position suggested that all of the traits that had previously been viewed as the essential core of woman now had to be undone, leaving her free to 'do her own thing.'

At the present time, the romanticist tradition lives on in the structures of society and in the interpersonal relationships and psyches of its inhabitants (and perhaps, most prominently, in the ideology of the New Right). The alternative, 'you do your thing and I'll do mine,' is also apparent in current thinking. It has provided a breath of relief for some women and has relevance as a therapeutic goal for troubled women, but has not really replaced traditional views in our minds and lives, and, to the extent that it ignores connection and social responsibility, is not woman-centered.

Valuing the 'female voice'

During the last decade, advances in feminist thought have suggested that, in some respects, many of the 'feminine traits' can be seen as positive, and even that women's greater socialization toward affiliation, emotional openness, and assuming responsibility for the well-being of others can be seen as more socially advanced than the competitive egocentricity encouraged in men (e.g. Bricker-Jenkins and Joseph 1982; Schaef 1981; Wetzel 1985). Carol Gilligan's (1977, 1982) investigation of women's moral development has been extremely influential in both shaping and articulating this growing sense of pride in 'women's nature.' Making the assumption that male stages of moral development are not the proper criteria for gauging female morality, Gilligan set out to identify the characteristically feminine voice in the moral domain. In conducting her research, the language that Gilligan heard repeatedly focused on themes of care, responsibility, and worries about selfishness. Gilligan reports three major ways in which women think about responsibility: (a) self-care in terms of survival; (b) self-sacrifice for the good of others; and (c) applying the principle of non-violence to both the self and others. In the first instance, survival needs preclude a moral dilemma; constrained by a sense of powerlessness, one simply acts out of necessity. At the second level – a position which reflects an elegant internalization of the romanticist perspective and encompasses the core of much psychosocial anguish – the woman equates responsibility with self-sacrifice and caring only for others. Disguising the passivity of dependence through the activities of care, the woman believes she is motivated only by compassion; but underlying her self-sacrifice is the expectation that she will be loved and protected in return. Threatened by abandonment and criticism, as well as her own power to hurt, she often ends up stuck in her victimization. Having relinquished overt control and failing to see the choices she makes, she gets 'suspended in an immobility of both judgement and action' (Gilligan 1977: 498). According to Gilligan, the transition to the third level of moral development begins when the woman questions whether or not it might be moral and responsible to include her own needs within the 'compass of care' and whether it might be responsible to at least be honest about what she is doing, getting, and avoiding. The trick is to care about others – to be 'good' – but also to be responsible to oneself and thus to be 'honest' and 'real.' The balance is sometimes hard to find, and in fact there is never a clearly 'right' solution or perfect balance. Rather, at this higher level of morality, one learns to live with ambiguity.

This articulation of 'the feminine voice' in the moral domain is one piece of an evolving alternative perspective on women in society that has relevance for conceptualizations about women's mental health. Without extreme care, however, this current trend in thinking could easily be subverted to result in an idealization of traits that are sometimes dysfunctional, to a false sense of what is 'naturally' female, and thus to a false moral prescription of how to be an ideal, natural woman – in short, another rendition of the old romanticist position.

Recently, social work authors have used Gilligan's notions about differences in morality between men and women to differentiate between male and female aspects of social work ethics (Rhodes 1985) and between academic research and clinical practice (Davis 1985). In focusing on women's sensitivity to issues of relationship, both of these authors seem to miss a critical aspect of Gilligan's analysis: it is the attention to the needs of the autonomous self, along with the needs of others, that signals higher levels of moral development. Following from Davis's discussion of the 'maleness' of the world of academic research and the 'femaleness' of the world of practice, it would be a small (but excessive and dangerous) leap to conclude that 'natural' women should forget about autonomy and that connectedness has no meaning for the 'natural' man. Davis does go on to emphasize the importance of making both 'voices' audible in the profession, and thus the importance of women speaking in their own voice, believing in their own reality, and making themselves heard. Herein lies the dilemma: speaking in one's own voice is an independent act, requires toleration of separateness.

We are led to believe (and indeed, many of us have a deep sense of the notion) that if we are independent, autonomous individuals we have to give up relationship and connectedness. Such a sacrifice is not easily undertaken nor advised. Instead, it seems that the best hope is to try to stay both free *and* connected. As far as we know 'nature' would not prohibit it, for women *or* men. The 'female voice' needs to be heard, but not restricted to a narrow and ultimately degrading range of expression.

Integrating the polarities

Recently, Benjamin (1979, 1982, 1984, 1985a, 1985b) has developed a model (Structural Analysis of Social Behavior – SASB) for understanding interpersonal/ intrapersonal behavior which provides an alternative to polarizing autonomy and connectedness. According to her, all human interaction can be understood along the two basic dimensions of affiliation and interdependence, and is made up of communications conveying varying degrees of friendliness and autonomy. A distinguishing and important feature of SASB is that these characteristics are viewed as orthogonal to, rather than opposite from, each other. As shown in *Figure 13.1*, the intersection of the affiliation and interdependence dimensions creates four main categories of communication behaviors (these are broken out into more specific clusters of behaviors or single behaviors in more complex versions of the model – see Benjamin 1979). The diamond at the top of *Figure 13.1* shows the four categories (quadrants) of interpersonal communication when the communication is directed toward another person. Communications that fall into the first quadrant are those which are both high in autonomy and high in bonding and basically encourage the other person to be her best self. The second diamond-shaped surface shows the reciprocal communication position when the focus is on oneself and the content reflects one's state. According to Benjamin's (1984) complementarity hypothesis, a communication that encourages autonomy in a friendly, bonded way (surface one, quadrant one) is likely to draw a friendly, assertive, disclosive response that shows a toleration of separateness as well as trust in the interpersonal relationship (surface two, quadrant one). Finally, the third surface represents self-concept or internalized interpretations of communications received over the course of development. If an individual has consistently received communications encouraging her to develop her

Figure 13.1 Chart of social behavior (quadrant version)

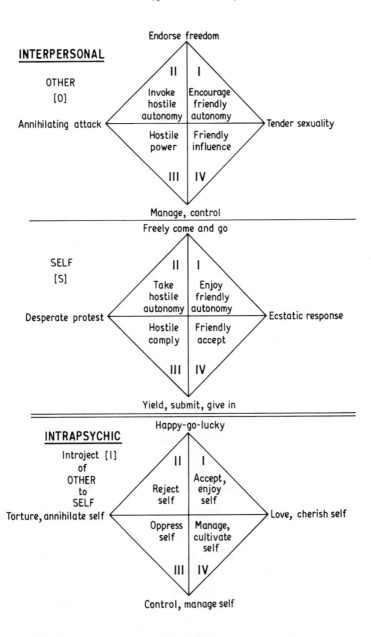

Source: Benjamin, L.S. (1979) Structural Analysis of Differentiation Failure. *Psychiatry* 42: 1-23.
© 1979, William Alanson White Psychiatric Foundation.

potential and to trust her 'instincts,' basic goodness, and abilities, making it clear that she is loved (surface one, quadrant one), she is likely to experience a fairly solid sense of worth, an acceptance of who she is, and a willingness to grow (surface three, quadrant one). Although the healthy adult takes positions in all of the quadrants – has the flexibility to express anger, take control, withdraw, ignore, protect, and show tenderness – 'home-base' is optimally somewhere in the 'warmer' ranges of quadrant one where the individual is both free and connected (Benjamin 1979).

Overall, SASB provides a guide for understanding psychosocial dilemmas, describing better alternatives, and determining what is required in order to get from the problem to the goal. Exploring the detail and implications of the model is well beyond the scope of this discussion. The point of relevance here is that Benjamin's schema operationalizes ways of being with others and oneself that allow a full range of human behaviors and locates the core of psychological health not in polar extremes, but in the mix, in the moderate zone, in Gilligan's 'level three.' And although level three resolutions rarely leave one with an unambiguous sense of being right and don't mean that one can always have it all, it is the overall commitment to being both self-respecting and interpersonally connected that provides the anchor point and the vision. Thus, a therapeutic goal for many women may be to move from a position that is either extremely dependent, fearful, angry, or controlling, to one that reflects both affiliation and freedom. The upcoming sections of this chapter will focus on each of the problematic positions, discuss their adaptive intent and maladaptive aspects, and briefly highlight broad intervention strategies that may be used to promote more adaptive responding.

Passive and dependent women

'Dependency needs are a universal aspect of human experience' (Lerner 1983: 697). Even though the desire to be loved and cared for is an integral part of human nature, dependency is often viewed in some pejorative sense: as regressive, weak, or childlike (Bowlby 1977). Despite the universality of dependency needs, there is also a widespread inclination to assume that women are primarily the ones who experience them. While women in heterosexual relationships often nurture, soothe, encourage, and support their partners, it is less likely that they receive reciprocal treatment. From this perspective, it is not that women have such voracious needs, but rather that their needs are not being adequately met. Lerner also points out that marital partners tend to be similar in terms of the actual level of autonomy or 'differentiation of self' achieved. For a variety of reasons the woman may be expressing more dependent behaviors than her male partner, but it is also likely that the proverbial 'rational, controlled, independent' husband and his 'crazy, clinging' wife are fairly well matched in terms of differentiation or independence (Bowen 1978).

Integrating the desires for connectedness and autonomy is a lifelong task for both men and women, made difficult, some theorists suggest, by the structure of the family of origin. In the case of females, a prevalent opinion is that because they are primarily reared by a caretaker of the same sex, it is harder for them to develop a differentiated sense of self (cf. Chodorow 1978). Miller takes issue with this view, saying that such a conceptualization ignores the likelihood that 'the only possibility of having any sense of self at all is built on this core [relational] process' (Gordon 1985: 44). The issue, she says, is not so much one of developing a separate sense of self, but 'rather a more complex sense of self that becomes defined and refined as [individuals] enter into ever more complex relationships to others' (Gordon 1985: 44). Other theorists attribute the tendency of some women to ignore the needs of the self to broad cultural prescriptions and to their current marital interactions. For example, Fodor (1974) presents a convincing argument that common cultural stereotypes of women as helpless and dependent leave them vulnerable to phobic conditions; and Lerner (1983) addresses the possibility that many women's difficulties in synthesizing dependence and autonomy may also stem from their accurate perception that their main relationships will not tolerate increases in autonomous functioning. Women may fear that men will not tolerate autonomous women as long as they perceive the possibility of obtaining dependent, compliant ones.

When the problematic manifestations of dependency (muting one's own opinions and preferences out of fear of disapproval, not taking action to solve problems, side-stepping challenges, and avoiding all expressions of autonomous functioning) become the focus of treatment, the clinician is not advised simply to try to wrest them away. Even these maladaptive behaviors have an adaptive intent, some reason behind their repeated expression. Rather than putting the client in a position between a family system (and/or an intrapsychic system) that makes one set of demands and a clinician who makes another, the clinician and client need to work together to find out what function the dependent behaviors serve (Benjamin 1984; Lerner 1983). In many instances, the motivation for the dependency is an often unconscious sense that the woman needs to under-function in order to bolster her partner and protect her relationship (Lerner 1983). If one partner under-functions, the other appears solid and strong by comparison; and if the 'under-functioner' moves in the direction of autonomy and certitude, the 'over-functioner' may act more oppressively in an attempt to maintain the old equilibrium in order to avoid becoming 'low-man' on the see-saw (Bowen 1978). A main strategy, then, for helping women move to the kind of friendly and autonomic experience described by Gilligan and Benjamin is to begin by helping them identify what keeps them tied to their current position.

'Paradoxically, a patient may become free to relinquish a dependent position when her therapist can identify and respect the adaptive functions that are served ... and appreciate with her the actual risks and potential losses that she and others face if she permits herself to behave in a more ... self-directed fashion.'

(Lerner 1983: 701–02).

Giving up what one had hoped to gain via the problematic behaviors and then envisaging and practicing an alternative stance constitute the second phase of the process. Although it seems likely that at least part of this work would be accomplished in individual or group sessions, in many situations couples counseling, family work, or environmental restructuring may be the best means for taking the new possibilities into the day-to-day lives of the women.

Not surprisingly, an unswerving adherence to passive and dependent expressions – particularly submission, withdrawal, and self-doubt – is associated with depressive disorders (Benjamin 1985a). Since the current literature contains several excellent references on explanations of and interventions for depression in women (e.g. Belle 1982; Brown and Harris 1978; Wetzel 1984), these topics will not be specifically addressed here. However, depression is not the only pernicious outcome of failure to attain the bonded/autonomous mix. For example, the fears of loneliness and constraint (and the attendant unattained needs for both connection and freedom) typify the dilemma of the agoraphobic woman (cf. Chambless and Goldstein 1982).

Dependency and anxiety

Whereas the depressed woman seems to have given up in the face of having 'tried her best and failed' to make up for what has been lost and to 'fight off the fate of misery and isolation' (Guidano and Liotti 1983: 190), the anxious woman, especially the agoraphobic woman, still struggles to overcome her particular 'weaknesses' and, from her perspective, must be constantly ready to take action against their reappearance. To this 'fearful coper,' any small sign of frailty – inability to control her behavior, physical functions, health, emotions, or the environment – signals danger, signals the possibility of being alone and humiliated in a hostile, judging, critical world. She wants to feel free, but is constrained by the anticipation of relentless obligations and hostile judgments.

Several theorists (e.g. Chambless and Goldstein 1982; Guidano and Liotti 1983) suggest that early in her life, the individual with agoraphobic symptoms was led to believe that the extradomestic environment was a dangerous place. Having been constrained in her early attempts at autonomous exploration (Bowlby 1973), she retains a conception of herself as being worthy of love but incapable of managing the danger and indifference of the world on her own. Thwarted in executing the natural press toward active exploration, she can hardly tolerate constriction; but neither can she tolerate being alone in such a difficult world. The claim that agoraphobic persons have been reared in overly restrictive families has been examined with mixed results (cf. Chambless 1982).

There is also frequent speculation regarding the contribution of marital interactions to agoraphobia. Guidano and Liotti (1983) suggest that one solution to the fear of loneliness/fear of constraint dilemma is to find a protector whom one can control. If this is the case, the search for a strong, stable, protective man is already undermined by the unconscious proviso that he must also be controllable. Several researchers (cf. Hafner 1982) cite evidence indicating that spouses of women with agoraphobic symptoms are immature men with many personal problems. Moreover, there is also support for the notion that the insecure husband of the agoraphobic woman feels better about himself because of his wife's helplessness. His tendency is to exert authority over his wife in order to obscure or deny his own adjustment problems. It is not uncommon for the woman with agoraphobic symptoms to experience strong urges to leave her marriage, but be unable to initiate alternatives to remaining (Goldstein 1973).

In a recent study of the marital repercussions of behavioral treatment for agoraphobia among thirty-two couples, Hafner (1984) uncovered two patterns of post-treatment adjustment. In one pattern, during the first six months following treatment couples experienced intensified conflicts around marital roles and increases in wives' autonomy, confidence, and assertiveness. In response, husbands developed psychological symptoms which tended to impede further improvement in wives' progress. By one year after treatment, conflicts had decreased and both partners were relatively autonomous within the adapted marital system. In the second pattern, stereotypic sex-role patterns were maintained, couples experienced little marital conflict, and husbands' psychological symptoms decreased during the first six post-treatment months. However, after one year, conflicts over roles had emerged and wives' agoraphobic symptoms were contingent on the extent to which these conflicts were resolved.

Although a central implication of Hafner's report for mental health curricula is that students should be taught to examine the current interpersonal context of women's problems, it needs to be noted that the evidence regarding dysfunction in the marital interactions of agoraphobic women and their spouses is not conclusive (cf. Chambless 1982). Still, there is enough question about spouses' roles in maintaining women's symptoms to warrant taking care to understand marital interactions and to avoid reinforcing the pattern of paternalistic control, especially in exposure-based treatment programs that use husbands as coaches who help their wives encounter previously feared situations (cf. Barlow and Beck 1984).

In summary, the profound ambivalence encompassed in the agoraphobic dilemma can be traced to cultural values, prevailing family structures, and marital interactions. All of the above shape the consciousness of women who then participate in perpetuating their own limited existence. And all of the above can be usefully probed as factors which stand in the way of integrating connection and freedom.

Angry and controlling women

For some women, the solution to being dominated, disrespected, and/or not properly cared for takes the form of expressions of anger. The anger may be expressed with varying intensity and for different purposes: for example, as covert snipes aimed at diminishing a stubborn yet ineffectual spouse, in the case of a woman attempting to establish counter-control while minimizing risks of rejection; as rageful attacks against an 'inadequate' caregiver, in the case of the woman with borderline symptoms who attempts to coerce her significant others into providing better care; as clear and emphatic statements of limits, intents, desires, and reactions, in the case of the woman who is taking an 'out-front,' autonomous, and essentially non-violent stand. Clearly, the efficacy and con-comitants of the anger solution will vary across these situations, but in general, both women and mental health care providers get confused about how 'okay' it is for women to be angry.

There are differing notions about the utility of anger, ranging from a view which says that in order to experience their own strength and power women need to 'get in touch' with their hidden rage, to the view that says it is okay for women to be assertive but they must not be angry (cf. Gaylin 1984; Tavris 1982). Similarly, there are different ideas about the origins of angry feelings and about the forces that subvert their open expression. For example, Lerner (1980) traces prohibition of anger in women both to the early mother–child relation-ship and to cultural forces designed to protect the patriarchy. By contrast, Miller de-emphasizes the early developmental origins of anger. She suggests that the anger we know is developed by a cultural structure which incites an angry response, then denies its legitimacy and/or expression, and finally ascribes it to a dangerous drive that must be controlled (Gordon 1985).

Although there is no current basis on which to resolve questions about the ori-gins of prohibition of female anger, the continuing exploration of these issues seems likely to generate useful knowledge and bears following. What seems more readily apparent now is that a main consequence of fear and/or denial of anger is the absence of crucial information about what the matter is and what kind of corrective action might be taken. But if the mental health problem involves suppression of anger, the therapeutic task is not necessarily the facilitation of full-flooded rage (Berkowitz 1972). We all know too many women for whom the expression of anger and resentments seems self-perpetuating. While it is very likely that identifying and experiencing strongly felt differences, preferences, and limits are helpful moves, 'getting the anger out' is not always freeing, and in some cases is an enmeshing maneuver undertaken to avoid an autonomous stance. For example, a woman currently participating in therapy has disclosed a long history of using venomous expressions of resentment and blaming to get her husband to do 'right by her' so that she would not ever have to stand separately from him in going ahead and getting what she needed. In the course of the work, it was discovered that this powerful, scrappy, aggressive woman is *afraid* of being direct about taking care of her needs and is subverted in her attempts by overwhelming feelings (feeling childlike, ashamed, bad, judged, and in jeopardy of being punished or abandoned).

Lerner (1980) suggests that showing hurt has the intent of drawing the other person closer, while expressing anger emphasizes differences between people and 'elicits a heightened sense of standing on one's own two feet, separate and apart from a relational context' (p. 140). This client, however, retrieves no such experience from her angry confrontations. Instead she uses her anger to establish control – the adaptive intent of which is to shore up a growing sense of vulnerability. Indeed, the vulnerability needs to be shored up, to be examined as to its components and sources, and then taken care of through self-respecting, 'level-three' actions. As it stands, her attempts at aggressive persuasion keep her helpless, underscore her dependence on the 'relational context,' and are not solutions to feeling helpless and alone.

In this woman's case, and probably in general, anger seems to work better when it is used in the way Lerner (1980) describes: to emphasize one's own positon apart from another rather than to instigate a kind of coercive togetherness. Among other therapy strategies, one guiding tactic is that the client will use her feelings of resentment as a cue to retreat for a moment, think about what it is that she wants, and then assert her interests and opinions clearly and without blaming her husband for not sharing them. The idea is not to subvert the anger, but to experience it and then go on to express a separate position.

If establishing coercive control (over oneself or another) is not an ultimately useful solution, that does not imply that exercising power is necessarily 'bad.' SASB sheds light on the issue of power and control in its representation of assertive communication as an autonomous, self-disclosive, and sometimes powerful description about one's own state. It is not focused on influencing another person, is not an action designed to control (Benjamin 1984). Coming to a similar conclusion in her essay on 'Women and Power,' Miller (1984) differentiates power that is used to dominate from power that is used to make a change happen: that is, to act in one's interests, to empower others, to state a position, to solve a problem. Although women have often been characterized as powerless and weak, Miller (1983) suggests that they have excelled in using power to enhance the power of others. While this valid and important position need not be abandoned, it could usefully be expanded to include using power for oneself.

Miller's (1984) experience is that women tend to avoid this latter use of power because they equate it with selfishness, or destructiveness, or being abandoned.

About all of this, Lerner (1980) says:

'It is perhaps simpler for all of us to direct our energy toward seeking love and approval from others, to enter into relationships comprised of endless cycles of guilt and blame toward the person who is failing to provide for our happiness, and to preserve forever the fantasy that some other person can complete and fulfill us.'

(Lerner 1980: 146, 147)

Indeed, if we continue to equate autonomy with isolation, power with selfishness and destruction, and anger with domination, we are back to choosing among the dichotomous extremes encompassed in the equally bankrupt romanticist and rationalist positions on the 'woman question.' Getting stuck on either side is not in our best interests. Although we have not contrived our own 'stuckness,' our internalization of important cultural and familial messages puts us in conflict between our press for competence and connection. If the bipolarities are autonomy and enmeshing control (or counter-control) rather than autonomy and loving interaction, the dimensions of a real solution emerge.

Curriculum considerations

What has been proposed so far is that content addressing more encompassing conceptualizations of mental health for women be included in social work curricula. The issues addressed in this chapter certainly do not exhaust the topics that should be considered in a careful exploration of mental health services for women. Rather, they are viewed as potentially useful ingredients in such an endeavor. As an alternative to laboring under one of several narrow views of women's nature, it is presumed that mental health practitioners and their women clients would benefit from learning a broader (but still individualized) conceptualization of what women can do. There is much that students can learn from the recent feminist thinking that puts high value on women's affiliative, caring, and emotionally open characteristics. But a main message of this discussion is that viewing those traits as constituting women's nature, while viewing self-reliance and autonomy as outside of women's potential, is limiting. Indeed, it is suggested that such a perspective is not unlike the one that keeps women clients tied to their well-intended but essentially dead-ended solutions, for example, the passivity solution, the resentment solution, or the agoraphobic solution.

Considerations about the relevance of the forgoing analysis to the range of women who experience mental health problems need to be a part of any presentation of these ideas. While it is assumed that almost everyone feels better and does better when they are both bonded to others and able to act in their own behalf, it is not assumed that these issues have the same immediacy for every woman, nor that achieving the balance discussed here should be the major goal of every mental health intervention. In many instances, however, the barriers to autonomy and affiliation (e.g. absence of economic opportunity, institutional and interpersonal supports, or particular life skills) are the relevant foci of attention. There is little systematic information about differences in perceptions of their own mental health problems and perceptions of the nature of help among groups of women, including poor women, minority women, and lesbians. Nonetheless, it is assumed that there are some important differences. These need to be addressed by integrating the information that does exist on the particular concerns and characteristics of women in each group into course content. For example, Belle and associates (1982) describe the relationships between chronic life stress and depression in their sample of low-income mothers and discuss the women's own perceptions that the concrete hardships of their lives constitute their emotional problems; and Loewenstein (1980) refers to some of the issues in attaining a balance between intimacy and autonomy among lesbian couples. Moreover, students need to be taught to look for differences, to hear and respect women's own ideas about where the trouble is coming from.

Although the content explored here might optimally be elaborated to form the central aspect of an advanced direct practice course on women and mental health, it could also be taken up with varying degrees of detail in several different parts of the curriculum. For example, such content could be addressed in field practice in which students are working in mental health settings with women clients; it belongs in human behavior and social environment courses addressing the developmental issues of particular groups of people; it could be introduced in first-year practice methods courses; it has a place in concentrations focusing on women, mental health, families, or direct practice (cf. Berlin 1980). Along with the usual teaching methods – providing students with pertinent theoretical and empirical literature, engaging them in thoughtful discussion of major issues, asking them to apply concepts to their own personal and practice experience – students seem to derive special benefit from conducting an analysis of the situation of a particular woman or group of women using some or all of the concepts introduced here, e.g. Gilligan's analysis of women's moral development, Benjamin's system of pinpointing problems and goals, the adaptive intent of dysfunctional behaviors.

Rather than attempting an overview of the complex and multidimensional topic of women and mental health, this chapter has focused on just a few points. It has not said exactly how mental health services should be provided nor exactly how content should be introduced, but rather it has offered a loosely woven perspective that can alter the tone and direction of curricula for mental health services for women and of the services themselves.

References

Barlow, D. H. and Beck, J. G. (1984) The Psychosocial Treatment of Anxiety Disorders: Current Status, Future Directions. In J. B. W. Williams and R. L. Spitzer (eds) *Psychotherapy Research*. New York: Guilford Press.

Belle, D. (1982) *Lives in Stress: Women and Depression*. Beverly Hills, CA: Sage Publications.

Benjamin, L. S. (1979) Structural Analysis of Differentiation Failure. *Psychiatry: Journal for the Study of Interpersonal Processes* 42: 1–23.

—— (1982) Use of Structural Analysis of Social Behavior (SASB). In J. Anchin and D. Kiesler (eds) *Handbook of Interpersonal Psychotherapy*. New York: Pergamon.

—— (1984) Principles of Prediction using Structural Analysis of Social Behavior (SASB). In R. A. Zucker, J. Aronoff, and A. J. Rabin (eds) *Personality and the Prediction of Behavior*. New York: Academic Press.

—— (1985a) Using SASB to Add Social Parameters to Axis I of DSM–III. In T. Millon and G. L. Klerman (eds) *Contemporary Issues in Psychopathology*. New York: Guilford Press.

—— (1985b, in draft) *Interpersonal Diagnosis and Treatment, the SASB Approach*. New York: Guilford Press.

Berkowitz, L. (1972) Two Cultures of Violence: Some Opposing Views of Aggression in Therapy. Presidential address to Division 8, Personality and Social Psychology, American Psychological Association, Honolulu, Hawaii.

Berlin, S. (1980) Content on Women in Integrated Practice Methods, Research, and Field Courses. Paper presented to Annual Program Meeting, Council on Social Work Education, Los Angeles.

Bowen, M. (1978) *Family Therapy in Clinical Practice*. New York: Aronson.

Bowlby, J. (1973) *Attachment and Loss*, vol. 2: *Separation: Anxiety and Anger*. New York: Basic Books.

—— (1977). The Making and Breaking of Affectional Bonds: II. Some Principles of Psychotherapy. *British Journal of Psychiatry* 130: 412–31.

Bricker-Jenkins, M. and Joseph, B. (1982) Social Control and Social Change. Paper presented to the Regional Conference on Women and Social Action, National Association of Social Workers, New York.

Brodsky, A. M. and Hare-Mustin, R. (eds) (1980) *Women and Psychotherapy*. New York: Guilford Press.

Brown, G. W. and Harris, T. (1978) *Social Origins of Depression: A Stydy of Psychiatric Disorder in Women*. New York: Free Press.

Carmen, E. H., Russo, N. F., and Miller, J. B. (1981) Inequality and Women's Mental Health. *American Journal of Psychiatry* 138: 1319–330.

Chambless, D. L. (1982) Characteristics of Agoraphobics. In D. L. Chambless and A. J. Goldstein (eds) *Agoraphobia: Multiple Perspectives on Theory and Treatment*. New York: John Wiley.

Chambless, D. L. and Goldstein, A. J. (eds) (1982) *Agoraphobia: Multiple Perspectives on Theory and Treatment*. New York: John Wiley.

Chodorow, N. (1978) *The Reproduction of Mothering: Psychoanalysis and the Sociology of Gender*. Berkeley: University of California Press.

Davis, L. V. (1985) Female and Male Voices in Social Work. *Social Work* 30: 106–13.

Ehrenreich, B. and English, D. (1979) *For Her Own Good: 150 Years of the Experts Advice to Women.* New York: Anchor Books.

Fodor, I. G. (1974) The Phobic Syndrome in Women. In V. Franks and V. Burtle (eds) *Women in Therapy.* New York: Brunner/Mazel.

Gaylin, W. (1984) *The Rage Within: Anger in Modern Life.* New York: Simon and Schuster.

Gilligan, C. (1977) In a Different Voice: Women's Conceptions of Self and of Morality. *Harvard Educational Review* 47: 481–517.

—— (1982) *In a Different Voice.* Cambridge, MA: Harvard University Press.

Goldstein, A. J. (1973) Learning Theory Insufficiency in Understanding Agoraphobia – A Plea for Empiricism. In J. C. Brengelman and W. Tunner (eds) *Proceedings of the European Association for Behaviour Therapy and Modification, 1971.* Munich: Urban and Schwarzenberg.

Gordon, S. (1985) Anger, Power, and Women's Sense of Self: New Thoughts on a Psychology for the Future from Jean Baker Miller. *Ms. Magazine* 14: 42–4.

Guidano, V. F. and Liotti, G. (1983) *Cognitive Processes and Emotional Disorders* New York: Guilford Press.

Hafner, R. J. (1982) The Marital Context of Agoraphobic Symptoms. In D. L. Chambless and A. J. Goldstein (eds) *Agoraphobia.* New York: John Wiley.

—— (1984) Predicting the Effects on Husbands of Behaviour Therapy for Wives' Agoraphobia. *Behaviour Research and Therapy* 7: 217–26.

Kaplan, M. (1983) A Woman's View of DSM–III. *American Psychologist* 38: 786–92.

Lerner, H. E. (1980) Internal Prohibitions Against Female Anger. *The American Journal of Psychoanalysis* 40: 137–48.

—— (1983) Female Dependency in Context: Some Theoretical and Technical Considerations. *American Journal of Orthopsychiatry* 53: 697–705.

Loewenstein, S. F. (1980) *Social Casework,* January: 29–30.

Miller, J. B. (1976) *Toward a New Psychology of Women.* Boston: Beacon Press.

—— (1983) The Necessity of Conflict. In J. H. Robbins and R. J. Siegel (eds) *Women Changing Therapy: New Assessments, Values and Strategies in Feminist Therapy.* New York: Haworth Press.

—— (1984) Women and Power. *Social Policy* 13: 3–6.

President's Commission on Mental Health (1978) *Report of the Task Panel on Mental Health and American Families: Sub-Task Panel on General Issues and Adult Years,* vol. 3.

Rhodes, M. L. (1985) Gilligan's Theory of Moral Development as Applied to Social Work. *Social Work* 30: 101–05.

Schaef, A. W. (1981) *Women's Reality.* Minneapolis: Winston Press.

Stimpson, C. R. (1981) Gerda Lerner on the Future of our Past. *Ms. Magazine* 10: 50–2, 93–5.

Tavris, C. (1982) *Anger: The Misunderstood Emotions.* New York: Simon and Schuster.

Walker, L. E. (1984) *Women and Mental Health Policy.* Beverly Hills, CA: Sage Publications.

Wetzel, J. W. (1984) *Clinical Handbook of Depression.* New York: Gardner Press.

—— (1985, in press). A Feminist World View Conceptual Framework. *Social Casework.*

14 Women's combined use of alcohol and other mind-altering drugs

Eileen M. Corrigan

Introduction

The extensive combined use of alcohol and other mind-altering drugs by women and the differing and frequently more negative impact of such use on women than men lead to practice and policy issues which are in need of examination. In this chapter the effects achieved by alcohol as a central nervous system depressant are emphasized since it is the primary mind-altering drug used by women. Next the epidemiology of alcohol and multiple drug use, and the consequences of such use, including drug overdoses, will be described.

There are two related purposes of this chapter. The first is to introduce the reader to the widespread use of alcohol and other drugs by women with emphasis on alcohol as the primary drug used. Second, based on this introductory material, curriculum implications are detailed.

Mind-altering drugs: a perspective on women's use of alcohol

Knupfer (1982) has argued that there has been little change in the normative standards for toleration of drunkenness in women and that drinking behavior is more stigmatized for women than for men. If it is true that there is a more rigorous standard for women's drinking behavior, then women who drink and develop a pattern of abuse may need to hide such a pattern even more than the male drinker.

In an earlier study it was reported that 37 per cent of a sample of alcoholic women in treatment were attempting to hide their drinking as they entered treatment (Corrigan 1980). Many of the women did much of their drinking alone and drank less than usual with others. Many drink their usual quantity only when with close friends and even change friends to accommodate their drinking. Comparable data are not available for a male treated population.

These data on women in treatment are consistent with findings reported in community surveys where almost two-thirds of the heavy drinking men go to a bar or tavern at least once a week whereas only about one-third of the heavy-drinking women report similar bar or tavern visits. Women are less likely than men to drink in a bar even when they are heavy drinkers and especially if forty years or older (Clark 1981). Fisher has observed that such 'sex differences in drinking behavior are probably due to divergent social norms for public drinking' (Fisher 1981: 44).

The greater likelihood of private drinking by heavy-drinking women is the psychosocial context within which drinking combined with other drug use by women must be viewed. The social isolation of women is also the context for the finding that women who drink heavily are more likely than men to report symptoms of depression. As Hill notes, however, this finding may well be due to selection bias in the samples, since heavy drinkers as a group may be more likely to require treatment and thus might be over-represented in hospital samples (Hill 1982: 63).

Alcohol equivalency of distilled beverages, wine, and beer

Most women are not aware that the dosage of alcohol they consume should be regulated for such factors as gender, age, body weight, fatigue, duration and quantity of past drinking, expectations, and individual sensitivity (Ray 1983). Many women lack basic information about the alcohol content of beverages; it is not uncommon for both women and men to believe that beer and wine are less powerful in their effect because they contain less alcohol per ounce. Yet the alcohol content contained in twelve ounces of beer, an ounce of spirits such as gin or whiskey, or a four-ounce glass of wine is approximately the same (Ray 1983).

The interaction of alcohol with other mind-altering drugs

It is no longer possible to describe alcohol use by women without referring also to their possible use of other drugs and the resulting combined effects. A number of different types of drug interactions have been identified. As Kissin (1974: 110) points out:

'Two drugs may be similar or opposite in their pharmacological effects in which case the co-administration of another drug with ethanol would cause either an increase or decrease in the ethanolic effect. The effect of the other drug would be considered either "synergistic" (additive) or "antagonistic". However, the "additive" effect may be the sum of each of the drugs administered separately or it may be greater, i.e. "supra additive".'

The supra-additive effect is, of course, what makes the combination of alcohol with other drugs so lethal. The combination results in many unplanned deaths.

Understanding alcohol's effects
Knowledge of the action of alcohol is especially important for women since alcohol is classified pharmacologically as a depressant and depression is a more frequent diagnosis for women than men. Alcohol, along with other depressants such as barbiturates, often used to induce sleep, are widely used by women. The relationship between alcohol and depression is not certain. There may be two separate conditions present, alcoholism and depression, or there may be an interaction between alcohol use and depression that is as yet not fully understood. This dimension of women's use of alcohol in combination with other depressants continues to be studied (Schuckit and Morrissey 1976; Turner, in progress).

Depressants act on the central nervous system, specifically the brain. The brain controls such critical functions as memory, judgment, and co-ordination. The initial sense of 'feeling good' achieved by drinking is fleeting. After several drinks, feelings associated with depression are heightened. Inability to sleep and irregular sleep patterns are commonly observed following the consumption of alcohol. Broken patterns of sleep are not unusual among heavy drinkers, and these patterns seem to be related to irritation of the brain. Because of this difficulty with sleep women frequently take other drugs. In this sleepless and possibly confused state women may take other drugs in an excessive amount. Even if they consume a dose that is normally 'safe,' the safety margin may be diminished because alcohol is already present in the bloodstream.

Epidemiology

The epidemiology of a problem focuses on its distribution in the population and indicates differential impact on groups. Considerable literature points to higher alcohol abuse by males (Cahalan, Cisin and Crossley 1969; National Institute on Alcohol Abuse and Alcoholism 1981). A growing body of evidence, however, points to a high abuse of prescription and over-the-counter drugs by females (Drug Abuse Warning Network 1980: 18). Data on prevalence of the abuse of non-opiate drugs in America conservatively estimate that 2 million adults may be abusers (Lau and Benvenuto 1978).

Alcohol
Fewer women than men are identified as heavy drinkers in either the general population or clinical samples. A male-to-female ratio of 3:1 has been cited for psychological dependence on alcohol. Fillmore (1984) offers a historical analysis

of the assessment of the number of women with drinking problems by researchers, public officials, and others.

A recent publication of surveys (Wilsnack, Wilsnack, and Klassen 1984/85) conducted between 1971 and 1981 is useful in portraying the stability of women's drinking over this most recent time-frame. As shown in *Table 14.1*, in both 1979 and 1981, the proportion of heavy drinkers is similar for each of the four age cohorts shown. It ranges from a low of 2 per cent for those aged 65 and over to a high of 9 per cent for the pre-middle-aged group of 35–49. Tolerance, i.e. needing more of a drug to achieve the same effect, usually develops during this age period (35–49) if there has been regular prior heavy drinking. The

Table 14.1 *Percentages of women at different drinking levels, by age group, 1971–81*

Age group	Harris 1971	Harris 1972	Harris 1973	Harris 1973	Harris 1974	ORC 1975	RAC 1976	SRG 1979	9-year Avg.	UND 1981	N 1981[a]
21–34											[847]
% drinkers	71	67	62	65	71	68	71	77	69	70	(356)
Lighter drinkers	47	37	46	40	36	44	51	46	43	41	
Moderate drinkers	18	26	21	22	29	19	15	26	22	24	
Heavier drinkers	6	4	5	3	6	5	4	5	5	6	
35–49											[670]
% drinkers	64	56	63	55	65	57	73	65	62	72*	(243)
Lighter drinkers	45	38	36	32	34	25	50	39	37	43	
Moderate drinkers	14	14	19	17	26	28	19	19	20	20	
Heavier drinkers	5	4	8	5	6	3	3	8	5	9	
50–54											[588]
% drinkers	47	44	43	50	49	48	50	49	48	52*	(190)
Lighter drinkers	32	28	24	28	27	40	36	30	31	37	
Moderate drinkers	10	13	13	18	18	16	11	16	14	10	
Heavier drinkers	5	4	5	4	4	1	3	3	4	4	
65 and over											[388]
% drinkers	26	42	29	28	36	32	37	40	34	33	(111)
Lighter drinkers	19	29	19	22	26	23	28	31	25	25	
Moderate drinkers	6	8	8	3	7	7	9	7	7	7	
Heavier drinkers	0	5	2	2	2	1	0	2	2	2	

Note: † Pre-1981 figures are from Johnson *et al.* (1977) for 1971–76 surveys and Clark and Midanik (1981) for 1979 national survey. Percentages are based on weighting.
[a] Weighted [ ] and unweighted ( ) numbers of cases in the 1982 survey.
* Linear trend, p < .05, one-tailed.

Source: Wilsnack, S. C., Wilsnack, R. W., and Klassen, M. A. (1984/85).

development of tolerance is one of the possible explanations for the higher concentration of heavy drinkers in the 35–49 age group. It has been hypothesized that the recent increased freedom in women's changing roles has also had an impact on women's drinking behavior. Fillmore (1984), in fact, presents a detailed analysis of three national surveys spanning fifteen years (1964, 1967, and 1979) which demonstrates an increase in heavy drinkers among employed women aged 21–29. She speculates that this increase may signal a rise in heavy drinking among employed women who drink.

As indicated in *Table 14.1*, women under 50 have a considerably higher proportion of drinkers than women of 50 and over. Although abstainers are not shown separately from drinkers in *Table 14.1*, over the nine-year period those aged 65 and over have almost as many abstainers (66 per cent) as the youngest age group (21–34) has drinkers (69 per cent). Note the consistency of this finding in each year shown in *Table 14.1*.

The decrease in drinking over the four age cohorts likely reflects an 'aging out' of drinkers. Atkinson (1984) comments on the use and abuse of alcohol and other drugs declining with age. A number of complex explanations are offered in the literature to account for this decreased use. There is increased biological sensitivity as a result of physiological changes (e.g. with age there is an increase in body fat which prolongs the drug's effect); since the metabolic rate is lower, there may be less blood to the liver which would decrease the rate of detoxification (Ray 1983). The higher mortality rate for alcoholics and other drug users may also be a factor in the overall reduction in prevalence of use. Spontaneous recoveries, as well as the benefits of treatment where abstinence is encouraged, may contribute to this diminished use of alcohol and other drugs with age. Of considerable interest is the variation reported in the 1981 data by marital status in Wilsnack, Wilsnack, and Klassen (1984/85) (see *Table 14.2*). The pattern reported is similar to that found in earlier surveys, with the generally younger never-married and divorced or separated women having a higher proportion of heavy drinkers than married or widowed women. The study for the first time reports on cohabiting women separately from other women. It shows cohabitors as having the highest proportion of heavy drinkers (18 per cent). The breaking with traditional roles and a lifestyle which supports drinking may account for this finding. No abstainers were found among cohabiting women surveyed, while 26 per cent to 62 per cent of other women were abstainers. Sampling variation needs to be considered, and future surveys may alter this finding.

Multiple drug use

Meaningful data on psychoactive drug use and abuse by women are difficult to obtain. In a recent comprehensive survey of households, physicians, health care facilities, employers, and insurance companies, it was reported that females are twice as likely as males to obtain a psychotropic drug (11.8 per cent versus 6.2

Table 14.2 *Drinking levels by marital status, for women*[a]

Drinking level	Married	Divorced or separated	Widowed	Never married	Cohabiting
Abstainers	41	26	62	27	0
Light drinkers[b]	40	38	28	38	49
Moderate drinkers	14	28	9	27	32
Heavier drinkers	5	7	1	9	18
Weighted N	1655	268	260	254	59
Unweighted N	542	121	81	116	41

[a] Percentages are based on weighting: rates may not total 100% due to rounding.
[b] Includes temporary abstainers (who drank in past 12 months but not past 30 days).

Source: Wilsnack, S. C., Wilsnack, R. W., and Klassen, M. A. (1984/85).

per cent) (Cafferata and Kasper 1983). Earlier studies found little difference by gender in the dispensing of prescription drugs (National Center for Health Statistics 1980: 40). Any differences were usually accounted for by the higher number of female visits to physicians. Balter and Levine reported that 67 per cent of all prescriptions for mind-altering drugs were written for women (Damman and Ousley 1978: 59). This may explain why high alcohol consumption by women, not men, is frequently associated with higher usage of other psychoactive drugs (Kaplan *et al.* 1980; Parry 1971). Further, race has been found to be significant in drug prescriptions only among women. White women were more likely than non-whites to purchase psychotropic drugs in 1977 (Cafferata, Bernstein, and Kasper 1981). Fairly typical is a study of a treated population where almost one-half of the women report using other psychoactive drugs while drinking, and black women were significantly less likely than white women to use these drugs (Corrigan 1980).

Consequences of alcohol and drug use by women

More is known about gender differences in the consequences of alcohol and drug use than is known about the reason for such differences. Women experience more severe consequences than men at lower dose levels and after a shorter period of time. Because women have relatively more fatty tissue than men (33 per cent versus 21 per cent), they cannot absorb alcohol as quickly. The result is higher concentrations of alcohol in the blood (Saunders, Davis, and Williams 1981). Hill's (1981) detailed analysis of research studies notes a wide range of physiological effects which are significantly higher for women than men. These include fatty liver, hypertension, anemia, and gastrointestinal disorders. Liver disorders, in particular, have been noted to be higher in women. A higher rate of liver disorders is reported for women with a younger age at death from portal cirrhosis. This increase has been especially striking among black women (Hill 1984). The key finding here is that lower levels of alcohol consumption by women compared to men will lead to cirrhosis. This finding may be further complicated for women who receive estrogen since this hormone is known to affect liver functioning.

The literature repeatedly suggests the differential impact of alcohol and other drugs on women and men with the same body weight. Not only does a higher blood alcohol level (BAL) occur for women because of their higher body fat, but with less body fluid there is a slower rate of metabolism. The result is likely to be a longer-lasting effect on the central nervous system. Thus women run a higher risk of alcohol and other drug overdoses at a lower level of consumption.

Drug overdoses

Alcohol in combination with another drug is most frequently mentioned in the Drug Abuse Warning Network (DAWN) Data Collection System (1982). Women abuse alcohol in combination more often than they abuse alcohol and other drugs alone. *Table 14.3* indicates the five drugs most frequently mentioned in a random sample of DAWN emergency rooms. Four of the five drugs are over-the-counter (alcohol-in-combination, aspirin) or prescription drugs (diazepam, dalmane). Proportionately twice as many women as men use a prescription or over-the-counter drug in the overdoses reported. The one exception is the alcohol-in-combination category where somewhat similar proportions of women (46.1 per cent) and men (53.8 per cent) use alcohol in combination with another drug. It is only in the illicit drug category of heroin and morphine that male use substantially exceeds that of women, on the order of almost 2:1. For all emergency room episodes reported by DAWN, women account for 53.5 per cent as compared to 46.5 per cent of episodes for men.

The reason given for these overdoses also points to gender differences. More women than men take drugs to commit suicide. Alcoholic women clearly are at high risk for suicide. The rate of completed suicides among female alcoholics is reported to be twenty-three times the general population rate (Adelstein and White 1977).

Approximately one-third of the cases which become known to medical examiners in the DAWN sample were the result of accidental overdoses. Shader and

Table 14.3 *Five drugs highest in frequency of mentions in drug overdoses in DAWN emergency rooms: percentage distribution by gender*

Rank of drug mention	Total %	Female %	Male %
O-C 1. Alcohol-in-combination	100	46.1	53.8
P 2. Diazepam (valium)	100	60.1	39.8
O-C 3. Aspirin	100	70.9	29.1
P 4. Flurazepam (dalmane)	100	70.6	29.3
I 5. Heroin-morphine	100	30.3	69.5

I = illicit, O-C = over-the-counter, P = prescription

The five drugs shown account for approximately 33 per cent of all drug mentions in the DAWN emergency rooms.

A study of the validity of the DAWN system reports a relatively low error rate, 11 per cent, although the under-reporting is rather serious and quite high, 50 per cent. The authors note that alcohol was the most commonly reported and detected drug in their study (Ungerleider *et al.* 1980).

Source: DAWN (1980), p. 20.

Anglin note a substantial group who anticipate surviving drug overdoses (Shader and Anglin, in press).

Educational issues

Preparation of students
Women's use of alcohol and other drugs is of prime interest to a profession which consists primarily of women helping other women. Social workers themselves also experience the disabling consequences of excessive use. Increasingly, agency administrators, as they become aware of a staff member's excessive use of alcohol or other drugs, actively seek consultation for such an employee.

Organized social work education, however, has not taken a leadership role in preparing students to practice in alcohol and drug settings, and such preparation is not mandated by its accrediting body. The social work curriculum in a number of schools has begun to reflect the importance of this area. Of 69 schools of social work responding to a survey in 1984, 68 report some content on alcohol and other drugs in the curriculum (Corrigan and Humphreys, in progress). State requirements of alcohol certification provide an added impetus for schools to incorporate such content. A curriculum with a focus on alcohol and other drugs is useful in attracting students at times of shrinking enrollment.

Students are particularly alert to alcohol and other drug use among their clients. In every setting they report a substantial number of individuals and families with alcohol and drug problems and are acutely aware of the lack of competencies experienced by many staff. The expansion of employee assistance programs where alcohol and drug problems are emphasized gives additional incentive to schools to offer this content. Such employee assistance programs are especially interested in identifying and referring women employees who experience alcohol and drug problems. Supervisors require training from the staff of the program to be able to achieve a successful referral. Students are also keenly interested in this subject in relation to their own alcohol and drug use and sometimes because it has been a problem for family or friends.

A major impediment students report to applying this new knowledge is the fact that practitioners persist in diagnosing drug dependence as reflecting an underlying problem. This approach runs counter to current knowledge and research which focus on alcohol as the primary problem (Bean and Zinberg 1981). A further stereotype that persists is the belief that there is a personality type which leads to alcohol dependence. Again there is no support for this belief (Pattison and Kaufman 1982). Predicting who will become alcoholic or drug-dependent based on personality alone remains elusive.

The cause and effect aspects of mind-altering drugs have been debated extensively in the alcohol and drug literature (Blum 1984; Kalant 1980; Kissin 1974; Pattison and Kaufman 1982). Khantzian (1982: 594) has observed:

'the use of alcohol as a solution to . . . problems eventually becomes a devastating and destructive problem in and of itself. It is little wonder then that debate continues whether psychopathology causes alcoholism or alcoholism causes psychopathology. Both are true.'

Earlier he noted:

'With few exceptions, most diagnostic reports on alcoholics show a low incidence of neurosis or psychosis. However, a number of investigators have debated whether alcoholism might mask psychopathology involving depression, neurosis and psychosis.'

(Khantzian 1982: 583)

New knowledge for practitioners

Many able and interested social workers hesitate to apply their generic skills and knowledge to individuals who are drug-dependent. In many settings drug-dependent clients continue to be referred to specialized services (Zimberg 1982). Those who teach in this field of practice must not only engage students in this learning but must also assist them to become trainers so that they can communicate this new knowledge to agency staff and possibly even other faculty members.

Social workers are expected to be able to intervene with women clients and their significant others and to facilitate program development in agencies and hospitals for those who are dependent on alcohol and other drugs. Many women may need help with a variety of social and intrapsychic problems. If they are living with a heavy-drinking or drug-dependent person the complexities of a possible mutually destructive relationship may loom as a major issue in treatment. If children are present, issues of adequate child care also need to be examined. If the woman is sexually active and at an age of procreation, the effect on a fetus of drinking and other drug use may well be a treatment issue.

Policy issues

Placing warning labels on all alcoholic beverages and other drugs to alert women to drug interactions is an obvious public health issue. A modest public health goal could be to inform women of the particular consequences to them of multiple drug use, namely the risk of overdoses and the possibility of fatalities. To date warning labels on alcoholic beverages have been put aside as a result of vigorous lobbying efforts (US Department of the Treasury and US Bureau of Alcohol, Tobacco, and Firearms 1979).

The regulation of the liquor industry remains problematic. The lack of a label on beverages such as beer stating the alcohol content in the container has kept many people in ignorance. In addition, there has been no systematic effort to inform the public, especially women, of the differential and more negative effect of alcohol and other drugs on women.

Research issues

The basis for the more powerful and rapid impact of drugs on women is insufficiently understood and warrants a focused research effort. Yet the whole area of research as it relates to women has received uneven and often only cursory support. This is most apparent as it relates to subgroups of women. For example, in a recent review of the literature over a ten-year period only thirteen research studies could be located relating to black women (Corrigan 1985). This same omission applied to Hispanic women, the elderly, the homeless, and lesbians.

A related issue concerns the decision-making process in reviewing grant applications for research support. Relatively few women scientists sit on review committees, and even fewer women chair such committees.

Future curriculum directions

Many students retain the popular image of the alcoholic as male. The 'drug addict,' too, is most often perceived as male. The educator is first faced with sensitizing students to viewing women as drug-dependent. This sensitization process includes the form of dependence (alcohol and other mind-altering drugs, particularly legal prescription and over-the-counter drugs), indicators of dependence, and an understanding of how drugs work. Once a woman's drug dependence is recognized it is possible to carry out early case finding and treatment, frequently within the setting where the woman has been identified.

The usual first goal of treatment for women with any drug dependence is withdrawal from the drug. Detoxification in a medical setting may not always be necessary, but this should be a decision based on sound knowledge. It may be helpful for some women to enter a brief detoxification program; on the other hand, withdrawal from alcohol and/or other drugs may occur without any untoward effects outside an inpatient program. Usually the woman has made prior attempts to reduce her intake and is aware of any withdrawal symptoms that have occurred. Options need to be explored, and a medical consultation is usually in order. It is also important to assess whether there have been any physical effects of prolonged alcohol and other drug use, e.g. liver damage.

The interrelation between the physical, psychological, and social consequences of alcohol and other drug dependence is well articulated in Ray (1983). Ray is especially clear about gender differences, emphasizing repeatedly the differing effects for women as compared to men. A scholarly series of readings in the biochemistry, physiology, behavior, clinical pathology, social aspects, and treatment of alcoholism became available in the early 1970s (Kissin and Begleiter 1971–83). More recently a handbook on alcoholism (Pattison and Kaufman 1982) and several books which give attention to both alcohol and drug abuse have been published (Blum 1984; Schuckitt 1979; Solomon and Keeley 1982).

Two books are now available that relate specifically to women (Kalant 1980; Wilsnack and Beckman 1984). The Kalant (1980) collection was initiated by the women staff of the Addiction Research Foundation in Canada and addresses both alcohol and drug use by women. Sex differences are noted in the various chapters on prevalence in drinking or other psychoactive drug use. Genetic and biological aspects for women are also discussed. A chapter by Annis and Liban on treatment modalities and outcome for women treated for alcoholism should be of prime interest to practitioners. In contrast the Wilsnack and Beckman readings (1984) focus almost entirely on alcohol problems in women, addressing the antecedents, consequences, and intervention. Readings in both books could well form the beginning basis for courses relating to women's alcohol and other drug use.

A new book which addresses social work practice with clients who have alcohol problems (Freeman 1985) should serve as a useful resource to practitioners and in curriculum development. A wide range of treatment issues are examined and course material for both direct practice and human behavior courses is included which could be modified for courses focusing specifically on women's alcohol and other drug use. In all, the area of women's excessive use of alcohol and other drugs is now rich in resources to assist those who wish to practice or guide practice for this significant problem for women in our society.

Conclusions

Greater multiple drug use by women than men has now been amply documented in treatment settings and emergency rooms. The evidence points to twice as many women as men receiving mind-altering drugs in the general population. The use of prescription and over-the-counter drugs with alcohol (the most extensively used of all mind-altering drugs) constitutes a major threat to women since they are at risk of overdoses at a lower level of consumption than men. The reasons for this greater risk are incompletely understood and may be embedded in both a physiological and social context.

The physiological aspects have not been receiving the needed research attention nor has there been adequate public policy debate concerning the impact of drug interactions, especially for women who are at much greater risk. Warning labels on alcohol and drugs focusing on unpredictable interactions are now overdue.

Social workers are well situated to apply their practice knowledge and skills to women who are dependent on alcohol and/or other drugs. The fact that most schools of social work now have courses focusing on both alcohol and drugs reflects the institutionalization of this old but newly discovered practice concern.

References

Adelstein, A. and White, G. (1977) *Population Trends* 6: 7–13.

Atkinson, R. M. (ed.) (1984) *Alcohol and Drug Abuse in Old Age.* Washington, DC: American Psychiatric Press.

Bean, M. H. and Zinberg, N. E. (1981) *Dynamic Approaches to the Understanding and Treatment of Alcoholism.* New York: Free Press.

Blum, K. (1984) *Handbook of Abusable Drugs.* New York: Gardner Press.

Cafferata, G. L. and Kasper, J. A. (1983) *National Health Care Expenditures Study*, data preview 14: *Psychotropic Drugs: Use, Expenditures and Source of Payment.* DHHS Publication No. (PHS) 83–335. US Department of Health and Human Services, National Center for Health Services Research.

Cafferata, G. L., Bernstein, A. B., and Kasper, J. A. (1981) *Family Structure, Stressors and the Use of Psychotropic Drugs*, mimeo. Presented at the Annual Meeting of the American Health Association.

Cahalan, D., Cisin, I. H., and Crossley, H. M. (1969) *American Drinking Practices.* New Brunswick: Rutgers Center of Alcohol Studies.

Clark, W. B. (1981) Public Drinking Contexts: Bars and Taverns. In *Research Monograph No. 7, Social Drinking Contexts.* Rockville: NIAAA, pp. 8–33.

Clark, W. B. and Midanik, L. (1981) *Alcohol Use and Alcohol Problems Among US Adults: Results of the 1979 Survey.* (Working draft.) Berkeley, CA: Social Research Group, School of Public Health, University of California.

Corrigan, E. M. (1980) *Alcoholic Women in Treatment.* New York: Oxford University Press.

—— (1985) Research on Women's Use of Alcohol and Other Drugs, 1974–1984. Presented at Interdisciplinary Alcohol/Drug Studies Center, Jackson State University, Jackson, MS.

Corrigan, E. M. and Humphreys, N. (in progress) *Survey of Schools of Social Work: Alcohol and Drug content.*

Damman, G. and Ousley, N. (1978) Female Polydrug Abusers. In D. R. Wesson, A. S. Carlin, K. M. Adams, and G. Beschner (eds) *Polydrug Abuse.* New York: Academic Press, pp. 59–96.

Drug Abuse Warning Network (1980) *Project DAWN Annual Report – 1980.* Rockville, MD: National Institute on Drug Abuse.

—— (1982) *Project DAWN Annual Report – 1982.* Rockville, MD: National Institute on Drug Abuse.

Fillmore, K. M. (1984) 'When Angels Fall': Women's Drinking as Cultural Preoccupation and as Reality. In Sharon C. Wilsnack and Linda J. Beckman (eds) *Alcohol Problems in Women.* New York: Guilford Press.

Fisher, J. C. (1981) Psychosocial Correlates of Tavern Use: A National Probability Sample Study. In *Research Monograph No. 7, Social Drinking Contexts.* Rockville, MD: NIAAA, pp. 34–53.

Freeman, E. M. (ed.) (1985) *Social Work Practice with Clients Who Have Alcohol Problems.* Springfield: Charles C. Thomas.

Hill, S. Y. (1981) A Vulnerability Model for Alcoholism in Women. *Focus on Women* 2(2): 68–91.

—— (1982) Biological Consequences of Alcoholism and Alcohol Related Problems in Women. In *Alcohol and Health Monograph 4, Special Population Issues.* Rockville, MD: NIAAA, pp. 43–76.

—— (1984) Vulnerability to the Biomedical Consequences of Alcoholism and Alcohol-Related Problems among Women. In Sharon C. Wilsnack and Linda J. Beckman (eds) *Alcohol Problems in Women.* New York: Guilford Press, pp. 121–54.

Johnson, P. Armor, D. J., Polich, M., and Stanbul, H. (1977) *US Adult Drinking Practices: Time Trends, Social Correlates and Sex Roles.* (Working notes prepared for the National Institute on Alcohol Abuse and Alcoholism.) Santa Monica, CA: Rand Corporation.

Kalant, O. J. (ed.) (1980) *Alcohol and Drug Problems in Women. Research Advances in Alcohol and Drug Problems,* vol. 5. New York: Plenum Press.

Kaplan, H. L., Sellers, E. M., Marshman, J. A., Giles, H. G., MacLeod, S. M., Kapur, B. M., Stapleton, C., Sealey, F., and Busto, U. (1980) Alcohol Use by Patients Admitted to Hospital Emergency Rooms for Treatment of Drug Overdose and Misuse. *Journal of Studies on Alcohol* 41(9): 882–93.

Khantzian, E. J. (1982) Psychopathology, Psychodynamics and Alcoholism. In E.

Mansell Pattison and Edward Kaufman (eds) *Encyclopedic Handbook of Alcoholism*. New York: Gardner Press, pp. 581–97.

Kissin, B. (1974) Interactions of Ethyl Alcohol and Other Drugs. In Benjamin Kissin and Henri Begleiter (eds) *The Biology of Alcoholism. Clinical Pathology*, vol. 3. New York: Plenum Press, pp. 109–62.

Kissin, B. and Begleiter, H. (eds) (1971–83) *Biology of Alcoholism*. 7 vols. New York: Plenum Press.

Knupfer, G. (1982) Problems Associated with Drunkenness in Women: Some Research Issues. In *Alcohol and Health Monograph 4, Special Populations Issues*. Rockville, MD: NIAAA, pp. 13–42.

Lau, J. P. and Benvenuto, J. (1978) *Three National Estimates of Non-Opiate Drug Use*. In D. R. Wesson, A. S. Carlin, K. M. Adams, and G. Beschner (eds) *Polydrug Abuse*. New York: Academic Press.

National Center for Health Statistics (1980) Office Visits by Women. *The National Ambulatory Care Survey, United States, 1977*. Hyattsville, MD: Public Health Service.

National Institute on Alcohol Abuse and Alcoholism (1981) *Fourth Special Report to the US Congress on Alcohol and Health*. Washington, DC: US Government Printing Office.

—— (1983) *Fifth Special Report to the US Congress on Alcohol and Health*. Rockville, MD: NIAAA.

National Institute on Drug Abuse (1980) *Alcohol Related Emergency Room Visits*. Forecasting Branch Division of Resource Development (mimeo), p. 8.

Parry, H. J. (1971) Patterns of Psychotropic Drug Use among American Adults. *Journal of Drug Issues* 1(4): 269–73.

Pattison, E. M. and Kaufman, E. (eds) (1982) *Encyclopedic Handbook of Alcoholism*. New York: Gardner Press.

Ray, O. (1983) *Drugs, Society and Human Behavior*, 3rd edn. St Louis: C. V. Mosby.

Saunders, J. B., Davis, M., and Williams, R. (1981) Do Women Develop Alcoholic Liver Disease More Readily Than Men. *Brit. Med. J.* 2(82): 1140–143.

Schuckit, M. A. (1979) *Drugs and Alcohol*. New York: Plenum.

Schuckit, M. A. and Morrissey, E. R. (1976) Alcoholism in Women: Some Clinical and Social Perspectives with an Emphasis on Possible Subtypes. In Milton Greenblatt and Marc A. Schuckit (eds) *Alcoholism Problems in Women and Children*. New York: Grune and Stratton.

Shader, R. and Anglin, C. (in press) *Emergency Room Study of Sedative-Hypnotic Overdosages: A Study of the Issue*. Rockville, MD: National Institute on Drug Abuse.

Solomon, J. and Keeley, K. A. (eds) (1982) *Perspectives in Alcohol and Drug Abuse: Similarities and Differences*. Boston: J. Wright, PSG.

Turner, S. G. (in progress) *Alcoholism and Depression in Women*. Doctoral dissertation, Rutgers University, School of Social Work.

Ungerleider, J. T., Lundberg, G. D., Sunshine, I., and Walberg, C. (1980) The Drug Abuse Warning Network (DAWN) Program: Toxologic Verification of 1,008 Emergency Room Mentions. *Arch. Gen. Psychiat.* 37: 106–09.

US Department of Treasury and US Bureau of Alcohol, Tobacco, and Firearms (1979) *The Fetal Alcohol Syndrome Public Awareness Campaign: Progress Report Concerning The Advance Notice of Proposed Rulemaking on Warning Labels on Containers of Alcoholic Beverages and Addendum*. Washington, DC: Supt. of Docs., US Government Printing Office.

176 *The Woman Client*

Wilsnack, S. C. and Beckman, L. J. (eds) (1984) *Alcohol Problems in Women.* New York: Guilford Press.
Wilsnack, S. C., Wilsnack, R. W., and Klassen, M. A. (1984/85) Drinking and Drinking Problems Among Women in a US National Survey. *Alcohol Health and Research World* 9 (2, Winter): 3–13.
Zimberg, S. (1982) Psychotherapy in the Treatment of Alcoholism. In E. Mansell Pattison, and Edward Kaufman (eds) *Encyclopedic Handbook of Alcoholism.* New York: Gardner Press, pp. 999–1010.

15 The female offender and the criminal justice system

Rosemary C. Sarri

Introduction

Despite the interest in sex-role differences in recent decades, one of the areas in which gender differences are most pronounced, but largely ignored, is that of crime. Neither female criminality nor offenders attracted the attention of policy-makers, correctional administrators, or even criminologists until the late 1970s. Surprisingly, the social work community also ignored them despite the fact that much female crime was associated with the family. The fact that male crime was so much more extensive appears to have resulted in the lack of attention. In 1983, 8,851,823 males were arrested compared with 1,705,486 females, a ratio of nearly 6:1 (United States Department of Justice 1984). A similar pattern was obseved among juveniles, although the ratio of four to one was somewhat lower (987,435 males and 265,793 juvenile females).

Although there are sex differences in criminal behavior, it should not be assumed that female offenders have been dealt with justly, benignly, or humanely by society and its agents. Anyone familiar with the plight of the female offender quickly observes that this lack of attention has not operated to her advantage. Instead it seems clear that the inequities faced by the majority of women in this society are magnified a hundredfold in the lives of female offenders. The situation has deteriorated in the 1980s with the rapidly increasing incarceration of women offenders despite the fact that their criminal behavior is not increasing in frequency or seriousness to any marked degree. In fact, just the opposite has occurred. A female minor offender has far greater likelihood of incarceration in 1985 than she did when committing the same offense in 1975.

It is perhaps no coincidence that the 1980s has produced rapidly increasing female single parenthood accompanied by high poverty rates for these women and their children as well as increasing criminal justice processing of women, especially for property crimes. Women are being subjected to more and more coercive social control at the same time that social welfare supports for them are being reduced or terminated. There appears to be a deliberate attempt to blame the victim for her plight and to force her back to traditional female roles.

Despite the opportunity for significant advances in knowledge about gender differences, relatively few social scientists have attempted to identify the basic issues related to crime causation in females and males, frequency of participation, offense patterns, or the manner of processing females versus males into and through the criminal justice system. Instead, the literature consists largely of descriptive studies or untested theories of female criminal behavior. Most of the comparative empirical studies have relied on secondary data (predominantly case records). Given the well-known problems in the reliability and validity of these data, their conclusions are limited and tentative. There are few exemplars of systematic and comparative longitudinal studies of sex differences in criminal behavior, of justice system processing, or of intervention programs for offenders.

This chapter summarizes what is known about female crime in the United States, about the female offender and victim, and about the operation of the criminal justice system as it affects women. It also outlines the critical issues for social work intervention and offers some recommendations for policy and intervention strategies.

Theories of female crime: a historical perspective

In the midst of growing interest in the female offender it is easy to forget that she is not a new phenomenon. One hundred years ago Lambert Quetelet, the Belgian statistician, noted that females accounted for about 25 per cent of all arrests (Hindelang 1979). As of 1985 the percentage has declined in the United States to 16.6 per cent (US Department of Justice 1985a).

One can profitably examine theories of female criminality from a historical perspective because these theories so often coincided with the development of other social science theory and intervention in the nineteenth and twentieth centuries (Lombroso and Ferrero 1916). The earliest theories of crime contended that female offenders were evil, immoral, or possessed of demons; but they were viewed as a minor problem in most communities because of their small numbers (Erikson 1966; Rasche 1974). Following that there was a search for constitutional or physiological causes, represented in the work of Lombroso and Ferrero (1916). They argued that female criminality was an inherent tendency which deserved punishment because such women violated their womanhood. These women were said to be more wicked and perverse than their male counterparts. Both Freud and Lombroso emphasized that the intellectual inferiority of women made them susceptible to crime. Others emphasized genetic factors, asserting that criminality was inherited (Fernald, Hayes, and Dawley 1920; Healy and Bonner 1926).

In the early twentieth century the Gluecks (1934) viewed female crime as a function of the interaction between constitutional and environmental factors. They did their studies almost exclusively in institutions, and their work set the stage for gender-based services which emphasized the training of women in traditional social roles. Later, Pollak's work (1950) had a significant impact on subsequent research, especially on adult female offenders. He argued that there were no real male/female differences in criminality, but that what differentiated them was the inherent deceitfulness of the female. Like Freud, Pollak also emphasized sexual factors as paramount, for he saw criminal women as trying to extend their sexual role. This emphasis on sexuality and crime grew rapidly and pervaded the literature (Konopka 1966; Sarri 1978; Vedder and Somerville 1970). Following Sutherland's development of the theory of differential association for male crime (Sutherland and Cressey 1966), Morris (1964) and Konopka (1966 and 1975) argued that adolescent female deviance was the result of ineffective family socialization.

Studies of the processing of women and men through the criminal justice system led to emphasis on differentiation, discrimination, and disparity in the treatment of female offenders, particularly in prisons. For example, studies of inmate social systems attempted to distinguish male/female differences in response to incarceration, but results were mixed because of variable study foci and theories (Giallombardo 1974; Heffernan 1972; Propper 1981; Tittle 1972).

When attention was directed more toward court processing and sentencing differentiation, issues of discrimination and disparity became more central as the work of Adler and Simon (1979), Figueira-McDonough (1984), and Nagel and Hagen (1983) illustrate. The criminology literature of the 1970s and 1980s suggested a relationship between the women's movement, changed sex roles, and crime (Adler and Simon 1979; Klein 1973; McCord and Otten 1983; Steffensmeier 1978). This question has been studied from a number of perspectives and in a variety of ways. Two more general theories appear to predominate in this literature: 'discriminatory control' and 'equal opportunity.' The latter suggests that with greater equality females are more likely to engage in criminal behavior because they have the opportunity to do so. Discriminatory control theories assert that women receive biased treatment from social control agencies in arrest, detention, and disposition, as for example the processing of prostitution or family violence where only the woman is charged with offending against her attacker. Figueira-McDonough (1984) tested the equal opportunity theory and found at best a weak link between feminist orientation and delinquency. She concluded that the influence was complex and tenuous, requiring a multidimensional approach to research.

Noting that the gender gap in crime is as great as ever despite sex role changes,

Wilson and Herrnstein (1985) speculate that sex differences in aggressive and other primary drives which flow into basic definitions of sex roles provide the basic explanation. The emphasis on interpersonal, moral, and sexual behavior as more characteristic of female offenders resulted in two major streams in theories of female and male crime. Male crime was viewed as provoked by utilitarian motives and as a result of social structural factors such as social class, access to legitimate opportunities, and differential association – at least those theories predominated until the return of the constitutional theories of the 1980s (Wilson and Herrnstein 1985). Female crime, on the other hand, was explained almost wholly in sociopsychological terms despite the fact that the sociodemographic characteristics of both groups of offenders were similar. Both were poor, young adults, under-educated, of minority status, and likely to have been exposed to neglect and/or abuse.

Lastly, an alternate view of gender and crime can be found in radical social theory which asserts that what counts as crime is established by powerful persons in society (Smart 1977). Public control of abortion exemplifies this approach as does the reluctance of society to deal forcibly with rape in marriage. Feminist theories of crime are equally concerned with victimization as they are with offending.

Who are the female offenders?

Because of the great variation in local, state, and federal statutes, the definitions of female crime and female offenders differ substantially by jurisdiction. There is variation depending upon whether one measures crime according to the official reports of law enforcement agencies or according to the reports of victims or offenders. Official crime reports include only persons arrested regardless of subsequent outcomes. They reflect the administration of criminal law, not the actual differences in criminal behavior (Hindelang 1979). On the other hand, self-report surveys of offenders indicate that while the vast majority of adults have committed one or more misdemeanors or felonies, the prevalence and frequency of all crime are far less for females than for males (Elliot and Ageton 1980; Short and Nye 1970).

Information from various sources provides the following profile of the female offender:

1. Two-thirds of women prisoners are under thirty years of age.
2. Nearly two-thirds of the prisoners are from minority groups although they compose only about half of the arrestees.
3. Offenders are educationally 'poor' – half not having completed high school.
4. The majority of prisoners are single, separated, widowed, or divorced, but most are mothers.

5. The majority have sporadic work histories in low-income service industries.
6. Over half have been recipients of public welfare, and many have had extended psychiatric and/or substance abuse treatment
    (Figueira-McDonough, Sarri, and Iglehart 1981; Glick and Neto 1977)

Table 15.1 *Arrest patterns in the United States, 1974 and 1983*

	1974			1983		
	Total arrests	Female		Total arrests	Female	
		Total %	Under 18 %		Total %	Under 18 %
Property[a]						
Females	139,169	22.5	41.7	384,906	22.5	34.5
Males	497,676			1,322,508		
Index[b]						
Females	159,011	19.4	40.3	432,809	20.1	32.9
Males	660,351			1,718,311		
Violent Crime[c]						
Females	19,720	10.9	22.1	47,903	10.8	16.8
Males	161,803			395,783		
Total						
Females	540,987	16.9	31.6	1,705,486	16.6	21.4
Males	2,655,339			8,581,823		

[a] Includes burglary, auto theft, larceny, theft, and arson.
[b] Includes criminal homicide, rape, robbery, aggravated assault, burglary, larceny and auto theft.
[c] Includes criminal homicide, rape, robbery, aggravated assault.

Source: *Crime in the United States, 1974.* Uniform Crime Reports (Washington, DC: Federal Bureau of Investigation, 1975 and 1984), pp. 184–86 (1974) and pp. 179–87 (1984).

Examination of arrest data from official reports in *Table 15.1* indicates that both in 1974 and ten years later in 1983 female crime was only a small proportion of adult crime, with the differences most pronounced for the more serious violent crimes. While arrests for both males and females increased substantially, increases were more rapid for females than males. However, their comparative position remained essentially unchanged. Overall arrest rates declined only from 16.9 per cent to 16.6 per cent. Younger women under eighteen show the most change. The percentage of females under eighteen arrested declined by 5–12 per cent for all the major crime categories (see *Table 15.1*). Most of the decline can be attributed to the decline in the size of the population under eighteen. Contrary to many public statements, male and female juveniles under eighteen comprised only 16 per cent of all arrestees in 1983 (United States Department of Justice, Federal Bureau of Investigation 1984). Examination of specific offenses indicates that only in the instances of fraud (40 per cent), forgery (33 per cent), and larceny (29.5 per cent) do females approach males in frequency of arrests. Most of these offenses are relatively petty although the offender may have a record of frequent and chronic criminal behavior.

Steffensmaier's (1978) longitudinal analysis of female criminal behavior supports the patterns observable in the official crime reports. Females made few gains in traditional 'male' crimes. He also noted that reporting patterns need careful examination because they vary over time, by geographical area, and by organizational attributes of processing agencies. Women are viewed less paternalistically today and, therefore, may not be dismissed from official processing as readily as they might have been in the past (Steffensmaier 1980).

Women of color

Historically, black women have been over-represented in correctional populations. In 1980, when black women comprised only 14 per cent of the female population in the United States, they made up almost half (1,989) of the total female prisoner population (4,304). In addition, it was not unusual for black female commitments to surpass those of white females. For example, in 1923, 6,399 black women were committed to prison from 1 January to 30 June as compared with 5,030 white women (Iglehart 1977).

Several researchers point to differential processing to account for the seemingly high crime rate among black women. In a study of women offenders at a New York State workhouse, Fernald, Hayes, and Dawley (1920) observed that the larger proportion of black women in the workhouse was probably due to the practice of giving workhouse terms to first or second offenders who might, if they had been white, have been given a chance on probation. More recently, numerous scholars acknowledge that black women have never been afforded protection from the criminal justice system as have non-minority women. Indeed, Klein (1973) asserts that chivalry has never been extended to women of color.

In addition to being over-represented in the criminal justice system, black women have been viewed as more criminal than the non-minority female. 'More criminal' refers to the tendency for black women to engage in more serious offenses. Again, historical data support this difference. Census data on prison populations from 1890 to 1936 show that a higher percentage of black women committed crimes against property and person than did white women. A larger percentage of white women were arrested for sex offenses, disorderly conduct, and drunkenness.

Institutional commitment patterns from 1900 to 1923 also show different patterns for white and black women. White women were more likely to be found in county jails and workhouses while black women were more likely to serve time in state prisons and penitentiaries. Because large percentages of the commitments for serious offenses were to state facilities (US Department of Justice, Bureau of the Census 1926: 32), it was said that black women were, no doubt, sentenced in accordance with the types of crimes they committed.

As early as 1904, sentencing differences were observed for these two groups of women. Among black women, almost half received a year or more of confinement. For white women, however, just over half served less than one year. Of course, length of time served should be reflective of the degree of seriousness of the crime committed, but, as will be noted, that often is not the case.

Table 15.2   *Arrest ratios per 100,000 persons in the general population, according to sex and race, New York State, 1940*

Sex and Race	Ratio per 100,000
White female	117
Black female	181.1
White male	263.5
Black male	1,890

Source: Pollak (1950): 116.

Table 15.3   *Rates of prisoners received from courts by state and federal prisons, per 100,000 persons in the United States, 1940 and 1980*

Sex and Race	1940 rates	1980 rates
White female	3.6	6
Black female	20.9	47
White male	95.3	178
Black male	384.7	1148

Source: United States Department of Justice, Bureau of Justice Statistics, *Prisoners in State and Federal Institution* on 12/31/80, p. 21; and Pollak (1950): 117.

Regardless of the theories of causation, black females are more likely than their white counterparts to be arrested, charged, convicted, and sentenced to prison. These trends have existed since the first years official statistics were recorded. *Tables 15.2* and *15.3* illustrate the gap between black and white women in arrest rates and incarceration rates. In 1940, for the state of New York, 181 black women were arrested per 100,000 in New York; the rate for white women was 12. Black women were also more likely to be processed through the criminal justice system from arrest to imprisonment than were white women. The incarceration rate for black women was 21 as compared to 4 for white women. Rates from 1932–36 for the United States support these gaps. For this period, white women had an incarceration rate of 6 per 100,000 while black women had a rate of 21 (von Hentig 1948: 236). By 1980 these ratios had changed substantially, producing even greater racial differences.

More recent attention on female criminality has acknowledged the special case of the black female offender while moving on to explain the causes of the recent rise in crime rates among non-minority women (Figueira-McDonogh, Sarri, and Iglehart 1981). Theories of changing opportunity structures and women's liberation ignore the fact that the women most likely to be processed through the criminal justice system are the least likely to respond to ideologies of sex-role equality.

Women as victims

This chapter primarily addresses women as offenders and their treatment in the criminal justice system. It would be remiss, however, not to note women as victims or the interactions in some instances between victim and offender statuses. All too often women become offenders because of the 'blame the victim' phenomenon, as in the case of sexual abuse, assault and violence, or sexual harassment. Space limitations prevent more than a brief mention of this problem but it is a matter of great concern (Rafter and Stanko 1982).

Crime is supposedly a violation against society as well as against an individual. However, the criminal justice system trivializes the harm of certain behavior – particularly wife-battering and sexual assault. This trivialization is particularly tragic in its consequences since being female reduces the ability of victims to be taken seriously by law enforcement officials. The National Crime Survey reports that women are less likely to be victimized by crime than are men. However, this annual survey, which receives much public attention, excludes the critical issues of family violence against women: wife-battering or sexual abuse. Violence against women is based on the political and economic powerlessness of women as well as on their lesser physical size and strength. This powerlessness is well illustrated by the gap in this survey. Reducing or stopping violence against women is inevitably linked to the liberation of women from oppressive social and economic relations at home, in the community, and in the workplace.

Overall, black women and women between the ages of sixteen and twenty-four are the more frequent female victims of crime, especially violent crime. To some extent the conditions of poverty and single parenthood under which many of these women live place them at high risk for victimization. In a recent study of AFDC recipients, Sarri *et al.* (1984) observed high levels of victimization of women and their children following termination of welfare benefits which placed these families in poor housing and precarious living situations. The women who are least likely to be victims of crime are elderly women, although the media leads the public to think otherwise (Bowker 1981).

Law and criminal justice system processing

In a myriad of ways statutes governing criminal justice systems have discriminated against females. In some instances females are specifically mentioned with reference to differential treatment. Although many laws might not stand the test of a Supreme Court challenge, they are enforced because they are not challenged. The statutory treatment of prostitution and promiscuity illustrates the differential treatment. Both of these are behaviors for which women still are almost exclusively prosecuted. Discrimination arises because some laws confine prostitution to the activities of females and do not penalize males, whether customers or actors. But, when laws are enacted, they may not correct the situation. New York enacted a law stating that patronizing a prostitute was a violation with a maximum sentence of imprisonment of fifteen days. However, the penalty for the prostitute was far more severe – a maximum sentence of three months, an obvious double standard. Hewitt and Mickish (1983) observed that between 1900 and 1920 nearly equal numbers of males and females were arrested, tried, and convicted for prostitution in Muncie, Indiana. Then in the 1920s laws and practices changed so that males were no longer charged. Thus one can see that 'deviance' occurs in the context of social institutions that have the power to label some persons as deviants and others not so.

Juvenile delinquency laws have long discriminated against females for specific status offenses for which only females were charged. Variable age limits existed for females as compared with males. Most of the latter are unconstitutional today, but many states have not changed their codes accordingly. A further problem remains in the attitudes and ideologies of persons administering the laws (i.e. judges, probation officers, and other court staff). White males predominate in executive and leadership positions in the criminal justice system so that critical decision-making remains in their hands. Institutionalized sexism and racism in that decision-making have been frequently observed (Iglehart 1977).

Examination of gender patterns in court proceedings produces substantial variation in the processing of males and females. In a Washington DC study, Figueira-McDonough (1984) observed marked male/female differences in the processing of larceny, drug, and sex crimes, but few differences in the treatment of person or serious property crime. Men and women were treated similarly in crimes in which males predominated, but where females predominated there were large differences in plea bargaining, rates of guilty pleas, and in sentence bargaining. Women were less able to bargain effectively, less often represented by counsel, and were more often willing to plead guilty to the original charge. Seriousness of offense and prior record were weaker predictors of sentences for females. Overall, males received stiffer sentences. The reverse was true for larceny where females predominated. In fact, controlling for prior record, race, and residence, the probability of severe sentences for larceny and sex crimes by women was nearly the same as for violent offenses. Family and friendship ties to the victim predicted the incarceration of females, but the opposite was true for males.

Daly (1981) argues that both class and gender must be carefully examined if one is to understand differences in criminal court processing and outcomes. She notes that women more often appear to receive less harsh sanctions, but comparisons must be made within as well as between groups of males and females. She also suggests that feminist theories of patriarchy can be used to specify how the defendants' form and degree of family connectedness become critical dimensions in court adjudication. Court agents expect women to perform family labor, and as a corollary they expect that men will be the primary breadwinners. This expectation leads them to assume that the heterosexual marital state is a stable group. Bernstein's findings confirm the importance of traditional values in judicial decision-making (Bernstein, Cardascia, and Ross 1979). Personnel are woefully ignorant of the changed female roles in work and family.

Several states have attempted to reduce sentence discrepancies with statutory sentencing guidelines. Where these have been implemented they appear to have resulted in reduced incarceration of women because of their less serious criminal behavior. However, as Knapp (1982) points out, prosecutors and legislators often act subsequently to reinstate previous, more punitive practices. As Durkheim suggested, society seeks to establish social mechanisms for enforcing normative standards regardless of the objective reality of specific behavior. Therefore, women must be punished with incarceration even when their behavior does not warrant such action in order to 'protect the safety' of the public.

Women in custody

Despite the discrimination or inequities that exist among police, judges, and prosecutors, the single most serious problem in criminal justice in the United States in the 1980s is the rapidly increasing incarceration of men and women in jails, prisons, reformatories, lockups, and other residential facilities. Incarceration rates in the United States far exceed those in any of our Western peer countries, including our neighbor, Canada. Moreover, these incarceration rates are not related to crime rates per se, but instead to poverty, poor education, percent minority population, and availability of prison beds (Downs 1977; Nagel 1977).

The incarceration of adult women in separate prison facilities developed in the mid-nineteenth century; for adolescent females the use of separate institutions is of more recent origin, dating from the early 1900s. Prisons for women were purportedly established to provide female inmates with the same benefits of rehabilitation given their male counterparts. Prisons were also built to comply with reformists' beliefs that women needed sexual morality and sobriety if they were to resume their 'predestined roles as homemakers, mothers and wives.' There was no recognition that the majority of these women might well be single parents and the sole supporter of their family. Prisons for females were located in rural areas, and the public knew very little about the persons or events inside, in contrast to a voluminous popular and scientific literature about male prisons.

As of mid-1984 the United States' adult prison population totalled 463,866 of which 20,853 (4.5 per cent) were female. There has been a dramatic increase in the incarceration of adult women during the 1980s – averaging between 9 per cent and 15 per cent per year (US Department of Justice 1983). This population of offenders is not equally distributed among the states, for there are eleven states with more than 500 female prisoners: California, Texas, Florida, Ohio, New York, Georgia, North Carolina, Michigan, Illinois, Louisiana, and Alabama, and two states with less than 10: Vermont and North Dakota. The first five of these hold 40 per cent of all female prisoners in the country (US Department of Justice 1985a). Rates per 100,000 population also highlight the great inter-state variation, as *Table 15.4* indicates; the overall rate of incarceration of females in state prisons was 13 in 1981, but Texas and Florida had rates of 20 while North Dakota and Vermont had less than 10 female prisoners, or less than 1 per 100,000 resident population (United States Department of Justice 1983).

Table 15.4 *Highest and lowest states in female incarceration rates, 1981*

Highest five states	Rate	Lowest five states	Rate
Texas	20	North Dakota	(1)
Florida	20	Vermont	(1)
Ohio	14	Minnesota	3
California	12	Maine	4
New York	8	West Virginia	4

Source: United States Department of Justice, Bureau of Justice Statistics, *Sourcebook of Criminal Justice Statistics*, 1983, p. 574.

The juvenile justice system incarcerates young women at far higher rates than the adult system (Sarri 1978). Moreover, they are held in private as well as public facilities. *Table 15.5* presents information on admissions and single-day population counts for juvenile females in 1982. There was a decline of just over 4,000 females between 1974 and 1982, largely attributable to two factors: the decline in the adolescent population (8 per cent) and the impact of the Juvenile Justice Act of 1974 which discouraged the incarceration of status offenders.

Table 15.5   *Female delinquents in correctional facilities, 1982*

	1974		1982	
	Admissions	*Single day count*	*Admissions*	*Single day count*
Private	20,297	9,645	34,367	9,148
Public	180,994	10,139	107,183	6,519
Total	201,291	19,784	141,550	15,667

Source: United States Bureau of the Census, *Children in Custody*, 1984.

The largest decline in the incarceration of females occurred in detention facilities (45 per cent), but there was also a substantial decline in training school populations. Private institutions, on the other hand, rapidly increased their female population because federal foster care monies were available and judges still preferred out-of-home placement (Lerman 1984). Information is not available about the transfer of juvenile females to mental health facilities, but that is estimated to have been substantial in this time period. In contrast to the decline in juvenile females, the juvenile male population incarcerated increased substantially, as did the proportion of youth who were black and Hispanic (41 per cent to 51 per cent). On a given day in the mid-1980s there were 50,382 women incarcerated, of whom 15,829 were juveniles. The rate for juveniles is far higher than for the adults because the age range is relatively small (14–17 years) for juveniles compared to adult women (17–60). Juvenile females compose 20 per cent of all incarcerated juveniles, whereas adult women compose 4.5 per cent of all adults in prison. Given the fact that the female juvenile arrest rate is less than 25 per cent of all juveniles arrested, these data suggest that chivalry has certainly not been shown to juvenile females.

Women, as well as men, are disproportionately incarcerated in Southern states compared with the more populous North and West. Blacks and Hispanics are being incarcerated at increasing rates as the data in *Table 15.2* revealed. When one examines the rates for females, even greater racial discrepancies are noted than for the total population.

One could speculate about the reasons for this difference in incarceration rates, but it seems clear that economic and racial discrimination are strong contributory factors. This pattern suggests particular directions for social work intervention if these inequities are to be reversed. These directions will be considered in the next section. Prior to that we will examine briefly the characteristics and needs of incarcerated females.

The mean age of female adult inmates is 29 and that of juveniles 15.7 years. More than half are non-white. Women inmates have a mean of 1.7 children which is nearly identical to current national fertility levels. The vast majority of women offenders are in prison for property crimes: larceny, forgery, fraud, followed by drug use and abuse. Homicide represents less than 10 per cent of the annual female commitments to prison, although at any given point in time this population is larger because of their longer length of stay. The average adult sentence is five years, but the median length of stay in 1983 was sixteen months for adult women. For juveniles the sentences were indeterminate, but the average length of stay was ten months, and in many states it far exceeded the average length of stay of males regardless of the males' more serious offenses.

Health care is one of the most important needs of incarcerated females because most facilities have poor services for a population that is at high risk for poor health because of poverty, substance abuse, and other factors (Resnik and Shaw 1980). Few correctional institutions have any primary care and often only have health professionals on call. They thus deal only with life-threatening situations or concern themselves about determining sexual misconduct or possession of contraband. One of the more serious health problems of female offenders stems from substance abuse – alcohol, narcotic drugs, and psychotropic prescription drugs. Using national survey data Goetting and Howsen (1983) noted that nearly 75 per cent of female prisoners reported having used heroin, 52 per cent barbiturates, 50 per cent cocaine. Thirty-three per cent reported having been in at least one drug treatment program. Overall, female prisoners report higher rates of serious drug abuse than do male prisoners.

A second need in women's prisons is for educational and experiential programming to increase the likelihood of their successful participation in the labor force. The vast majority of juvenile and adult female offenders have had serious problems in education and/or employment. Yet, most correctional institutions in 1985 still offer limited traditional programs which reinforce the disadvantaged status of these women. This situation persists despite the fact that resources are available through JPTA and vocational training programs.

Because the majority of female offenders have been or will be parents, they need assistance in developing and maintaining meaningful family relationships. Model programs have been developed in several European countries but seldom even experimented with in the United States. The European programs have made it possible for women to continue at least some of their parental functions.

Alternatives to incarceration

Female offenders have had less access than male offenders to programs which are alternatives to incarceration, despite their less serious offenses (Chapman 1980). Mechanisms such as police warnings, community panels, community service, dispute resolution, and restitution are unavailable to the average offender. These programs are far less costly than incarceration, but they still have not been developed. Women also have less access to halfway houses and transition programs when they leave prison.

One can safely argue that 75 per cent of female offenders could be handled effectively and safely in community-based programs at a far lower cost to society, to the woman, and to her family. According to their own reports, judges would utilize such programs more frequently for sentencing if they existed. What is particularly disturbing is the fact that the least serious female offenders are incarcerated in jails which have the poorest programs and the highest security (Chapman, 1980; Glick and Neto 1977). States with low incarceration rates such as Minnesota, Vermont, and Wisconsin are the ones where there has been the most experimentation with the development of a variety of diversion programs for female offenders.

Issues for social work

Social work, along with most of the helping professions, has ignored the female offender in police stations, probation, jails, prisons, and community programs despite the fact that her needs are exactly those which social workers should be able to address and deal with effectively. Poverty, single parenthood, poor health, inadequate education, and lack of employment are all problems which social workers are trained to address. Moreover, as a profession social work should call public attention to the dangers of the overuse of coercive social control as practiced in the United States today.

The lack of social workers in female correctional programs is partly a response to the profession itself which has been far more willing to serve middle-class clientele in mental health, family service, and medical settings. It is also the result of inadequate attention by schools of social work to the development of curricula to train professionals for criminal justice. Lastly, it reflects societal values which suggest 'out of sight, out of mind,' or 'there's nothing that can be done for these people.'

The requests for equal treatment under the law by plaintiffs in federal class-action suits such as Glover v. Johnson (1979) or Canterina v. Wilson (1983) reflect the almost total lack of rehabilitation/educational programming for adult female offenders. Social workers are needed in administrative, program design, and supervisory positions more than they are needed in direct service, although the latter is important. Without well-designed programs, casework and counseling will never be effective (Figueira-McDonough, Sarri and Iglehart 1981; Glick and Neto 1977). Female social workers are also needed who have strong commitments to the feminist movement and equality for women to counter the dominance of male executives who set up programs based on their work with male offenders or on their traditional conceptions of appropriate female social roles (Iglehart and Stein 1985).

Among the programs for which social work could assume primary responsibility are the following:

(a) Service in police agencies in the areas of family violence, sexual assault, substance abuse, promiscuity and prostitution, and runaways;
(b) Supportive services for families of victims and offenders in all law enforcement agencies;
(c) Educational programs to meet basic educational needs and contemporary career opportunities for women;
(d) Health care and substance abuse treatment;
(e) Self-help and mutual support programs for offenders so that they can be empowered to take control of their lives and have legitimate personal and occupational careers;
(f) Programs which break down the barriers between society and criminal justice so that incarceration can be reduced with the development of alternative community-based programming.

If social work is to play a more significant role in correctional programs for female offenders, social work education must make substantial changes. Most schools do not have a course on the female offender or even one on the administration of criminal justice generally. There needs to be a justice component in the curriculum in social welfare policy and services sequence. Curricula in human growth and behavior must include more knowledge about low-income and minority women's life stages and styles, about deviance and social control, and about alternative family patterns. Lastly, methods and practicum training must prepare social workers for sophisticated practice in criminal justice. One can no longer be trained in a voluntary community agency and then expect to be able to function effectively in a coercive social control organization with highly sophisticated custody and management technologies. Lastly, all social workers expecting to work in criminal justice need training in community organization and action if alternatives to the present system are to be developed. States which have made progress in this task have had such practitioners.

Conclusions

The plight of the female offender in the United States in the 1980s is such that it demands priority concern of the social work and social welfare community. This chapter has suggested that there are needs for changes in laws, policies, programs, and practice in criminal justice. Feminist perspectives argue that crime occurs in the context of gender, class, race, and age relations. An adequate understanding of crime and deviance requires analysis of the ways in which institutionalized patterns of gender behavior influence the behavior of all in society.

This chapter does not address broader issues confronting this society such as poverty, deficits and debts, unemployment, and peace and security, even though these issues are not unrelated to what is happening in criminal justice as are problems considered in other chapters of this volume. Along with many other countries of the world the United States has witnessed a dramatic change in families and in the roles and status of women. These changes have undoubtedly contributed to some of the problems being faced in criminal justice today. Whether recognition of these problems and their interrelationships will produce ad hoc custodial responses or a sound reassessment and the establishment of more comprehensive social policies is highly uncertain. It is this challenge which we hope that social workers will take up. It is time to rid society of the mentality represented by the message of the old nursery rhyme, 'Take the key and lock her up, lock her up, lock her up, my fair lady!'

References

Adler, F. and Simon, R. (1979) *The Criminality of Deviant Women*. Boston: Houghton, Mifflin.

Bernstein, I. N., Cardascia, J., and Ross, C. E. (1979) Defendant's Sex and Criminal Court Decision. In R. Alvarez, K. G. Lutterman, and Assoc. (eds) *Discrimination in Organizations*. San Francisco: Jossey-Bass, pp. 329–54.

Bowker, L. (1981) *Women and Crime in America*. New York: Macmillan.

Chapman, J. (1980) *Economic Realities and the Female Offender*. Lexington: Lexington Books.

Chesney-Lind, M. (1977) Judicial Paternalism and the Female Offender. *Crime and Delinquency* 23 (April): 121–30.

Daly, K. (1981) Gender Differences in Criminal Court Outcome: Towards a Theoretical Formulation Linking Class and Gender Relations. Paper delivered at the American Criminology Society Annual Meeting, Washington, DC, November. Amherst, MA: Department of Sociology.

Downs, G. (1977) *Bureaucracy, Innovation and Social Policy*. Lexington: Lexington Books.

Elliot, D. and Ageton, S. (1980) Reconciling Differences in Estimates of Delinquency. *American Sociological Review* 45: 95–110.

Erikson, Kai (1966) *Wayward Puritans*. New York: Wiley.
Fernald, M., Hayes, M. H., and Dawley, A. (1920) *A Study of Women Delinquents in New York State*, 1968 edn. Montclair, NJ: Patterson Smith.
Figueira-McDonough, J. (1982) Gender Differences in Informal Processing: A Look at Charge Bargaining and Sentence Reduction in Washington, D.C. *Journal of Research on Crime and Delinquency* 22(2): 101–33.
—— (1984) Feminism and Delinquency. *British Journal of Criminology* 24(4): 325–42.
Figueira-McDonough, J., Sarri, R., and Iglehart, A. (1981) *Women in Prison in Michigan 1968–1978: A Study of Commitment Patterns*. Ann Arbor, MI: University of Michigan, Institute for Social Research.
Giallombardo, R. (1974) *The Society of Impressed Girls*. New York: Wiley.
Glick, R. and Neto, L. (1977) *National Study of Women's Correctional Programs*. Washington, DC: United States Government Printing Office.
Glueck, E. and Glueck, S. (1934) *Five Hundred Delinquent Girls*. New York: Alfred Knopf.
Goetting, A. and Howsen, R. (1983) Women in Prison: A Profile. Unpublished paper. Bowling Green, KY: Western Kentucky University.
Healy, W. and Bonner, A. (1926) *Delinquents and Criminals: Their Making and Unmaking: Studies in Two American Cities*. New York: Macmillan.
Heffernan, E. (1972) *Making It in Prison: The Square, the Cool and the Life*. New York: Wiley.
Hewitt, J. D., and Mickish, J. E. (1983) The Legal Control of Female Sexual Behavior During the Progressive Era: A Local History. Paper presented at the Annual Meeting of the American Criminology Society, Denver, Colorado, 12 November. Muncie, IN: Ball State University, Department of Criminal Justice.
Hindelang, M. (1979) Sex Differences in Criminal Activity. *Social Problems* 27: 143–56.
Iglehart, A. (1977) Differences in Black and White Female Criminality. Unpublished paper, March. Ann Arbor, MI: University of Michigan School of Social Work.
Iglehart, A. and Stein, M. (1985) The Female Offender: A Forgotten Client? *Social Casework*, March: 152–59.
Klein, D. (1973) The Etiology of Female Crime. *Issues in Criminology* 8(2): 3–30.
Knapp, K. (1982) Impact of the Minnesota Sentencing Guidelines in Sentencing Practices. *Hamline Law Review* 5(2): 237–56.
Konopka, G. (1966) *The Adolescent Girl in Conflict*. Englewood Cliffs, NJ: Prentice-Hall.
—— (1975) *Young Girls: A Portrait of Adolescence*. Englewood Cliffs, NJ: Prentice-Hall.
Lerman, P. (1984) Child Welfare, the Private Sector and Community-based Corrections. *Crime and Delinquency* 30(1): 5–38.
Lombroso, C. and Ferrero, W. (1916) *The Female Offender*. New York: D. Appleton.
McCord, J. and Otten, L. (1983) A Consideration of Sex Roles and Motivations for Crime. *Criminal Justice and Behavior* 10: 3–12.
Morris, R. (1964) Female Delinquency and Relational Problems. *Social Forces*, October: 82–9.
Nagel, I. and Hagen, J. (1983) Gender and Crime: Offense Patterns and Criminal Court Sanctions. In M. Tonry and N. Morris (eds) *Crime and Justice*, vol. 4. Chicago: University of Chicago Press: pp. 91–144.
Nagel, W. (1977) On Behalf of a Moratorium on Prison Construction. *Crime and Delinquency* 23(2): 154–72.
Pollak, O. (1950) *The Criminality of Women*. Philadelphia, PA: University of Pennsylvania Press.

Propper, A. (1981) *Prison Homosexuality*. Lexington: Lexington Books.

Rafter, N. and Stanko, E. (1982) *Judge, Lawyer, Victim, Thief: Women, Gender Roles and Justice*. Boston: Northeastern University Press.

Rasche, C. F. (1974) The Female Offender as an Object of Criminological Research. *Criminal Justice and Behavior* 1: 301–02.

Resnik, J. and Shaw, N. (1980) Prisoners of Their Sex: Health Problems of Incarcerated Women. In J. Robbins (ed.) *Prisoners Rights Sourcebook*, volume 2. New York: Clark Boardman.

Sarri, R. (1978) Gender Issues in Juvenile Justice. *Crime and Delinquency* 29(3): 381–98.

Sarri, R. (ed.) (1984) *The Impact of Federal Policy Change on AFDC Recipients and Their Children*. Ann Arbor: University of Michigan Institute of Social Research, Center for Political Studies.

Short, J. and Nye, F. (1970) Extent of Unrecorded Juvenile Delinquency. In J. E. Teele (ed.) *Juvenile Delinquency Reader*, Ithaca, IL: F. E. Peacock.

Smart, C. (1977) *Women, Crime and Criminology*. London: Routledge and Kegan Paul.

Steffensmeier, D. (1978) Crime and the Contemporary Woman: An Analysis of Changing Levels of Female Property Crime, 1960–1975. *Social Forces* 57(2): 566–84.

—— (1980) Assessing the Impact of the Women's Movement on Sex-Based Differences in the Handling of Adult Criminal Defendants. *Crime and Delinquency* 26 (3 July): 333–43.

Sutherland, E. and Cressey, D. (1966) *Principles of Criminology*, 6th edn. Philadelphia: Lippincott.

Tittle, C. R. (1972) *Society of Subordinates: Inmate Organization in a Narcotics Hospital*. Bloomington: Indiana University Press.

United States Department of Justice (1983) *Sourcebook of Criminal Justice Statistics*. Washington, DC: United States Government Printing Office, p. 574.

—— (1985a) *Prisoners in 1981, 1982, 1983, 1984*. Washington, DC: United States Department of Justice, Bureau of Justice Statistics.

—— (1985b) *Prison Admissions and Releases 1982*. Washington, DC: United States Government Printing Office.

United States Department of Justice, Bureau of the Census (1926) *Prisoners in State and Federal Institutions*. Washington, DC: United States Government Printing Office.

—— (1984) *Children in Custody*. Washington, DC: United States Government Printing Office.

United States Department of Justice, Federal Bureau of Investigation (1975 and 1984) *Uniform Crime Reports*. Washington, DC: United States Government Printing Office.

Vedder, C. and Somerville, D. (1970) *The Delinquent Girl*. Springfield, IL: C. Thomas.

von Hentig, H. (1948) *The Criminal and His Victim: Studies in the Sociology of Crime*. New Havin, CT: Yale University Press.

Welch, S., Gruhl, J., and Spohn, C. (1984) Sentencing: The Influence of Alternative Measures of Prior Record. *Criminology* 22(2): 215–28.

Wilson, J. and Herrnstein, R. (1985) *Crime and Human Nature*. New York: Simon and Schuster.

16 Women and work

Katharine Hooper Briar, Marie D. Hoff, and Essie Tramel Seck

The social work profession has a major role to play in helping women cope with the stresses associated with their roles in the home and the labor market. Increasing family responsibilities and labor market inequities necessitate multi-dimensional social work interventions. For example:

> Susan is a 38-year-old single parent suffering from depression and sleeping disorders. She attributes her problems to her inability to find a better job. Currently, she works in a temporary secretarial service company. She figures that if she were seen as a desirable worker she would have been hired by one of the companies for which she provides temporary filing and typing services.

In the past, if Susan were to seek help from a social service agency it is possible that only her depressive symptoms and sleeping problems and not her occupational stresses, needs, and rights would be addressed. This is due in part to the uneven attention the profession has paid to the meaning of work and to the effects of job inequities and stress, especially on women's lives. It is understandable that work and work problems have not been explicitly addressed, as only recently has there been a resurgence in professional concern for work roles of clients and the workplace as a practice domain. Coinciding with the emerging interest of social workers in work problems and rights of clients has been the unparalleled involvement of women in the labor market, increasing from 27 to 51 per cent between 1940 and 1980 (Quarm 1984).

Paid employment has long been a pressing women's issue, especially among ethnic and racial minorities as well as working-class women (US Department of Labor 1975). In recent years economic and social necessity along with assertion of rights to full participation in society have increasingly made market work an issue for most women. Because women's work roles have historically centered around family caregiving as well as paid employment, perspectives on work must be broadened to capture distinct dimensions of women's experience. Moreover, women's work cannot be understood solely through the application of knowledge derived from traditional research work. Most of that literature pertains to men whose economic and occupational functioning have historically been determined by their paid employment. In fact, traditional research has focused on the deleterious effects of unemployment for men and employment for women (Mortimer and Sorensen 1984). Clearly, women's work life must be understood as fundamentally different from men's, not just because of the variance in wages, socialization, and occupational opportunities, but also because women are unable to relinquish their family work responsibilities when they enter or retire from the labor market. Women as workers are obviously not a monolithic group. Research developments on women and work are relatively recent and incomplete, and cannot be generalized to many women who may differ by virtue of their class, ethnicity, race, age, sexual and affectional preferences, or disability.

Despite such knowledge gaps, this chapter will address several significant dimensions of work-related problems and demonstrate how they can be alleviated by multidimensional social work interventions. This chapter will address such stress-producing conditions and inequities as the economic vulnerability of women as providers and caregivers, wage and occupational segregation, and women's occupational development. In addition, this chapter will focus on the costs and benefits of employment as well as occupational interventions and occupational arenas as practice domains. Curriculum implications and conceptual and empirical challenges are also discussed.

Provider and caregiver work roles

Gender-role division and stratification, accelerating with the industrial revolution, have historically consigned women to unremunerated domestic work roles and men to paid employment in the labor market. Thus the influx of women into the workforce does not signify a role shift as much as a role addition for women who increasingly combine provider as well as caregiver roles. Despite societal ambivalence and ambiguity regarding women's labor force participation, women's own individual and family economic needs and rights to occupational participation have intensified their out-of-home employment. As a result, it is expected that by the 1990s, 60–65 per cent of working age women will be in the labor force (US Department of Labor 1977).

A number of factors account for the accelerated movement of women into the labor market. These include economic necessity created by inadequate spousal income, the increasing incidence of single or never married women, and the desire for self-actualization, inspired in part by the women's movement. With about 50 per cent of all first marriages ending in divorce, women are increasingly vulnerable to economic insecurity and its consequent social, emotional, health, and family devastation. Second marriages are not conduits to long-term economic security either, as 60 per cent of second marriages fail. Black women are less likely to remarry, perpetuating their precarious economic situation. Women as widows are less likely than men widowers to remarry, intensifying their vulnerability to economic insecurity due to increasing risk of poverty among aged women. In fact, both a job and a spouse are disproportionately inaccessible to older women compared to their male counterparts.

The restructuring of both the institutions of work and family in the past two decades has eroded support for women in their caregiving capacities and for men in their economic provider role (Ehrenreich 1983). Caregiving responsibilities, historically subsidized through marriage, relegated women to almost total economic dependence on men. Ironically, as complete economic support via marriage has been diminishing, the multigenerational caregiving responsibilities for women are intensifying, and these family responsibilities may span several generations of family members. Single adolescent mothers, for example, may add to caregiving strains by looking to their mothers for their own continued rearing as well as for help in caring for their child.

Despite women's entrance into the labor market there has been little decline in the caregiving and housework tasks they perform (Kreps and Clark 1975; Oakley 1974; Robinson 1980). Neither has there been a more equal division of family work tasks in two-parent families. Women perform 70 per cent of family work, compared to 15 per cent for men and 15 per cent for children (Hartman 1981). Black couples (McAdoo 1983) and homosexual couples (Blumstein and Schwartz 1983) tend to be more egalitarian in their division of family work roles. The United States is not unique; caregiving as a women's domain and unpaid job is a world-wide issue. In fact, it is estimated that two-thirds of the world's work is done by women, while only 10 per cent of the world's income is received by women (Scott 1984).

In recent years, men's overall economic power has declined with inflation, recessions, and permanent job loss. The shift from an industrial to a service economy has created convulsions among manufacturing industries, dislocating workers and their families from their intergenerational dependence on a single industry such as mining, steel, auto, timber, textiles, and agriculture. Frequent and deepening recessions coupled with the complete loss of jobs have not only reduced the economic stablity of families but have been a major contributor to ruptured family structures (Briar 1983).

Unemployment of the male wage-earner is not only a precipitant of divorce, but may trigger a chain of economic, emotional, and social disruption in the family. Women may have to contend with the toll of their husbands' unemployment, as well as the battering, substance abuse, or eviction which unemployment may precipitate. Women may further experience downward economic and social skidding through low wages or the bare subsistence of welfare (Briar 1978).

Work, wages, and occupational segregation

While single women have traditionally had higher rates of labor force participation than other women, the greatest recent increase in women workers has been among married women. Many women are employed because dual wage-earners are needed to generate an adequate family income. Two-thirds of working women are single, divorced, widowed, separated, or are married to men who earn less than $10,000 per year (Westley and De Gooyer 1982). In sharing the provider role, women's contributions in many cases are crucial to raising the family standard of living above poverty level (Smith 1979). Married women work to stabilize their family resources, to curb the effect of inflation and to enhance children's opportunities for college, for decent housing, or for a more desirable lifestyle. In addition, women's labor market participation intensifies with their perceived rights to occupational development and mobility. Black women are more likely than white women to experience divorce, single parenthood and early widowhood, profoundly deepening their economic insecurity (Freudiger and Almquist 1983). The adage that women with children are a man away from poverty is for the most part true.

Marital status, income, and class differences may explain why some women work for sheer economic survival, while others see their jobs as tools for self-expression and self-development. Nevertheless, despite increasing expectations for labor market participation, women generally remain 'on loan' to the workforce as, at any juncture, illness, disability, or dependency of a family member may conscript them into their full-time caregiving roles unless they have unusual powers of resistance.

Despite women's strides in entering non-traditional jobs, the overall status of women as workers remains precarious. They often cannot rise above subsistence wages and must manage both provider and caregiver roles. On the average, women's earning power is substantially less than men's, white women earning 64 cents, black women 57 cents, and Hispanic women 50 cents to every dollar earned by white men (Editorial 1985). Black women earn 23 per cent less than black men, a smaller differential than between white men and women because black men earn less to begin with (Ferber and Birnbaum 1982). Such inequitable earnings among white, black, and Hispanic women are due less to time out for caregiving than to pay inequities for the same job and for jobs of comparable worth.

Despite the increase in the numbers and proportions of women in the paid workforce, they are disproportionately relegated to low-wage jobs in 'female' occupations and their occupational distribution has not changed during this century. Occupations which were predominantly female in 1900 remain so today. Sixty per cent of women remain crowded into ten traditional female jobs and occupations (Pearce 1979; US Commission on Civil Rights 1983). Nurturant occupational roles such as nurses, librarians, teachers, social workers, and child care providers are disproportionately dominated by women who accounted for 73 per cent of the workers in these fields (England 1984). Such occupations provided jobs for 5 per cent of males and 19 per cent of females in the labor force. In one study of 419 identified occupations, there were 41 in which 50 per cent were women, while there were 179 occupations in which 90 per cent were men (Rytina 1981).

Occupational sex segregation has been explained in terms of a dual or secondary labor market which maintains women in jobs without benefits and without opportunities for advancement – jobs that fluctuate with the economy perpetrating the 'last hired, first fired' syndrome, a phenomenon disproportionately experienced by ethnic and racial minority women (Almquist 1979).

Women's gains in blue-collar and technical occupations have been significant but ephemeral. Given the loss of manufacturing jobs, two-thirds of blue-collar women who were able to position themselves in high-paying jobs are now permanently displaced. Some must work two jobs, for example, in fast food industries, just to sustain the standard of living to which their families had been accustomed during their employment in the manufacturing industry (Snyder and Nowak 1984).

Since women have increasingly broken through barriers to enter the labor market and because legislative initiatives have accompanied their progress, it is assumed that many have achieved special status and gains. This is a myth, especially affecting black women (Malveaux 1983). Efforts to prevent and reduce discrimination have been promoted by the Equal Opportunity Commission and in education through Title IX of the Civil Rights Act, but differential treatment of women is perpetuated in social security, health insurance, pension plans, and credit access (Grubb and Lazerson 1984). Despite efforts to advance women's rights through the Security Employee Retirement Income Act of 1974, women as retirees are most vulnerable because their employment has been so frequently interrupted by full-time caregiving episodes (Glazer 1984). Such legislation is merely a beginning point given the discrimination experienced especially by disabled, racial and ethnic minority, and overtly lesbian working women.

Employment as a focus for social work intervention

Barriers to labor market participation and to socialization and preparation for labor market work involve societal discrimination against women as workers, heightened by oppression due to race, ethnicity, age, disability, and sexual pre-ference. Societal ambivalence about women's labor market participation is reflected in additional impediments to employment, such as the absence of com-prehensive child care and related caregiving resources, and the continuing socialization of women primarily for family rather than for dual family and workforce roles. Social workers have major responsibilities to address the struc-tural sources of women's labor market problems as well as the stresses which these problems engender. A profession and its practitioners can have multiple impacts on work institutions and labor market policies. This section will address only a few of the many interventions social workers can pursue to advance women's rights as workers more adequately and to mitigate some of their employment-related stresses.

Clearly, work can be seen, at one extreme, as a critical social work resource promoting self-development and even self-actualization, or from the other extreme as an instrument of social injustice which inflicts harm. On the one hand women's work and work-role problems may be compounded not just by all the work-related stresses that men endure, but by the overload of carrying out full-time paid employment along with family caregiving (Glazer *et al.* 1977). On the other hand, social workers may find that in addressing women's work-role overload some of these stresses may be mitigated by advocacy for improved comprehensive caregiving support, and by corporate and union policies and benefits, e.g. sick child care and family leave policies.

Social work practice itself may inadvertently regulate and restrict some aspects of women's occupational development because interventions may exclude voca-tional assessment, counseling, job placement, and advocacy for equitable employment opportunities. Countless women seek help every year, for depres-sion, for marital conflict, for substance abuse, and for help with child manage-ment. Are such problems by-products of unemployment or under-employment, or do they stem from the inequitable burdens of double work roles?

Since direct service workers' primary focus is psychological and not employ-ment-related, it is understandable that client problems are 'framed' in terms that fit the intervention resources of the social worker. Moreover, social work inter-ventions have been mainly limited to the family domain. Within that domain, service may center on more efficient methods of communication, behavior management of children, or negotiation skills with adolescents or partners rather than on role shifts and sharing, or task reallocation with partners or children. The case below illustrates some of these potential practice pitfalls.

Mary seeks counseling for her lethargy and frequent spells of crying. Her life seems empty even though she feels some satisfaction in having raised two healthy children and having seen her husband through his job woes. With her children performing well in high school and the recent improvement in her husband's job, it seems to her that everyone's life is moving on but hers. Mary hopes that social work counseling will make her a better adjusted wife and mother.

Mary may seemingly be a perfect candidate for the psychological interventions that have dominated social worker's repertoires. A better approach, however, might be career assessment and occupational development. A job may not only be an antidote for her depressive symptoms but for her possible under-employment created by her family work role (Weissman *et al.* 1973). 'Housewife depression' may be a by-product of under-employment which for some may be as crippling as unemployment. Meaningful use of time, structure to one's day, a sense of productivity as well as a sense of social connectedness may help to provide a therapeutic base for Mary's functioning.

Addressing work problems: toward multidimensional practice

As social workers develop a multifocused practice modality, their skills will span micro and macro levels of intervention. At the clinical level social work skills need to address the cognitive barriers that may make job search, job acquisition, and job advancement seemingly insurmountable. At the macro level, social workers need legislative advocacy skills and community organization and program development skills.

Social work practice can be aided by feminist and multi-cultural perspectives which offer new frameworks and insights for combating the effects of oppression. These include empowerment, systematic consciousness-raising, and group-based collective action among women, but they may not be sufficient to help women find jobs and achieve occupational growth. Another set of interventions is needed.

As is true of all workers, women should have rights to occupational aids which recast their skills in marketable terms and provide short- and long-term occupational goal planning and valid labor market data. Without knowledge of the frequencies of openings in the kinds of jobs they seek, the job search may not only be prolonged but may be so aversive that withdrawal from the job search may occur altogether. All clients have a right to knowledge about job-seeking skills, about coping strategies for dealing with the many months of rejection before an interview is landed, and with the many interviews before an offer occurs. The fact that 12 per cent or fewer open jobs are listed with employment services necessitates hard work at 'informational interviewing' to locate the hidden job market. These involve interviews with key informants including prospective employers regardless of whether they have jobs open at the time. The three steps to job acquisition – (a) self-assessment, (b) labor market assessment, and (c) self-promotion – must be part of every job-seeking repertoire (Gentry 1985).

Social workers may find that for some depressed women, the stress of the job search may itself aggravate their symptoms. To have one's confidence elevated enough to seek a job and then to endure discrimination and multiple rejections leaves women clients at great risk of either taking any job offered or else giving up and succumbing to the human costs of unemployment.

For many women, a secure employment future requires that they advance their educaction as well as their employment skills. Increasingly, women are not just balancing the workplace and family domains but full- or part-time education as well. Social workers must be prepared to mobilize help from the educational community including such resources as vocational testing and preference guides, grants and scholarship aid, and various education, training, and job placement programs.

Social workers should also be familiar with specialized programs such as those for displaced homemakers, the Job Training Partnership Act (JTPA), Women's Resource Centers on campuses, and special programs which give credit for prior learning. Apprenticeship programs in unions may also expand occupational avenues and must be part of the social worker's resource inventory.

Just as many women have sought help with their family work roles from social service agencies, they increasingly seek aid for employment stress, stemming from such issues as work conditions, leave policies and benefits, or sexual harassment. Social workers will also see clients with stress from under-employment. As with unemployment, most women who are under-employed blame themselves for being trapped in a job that doesn't tap their talents, skills, or prior earning capacity.

Rigid work systems and schedules, the absence of flextime policies or permanent part-time work during child-rearing years, and inadequate health, leave, and related benefits are severe stressors to women in their dual work roles. Not surprisingly, symptoms such as exhaustion, depression, alcohol abuse, absenteeism, sickness, and accidents may be the presenting problem the woman worker brings to the social service agency. The clinical challenge for the future will be to find ways to deal with these symptoms in relationship to their occupational causes.

Social workers need to be aware that working women clients are victimized by various forms of harmful work conditions and they need to support self-protective actions by women. Since the passage of the Occupational Safety and Health Act of 1970, employed women are more aware of their rights to protection from toxic and dangerous work conditions. Social workers are increasingly advocating for clients seeking workman's compensation and helping with labor market re-entry. Since women workers have historically been afforded less union protection due to comparative lack of organizing in women's occupations, they may be more vulnerable to capricious workplace policies and often to the risk of being blamed for their plight. The absence of recourse may cause them to personalize rather than politicize their work problems.

The auspice for social work practice will obviously dictate and limit the types of problem-solving and social change avenues open to practitioners. A social worker based in a community social service agency serving women telephone workers whose jobs are to be terminated may have different problem-solving options than the union-based social worker.

The growing numbers of Employee Assistance Programs in public and private sector workplaces offer new programmatic contexts for problem-solving on behalf of women workers. Public policy initiatives are also needed to promote child care facilities. Also needed is social activism for improved work conditions and workplace supports for caregiving responsibilities. A professional organization such as the National Association of Social Workers that actively promotes equal rights, justice on the job, and full employment at living wages for all will reinforce efforts by individual practitioners. Unless practice promotes such multilevel public policy initiatives for working women clients, social work strategies may inadvertently make clients adjust to unjust conditions.

Clearly, one major avenue for activism on behalf of women employees is through the recent resurgence in labor union organizing in women's workplaces and industries. Intensified agendas for mobilizing and supporting women as workers are fostered by the Coalition for Labor Union Women, clerical worker union organizing, and renewed consciousness about women's historic contributions to unions (Hunt 1982; Milkman 1985). These and similar organizations may represent some of the most progressive alliances and forces available to counteract the low wages, occupational insecurity and immobility, and harmful work conditions inherent in many occupations dominated by women. Social workers will also be building new alliances with representatives from personnel, affirmative action, employee relations and corporation foundations as they develop new bridges to the workplace on behalf of women as well as men clients.

As the speciality area of occupational social work evolves, the profession also may be looking inward at social workers as a class of workers experiencing deficits in workplace personnel practices, benefit provisions, and work conditions. Not only have few social service agencies adopted an integrated view of the workplace and family life, but the disproportionate number of women in direct service, non-managerial roles may be subject to some of the same discriminatory problems as their clients experience. Thus, professional concern with women as workers may generate new employee practices and occupational opportunities for women and men in social work as well.

Curriculum implications of women and work

Much work lies ahead for social work educators who may want to explore the extent to which the problems for which clients seek help stem from occupational stress derived either from unemployment/under-employment, harmful work conditions, or from the stress of both paid work and caregiving roles. Social workers are in prime positions to question the effects of job stress in the labor market.

Beginning efforts in raising such questions and promoting the infusion of work content into the curriculum have been undertaken by Akabas and Kurzman (1982), especially in their advancement of occupational social work. Concern with work issues must be generic to the profession and not just left to this emerging speciality area. Ideally all social workers would be equipped to use an inventory of occupational stresses. Such an intervention framework may begin to pinpoint whether a woman needs help in searching for a better job, improved work conditions, aid with unemployment or with the reallocation of tasks and responsibilities. Just as environmental, social, and psychological attributes of one's job can impair functioning, some forms of caregiving can be most deleterious to health and human functioning. Research has shown that family caregivers of infirm elderly people may become more impaired than those for whom they are caring (Briar and Ryan 1986). Practitioners can promote support groups so that women with caregiver-provider roles can collectivize their distress, share coping tips, and organize for respite services.

Infusion of content on women and work can occur in such core courses as social policy. Here an examination can be made of the ways that the government regulates the domestic life of women. For example, inadequate funding for programs for deinstitutionalized patients has an immediate impact on women who, for the most part, provide the family's care of such patients (Briar and Ryan 1986). Moreover, social policy content has tended to focus on public sector decisions and less on private sector policies and their consequences, thereby overlooking the impact that work organizations have on human functioning. Content on women and work provides a good example to convey understanding of the many dimensions of the American distinction between the public and the private spheres of life.

More systematic attention to workers, especially women as workers, will assess the deficits in policies and services which sustain women's unequal income, job, and occupational entitlements and pursuits. Social policy courses must address the consequences of inadequate caregiving resources for employed women. Students should be aware of the fact that child care tax credits cover only 20–30 per cent of the costs of care through income tax deduction, heightening the financial burden on low-wage single mothers (Grubb and Lazerson 1984). Fewer than one out of three working mothers with children under the age of thirteen have access to child care. In fact, six to seven million children must care for themselves some part of the day (Martinez 1985). Moreover, as Abramovitz has shown, a historical examination of social welfare depicts how women have been regulated by the welfare state according to a 'family ethic' compared to policies binding men primarily to a 'work ethic.' In fact, historical antecedents to women's condition, especially as single parents, can be thoughtfully charted in the study of mother's pensions, AFDC, social security, and child care legislation. Societal ambivalence regarding women's 'proper' roles can be clearly analyzed in the current debates over welfare work requirements and workfare programs. Attention in the curriculum to current policy debates may help to sharpen students' awareness of the reform efforts needed to shape the future (National Advisory Council on Economic Opportunity 1981). These debates include the need for full employment, equity in occupational access and rights to occupational self-development.

The human behavior and social environment curriculum fosters an examination of the developmental effects of prescribed societal roles for men and women and the consequent scripts they enact in their school, cliental, and family activities. Of empirical interest are the developmental effects of the 'superwoman' syndrome on the socialization of young women and men. Expectations embodied in this syndrome may 'normalize' double-duty round-the-clock work as women's new calling, while denigrating women who are unable or choose not to acquire paid work, or alternatively who reject caregiving roles. Work and income must be addressed as powerful shapers of human behavior, and work roles must be examined as key determinants, not just correlates, of developmental processes and outcomes.

Clinical methods courses can promote employment as a new focus of social work intervention. These courses should question traditional gender-role assumptions about family and market work. In these courses, new conceptions of women's work problems can be examined. For example, it can be debated whether marital conflict stems from communication, power, or inequitable work allocation issues. Students might question whether unemployment or harmful work systems and work conditions contribute to substance abuse and emotional, health and interpersonal problems. Clinical responses may be expanded to address not just such problems, but the economic and employment precipitants themselves. Paid employment under good working conditions may be a powerful intervention to treat symptoms once attributed to intrapsychic and interpersonal problems.

Content in macro practice, whether offered within generalist or specialist curricula, must address the social change implications of the problems of women workers. What new policies and services need to be fostered to address the fact that women are exploited in low-paying, dead-end jobs or for their free caregiving labor? Few social agencies have participated in community efforts to stop plant closures, to promote economic development, or to organize services for unemployed or under-employed workers, let alone women workers. As lay-offs and plant closures occur, social service agencies have major roles to play in preventing and alleviating the human cost of unemployment while advancing the caregiving needs of families through public and private sector innovations.

Research courses offer major avenues to formulate the significant empirical questions regarding work needs and problems of women and the consequent effects of sexism, racism, agism, homophobia, and discrimination due to disability. All too often research on women has ignored the extent to which economic and employment variables shape women's behavior and contribute to their problems.

Much of the work of disciplines such as economics has involved the quantification of women's economic behavior, sometimes to the exclusion of related psychological, social, health and occupational dimensions. Social workers' empirical research skills and a multidisciplinary focus can offset some of the reductionism in traditional economic measures by the formulation of broader bases for understanding and measuring women's market and family work contributions and their costs.

As social workers more systematically employ an occupational lens, the benefits and the injustices inherent in women's work conditions should foster a new level of dialogue in the profession about justice in the market and in the family. Understanding the way in which economic policies have maintained women as caregivers, may prompt more proactive agendas for the future. The occupationally astute social worker may become a leading voice in formulating and advancing policies and practices that promote equity for women in the workplace and address the inequities and stresses of combined market and family work roles in women's lives.

References

Abramovitz, Mimi (1985) The Family Ethic: The Female Pauper and Public Aid, Pre-1900. *The Social Service Review* (59): 121–35.

Akabas, Sheila, H. and Kurzman, Paul A. (1982) *Work, Workers and Work Organizations*. Englewood Cliffs: Prentice-Hall.

Almquist, Elizabeth M. (1979) *Minorities, Gender and Work*. Lexington: D. C. Heath.

Blumstein, Philip and Schwartz, Pepper (1983) *American Couples: Money, Work, Sex*. New York: William Morrow.

Briar, Katharine (1978) *The Effect of Long-Term Unemployment on Workers and their Families*. San Francisco: R&E Research Press.

—— (1983) Layoffs and Social Work Intervention. *Urban and Social Change Review*. 16(2): 9–14.

Briar, Katharine and Ryan, Rosemary (1986) The Impact of Deinstitutionalization and Diversion on Women as Family Caregivers. *Women and Social Work*, in press.

Editorial (1985) From 59¢ to 64¢: Economic Decline closes the Wage Gap – A Little. *Dollars and Sense* 107 (June): 8–9.

Ehrenreich, Barbara (1983) *The Hearts of Men: American Dreams and the Flight from Comment.* Garden City, NY: Doubleday/Anchor Press.

England, P. (1984) Socio Economics and Explanations of Job Segregation. In Helen Remick (ed.) *Comparable Worth and Wage Discrimination.* Philadelphia: Temple University Press.

Federal Child Care Legislation (1985) *Washington Social Legislation Bulletin* (29). Washington, DC: Child Welfare League of America.

Ferber, M. A. and Birnbaum, B. (1982) The Impact of Mother's Work on the Family as an Economic System. In Sheila B. Kamerman and Cheryl D. Hayes (eds) *Families that Work: Children in a Changing World.* Washington, DC: National Academy Press.

Ferree, M. M. (1984) Sacrifice, Satisfaction, and Social Change: Employment and the Family. In Karen Brodkin Sacks and Dorothy Remy (eds) *My Troubles Are Going to Have Trouble with Me.* New Brunswick, NJ: Rutgers University Press.

Freudiger, P. and Almquist, E. M. (1983) Sources of Life Satisfaction: The Different Worlds of Black Women and White Women. In E. Matthews (ed.) *Black Working Women.* Berkeley: Center for Study of Education and Advancement of Women, University of California.

Gentry, Mary (1985) Job Search Strategies. Unpublished material, South Seattle Community College, Seattle.

Glazer, Nona Y. (1984) Paid and Unpaid Work Contradictions in American Women's Lives Today. In Kathryn M. Borman, Daisy Quarm, and Sarah Gideonse (eds) *Women in the Workplace: Effects on Families.* Norwood, NJ: Ablex Publishing.

Glazer, Nona, Majka, L., Acker, J., and Base, C. (1977) The Homemaker, the Family and Employment. *American Women Workers in a Full Employment Economy.* Washington, DC: Joint Economic Committee, Congress of the United States. 95th Congress, 1st session.

Grubb, W. Norton and Lazerson, Marvin (1984) Gender Roles and the State. In Kathryn M. Borman, Daisy Quarm, and Sarah Gideonse (eds) *Women in the Workplace: Effects on Families.* Norwood, NJ: Ablex Publishing.

Hartman, H. (1981) The Family as the Locus of Gender, Class and Political Struggle: The Example of Housework. *Signs* 6(3): 366–94.

Hunt, J. (1982) A Woman's Place in Her Union. In Jackie West (ed.) *Work, Women and the Labour Market.* New York: Routledge and Kegan Paul, pp. 154–71.

Johnson, Beverly L. and Waldman, Elizabeth (1983) Most Women Who Maintain Families Receive Poor Labor Market Returns. *Monthly Labor Review* 106(12): 30–4.

Kreps, Juanita and Clark, Robert (1975) *Sex, Age and Work.* Baltimore: Johns Hopkins University Press.

McAdoo, Harriet (1983) Stress and Support Networks of Single Black Mothers. In E. Matthews (ed.) *Black Working Women.* Berkeley, CA: Center for the Study, Education and Advancement of Women, University of California.

Malveaux, Julianne (1983) Shifts in the Occupational and Employment States of Black Women: Current Trends and Future Implications. In E. Matthews (ed). *Black Working Women.* Berkeley, CA: Center for the Study, Education and Advancement of Women, University of California.

Martinez, S. (1985) Federal Child Care Legislation. *Washington Social Legislation Bulletin* (Child Welfare League of America) 29: 7.

Milkman, R. (ed.) (1985) *Women, Work and Protest*. Boston: Routledge and Kegan Paul.

Mortimer, Jeylant and Sorensen, Glorian (1984) In Kathryn M. Borman, Daisy Quarm, and Sarah Gideonse (eds) *Women in the Workplace: Effects on Families*. Norwood, NJ: Ablex Publishing.

Mott, Frank L. (1979) Racial Differences in Female Labor-Force Participation. In Karen Wolk Feinstein (ed.) *Working Women and Families*. Beverly Hills, CA: Sage.

National Advisory Council on Economic Opportunity (1981) *The American Promise: Equal Justice and Economic Opportunity*. Washington, DC: Superintendent of Documents.

Oakley, Ann (1974) *Women's Work*. New York: Vintage Books.

Parnes, Herbert S., Shea, J. R., Roderick, R. D., Zeller, F. A., Kohen, A. I., and Associates (1970) *Years for Decision: A Longitudinal Study of the Educational and Labor Market Experience of Young Women*, vol. 1, Manpower Research Monograph 24. Washington, DC: Government Printing Office.

Pearce, Diane (1979) Women, Work and Welfare: The Feminization of Poverty. In Karen Wolk Feinstein (ed.) *Working Women and Families*. Beverly Hills, CA: Sage Publications.

Quarm, Daisy (1984) Sexual Inequality: The High Cost of Leaving Parenting to Women. In Kathryn M. Borman, Daisy Quarm, and Sarah Gideonse (eds) *Women in the Workplace: Effects on Families*. Norwood, NJ: Ablex Publishing.

Read, Sue (1982) *Sexual Harassment at Work*. Middlesex, England: Hamlyn Paperbacks.

Remick, Helen (ed.) (1984) *Comparable Worth and Wage Discrimination*. Philadelphia: Temple University Press.

Robinson, J. (1980) Housework Technology and Household Work. In S. F. Berk (ed.) *Household Labor*, Sage Yearbooks in Women's Power Studies, vol. 5. Beverly Hills, CA: Sage Publications.

Rytina, Nancy F. (1981) *Monthly Labor Review* 10(1): 49–53.

Scott, H. (1984) *Working Your Way to the Bottom*. Boston: Pandora Press.

Smith, Ralph E. (1979) The Movement of Women into the Labor Force. In Ralph E. Smith (ed.) *The Subtle Revolution: Women at Work*. Washington, DC: Urban Institute.

Snyder, Kay A. and Nowak, Thomas (1984) Job Loss and Demoralization: Do Women Fare Better than Men. *International Journal of Mental Health* 13: 92–106.

US Commission on Civil Rights (1983) *A Growing Crisis: Disadvantaged Women and their Children*. Washington, DC: US Government Printing Office.

US Department of Labor (1975) *Handbook on Women Workers*. Washington, DC: Bureau of Labor Statistics.

—— (1977) *U.S. Working Women: A Databook*. Washington, DC: Bureau of Labor Statistics.

Weissmann, Myrna, Pincus, Cynthia, Radding, Natalie, Lawrence, Roberta, and Siegal, Rise. (1973) The Educated Housewife: Mild Depression and the Search for Work. *American Journal of Orthopsychiatry* 43(4): 565–72.

Westley, L. and De Gooyer, J. (1982) *Women's Work: Undervalued, Underpaid*. Washington, DC: National Commission on Working Women.

17 Battering and abuse of women in intimate relationships

Ginny NiCarthy, Addei Fuller, and Nan Stoops

Introduction

Women throughout the world are subjected to rape, clitoridectomies, battering, forced childhood marriages, sexual slavery, and bride burning. Only in the last ten years have there been world-wide efforts to end these practices (Russell and VandeVen 1976; *Victimology* 1978). In the United States and Western Europe acts of violence by men against women, ranging from verbal harassment to murder, are now widely recognized as serious and pervasive problems. They are not isolated, 'senseless,' 'random' crimes, as newspapers often characterize them. Verbal, sexual, and physical abuse of individual women by individual men are part of a pattern which can be understood by placing them in the framework of gender power differentials, sex-role socialization, and discrimination against women.

In this chapter we will focus on battering as one form of male violence against women and offer an analysis which underscores the need for a feminist approach to social work with abused women. The response to woman abuse, like the abuse itself, will be viewed from political, social, and individual perspectives.

Until the 1970s most professionals, as well as the general public, closed their eyes to the existence of battering (Dobash and Dobash 1979). Those few who did recognize the problem tended to view female victimization by males as an individual problem and assumed that traditional treatment models would adequately meet the needs of those seeking help. Feminists were the first to call violence against women a social problem and to issue the challenge for large-scale change (Schechter 1980).

The grassroots movement against woman battering began with two women talking at the kitchen table, then two more and two more. As political analysis and feminist vision were added to personal experience, the movement grew and became mobilized in a national network of active state coalitions, local programs, and individuals working twenty-four hours a day, seven days a week to provide safety, information, and emotional support to victims of battering (Schechter 1980).

Activists quickly identified a number of fundamental issues previously ignored or misconstrued by traditional services and treatment models. They challenged mental health professionals' emphasis on family pathology or individual mental illness as the cause and justification for battering (Dobash and Dobash 1979; Prescott and Letko 1977). Instead, priority was given to essential survival needs and education which places responsibility for violence on the perpetrator and asserts a woman's right to live free from violence and the threat of it.

The basic unit of the movement is the shelter for battered women and their children, and there are now more than 800 of them around the country. In 1983 alone an estimated 91,000 women and 31,000 children found safety and support in shelters, while 264,000 women and children were turned away due to lack of space (Medley 1985). Shelter services vary, but most offer: temporary housing, food, and clothing; individual and group counseling for both women and children; a twenty-four-hour crisis line; information and referral; and assistance in obtaining financial aid, medical care, legal counsel, and low-cost housing.

An alternative form of shelter, most commonly found in rural areas, is the safe home system, in which a family takes in a battered woman and her children for a few days, while a trained advocate helps the victim obtain legal aid and plan for her future.

Community-based support groups provide information about the dynamics of battering relationships, help women evaluate the danger of their situations and, perhaps most importantly, learn that they are not alone in being abused. For many, the group serves a transitional purpose, giving each woman time and support during that uncertain period when she wrestles with the decision of whether to stay with the abusive man or to leave him.

Woman-battering cuts across all lines of race, culture, sexual preference, class, and age. Individual grassroots workers are typically committed to providing space that is psychologically and physically safe for all battered women. Yet workers are products of a biased and discriminatory society, and they do not always meet their goals. The fears of women of color and lesbians that shelters, safe homes, or groups won't be able to provide safety for them are grounded in their knowledge of pervasive racist and homophobic institutions. It is essential for all human service workers to examine closely the ways in which racism and homophobia exacerbate the issues of battering for women of color and lesbians. It is equally important for social workers in established agencies to explore the degrees to which local grassroots services provide safety for all battered women.

Social context of battering

Woman-battering – its causes, consequences, and prevention – is an expanding field, still in its infancy, so each discovery opens up many more questions. Even estimates of the extent of battering vary widely. Straus, Gelles, and Steinmetz (1981) found that two-thirds of American couples experience violent incidents at some time in their marriages and about one-third experience violence every year. They estimate an annual marital assault rate of 6,100 per 100,000, compared to the 190 aggravated assaults per 100,000 known to the police each year. Walker (1979) estimates that up to 50 per cent of all women will be battered at some time in their lives.

Battering results from a historically created gender hierarchy in which men dominate women (Schechter 1980). Historically, men have had explicit or implicit permission to batter women as a means of control, regardless of race or class. 'Men [who batter] are not necessarily consciously aware of their need to dominate, rather they are socialized to feel uncomfortable when not in control and they turn to violence as a response to their discomfort' (Schechter 1980: 219). There is still much to be learned about why pervasive institutional socialization – in this case sexism, male control of women, and the use of violence to implement control – affects the attitudes and behavior of some men much more than others. Numerous hypotheses have been offered for why certain men batter their intimate partners: sexism and the resultant unequal power between husbands and wives (Straus 1977), patriarchal institutions' designation of the wife as the 'appropriate victim' (Dobash and Dobash 1979), alcohol, drugs, jealousy, and sexual and financial problems (Roy 1982), lack of other power resources (Goode 1974), sex-role learning in the nuclear family (Stacey and Shupe 1983), and numerous others (Breines and Gordon 1983).

Regardless of the causes of battering certain characteristics stand out. Men who batter tend to minimize the seriousness of their violent behavior, to see their lives as being externally directed, to express most emotions as anger, to 'need' to control, and to be isolated, dependent, and possessive. In addition some are depressed and prone to suicide (Ganley 1981).

Women see two sides of the abusive man's behavior. Sometimes abusive partners are charming, boyishly lovable, bright, exciting, and even nurturing and protective when they are not being violent. An abusive man's emotional dependence and low self-esteem may be hidden under a facade of self-confidence or 'cool.' If his intimate partner is the only person who is aware of his feeling of vulnerability as well as his violent actions she may doubt her perceptions or blame herself for the battering, since no one else sees the man as she does, and she may not mention the contrasts.

Both men who batter and their women are acutely aware that most women are still economically dependent on men, if not for their entire support, at least for the means to live comfortably. Men who batter often maintain complete economic control, either forbidding the woman to earn money or allowing her no say over how her earnings are allocated. Since women know that child support would be unreliable at best (Rich 1984), women who have never earned a wage adequate to support a family are fearful of leaving a man who earns a good salary. Even women who have good jobs or careers know they will suffer a severe drop in income when they leave a man.

Role modeling of violence in the family has frequently been mentioned as a contributing cause of battering (Stacey and Shupe 1983). Children who observe problems solved by manipulation, intimidation, verbal abuse, or physical violence do not develop other problem-solving skills. Their experience is that anger in intimate relationships frequently leads to violence, and that the most severe violence is usually directed at the woman (Straus 1977: 43), the partner with the least amount of power. They learn that violence is an appropriate problem-solving technique, and some of them bring what they have learned as children to their adult relationships. Yet some men batter who did not grow up in abusive environments (Pagelow 1984). Dobash and Dobash (1979) found that only 12 per cent of siblings of men who batter were known to be violent to spouses. Nor is there an explanation for why female children who observed their mothers being battered do not, as adults, become battered with any more frequency than other women.

Social supports frequently exist for excusing otherwise unacceptable behavior when the perpetrator pleads innocence by reason of drunkenness. Men who batter often blame alcohol for their abusive behavior. Although alcohol lowers inhibitions and makes it easier to vent previously pent-up rage, it is not the cause of violence (Ganley 1981). It may be more accurate to say that, in some instances, the intent to be violent causes alcohol consumption, since some men admit they drink as an excuse to become violent. The violent alcoholic partner must be held responsible for his behavior and helped to realize that he has two problems: he abuses his partner and he abuses alcohol.

Therapists, researchers, and the general public move quickly from the question of how to stop the battering to asking why the woman stays, sometimes implying that it is her fault she is battered since she chooses not to leave. The many reasons for staying stem from social proscriptions as well as individual situations and values. Regardless of the reasons the woman stays with a violent man, the battering is his responsibility, not hers. Lenore Walker's theories of the cycle of violence and learned helplessness have been described extensively elsewhere (Walker 1984). Theories about women's delay in leaving include addictive love (NiCarthy 1986), childhood bonding through positive and negative reinforcement (Dutton and Painter 1982), hopefulness (Gravdal 1983) and brainwashing (NiCarthy, Merriam, and Coffman 1984) among others. Women try many solutions before they face the necessity of leaving their men, although for most women that is the only safe answer to violence (see Bowker 1983 for exceptions). Many women who appear to be staying and going back in a purposeless repetitive pattern may be gradually gaining strength and learning to use resources in preparation for the final separation. It is important for social workers to understand why each woman made the choice she did within the context of her own values and options.

Religious beliefs have caused many women to remain with abusive men. Violent men often persuade their women that scriptures say women are:

'inferior in status before husband and God, and deserving of a life of pain. . . . No sooner do women in violent relationships begin to develop an ideological suspicion that their subordination is wrong than they are told that resistance is unbiblical and unchristian [sic], . . . that Christian women are meek, and that to claim rights for themselves is to commit the sin of pride.

. . . The seeds of wifebeating lie in the subordination of females and in their subjection to male authority and control . . . supported by a [religious] belief system that makes such relationships seem natural, morally just and sacred.'
(Dobash in Thistlethwaite 1981: 308)

Those women who are fortunate encounter religious leaders who help them realize that the scriptures do not support battering.

Traditional ideas about loyalty, duty, and a woman's desire to nurture her family are often imposed on women by men who batter, reinforcing societal messages and individual values, so that a woman stays with her partner to try to 'fix' whatever is wrong with the relationship. Moral imperatives and the desire to maintain connections with loved ones even at great cost to themselves often have negative long-term consequences for women. They may also be examples of an ethical perspective peculiar to the female gender (Gilligan 1982), one that makes a significant contribution to society. It is important for social workers to let clients know that those qualities can be appreciated as strengths, even though the same qualities are also potential sources of danger.

Although the man's violence may at times be primarily expressive it is also instrumental in making the woman afraid to do anything that may result in another beating. It is often backed up by his quite believable threat to murder her if the woman leaves, so that she may feel less danger in continuing to live with him than in leaving. At least when they live together she often knows his whereabouts and his moods, rather than having to cope with the fear, when living alone, that each strange sound in the night might be her partner coming to kill her. A familiar threat may seem relatively unthreatening compared to a new unpredictable one, whether it is being stalked by an abandoned partner or creating a new independent lifestyle. The social worker needs to understand and accept the client's realistic fears as well as the exaggerated ones and to help her distinguish between them. She can then help the woman cut through her denial of current danger while helping her explore ways to maximize safety, whether the woman stays or leaves.

A man who batters often emotionally abuses or 'brainwashes' his partner in ways that are similar to the methods military personnel use to control prisoners of war: isolation, demonstrations of omnipotence, threats, monopolization of perception, enforcement of trivial demands, humiliation, imposed debility, and occasional indulgences (Russell 1982). The woman never knows what to expect of her partner, which leaves her constantly 'walking on eggshells,' trying to anticipate his 'Dr Jekyll/Mr Hyde' behavior. These reactions sometimes cause the woman to feel 'crazy' and blame herself, so that she doesn't see separation as a solution.

Women of color
While the above aspects of battering apply to all women, there are additional issues for women of color, some of which make it more difficult for them than it is for white women to leave abusive men. In many Latino, Asian, and Native American communities, physical abuse is held in greater secrecy than in white communities (Belden 1980; Warren 1982). For fear of bringing shame on the family and the community, violence is often treated as a private problem. In addition, stereotypes that characterize black women as strong, resilient, and matriarchal or Asian women as stoical reinforce those women's reluctance to acknowledge the abuse. They believe they must be resilient or stoical, which they interpret as enduring abuse and keeping it to themselves. Their determination not to speak up about the battering deprives them of family and community support.

One result of these interlocking factors is that when a woman of color seeks refuge in a shelter she not only runs the risk of being in an unfamiliar environment, where her culture and heritage may not be understood, but also of being ostracized by her community for breaking the silence. That isolation places women of color in a position of total dependence on an abusive man (Belden 1980; Ginorio and Reno 1985).

Each woman of color who has been abused responds to the violence in her life and her interactions with social workers in an individual way. In part her responses depend on how much she identifies with the values of her ethnic and cultural group, especially in regard to marriage, family, communication styles, and problem-solving methods (Zambrano 1985). With this in mind, the social worker should be aware of some important factors:

1. A woman of color may have negative feelings about reporting to police and other agencies because of a personal or cultural history of oppression by institutions (White 1985). For instance, because proportionately many more black than white men are jailed, black women may believe they are betraying the community if they call the police to arrest their men.

2. Different kinds of extended family systems available to a woman of color have the potential to be especially helpful or to hinder her in gaining control of her life. A Hispanic family may put pressure on the violent husband to change his behavior or they may present a solid front that the woman must obey regardless of the treatment accorded her by her man.

3. Separation from the violent partner may ultimately mean separation from the extended family, church, or community. In some cities the segregation of racial groups into certain neighbourhoods means that to avoid the man who batters the woman must avoid the services, churches, and community centers he frequents, which are usually the same places her extended family goes to. In a highly segregated city, they may be the only places the woman feels comfortable.

Professionals should be prepared to consult with or refer to specialized agencies or individuals in the specific ethnic community that will meet the cultural needs of women of color, as well as understand the dynamics of battering and safety issues.

Lesbians

Some lesbians are battered by their partners (Lobel 1986, Paisley and Krulewitz 1983). This phenomenon cannot be explained by theories of gender hierarchy and social permission, and the explanation of this dynamic is not yet clear. Like their heterosexual counterparts, battered lesbians are sometimes uncertain who should be held accountable for the violence. Their responses to battering are sometimes ambivalent because of denial of the abuse, fear of greater violence, and loyalty to the partner. There may be an additional burden of guilt caused by the belief that women, especially feminists or especially lesbians, are different from men and should exercise power and control through non-violent means.

In addition to physical safety, psychological safety is a primary concern for battered lesbians. In acknowledging the battering, a lesbian will probably have to admit her sexual preference which necessitates a dual 'coming out' to family, friends, or counselor, who may blame or reject her either for the battering or for being a lesbian. Fear of that rejection keeps many lesbians trapped in abusive relationships.

Current services for lesbian victims of battering are incomplete at best, nonexistent at worst. But as the awareness of lesbian battering grows, so do the services. The social worker should be aware of the diversity of women who seek help in escaping from battering, and until a woman has identified her abuser in some specific way should not assume the abuser is male. Nor should it be assumed that shelters and other social services do, or do not, address the needs of lesbians. Workers will need to familiarize themselves on a periodic basis with lesbian organizations, domestic violence agencies and individuals who can provide sensitive and adequate assistance.

The role of the social worker

Human service workers

A sensitive social worker is attuned to a number of cues that may point to abuse. Among many physical signs, chronic illness or injury stand out (Stark, Flitcraft, and Frazier 1981). A client who has been abused may relate to the social worker in a way that seems defensive, submissive, or fearful. She may seem depressed, hopeless, helpless, or confused. Many workers believe that most women cannot sustain battering without a severe lowering of self-esteem, though Walker's recent (1984) research has called that judgment into question. None of these traits are causes of abuse, but they may be results of abuse, and should be viewed as red flags for further inquiry.

When the worker recognizes probable signs of abuse it is essential that she confront the woman with what she sees or suspects. Many women want to be confronted, to be 'found out,' but not until they trust the worker, so timing is of great importance. The worker must develop sensitivity to the degree of trust her client has for her and her agency. She should ask the client about her fears of confiding in an agency representative and openly discuss whether these fears are based on outmoded practices, current policy, or other experiences.

Blanket assurances that records are completely confidential should not be made without careful thought. Because violent men often harass their ex-spouses through litigation, a client should be informed that if she becomes involved in divorce or child custody conflicts, records may be subpoenaed. The worker and client should discuss what information can safely go into case notes, always erring on the conservative side and keeping in mind that what is obviously fair is not necessarily what will happen in court. The worker should avoid assuring the client that the people to whom she is referred will be understanding and not victim-blaming, unless the worker has specific information about the attitudes of such people. In some communities services for abused women are only available from victim-blaming service providers. The worker can meet the client's skepticism about the agencies or other workers with honest, realistic assessments, and suggestions for how the client can maintain her self-respect even if she must deal with professionals who don't respect her.

Even after a woman has admitted to being abused, she frequently minimizes the physical damage her partner has done to her. She is especially likely to overlook the impact of emotional abuse on herself and children in the household. The worker can play a crucial role in helping the woman appraise her situation realistically. She can ask the client to make one list of dangerous and humiliating things her partner has done to her, and another of the good times and his lovable traits. The two lists will provide a balanced perspective and help the woman realize that she tends to deny the danger when things are going well, in the 'honeymoon phase,' and to forget, during and immediately after the 'acute battering phase,' that there are reasons she stays with her partner (Walker 1979). Many women believe they are alone in being victimized by the men who say they love them. The social worker raises their awareness of women's abuse by men as a historical commonplace (Davidson 1977; Dobash and Dobash 1979) and cross-cultural phenomenon (Gelles and Cornell 1983; Russell and VandeVen 1976). This enables the client to see her situation not as an individual problem for which she alone is responsible, but as a social and political problem which, however, is losing institutional supports.

In order to discuss fruitfully whether to report violence to police and follow through with prosecution, the worker should be familiar with state and local laws and services. Some states now have laws that require the arrest of violent family members, whereas in others there are many loopholes for violent partners to escape the attention of the law. Even where laws are strict, in specific localities police may be lax in implementing them or may even use them in ways that are injurious to the women who are battered. In some jurisdictions men convicted of battering may get stiff sentences, whereas in others they may be let off with a warning or sentenced to a group for men who batter. Although she cannot give guarantees, the worker, in consultation with legal workers who are expert on the latest laws and their local implementation, should be able to provide information about the probable consequences should the woman decide to report battering to the police. In addition, she should be familiar with non-sexist, non-victim-blaming counseling, legal, and housing resources in the community.

A major role for the worker is to assist the client in deciding whether to stay with or leave the partner. If the client's choice is to leave permanently, the worker helps her to make the safest possible plan, keeping in mind that she will be in most serious danger right after she leaves (Walker 1979). She should be urged to stay in a shelter or other safe and secret place until her partner has been served with papers or arraigned in court, and she has reason to know he has calmed down. Even then, as many safety measures as possible should be implemented (NiCarthy 1986).

Couples counseling can be threatening for the woman because she may never feel free to speak the truth in the presence of her partner. Hence, the problem of her actual danger may easily become obscured by a therapist's emphasis on communication or 'mutual responsibility' for interactions between the couple. Even if the woman seems to have serious problems or is extremely difficult to communicate with, the abusive partner's anger management must be addressed first (Ganley 1981). He must take responsibility for being out of control, regardless of the woman's behavior. (If the woman is also violent, then she, of course, must take responsibility for controlling her behavior.)

Group sessions for men who batter are the treatment of first choice. They provide skills training in anger management, assertiveness, and relaxation and also facilitate a re-assessment of sex roles in the relationship. The group can also help the man to recognize his responsibility for his violence. Because men who batter tend to be emotionally isolated, the group also serves an important support function (Ganley 1981).

An increasing number of professional social workers in traditional agencies have begun leading groups for women who are battered. Groups are invaluable for those women who do not want or need shelter. The groups are most helpful when seen as 'mutual support' groups or 'problem-solving' groups, rather than as 'therapy groups' (NiCarthy, Merriam and Coffman 1984). While most such groups do not differentiate between past and current battering, 'second phase' groups are useful for women who have been separated for a period of weeks or months; they provide support and help in solving new problems for women who are striking out on their own for the first time or for the first time in many years. Other kinds of groups are designed to assist women with common characteristics. Some are based on age, ethnicity, or other characteristics that lend themselves to a double aspect of support, so that participants feel secure in being with people who in some important respects are like them (NiCarthy, Merriam, and Coffman 1984).

A social worker who wants to start a community group is well advised to begin by contacting grassroots battered women's organizations and to work with them in planning the group location, format, and a process for mutual referrals.

Community organizers
Within the feminist movement against battering much work has been done to change systems. Increased awareness of the role of institutions in fostering abuse was the first step. It has taken place on a national and local scale for ten years, and continues in additional cities and towns as community organizers learn about both the dimensions of the problem and the responses of their local institutions. How well does each institution respond to the needs of women who have been battered? What are the obstacles to better service? A social worker should look for the answers to those questions by surveying clients and former clients as well as staff and liaison agencies. Those who work directly with abused women will have the most information about their clients' interactions with all systems, so interviews with shelter and safe home workers are essential.

If the grassroots movement against domestic violence is to be completely effective in achieving its goals, it must have co-operation from the legal and medical systems to which battered women frequently turn for help. All levels of the criminal justice system, including legal statuses and procedures, are slowly

becoming more adequate in protecting women who are battered and in responding to battering as a crime. However, in many communities law enforcement
officials continue punitive treatment of victims, exacerbating their problems
rather than relieving them. Social workers who want to co-operate with police or
prosecutors in such localities will need to start communicating with them at a
basic level in order to reach agreements about definitions of battering and about
who is to be held responsible for it before addressing action plans.

Medical treatment for the abused victim varies greatly from hospital to hospital, but, increasingly, personnel are learning to use a special protocol to identify
and treat victims of battering (Stark, Flitcraft, and Frazier 1981). Medical social
workers can lead the way in examining more than physical injury and in insti-
tuting advocacy and referrals to shelters, safe homes, and crisis lines, as normal
standards of care.

Researchers

Early researchers reported data that implicitly or explicitly blamed the victim
(Gelles 1977; Lion 1977). In recent years non-sexist and feminist researchers
have asked different questions and have re-evaluated previous answers. The
quantitative work of Straus, Gelles, and Steinmetz (1981) has made the pervasiveness of the problem clear. Dobash and Dobash have emphasized the importance of the historical and patriarchal context of specific violent acts (1979).
Lenore Walker's extended interviews have enabled her to develop theories of the
cycle of violence and learned helplessness (Walker 1984).

The research of sociologists and psychologists has contributed greatly to our
understanding of battering, but it should be emphasized that the state of knowledge is embryonic. Walker (1984) found some of her hypotheses rejected, and
Straus (1977) uncovered hard-to-explain data. Researchers asking why a battered
woman stays with her abuser have found multiple answers. Little research has
focused on why she leaves or how she is able to stay away, nor on how to change
or counter social and economic power differentials that provide the context in
which men batter women. Nor has much research been addressed to the question of why a man batters the woman he 'loves' and how he can be stopped. So
far, the tentative answers to all questions about battering are far from complete
and often contradictory (Breines and Gordon 1983). It is important that we
remain open to the contributions of feminist and non-sexist research.

Curriculum issues

In training social work students for work with battered women role-plays are
particularly useful learning tools. For instance, students may be asked to use a
real situation from their lives that has been troublesome but not traumatizing, in
which they felt taken advantage of and helpless. One may play a client who is so
distraught that she is not even interested at the moment in solving her problem

or is too depressed to think clearly about it. The other may play an empathic social worker, whose initial task is to distinguish between when the client wants just emotional support and when she wants information or problem-solving. The instructor should expect that more than one student will talk about her own experience of being battered either to the instructor or to the whole class. Memories of their own abuse will be recalled by many students as they participate in role-plays or view films, so special sensitivity and acceptance are important. Films are often available from state shelter networks (La Beau 1982). Recommendations can be found through shelters and safe homes. Speakers from the various branches of the movement will enrich and broaden students' understanding of the problem. Students may find it particularly valuable to do volunteer field work in shelters and other organizations that provide services for battered women or to work toward social change in law or other systems.

The instructor and students should keep in mind throughout the course that the individual problems of each woman who is battered and each man who batters cannot be divorced from the political reality of a sexist society. Before the development of feminist therapy and the movement against woman-battering most police, social workers, medical personnel, and clergy unwittingly encouraged women's silence about their victimization and tended to react punitively ('What did you do to provoke him?') when abused women dared to mention what had been done to them. Thus agency personnel more often exacerbated the problem than eased it. Fortunately, much progress has been made in the past ten years, yet many institutional and individual changes must still be addressed.

Social workers are in a position to help individual women gain realistic perspectives on their dangerous partners and reduce their fear of the unknown and of becoming independent. They also can give practical assistance to each woman who decides to make constructive changes in her life. Because most women who are battered are isolated, the best way to assist them is through groups; and because men who batter also tend to be isolated the most effective way for them to change is through the support and confrontation of a group of men with similar problems.

Whatever treatment the worker chooses will be most successful if she keeps in mind the social context and helps the woman who has been battered see herself as one of many survivors of a pervasive social problem in the process of change.

References

Belden, L. (1980) Why Women Do Not Report Sexual Assault: Part II. *Aegis: Magazine on Ending Violence against Women*, Winter/Spring: 5–11.

Bowker, L. (1983) *Beating Wife-Beating*. Lexington, MA: Lexington Books (Heath).

Breines, W. and Gordon, L. (1983) The New Scholarship on Family Violence. *Signs* 8(3): 490–531.

Davidson, T. (1977) An Historical Perspective. In M. Roy (ed.) *Battered Women*. New York: Van Nostrand Reinhold.

Dobash, R. E. and Dobash, R. (1979) *Violence Against Wives: A Case Against the Patriarchy*. New York: Free Press (Macmillan).

Dutton, D. and Painter, S. (1982) Traumatic Bonding: The Development of Emotional Attachments in Battered Women and Other Relationships in Intermittent Abuse. *Victimology: An International Journal* 6(1–4): 139–55.

Ganley, A. (1981) *Court-Mandated Counseling for Men Who Batter: a Three-Day Workshop For Mental Health Professionals*. Center For Women Policy Studies, 2,000 'P' Street NW, Suite 508, Washington DC 20036.

Gelles, R. (1977) No Place To Go: The Social Dynamics of Marital Violence. In M. Roy (ed.) *Battered Women*. New York: Van Nostrand Reinhold.

Gelles, R. and Cornell, C. (eds) (1983) *International Perspectives on Family Violence*. Lexington, MA: Lexington Books.

Giles-Sims, J. (1983) *Wife-battering: a Systems Theory Approach*. New York: Guilford Press.

Gilligan, C. (1982) *In a Different Voice*. Cambridge, MA: Harvard University Press.

Ginorio, A. and Reno, J. (1985) Violence in the Lives of Latina Women. *Working Together* 5(3): 6–8.

Goode, W. (1974) Force and Violence in the Family. In Suzanne Steinmetz and Murray Straus (eds) *Violence in the Family*. New York: Harper and Row.

Gravdal, B. (1983) Battered Women: Learned Helplessness or Learned Hopefulness in Abusive Relationships. Paper delivered at Association of Women in Psychology (AWP) Conference, Seattle, Washington.

La Beau, C. (1982) *No Longer Alone*. MTI Teleprogram. Deerfield, IL: Simon and Schuster Communications.

Lion, J. (1977) Clinical Aspects of Battering. In M. Roy, (ed.) *Battered Women*. New York: Van Nostrand Reinhold.

Lobel, K. (ed.) (1986) *Naming the Violence: Speaking Out About Lesbian Battering*. Seattle, WA: Seal Press.

Medley, Donna (1985) Oral report to the National Coalition Against Domestic Violence Steering Committee, May, Washington, DC.

NiCarthy, G. (1986) *Getting Free: a Handbook for Women in Abusive Relationships*. Seattle, WA: Seal Press.

NiCarthy, G., Merriam, K. and Coffman, S. (1984) *Talking It Out: A Guide to Groups for Abused Women*. Seattle, WA: Seal Press.

Pagelow, M. D. (1984) *Family Violence*. New York: Praeger.

Paisley, C. and Krulewitz, J. (1983) Same-Sex Assault: Sexual and Non-Sexual Violence within Lesbian Relationships. Paper presented at the Association for Women in Psychology Conference, Seattle, WA, 5 March.

Prescott, S. and Letko, C. (1977) Battered Women: A Social Psychological Perspective. In M. Roy (ed.) *Battered Women*. New York: Van Nostrand Reinhold.

Rich, S. (1984) Enforcing Fathers' Rights. *Washington Post Weekly*, 19 March.

Roy, M. (ed.) (1977) *Battered Women*. New York: Van Nostrand Reinhold.

—— (1982) *The Abusive Partner: An Analysis of Domestic Battering*. New York: Van Nostrand Reinhold.

Russell, D. (1982) *Rape in Marriage*. New York: Macmillan.

Russell, D. and VandeVen, N. (1976) *Crimes Against Women: The Proceedings of the International Tribunal*. Millbrae, CA: La Femme.

Schechter, S. (1980) *Women and Male Violence*. Boston: South End Press.

Stacey, W. W. and Shupe, A. (1983) *The Family Secret*. Boston: Beacon Press.

Stark, E., Flitcraft, A., and Frazier, W. (1981) *Wife Abuse in the Medical Setting*. Rockville, MD: National Clearing House on Domestic Violence.

Straus, M. (1977) A Sociological Perspective on the Prevention and Treatment of Wifebeating. In M. Roy (ed.) *Battered Women*. New York: Van Nostrand Reinhold.

Straus, M., Gelles, R., and Steinmetz, S. (1981) *Behind Closed Doors: Violence in the American Family*. Garden City, NY: Anchor Press/Doubleday.

Thistlethwaite, S. (1981) Battered Women and the Bible: from Subjection to Liberation. *Christianity and Crisis* 41(8): 308, 311.

Victimology: An International Journal (1977–78) Issue on spouse abuse, 2 (3–4).

Walker, L. E. (1979) *The Battered Woman*. New York: Harper and Row.

—— (1984) *The Battered Woman Syndrome*. New York: Springer.

Warren, B. (1982) Issues Relating to American Indian Women. News. *Newsletter of the Minnesota Coalition for Battered Women* 2(4): 1–2.

White, E. (1985) *Chain, Chain, Change for Black Women Dealing with Physical and Emotional Abuse*. Seattle, WA: Seal Press.

Zambrano, M. (1985) *Mejor Sola Que Mal Accompanada: For the Latina in an Abusive Relationship*. Seattle, WA: Seal Press.

PART IV
Specialization by population group

18 Overview

Dianne S. Burden

This section on specialization by population group focuses on issues for women across the life-cycle. Developmental theories which address the life-cycle frequently are based on practice wisdom and empirical data about white, middle-class males. Female differences by comparison may be perceived as deviations from the 'norm.' The chapters in this section identify particular issues of concern to women at various stages in the life-cycle. They then discuss the implications of issues and concerns particular to female life stages for both social work practice and policy. A theme recurring in all three chapters is the invisibility of women's particular concerns. Because women have been studied in a secondary capacity relative to the primary male norm, and because women tend to be lower-income and lower-status and to provide unpaid caretaking functions, their particular life stage issues have not received adequate attention.

Diane de Anda and Ruth Zambrana in their chapter on 'Adolescent Development: A Re-examination of the Female Experience' assert, for example, that theories of adolescent development pay inadequate attention to gender, culture, social class, and sexual orientation issues. The chapter identifies gender biases within the developmental literature and points out that female differences from male norms are typically seen as 'deviant' and as hindering the progress of development. De Anda and Zambrana then explore areas of need specific to female adolescents which require more in-depth attention. The first area discussed is adolescent sexuality, particularly the lesbian adolescent and teenage pregnancy and parenthood. Another area which has received inadequate attention is health risks in adolescence, namely increased rates, particularly among females, of attempted suicide, depression, and substance abuse. Violence against young adolescent women is another area of the female development experience that has not received enough attention. Young women are at high risk for battery, rape, and incest. The pressure to be attractive and have a successful social life leaves young women particularly vulnerable to date rape. The risk of violence has major implications for the health and psychological development of adolescent women and as such needs to receive major attention in social work education.

Dianne Burden in her chapter on 'Women in the New Family' focuses on the changing structure of the American family in the last twenty-five years. This change has witnessed an influx of women into the workforce, an increase in dual-earner families and single-parent families, and major shifts of roles of men and women within the family and the workplace. It has also witnessed an increase in non-traditional, alternative family structures including cohabiting couples, both homosexual and heterosexual, and single persons living alone. Burden discusses the major factors related to the changing roles of women, including economic need, increased education, and changing expectations. She then identifies changes in marriage and kinship patterns which are major contributing factors to the new family. These include a high divorce rate, deferment of marriage, decreased birthrate, serial monogamy, decreased household size, and a trend toward independent living. These changing patterns have led to the near disappearance of the traditional family form of father at work and mother at home with young children. The changes have had serious repercussions for women as they are now providing a major share of the income-producing role in dual-earner and single-parent families, but continue to take care of traditional family responsibilities as well. Important practice and policy implications emerge as to who will care for children in a society where the great majority of adults are in the workplace. Burden examines the growing overlap between work and family and the policy conflict which results between traditional and non-traditional family structures.

Nancy Hooyman's chapter on 'Older Women and Social Work Curricula' posits that older women have been invisible in gerontological research and practice as well as in the women's movement. Aging is just now emerging as a feminist issue because old people are the fastest growing segment of the population, and they are primarily female. The chapter reviews older women's economic, health, and social statuses. It focuses on how the caregiving cycle for women shapes many of the problems they face in old age. In discussing the precarious economic situation of older women, Hooyman states that the lower-paid status of women throughout their work life follows them into retirement. Women's unpaid caregiving role has a major impact on career patterns due to the discontinuities it causes in women's work histories. Women are penalized at retirement for the time they take throughout their lives to care for others. Women's work and living patterns in turn put them at higher risk for health problems in old age because of reduced access to private health insurance and to high-quality medical care. Their lower socioeconomic status leads to a higher incidence of chronic diseases and disabilities as they get older. At the same time, low-income status leads to reliance on Medicaid and to the stigma and service problems associated with that program. Finally Hooyman addresses the social status of older women and in particular the greater probability that they will live alone and receive poor nutrition. Poor nutrition may in turn be related to depression, disorientation, and reduced capacity to respond to stress and be immune to disease. After a lifetime of caring for others, women may end up isolated and alone. The social isolation of older women may be changing, however, as women join together in support groups and use their considerable skills at forming and sustaining friendships with other women.

The chapters in this section focus on women's roles throughout the life-cycle and the impact these roles have on women's development. While women have traditionally been the caregivers of society, they are now assuming a major share of producing incomes as well. The result has been inequity for women in the new family where they are expected to fulfill both roles. The result has also been inequity for women in old age where their lifetime caregiving role has not been adequately rewarded. Issues for women specific to their life-cycles have received inadequate attention in both policy and practice because of women's secondary status in the power structure. This inattention has resulted in hidden problem areas for women at all stages of life, and it is these areas which are addressed in this section.

19 Adolescent development: a re-examination of the female experience

Diane de Anda and Ruth E. Zambrana

Theories of adolescent development suffer from 'conceptual homogenization;' that is, most developmental formulations present a single model or set of characteristics as applicable across adolescent populations irrespective of differences in gender, culture, social class, and sexual orientation. This narrow focus has resulted in a biased appraisal of these diverse adolescent populations. Most often, individuals not fitting within the 'norms' established with white, heterosexual, middle-class male samples have been viewed as deficient in various areas of development or as exhibiting pathology.

This chapter will focus on the female adolescent with reference to: (a) biases within the developmental literature, (b) exploration of particular areas of need, and (c) suggestions for appropriate areas of focus with regard to curricula, policy, practice, and research.

Biases in theories of adolescent development

Most theories of adolescent development provide an overall schema regarding psychosocial development with some indication that minor gender differences may occur in specific areas. In most cases, the points at which female development diverges from the general (i.e. male) model are viewed as 'deviant' and as hindering the progress of development.

According to psychosexual theories (Blos 1941, 1979; A. Freud 1948; S. Freud 1924), the primary developmental tasks of adolescence involve resolution of the Oedipal and pre-Oedipal conflicts of the earlier stages of infantile sexuality. With the physiological changes of puberty, the adolescent is viewed as entering the genital stage which rekindles the psychological struggle for dominance between the ego and the id. 'The painfully achieved psychic balance of latency is upset' (A. Freud 1948: 158) as the ego is buffeted by the instinctual impulses and demands of the id (now notably increased in quantity) and the restrictions of the superego. Successful resolution of these conflicts is achieved via a second individuation process, the development of ego continuity, and the achievement of a definite sexual identity (Blos 1941, 1979). However, according to this model, the female adolescent rarely achieves the psychosexual maturity of her male counterpart. Females are described as less individuated than males due to the maintenance of strong pre-Oedipal ties to the mother and a late and 'incompletely' resolved Oedipal complex (Blos 1941, 1979; S. Freud 1924).

Blos (1979) views regression as psychologically healthy and growth-producing during adolescence ('normative regression'). However, he views female development as more complex and prolonged than that of males because this 'regressive pull to the oedipal mother' (Blos 1979: 129) is more threatening to the female. This pull towards a same-sex love object is viewed as in conflict with the primary task of adolescence, the development of non-incestuous heterosexual love objects.

The basic underlying sex bias lies in the use of a male model as the criterion for psychosexual development. As Chodorow (1974, 1978) and Gilligan (1979) point out, separation and individuation from the primary (generally female) caretaker are necessary prerequisites for the development of male gender identity. However, female gender identity progresses as a result of identification with and attachment to the same-sex primary caretaker (the pre-Oedipal mother). The process, in fact, is posited to be an exact reversal of that hypothesized by Blos. Moreover, in Blos's conceptualization, as in so many traditionalist prescriptive discussions of women, the female adolescent is in a double-bind, no-win situation – moving away from progressive development toward heterosexuality if she engages in normative regression and demonstrating 'pathology' if she engages in heterosexual behavior, as this 'pseudoheterosexuality' is considered to be a defense against the pull toward the pre-Oedipal mother. While sexual activity is seen by this writer as the focus of female 'pathology,' no such value is placed on the sexual behavior of adolescent males.

These conceptualizations are problematic because female adolescent adjustment is judged according to inappropriately generalized male criteria. As a result, female adolescents are viewed as stymied in their development, and thus the 'woman-child' myth is perpetuated. Especially vulnerable is the gay female adolescent whose level of development is viewed as immature and pathological since the establishment of psychosexual identity based upon attachment to heterosexual love objects will never be completed.

Psychosocial theorists, most notably Erik Erikson (1963, 1968), reflect similar biases. While Erikson indicates that his formulations are based upon the adolescent male experience, he presents his model as characteristic of the adolescent experience as a whole. Based upon psychosexual formulations, Erikson's concept of identity implies the concept of individuation. Identity formation is given as the major task of adolescence and identity achievement as the hallmark of maturity and a prerequisite for the development of true intimacy. However, both the salience and the sequence of Erikson's model have been questioned with regard to adolescent female development. It has been hypothesized that female identity may be promoted by attachment rather than by separation and that the developmental sequence may be opposite for males and females (Gilligan 1979). The normative female developmental sequence may entail the development of intimacy prior to or jointly with the establishment of identity. In other words, for females, identity and intimacy or identity and attachment may not be incompatible experiences.

Marcia (1980) and Podd (1972) indicate that substantial empirical data exist regarding gender differences in personality characteristics and psychological adjustment. While identity achievement status and moratorium ('identity crisis') status are consistently associated with positive characteristics (e.g. high self-esteem) for males, identity achievement status and foreclosure (that is, parent-determined) status are associated with positive characteristics (and moratorium with negative characteristics) for females. Marcia (1980) hypothesizes that stability in one's identity status may be more significant for females than males. However, because foreclosure status was associated with positive outcomes for females, the Eriksonian view that healthy adult maturity must be preceded by a period of identity crisis can be seriously questioned at least in regard to female development. There may be a significant relationship between attachment and foreclosure status for the female adolescent. Furthermore, for the female adolescent foreclosure may not be a simple acceptance of one's parents' identity preferences but may involve a more subtle reappraisal of parental values and expectations.

The Eriksonian model may also have little applicability to ethnic minority and lower socioeconomic status adolescents, who may not have the luxury of a moratorium. Limited occupational opportunities do not allow these populations to expend much time and energy in speculation as to their occupational identity. While ideological issues may still be addressed, the range of potential experiences open to these groups is more limited than those available to the more affluent. Finally, in a homophobic society, what is perceived as a negative identity may actually be a progressive step towards resolving identity issues for the gay adolescent female.

Piagetian formulations of cognitive development also exhibit some elements of gender and sociocultural bias. For example, the movement from concrete to formal operations is claimed to occur more frequently and earlier among males than females and in white middle-class samples. However, two basic problems lie at the core of these assertions: (a) methodological problems in the measurement of formal operations and (b) the consideration of environmental context.

Piaget (1972) himself, in one of his later publications, indicated that there were serious methodological limitations to the procedures used to determine the exist- ence of formal operations. Piaget (1972), therefore, qualified his own findings, indicating that it is highly likely that the majority of individuals reach formal operations during adolescence but that these cognitive structures and modes of functioning are exhibited primarily in areas specific to the person's experience and occupational expertise: 'they reach this stage in different areas according to their aptitudes and their professional specializations' (p. 10). This leaves open for investigation the manifestations of hypothetico-deductive thinking within different ethnic-cultural and social class contexts. Areas requiring abstraction and projection of alternatives and possibilities may vary greatly given the cultural milieu and social realities of different populations. Elkind (1975) strongly criticizes the sociocultural and class bias of most cognitive research as 'meaningless when . . . interpreted independently of the sociocultural context in which they [the data] are obtained' (p. 59).

Given that female socialization experiences are different from those of males, areas in which formal operations might be employed might also differ to some extent. Elkind (1975) challenges those studies which claim that fewer females than males demonstrate formal operations. He claims that the testing procedures and context are related more to the interests and experiences of males than females and, therefore, demonstrate 'differential application of mental abilities and not . . . the absence of formal operational thinking' in females (p. 52).

Inasmuch as Kohlberg's (1969) theory of moral development is based upon Piagetian concepts of cognitive development, the same types of biases are also reflected in his approach. For example, the development of post-conventional morality is seen as dependent upon the development of formal operations. Moreover, Kohlberg's stage formulation automatically guarantees that a large proportion of the female population will be classified as being at a 'lower' stage of moral development than males; female socialization is focused more strongly on considering the interpersonal needs of others in making decisions and choices, and within Kohlberg's model, this perspective relegates women to a 'conventional' level of development. Yet taking the perspective of others into account in making a moral decision seems closer to recognizing the relative nature of indi- vidual values in relation to universal principles (a post-conventional level) than to the law and order perspective to which it is ascribed by Kohlberg.

According to Gilligan (1982), moral issues and dilemmas are conceptualized by women as 'problem[s] of care and responsibility in relationships rather than as one[s] of rights and rules' (p. 73). Therefore, women's moral development is more appropriately evaluated in terms of 'the integration of rights and responsi- bilities [that] takes place through an understanding of the psychological logic of relationships' (p. 100).

In Hoffman's (1980) conceptualization, empathy serves as the basis for moral development. While still in its formative stages, this theory may offer more promise for understanding female moral development because it incorporates issues of attachment and intimacy which are particularly salient for women.

Social learning theory conceptualizations of development may be less vulnerable to class, culture, and gender bias. The main reason for this reduced bias is the basic principle of reciprocal determinism which holds that all behavior is the result of an interaction between the individual and the (social and object) environment which mutually determine and shape one another. In this way all behavior is viewed in its sociocultural context. For females this approach reflects gender-specific experiences and responses within the sociocultural environment. One's behavior is explained as the outcome of a complex of reinforcing and punishing consequences, vicarious learning via models, rule-learning, and ultimately self-regulated responses. The theory explains idiosyncratic as well as culturally specific behavior within specific contexts and socialization experiences. However, the direct application of these heurestic principles is not always clear-cut. For example, what are the various reinforcement contingencies and models available for female versus male adolescents, and for different ethnic and class populations? In terms of moral development, social learning principles allow for explanations of the great diversity in behavior under different circumstances. However, one still needs to determine whether rules, reinforcement contingencies, or models are the most salient factors in moral development of different individuals or cultural groups.

The present empirical literature does not offer solutions to the issues discussed above. With the exception of Douvan and Adelson's (1966) sample of female adolescents during the 1960s, most studies are based upon white, middle-class, male samples. Presently, the theoretical formulations available can serve primarily as guides to areas which must be explored but do not provide a basis for explaining the dynamics of adolescent development in a context appropriate to the individual's gender, class, sociocultural experience, and sexual orientation.

Selected issues in adolescent development

Theoretical formulations are of particular importance in their application to adolescent populations whose developmental progress is significantly thwarted by idiosyncratic and environmental factors. There are a number of specific adolescent issues which have been identified in the last decade as social dilemmas, such as adolescent sexuality, health risks in adolescence, and violence. These authors have selected a number of these issues which most differentially impact adolescents on the basis of gender, ethnicity, class and social orientation.

Adolescent sexuality

The gay adolescent Given the degree of homophobia and discrimination against homosexuals in American society, the establishment of a positive homosexual self-image and interpersonal life is made particularly stressful and problematic for the lesbian adolescent. With few acceptable role models available, she may often feel alienated from the rest of her peers. As described by a client: 'You can be in conflict with yourself and in harmony with the world, or in harmony with yourself and in conflict with the world' (Lewis 1984). This conflict is further complicated by the fact that neither socialization processes nor an adequate vocabulary exist to facilitate dealing with the homoerotic and emotional feelings the gay adolescent is beginning to experience. Most often the development of one's identity must be accomplished simultaneously with identity management (remaining 'in the closet'), particularly with respect to one's family, resulting in a sense of loneliness and isolation (Martin 1982; Steinhorn 1979). This places the gay adolescent at particular risk for depression and suicide. A director of a gay and lesbian center in Los Angeles estimates that as many as 50 per cent of the runaways ('throwaways') daily entering the city are gay youth (Ogle 1985).

Literature regarding the lesbian adolescent experience is practically non-existent. If the needs of this population are to be met, concerted efforts need to be expended to move beyond clinical research models and to design research which would acquire data regarding the gay adolescent experience itself. Such an effort will ultimately provide more accurate guidance for helping professionals who deal with gay adolescent clients. In the meantime supportive efforts in services and education need to be directed toward this population at both the practice and policy levels.

Adolescent pregnancy and parenthood Increased concern during the last decade about adolescent sexuality and fertility stems both from the large number of teenage pregnancies and from the resultant risks and losses for this population. Superimposing pregnancy upon adolescence complicates a period already characterized by conflict. The need to adjust to the process of pregnancy and the demands of parenthood certainly closes the door on childhood, may block or distort the developmental tasks of adolescence, and produce obstacles in the negotiation of adulthood.

Over the past twenty years a national decline in fertility levels has characterized a broad range of social groups within the United States, including women from all socioeconomic levels, racial/ethnic groups, and religious backgrounds (Gibson 1976; Rindfuss and Sweet 1978). In contrast to this pattern, however, is the great increase in the number of pregnancies and births among unmarried adolescent girls. The percentage of teenage pregnancies rose from 8.5 per cent of 15–19-year-olds in 1971 to 16.2 per cent in 1979. In their study of sexually active teenage girls, Zelnik and Kantner (1979) found that from 1971 to 1976 there had been an increase of 50 per cent in those who never used contraceptives. In the 1980s the percentage of illegitimate births within the adolescent population has risen 60 per cent since 1965 and 300 per cent since 1942 (Bolton 1982; Zelnik and Kantner, 1980).

Teenage pregnancy and child-bearing have come to be viewed as significant problems with negative psychological, social, medical, educational, and economic impacts (Bacon 1974; Bolton 1982; Braen and Forbush 1975; Furstenberg 1976; Lewis, Klerman, and Currie 1977; Osofsky and Osofsky 1978). Adolescent pregnancy and parenthood have been found to carry a high risk of adverse consequences, both short- and long-term, for mother, child, and family, leading Furstenberg (1976) to label it a 'syndrome of defeat.' Pregnant adolescents have been found to be obstetrically at risk, with maternal and infant mortality higher amont teenage mothers than among other groups. Non-fatal health complications have been found to be more common than among the general population (Guttmacher Institute 1981; Osofsky 1968). Adolescent mothers are less likely to finish high school than other adolescents, and this fact combined with the lack of child care severely limits occupational opportunities (Guttmacher Institute 1981).

With few exceptions, empirical research on adolescent sexuality and pregnancy have studied black and white populations. Black adolescents were found to be more likely than white adolescents to have non-marital coitus without use of contraception, to become pregnant, and to keep their infants (Zelnik, Kantner, and Ford 1981). The early literature relied on explanations based only on race and socioeconomic background. Not until the late 1970s did research attention begin to focus extensively on the nature of the problem, i.e. socioeconomic antecedents, consequences, and intervention strategies. However, with the exception of recent research by Becerra and de Anda (1984), concern with adolescent sexual and reproductive behavior has almost totally neglected the large Latino population.

Latinos are one of the fastest-growing ethnic groups in the United States and sources indicate that they will become the largest racial/ethnic minority group in the country during the first decade of the twenty-first century (Andrade 1983). Almost half of the Mexican Americans who make up 60 per cent of the Latino population are under twenty years of age (US Bureau of the Census 1981). For many years Latinas have had the highest fertility rate of any group identified in census data (Ventura and Heuser 1981). Recent statistics show that a relatively large proportion, nearly one in five, of these births are to teenagers (Ventura 1982). Although interest in and use of contraception by Latinas have been reported by some studies to be high, unmarried Latina adolescents have far lower rates of contraceptive use than similar adolescents from other ethnic groups (Rochat 1981; Stein 1985; USDHEW 1979).

Previous research on adolescent sexuality and pregnancy has focused primarily on areas of risk and blocked opportunity. This research, while informative, has principally focused on the adolescent's liabilities. Insufficient attention, on the other hand, has been given to determining factors which might serve as strengths in the development of responsible sexuality (Becerra and de Anda 1984; de Anda and Becerra 1984; de Anda 1985).

In response to the high levels of adolescent pregnancy and increasing sexual activity, a few investigators have recently begun to focus on the sources, quality, and effectiveness of the preparation adolescents receive from the agencies typically involved in the sexual socialization process. Adolescent sexuality and fertility behavior develop in response to the capacities and values shaped by experiences within the family, peer group, school, media, and other social institutions. The historical framework as well as sociocultural values and norms, socioeconomic status, ethnicity, and religion all have been found to contribute to the development and expression of adolescent sexuality (Chilman 1983; Miller and Simon 1980).

Health risks in adolescence

While adolescents experience few chronic health problems, there is growing concern regrding mortality patterns and increased rates of attempted suicide, depression, and substance abuse among adolescents, especially females. Mortality patterns among youth include accidents, homicides, and suicides, which account for about three-fourths of all deaths in the 15–24 age group. While the accidental death rate for young white males is three times that of their female counterparts, young blacks of either sex are at least five times as likely to be murdered as whites. These rates have been linked to a number of factors: lifestyle, socioeconomic factors, and the misuse of alcohol and drugs (USDHHS 1980).

These same factors are related to suicide, which is now the third leading cause of death among 15–24-year-olds. While the suicide rate for males is four times higher than that for females, females are two to three times more likely to *attempt* suicide. A contributing factor to these differential rates may be sex-role differences. Adolescent females generally are more willing to seek help and are more revealing than males (Sommer 1984). Based on his observation and studies, Peck (1982) suggests that up to 10 per cent of youngsters in any public school classroom may be considered at risk for suicide. A number of factors have been suggested as influential in this behavior, such as depression, physical abuse by parents, family instability, and family alcoholism (Peck 1982). In another study, suicide rates among Latino youth in the five Southwestern states have been found to be higher than among youth of other ethnic groups (Carter-Lourens 1983). The findings are still contradictory and require further study.

There is mounting evidence that drug abuse is beginning at earlier and earlier ages. For example, Johnston, Bachman, and O'Malley (1984) found that half of their sample started using PCP before entering high school. There is also evidence that sex differences in terms of differential drug use remain, but are diminishing. Girls tend to use alcohol and marijuana less frequently than boys. However, in a study that examined the use of eleven different drugs among adolescents, females were found to use cigarettes and stimulants more frequently than males. The latter finding, however, was probably confounded by reports of diet pill use (Gritz 1984; Sommer 1984). Finally, there are significant differences in substance abuse patterns among adolescents of different ethnic groups. For example Latinos have been found to abuse inhalants significantly more often than other adolescent populations, fourteen times the estimated national rate (Padilla *et al.* 1979).

Depression has also been found to be prevalent among female adolescents and related to substance abuse. For example, in their longitudinal study of adolescent drug use, Kandel and Davies (1982) found that depressive mood was an important indicator of initiation into illicit drugs other than marijuana among adolescents who had already experimented with marijuana. The findings suggested that adolescents may use drugs to relieve their depressive mood states as a form of self-medication. A follow-up study was conducted with 8,205 adolescents from eighteen public secondary schools in New York State. Two findings were highlighted: first, adolescents from families with incomes of less than $3,000 were more depressed than any other group, and second, girls were more depressed than boys. Furthermore, the sex differences were greater in adolescents than in adulthood between males and females.

Violence as a health and psychological risk

Violent behavior toward young adolescent women has implications both for their health and their psychological development. The major forms of violence against female adolescents include battery, rape, and incest. A limited number of studies have been conducted which have identified violence in dating relationships among high school students, with first incidents usually occurring at the age of fifteen. The reported range has been from 12 to 35 per cent. Studies of college students found a surprisingly high rate of dating violence, ranging from 21 to 60 per cent of students (Southern California Coalition on Battered Women 1984). Non-stranger rape and battery are particularly important areas of exploration since the limited data available do not permit an understanding of the psychological impact on adolescent girls (Strickland 1985). It can be suggested that young adolescent girls are at a clear disadvantage since they are still determining what is appropriate in male–female relationships. There is little reliable data on rape and battery against young girls. Bureau of Justice statistics report a rate of 250 rapes per 100,000 females in the age category of 16–19-year-olds, although about one-fifth occur among 12–15-year-olds (US Department of Justice 1984).

Little empirical work has been conducted on incest in adolescence. The vast majority of studies have focused on childhood experiences. The extant studies report on clinical case examples which again do not provide insight into the antecedents or consequences of this experience for the adolescent (Burgess *et al.* 1978; Kempe and Kempe 1984).

Violence and sexual abuse appear to be significant precipitating factors for a significant portion (36 per cent) of the female runaway population (Office of Inspector General 1983). The National Statistical Survey on Runaway Youth has estimated that 733,000 adolescents were runaways in 1975; 47 per cent were girls between the ages of 16–17. It was estimated that 25 per cent are hard-core 'street kids' in serious trouble, of which three-quarters engage in some type of criminal activity and half in prostitution specifically. Runaways are more likely to come from low-income families (40 per cent). Racial difference in runaways do not seem significant. The white rate is 2.9 per cent, black 3.2 per cent, and Hispanic 4.6 per cent. The higher rate for Hispanics may reflect, in part, a cultural difference where children may leave to live with a relative (Nye and Edelbrock 1980).

Preliminary work on runaways has identified some of the characteristics of this population. For example, female runaways aged 12–16 years indicate a history of truancy, use of alcohol and drugs, suicidal talk, and attempted suicide (Sommer 1984).

The interrelationships between violence, runaway behaviors, and poor mental health clearly show the need for more supportive services to both parents and adolescents. At present there is a need to develop more appropriate research strategies so that policy and practice can be made more relevant to the needs of these youth. 'As with other self-destructive behaviors the wide range of etiology requires a multiplicity of treatment alternatives – family counseling, individual therapy, crisis centers, and shelters' (Sommer 1984: 136).

Policy and practice implications for social service to adolescents

Policy development needs to incorporate an understanding of the problems of adolescents as they relate to gender, race, class, and sexual preference. To date limited data exist on social issues such as teenage pregnancy among Latina adolescents, and educational and social issues encountered by homosexual teenagers. However, a number of policy issues and directions have recently been articulated which may begin to address the practice area for adolescents.

Policy for young teenage mothers needs to address their educational needs and how they can continue their educational endeavors while assuming parental roles. In several school districts in the nation, special outreach programs have been developed for adolescents to encourage them to complete their education after the birth of the child. However, many of these programs still require that the students be economically self-supporting and provide for their own day care resources. The lack of additional economic and day care support services clearly excludes a significant number of adolescents who either need to go to work to support their child and/or cannot afford to pay for day care services. Policy needs to be developed at two levels: (a) to provide information on contraception to both teenagers and parents, and (b) to develop a national system of special programs for adolescents who become parents. It seems essential to include the parents of teenagers so that the young adolescent can feel a sense of support for her decision.

The decision to have a child for a minor also raises a number of legal and ethical issues. Should the parents be informed? Can a young adolescent girl make a responsible decision? Who will carry the burden of the decision? The parents? The state? The law in some states has favored the individual right of choice. In other states, the right of the individual girl to make a choice as to whether to have the child or not has been denied. The issue cannot be answered the same way for everyone. While the law must guarantee the right, a mechanism must also be provided whereby the decision can be made taking into account and utilizing the supportive elements within the individual's sociocultural milieu.

Family planning services need to be developmentally and culturally sensitive to the needs of adolescents. The approach should provide informational services, opportunity for decision-making and thus an informed choice as well as continuous, comprehensive care. In the case of adolescents, service providers must keep in mind that young people need support and assistance during the decision time as well as during the prenatal and postnatal parental period. Groups can provide an important modality for intervention among young people.

Data indicate that adolescent pregnancy results in an abrupt and marked reduction of interaction with peers (de Anda and Becerra 1984). The pregnant adolescent and adolescent mother finds herself estranged from her peers during a period of development generally characterized by increased peer interaction and intimacy. Inasmuch as this peer interaction is viewed as enhancing one's social, psychological, and cognitive development, establishment of a network of peer support groups for adolescent mothers appears to be a particularly promising intervention. Moreover, one needs to take into account the developmental literature which repeatedly indicates that dyads or small intimate groups are more typical forms of female interactions than large groups. The use of multiple supportive dyads or small groups of three or four adolescent mothers should be explored. In addition, while the adolescent mother might be part of a network of several adolescent mother dyads, one dyad might pair the adolescent mother with a more experienced young mother who could serve as a model as well as provide a supportive relationship.

Finally, parenting programs need to be provided for adolescents, and these should incorporate information on health issues for mother and child as well as nutritional information and classes on how to parent.

Implications for curricula

Human behavior It is apparent from the introductory critique of the developmental literature that some alternative conceptualizations are needed to replace the traditional theoretical formulations that have formed the core of human behavior courses. The basic concepts of these theoretical models must be re-examined with respect to gender, social, cultural/ethnic, and sexual orientation biases. The aim should be to work towards developing theoretical models that are more fully applicable to the variation within human experience. Empirical research is needed to determine whether developmental processes are homogeneous across all populations or whether they vary significantly across subgroups. For example, in reappraising the dynamics postulated by psychosexual theories, it is important to re-examine the process of identification. Is the process of identification significantly different for males and females? Do similarities or differences between the gender of the child and the primary caretaker result in parallel or significantly different experiences for males and females? Furthermore, it is important to explore which developmental experiences are more strongly impacted by idiosyncratic and dyadic interaction factors and which by environmental variables such as cultural and class milieu.

For stage theories (e.g. those of Erikson, Piaget, Kohlberg), both developmental sequences and normative assertions must be critically evaluated. Empirical data are needed to provide information regarding the similarities and differences in the developmental timetables and processes of various cohorts to determine whether development is as homogeneous as stage theories portray it to be. More importantly, variations in developmental timetables need to be viewed as expansions of the conceptual frameworks, not as 'deviations' from normal and healthy patterns and sequences.

Lastly, theoretical models and empirical data need to be meshed to give meaning to abstract concepts. Linkages between theory and the specific behaviors of specified populations should be promoted. New models can best be derived from a dialectic of reciprocal influence between the theoretical and the empirical.

Research Because of the sex bias in the theoretical literature and the gaps in the empirical literature, there is a need to promote research aimed at both theory-building and the securing of empirical data on specific female adolescent populations. Students need to be taught how to evaluate critically the research literature for sex biases and how to use elements of this literature to generate research questions and hypotheses sensitive to gender differences. Ethnographic models are particularly useful to this end. This methodology requires that data be obtained from the perspective of the population under study. This increases the likelihood that the questions and hypotheses that will be generated and the measures that will be developed will tap variables most relevant to specific female adolescent populations.

Practice Inasmuch as practice is built upon an understanding of the dynamics of human behavior, the state of the theoretical literature offers a dilemma for the practitioner. However, the social work dictum, 'to begin where the client is,' provides a mechanism for constructively utilizing available and developing theoretical models. Rather than using theoretical formulations as normative criteria for evaluating behavior and developmental progress, theoretical constructs and principles can be used as guidelines or suggestions for factors to explore with the client. The relevance of the factors is determined by the needs, presenting problems, and sociocultural context of the client. For example, if the client is a sixteen-year-old female involved in delinquent gang activity and drug abuse, the following factors might be explored:

(a) relationship and attachment issues with respect to same- and opposite-sex caretakers;
(b) issues of identity and their impact upon the presenting problems;
(c) models (particularly female models) of delinquency or substance abuse within the family and broader environment;
(d) reinforcement provided within the environment for the specific behaviors;
(e) the norms for female behavior in the client's cultural milieu with respect to the presenting problems;
(f) the clash between norms of mainstream and minority cultures or between generations within the culture;
(g) issues of sexual development and identity and the mesh between individual, familial, cultural, and subcultural modes of expression.

Most important, a practice methodology needs to be taught that places the worker in the role of practitioner-researcher. Because it is the nature of social work to serve varied populations and deal with problems in advance of the availability of population or problem-specific interventions, students need to be taught how to formulate their clinical problems in a manner that allows for empirical evaluation. This approach requires that practice outcomes be specified (operationalized) in measurable terms, that functional hypotheses be generated, that interventions be specified to allow for replication with future clients and client populations, and that clinical outcomes be evaluated against the initially specified outcome criteria. In this way, not only can interventions with individual clients be evaluated, but this $n = 1$ 'research' can be cumulated to determine which interventions appear most effective with populations grouped by varying classifications, such as by presenting problem, gender, ethnic-cultural background, class status, or sexual orientation. This procedure is most effective if employed as a collaborative effort within an agency and ultimately in a broader network of practitioners focused on specific populations and/or problem areas. It also offers data for a more inductive approach to developing practice principles which can serve specific populations.

Electives One of the main functions of electives is to provide flexibility within the curriculum to deal with issues and populations of particular saliency to the local community as well as those of concern to the profession as a whole. However, how does one determine the focus of these concerns? For example, does one offer separate courses in the black, Hispanic, or Asian family or a course in the experience of the minority family in America? Because the Asian population in the United States is now so heterogeneous, are further courses needed for the various groups within this broader population? Should a general course be offered on the major problems of adolescent populations which touches upon adolescent pregnancy, substance abuse, and so forth, or should courses be problem-focused (e.g. substance abuse) and issues unique to adolescent development be incorporated? While the expertise of one's faculty, the most immediate needs of the community being served, and the material available in the area all help to determine which course of action to take, the dilemma is probably best served by breaking away from thinking of electives solely in terms of courses. Traditional courses might be just one of many options open to students to acquire more specialized knowledge. Other options include: intensive (one, two, or three all-day) workshops, several rotating modules that last a limited number of weeks during the quarter or semester, or group projects for a small core of students who share a common, more narrowly focused interest.

Finally, it is critical that issues related to gender, social and ethnic/cultural differences and sexual orientation not be included solely within the elective portion of the curriculum, but that these issues be emphasized and woven throughout the core curriculum. Only in this way can the centrality of these issues to the understanding of human behavior be demonstrated.

Conclusion

Although it appears that adolescence is more stressful for some youth than for others, the actual extent of social and health-related problems among female adolescents in modern society does represent a serious issue. For example, the interrelationship between adolescent female suicide, depression, and drug use needs to be explored. Teenage pregnancy is another area which carries serious consequences in terms of social, educational, and psychological costs for the adolescent. Adolescent pregnancy and motherhood limit the options and cause stress for this youthful female population.

Adolescence is a period in the life-cycle during which dramatic changes occur in all areas of development: physiological, psychological, cognitive, sexual, and social. The magnitude and rapidity of these changes and their simultaneous evaluation by the adolescent and those in her social environment offer potential for significant growth enhancement or for expending energies in destructive or growth-retarding directions. Policy, practice, research, and curriculum development needs to be directed toward this population to determine the theoretical frameworks most consonant with the female adolescent experience, particular areas of vulnerability and need, and the unique strengths that this population brings to its developmental experience.

References

Andrade, S. (ed.) (1983) *Latino Families in the United States: A Resource Book for Family Life Education.* New York: Planned Parenthood Federation of America.

Bacon, L. (1974) Early Motherhood: Accelerated Role Transition and Social Pathologies. *Social forces* 52(3): 333–41.

Becerra, R. and de Anda, D. (1984) Pregnancy and Motherhood Among Mexican American Adolescents. *Health and Social Work* 9(2): 106–23.

Blos, P. (1941) *The Adolescent Personality.* New York: D. Appleton Century.

—— (1979) *The Adolescent Passage, Developmental Issues.* New York: International Universities Press.

Bolton, F. G. (1982) The Pregnant Adolescent: Problems of Premature Parenthood. Beverly Hills, CA: Sage Publications.

Braen, B. and Forbush, J. B. (1975) School-Age Parenthood: A National Overview. *Journal of School Health* 45(5): 256–62.

Burgess, A. W., Groth, A. N., Holstrom, L. L., and Saroi, S. M. (1978) *Sexual Assault of Children and Adolescents.* Lexington: Lexington Books.

Carter-Lourens, J. (1983) Youthful Hispanic Suicides: Targeting Prevention Strategies and Policies for Adolescent Hispanic Suicides. Unpublished. Los Angeles: UCLA Bush Program.

Chilman, C. (1983) *Adolescent Sexuality in A Changing American Society.* New York: John Wiley and Sons.

Chodorow, N. (1974) Family Structure and Feminine Personality. In M. Rosaldo and L. Lamphere (eds) *Women, Culture and Society.* Stanford, CA: Stanford University Press.

—— (1978) *The Reproduction of Mothering.* Berkeley: University of California Press.

de Anda, D. (1985) The Hispanic Adolescent Mother: Assessing Risk Related to Stress and Social Support. In W. Vega and M. Miranda (eds) *Stress and Hispanic Mental Health.* DHHS publication no. 85–1410.

de Anda, D. and Becerra, R. (1984) Support Networks for Adolescent Mothers. *Social Casework* 65(3): 172–81.

Douvan, E. and Adelson, J. (1966) *The Adolescent Experience.* New York: John Wiley and Sons.

Elkind, D. (1975) Recent Research on Cognitive Development in Adolescence. In S. E.

Dragastin and G. H. Elder Jr (eds) *Adolescence in the Life Cycle: Psychological Change and Social Context*. New York: Wiley.

Erikson, E. H. (1963) *Childhood and Society* (2nd edn). New York: Norton.

—— (1968) *Identity, Youth, and Crisis*. New York: Norton.

Freud, A. (1948) *The Ego and the Mechanisms of Defense*, trans. C. Baines. New York: International Universities Press.

Freud, S. (1924) *A General Introduction to Psychoanalysis*. New York: Pocket Books, 1973.

Furstenberg, F. F. (1976) *Unplanned Parenthood: The Social Consequences of Teenage Childbearing*. New York: Free Press.

Gibson, C. (1976) The U.S. Fertility Decline, 1961–1975: The Contribution of Changes in Marital Status and Marital Fertility. *Family Planning Perspectives* 8: 249–52.

Gilligan, C. (1979) Woman's Place in Man's Life Cycle. *Harvard Educational Review* 49(4): 431–46.

—— (1982) *In a Different Voice*. Cambridge, MA: Harvard University Press.

Gritz, E. R. (1984) Cigarette Smoking by Adolescent Females: Implications for Health and Behavior. *Women and Health* 9(2/3): 103–15.

Guttmacher Institute (1981) *Teenage Pregnancy: The Problem Hasn't Gone Away*. New York: Alan Guttmacher Institute.

Hoffman, M. L. (1980) Moral Development in Adolescence. In J. Adelson (ed.) *Handbook of Adolescent Psychology*. New York: John Wiley and Sons.

Johnston, L., Bachman, J. and O'Malley, P. (eds) (1984) *Highlights From Drugs and American High School Students, 1975–83*. Ann Arbor, Mich.: University of Michigan, Institute for Social Research, National Institute on Drug Abuse.

Kandel, D. and Davies, M. (1982) Epidemiology of Depressive Mood in Adolescents. *Archives of General Psychiatry* 39.

Kempe, R. S. and Kempe, C. H. (1984) *The Common Secret: Sexual Abuse of Children and Adolescents*. New York: W. H. Freeman.

Kohlberg, L. (1969) *Stages in the Development of Moral Thought and Action*. New York: Holt, Rinehart and Winston.

Lewis, D. O., Klerman, L. V., and Currie, J. F. (1977) Experiences with Psychiatric Services in a Program for Pregnant School Age Girls. *Social Psychiatry* 8: 13–22.

Lewis, L. A. (1984) The Coming-Out Process for Lesbians: Integrating a Stable Identity. *Social Work* 29(5) 464–69.

Marcia, J. E. (1980) Identity in Adolescence. In J. Adelson (ed.) *Handbook of Adolescent Psychology*. New York: Wiley, pp. 159–87.

Martin, A. D. (1982) Learning to Hide: The Socialization of the Gay Adolescent. *Annals of the American Society for Adolescent Psychiatry* 10(4): 52–65.

Miller, P. Y. and Simon, W. (1980) The Development of Sexuality in Adolescence. In J. Adelson (ed.) *Handbook of Adolescent Psychology*. New York: John Wiley and Sons, pp. 383–407.

Nye, I. F. and Edelbrock, C. (1980) Some Social Characteristics of Runaways. *Journal of Family Issues* 1: 147–50.

Offer, D. and Sabshin, M. (1984) *Normality and the Life Cycle. A Critical Integration*. New York: Basic Books.

Office of Inspector General (1983) *Runaway and Homeless Youth: National Program Inspection*. Washington, DC: US Department of Health and Human Services.

244 The Woman Client

Ogle, A. J. (1985) The Plight of the Children Nobody Wants. *Lesbian News* 10(7).

Opinion Research Corporation (1976) *National Statistical Survey on Runaway Youth*, part 1. Princeton, NJ: ORC.

Osofsky, H. (1968) *The Pregnant Teenager: A Medical, Educational and Social Analysis*. Illinois: Charles Thomas Publishers.

Osofsky, H., Osofsky, J. D., Kendall, N., and Rajan, R. (1973) Adolescents as Mothers: An Interdisciplinary Approach to Complex Problems. *Journal of Youth and Adolescence* 2(3): 233–49.

Osofsky, J. and Osofsky, H. (1978) Teenage Pregnancy: Psychosocial Considerations. Clinical Obstetrics and Gynecology 21: 1161–173.

Padilla, E., Padilla, A., Ramirez, R., Morales, A. and Olmedo, E. (1979) Inhalant, Marijuana and Alcohol Abuse Among Barrio Children and Adolescents. *The International Journal of Addiction* 14(7): 987–92.

Paton, S. M. and Kandel, D. B. (1978) Psychological Factors and Adolescent Drug Use: Ethnicity and Sex Differences. *Adolescence* 13(50), Summer: 18–200.

Peck, M. (1982) Youth Suicide. *Death Education* 6: 29–47.

Petersen, A. C. and Taylor, B. (1980) The Biological Approach to Adolescence. In J. Adelson (ed.) *Handbook of Adolescent Psychology*. New York: John Wiley and Sons.

Piaget, J. (1972) Intellectual Evolution from Adolescence to Adulthood. *Human Development* 15(1): 1–12.

Podd, M. H. (1972) Ego Identity Status and Morality: The Relationship between Two Developmental Constructs. *Developmental Psychology* 6: 497–507.

Rindfuss, R. and Sweet, J. (1978) The Pervasiveness of Postwar Fertility Trends in the United States. In K. Taeuber, L. Bumpass, and J. Sweet (eds) *Social Demography*. New York: Academic Press.

Rochat, R. (1981) Family Planning Practices among Anglo and Hispanic Women in U.S. Counties Bordering Mexico. *Family Planning Perspectives* 13: 176–80.

Simon, W., Berger, A. S., and Gagnon, J. S. (1972) Beyond Anxiety and Fantasy: The Coital Experiences of College Youth. *Journal of Youth and Adolescence* 1: 203–22.

Sommer, H. (1984) The Troubled Teen: Suicide, Drug Use and Running Away. *Women and Health* 9(2/3): 117–41.

Sorenson, R. C. (1973) *Adolescent Sexuality in Contemporary America*. New York: World.

Southern California Coalition on Battered Women (1984) *Domestic Violence Fact Sheet*. Santa Monica, CA: Southern California Coalition on Battered Women.

Stein, S. J. (1985) Factors Related to Contraceptive Use Among Mexican-American Adolescents. Doctoral dissertation. Los Angeles: Wright Institute Los Angeles.

Steinhorn, A. I. (1979) Lesbian Adolescents in Residential Treatment. *Social Casework* 60(8): 494–98.

Stricklands, B. (1985) *Gender Differences in Health*. Unpublished presentation at Dept. of Psychology, U.C.L.A.

US Bureau of the Census (1981) Persons of Spanish Origin in the United States: March 1980 (advance report). *Current Population Report*. Series P–25, no. 351. Washington, DC: US Government Printing Office.

United States Department of Health, Education and Welfare (1979) *U.S./Mexico Border Survey of Maternal and Child Health/Family Planning*. Advanced Report.

United States Department of Health and Human Services (1980) *The Status of Children, Youth and Families, 1979*. Washington, DC: Office of Human Development Service.

—— (1983) *Runaway and Homeless Youth*. October.

—— (1985) *Stress and Hispanic Mental Health: Relating Research to Service Delivery.* DHHS publication no. 85–1410. Washington, DC: Public Health Service.

United States Department of Justice (1984) *Criminal Victimization in the United States, 1982.* Washington, DC: Bureau of Justice Statistics.

Ventura, S. (1982) Births of Hispanic Parentage, 1979. *Monthly Vital Statistics Report 32* (supplement). Hyattsville, MD: National Center for Health Statistics, Public Health Service.

Ventura, S. and Heuser, R. (1981) Births of Hispanic Parentage, 1978. *Monthly Statistics Report 29* (supplement). Hyattsville, MD: National Center for Health Statistics, Public Health Service.

Zelnick, M. and Kantner, J. (1979) Sexual and Contraceptive Experience of Young Unmarried Women in the United States: 1976 and 1971. In C. Chilman (ed.) *Adolescent Pregnancy and Childbearing: Findings from Research.* Washington, DC: US Government Printing Office, pp. 43–81.

—— (1980) Sexual Activity, Contraceptive Use and Pregnancy Among Metropolitan-Area Teenagers: 1971–1979. *Family Planning Perspectives* 12: 230–37.

Zelnik, M., Kantner, J., and Ford, K. (1981) *Sex and Pregnancy in Adolescence.* Beverly Hills, CA: Sage Publications.

20 Women in the new family

Dianne S. Burden

Introduction

A dramatic shift in the structure of the American family has been one of the most important social changes of the last twenty-five years. An influx of married women with young children into the paid labor force and a rapid increase in dual-earner families have created pressure for a major restructuring of job/home-life responsibilities and interpersonal roles between men and women. The continually increasing incidence of single-parent families primarily headed by women also marks the change in American families. The purpose of this chapter will be to examine the dynamics of the changing family and to assess the impact of such rapid change on social welfare policy and practice particularly as they pertain to women.

A key element contributing to new family structures and interactions has been the changing role of women. In addition to being the primary caretakers of the family, women are now assuming major roles in the family as breadwinners. Their participation in the labor force has become a vital factor in the national economy. The change in roles has led to a difficult transition period resulting in questions which must be addressed in social work practice and education. Who will care for the family as more and more women enter the paid workforce? Will women continue to fulfill their homemaking and child-rearing roles for free in addition to earning a major portion of the family income? What policies need to be developed to enable women to manage their multiple work/family responsibilities as well as to encourage men to share these responsibilities more equally? What social services need to be developed to provide support for the changing family, particularly for the growing number of single-parent families? What do social service providers need to know about the multiplicity of family forms in order to provide adequate service to dual-earner families, single-parent families, gay and lesbian families, families of various ethnic and racial backgrounds, families both with and without children?

Changing roles of women

The changing family in America is essentially the story of the changing role of women in recent years. Social work education for non-sexist practice cannot be complete without major attention being paid to the transformation which is occurring for women both within the family and in the world of work. Numerous factors have contributed to this change. To a large extent the change has been spurred by economic need and has been characterized by a major increase of women, and particularly of women parents, in the workforce. Currently more than half of all married mothers and almost three-quarters of all single mothers are employed (Hayghe 1981; Smith 1979). The only factor keeping most families in the middle class, and many families out of poverty, today is the presence of two incomes (Grossman 1982). Single-parent families are at high risk for poverty because they must subsist on the one income of a usually lower-paid woman. Projections for the 1990s are that the trend will continue and that by the end of the century only 25 per cent of women parents will be in the traditional homemaker role with a husband earning the total income.

Economic need is not the only factor exerting an influence on women's changing roles. Increased education and the women's liberation movement have combined to raise women's career expectations and overcome barriers to educational and career advancement. More than half of undergraduate college students are now women. More than a third of medical and law students are women. Women's changing roles have coincided with major shifts in marriage and kinship patterns and with significant changes in family composition such as reduced household size and an increase in single-parent and dual-earner families. Changing roles have also provided a more accepting atmosphere for the concerns of a range of alternative family forms including gay and lesbian families, couples choosing not to have children, single persons living alone, heterosexual cohabitation, and group living arrangements.

Change in marriage and kinship patterns

Marriage and kinship patterns have altered considerably over the last twenty-five years. These changes are of particular concern to social work practitioners as the stress which results from rapid social transition often leads to periods of family dysfunction. The divorce rate now stands at close to 50 per cent for first marriages and even higher (60 per cent) for second marriages (Glick and Norton 1980). Divorce has moved from a crisis of family breakdown for a 'deviant' minority to a stage of the adult life-cycle, a rite of passage, for half the married population. For teenage marriages the divorce rate is even higher, with 62–75 per cent of marriages before the age of twenty ending in divorce within the first six years (Moore 1981). The divorce rate is the major factor in making the single-parent family the current family form for one-fourth of American children.

Many have cited the high divorce rate as evidence that the American family is on the decline (Bronfenbrenner 1977). Others point out that divorce may simply have replaced the death of a parent as a disruption in a child's life (Bane 1976). Indeed the cause of divorce may have more to do with longer life expectancies than with unhappy relationships. Before modern obstetrics and gynecology, combined with other medical advances which have increased women's life expectancy, it was not unusual for a man to outlive two or three wives. According to Bane (1976), more children are living today with at least one natural parent than at any time in the history of the world. Short life expectancies may have provided a solution to unsatisfactory marriages. In today's world, it may simply be unrealistic to expect a married couple to stay compatible and remain together for sixty or seventy years. For many people serial monogamy may be the more satisfactory marriage pattern (Shorter 1977).

In spite of the high divorce rate, the popularity of marriage does not appear to be on the decline. A large majority remarry relatively soon after divorce – 85 per cent of men an average of two years after divorce, and 75 per cent of women an average of six years after divorce (Thornton and Freedman 1983). Divorce for women may lead to longer periods of singlehood than for men for a variety of reasons. Since women more frequently receive custody of children, they may be less likely to lose a sense of family and to feel a need to start a new one quickly. Divorced women with children may also be less 'marriageable' than divorced men. This may be so because women's incomes are lower, they have the liability of children to support, and they are not as young as the expanding pool of younger marriageable women still willing to marry older men. The frequency of remarriage leads to the issue of blended families and step-parenting, a phenomenon of increasing importance to social workers engaged in family practice. Remarriage brings its own stresses from dealing with ex-spouses and each other's children. It also brings an even higher divorce rate than first marriages (Glick and Norton 1980). Since women are traditionally responsible for maintaining the family kinship network and social life, they are faced with increasingly complex interactions among multiple sets of in-law and friendship networks.

Change in family composition

The higher divorce rate is only one factor which has led to an increase in the number of single-adult households. Young adults are deferring marriage until the late twenties or early thirties resulting in a delay of child-bearing (Masnick and Bane 1980). Fewer older people are living with their adult children, a consequence of the financial independence gained for older Americans by the Social Security Act of 1935 and subsequent indexing of benefits to the cost of living (Schottland 1967).

A major unanticipated consequence of the decline in average household size has been a critical housing shortage particularly in urban settings. High housing prices have a severe effect on lower-income women and children.

The dramatic decline in the birthrate since 1960 has also contributed to smaller household sizes (Glick and Norton 1980). In 1958, at the height of the baby boom, the average family was having 3.8 children. By 1978, the birthrate had been cut in half to 1.8 children per family, below the population replacement rate of 2.1. This rate has held steady for the last seven years. The decline in the birthrate when combined with a corresponding decline in the deathrate has resulted in a significant reduction of the proportion of American households with young children. The average woman now lives until seventy-six years of age, and yet only spends about twenty of those years with children at home and only about six or seven years with preschool-age children. Motherhood is no longer the prime focus of the lives of the great majority of women. Indeed, the typical American family no longer has children in it. Various sources put at 7 per cent the proportion of households representing the traditional form of father at work and mother at home with young children (Masnick and Bane 1980).

The decline in numbers of households with young children has had some negative effects on families. Now that the large numbers of children from the baby boom generation have moved into adulthood, society has become less child-centered and more adult-centered. As a result, support for public schools has declined in recent years. Community support for child welfare programs such as AFDC and Maternal and Child Health has also declined. Children may once again be viewed as the property and total responsibility of their parents, increasingly of their female parents. Not only are women increasingly responsible for young children, but as the population ages and housing prices increase, middle-aged women may be more frequently members of the sandwich generation – caring both for aging parents and for adult children who cannot afford to be totally independent. The implications for social work policy and practice are clear in the need to provide assistance to cope with the growing demands on women to assume increasing responsibility for family support, both financial and emotional.

Increase in single-parent families

The most compelling change in family composition for women, and particularly for black women, has been the tremendous increase in female-headed single-parent families since 1960. Currently a quarter of all American families with children are headed by women alone, but half of all families in poverty are headed by women (Grossman 1982). While 12 per cent of white children live with a single mother, 42.5 per cent of black children live with their mother only (USDHHS 1980). Poverty is also particularly a problem for non-white single-parent families, with 65.7 per cent of black, 68.6 per cent of Hispanic, but only 40.3 per cent of white female-headed families in poverty (USDHHS 1980). Employment appears to be an important factor in raising women out of poverty. Single parents are much more likely than married women parents to be employed (72 per cent compared with 51 per cent) (Smith 1979). Only 19 per cent of single mothers who work part-time and 7 per cent who work full-time are in poverty (Smith 1979).

The incidence of single parenthood is exacerbated by recent increases in out-of-wedlock teenage parenthood. Paradoxically, there has been no actual increase in child-bearing among teenagers in recent years. An increase in sexual activity and a subsequent increase in teenage pregnancy have generated a crisis mentality; however, the fact that one-third of all teenage pregnancies are terminated in abortion has prevented an increase in actual child-bearing. The key factor contributing to the crisis appears to be the fact that 95 per cent of teenage mothers are now keeping their babies rather than giving them up for adoption as they did in previous generations. Families headed by teenage mothers are at particular risk for poverty. Almost half (49.7 per cent) of all AFDC expenditures go to households in which women bore their first child as teenagers (Moore 1981).

The increase in single-parent families through divorce and out-of-wedlock child-bearing is the major factor contributing to the growing feminization of poverty in the United States. Social work as a profession has historically been concerned with poverty, its correlates and policy implications. A non-sexist curriculum for social work education requires a major focus on the changing roles of women in families and on the resultant hardships of women and children cause by the inequitable economic status of women in this society.

Social work practice at both the direct service and policy development levels has tended to view single parents' problems as primarily caused by the lack of a male family head (Burden 1980). As such, counseling is frequently aimed at helping a woman make herself more attractive on the marriage market. Policy goals are frequently intended to provide incentives for the maintenance of two-parent families. This focus is exemplified by the concern that providing economic independence to women through a guaranteed annual income or adequate AFDC benefits will encourage dissolution of marriages (Steiner 1981). This latent objective of social work practice and public policy that women and children should be cared for (and controlled) by male family heads, not by equal participation in the economy, raises serious questions when the sex ratio issue is considered. Particularly in the black community there are simply not enough marriageable men to go around for the available women (Guttentag and Secord 1983). This unevenness in the male/female ratio has multiple causes. The male lifestyle when combined with institutional racism is particularly lethal for young black males; they are killed off at alarming rates by homicide, suicide, and accidents. In addition, institutional racism disproportionately diverts black males into the prison system, state mental hospitals, and the military, thus further reducing the number of available men (McAdoo 1983). To suggest that the acquisition of a male partner holds the solution for the problems of single-parent families is simply not realistic social work practice or public policy formulation. Because of its prevalence in the culture, the single-parent family can no longer be viewed as a 'deviant' family form, the solution for which is remarriage.

Increase in dual-earner families

The most notable trend in the married family has been the increase in dual-earner couples in recent years (Grossman 1982). This trend has been caused by the influx of women into the workforce, particularly married mothers with young children. Working wives now earn 26–38 per cent of their families' incomes (Grossman 1982).

One result has been increased pressure on men to assume a more equitable share of child-rearing and homemaking responsibilities. In spite of this new pressure, however, as women have taken a larger share of the income-producing function in society, they have so far had to continue to bear the major responsibility for child-rearing, homemaking, and emotional support activities in the family (Burden 1983; Condran and Bode 1982). While women are spending more of their daily lives in the labor force, men have not yet assumed a corresponding share of family responsibilities. Studies indicate that married men show no difference in the amount of housework they do whether the wife works outside of the home or not (Bernard 1979; Burden 1983; Condran and Bode 1982; Fox and Nickols 1983; Kreps and Clark 1975; Nickols and Metzen 1982; Vickery 1979). Marriage tends to be less of a support system for employed women than for employed men (Bernard 1972; Burden 1985). The result is a serious inequity in the amount of discretionary time available to employed men and women when the interaction of work and family responsibilities is considered.

Social work and other mental health practitioners need to consider the impact of such inequity on marital and family dynamics. The high divorce rate may be an indication that women have been withdrawing the free grants they have provided to men within marriage (Bernard 1979). As American women gain in education, career aspirations, and career advancement, they may simply no longer be willing to accept traditional family patterns. The resulting conflict may lead to differential family patterns which include (a) more equitable sex-role neutral marriages; (b) more women living either by themselves, with their children, or in alternative family forms; or (c) an increase in the number of men seeking wives considerably younger or from Third World countries in an effort to find a compliant woman to maintain traditional sex-roles within marriage. The economic need of most families for two incomes may make this last option increasingly an upper-middle-class phenomenon, and it may founder on the increasing reluctance of younger women to accept a subservient role even in return for a high-status, high-income husband.

Alternative family forms

As the family continues to change in late twentieth-century America, social work education must focus on the alternatives to the traditional family that more and more people are choosing in order to meet their intimacy and economic needs. Alternative family forms are frequently not viewed as families at all and therefore do not receive societal sanction and support. These families include gay and lesbian families, families choosing not to have children, single persons living alone, group living arrangements, and friendship networks which function as families. A non-sexist approach to social work education views the family from a functional perspective outside the restrictive boundaries of traditional sex-role stereotypes about the family.

The particular situation of gay and lesbian families is inadequately addressed in most courses about families, and yet heterosexual couples may have much to learn from gay couples.[1] Gay relationships are frequently patterned on a best friend or roommate model rather than a heterosexual sex-role model. As such these relationships tend to be more egalitarian both in income-producing and homemaking responsibilities (Walsh 1983). A major issue for gay couples is their rights as parents. About 20 per cent of gay men and 22–24 per cent of lesbian women have been married. Of these, 52 per cent of men and 56 per cent of women have children. Comparison studies of children living with lesbian mothers and children living with single heterosexual mothers have found no differences with regard to emotional disturbance, toy preferences, or gender identification (Macklin and Rubin 1983). Similarly, data suggest no disproportionate incidence of homosexuality among children of homosexual parents. Yet in contested custody cases where a parent's sexual orientation is an issue, gay fathers rarely win custody and lesbian mothers win in only about 15 per cent of cases.

Loss of custody of children is clearly an issue of overriding concern for gay and lesbian families. Gay and lesbian couples are denied the legal rights and benefits of marriage such as income tax deductions, social security survivors benefits, and family health insurance. Institutional homophobia frequently denies homosexual couples the opportunity to be parents through adoption or foster care.

The cohabiting heterosexual couple is an increasingly common family form that faces many of the same barriers as gay and lesbian couples, with the significant exception of homophobia.[2] The incidence of cohabiting couples tripled from 1970 to 1980 and doubled from 1975 to 1980 alone (Glick and Spanier 1980). In 1981, 1.8 million couples were unmarried – 4 per cent of all couples living together (Spanier 1983). Couples who live together outside of marriage tend to be young, white, and urban. The women in these relationships are more likely than their married counterparts to be employed, and they provide a larger proportion of the family income. Cohabiting relationships are characterized by more androgynous roles, less commitment to the relationship, but greater life satisfaction, particularly for women (Macklin 1980). Although cohabiting relationships (both homosexual and heterosexual) have on average a shorter duration than married relationships, they are important family forms which appear particularly supportive for women and need to be addressed seriously in social work courses on the family.

Singlehood is another family form which has been gaining in frequency and is of particular import to women.[3] Fewer women than men remarry after divorce (75 per cent as opposed to 85 per cent). Both women and men are deferring first marriages until later ages. In 1980, 50 per cent of all women aged 20–24 had never married, compared to only 30 per cent in 1970. Education is the strongest predictor of singlehood for women (Cargan and Melko 1982; Stein 1983). During the 1970s the number of persons living alone increased by 60 per cent. Currently 23 per cent of all households are single-person households accounting for 58 million American adults over eighteen. Since the sex ratio (proportion of men to women) decreases as age increases, women are far more likely than men to live in single-person households for significant periods of their lives. Yet single persons are traditionally not even considered to be living in families. A nonsexist approach to social work practice would view a single person and her friendships/extended family network as a family for the purposes of providing functional and emotional support. However, the members of the single person's extended family network are currently excluded from the benefits of legal marriage in the same way that cohabitators are (Stein 1983).

Work/family interaction

Another major factor affecting the family in recent years has been its changing relationship with the world of work outside the home. Since more than half of all women now work outside the home, pressure has been mounting to break down the traditional barriers between work and family. Women find themselves in an inequitable double-bind where they bring home substantial portions of the family income or head families themselves, but are still expected to take the primary responsibility for homemaking, child-rearing, and emotional support activities. The increase in roles and responsibilities of women has not been followed by corresponding societal provisions for working families such as maternity and paternity leave, child care, and family leave.

Social work education has traditionally focused on the intrapsychic and interpersonal aspects of family members' lives. Little attention has been paid to the impact of carrying out multiple work/family responsibilities with inadequate institutional or interpersonal assistance. Changes in the family and corresponding changes in the workforce now make it necessary for social work to focus on the impact of employment on family dynamics and indeed to shift the locale of social work practice to the work setting where adult family members are now spending a large portion of their waking hours.

The traditional workforce consisted of married men with wives at home caring for the family and single women who either had not yet married or who never married. The majority of the new workforce consists of dual-earner couples or single employees who must balance multiple job and family demands. Only 15 per cent of the workforce is now the traditional family form of married male with wife at home full-time (Burden 1985).

A key question for social services providers today is how family support functions will be fulfilled now that most women are in the paid labor force outside of the home. While women have been withdrawing their full-time support in the family, no corresponding source has emerged to replace that support. Employed women, therefore, are essentially left in the inequitable situation of having two full-time jobs – one in the labor force and one in the family. As stated earlier, men have not on average significantly increased the amount of time they spend on family responsibilities as wives join the labor force (Bernard 1979; Fox and Nickols 1983). Single fathers provide little support, either financially or in time spent on child care, to their children and ex-spouses (Jones, Gordon, and Sawhill 1976). Few family supports have ever existed for working parents in the community or in the public sector. Key among services which are not being provided by the public sector is child care for parent employees, many of whom cannot afford the high rates demanded in the private day care sector.

In recent years, the focus has turned to the private sector to take responsibility for the family support needs of its employees. It is in a company's own self-interest to minimize the amount of job–family role strain an employee experiences. Such an approach is likely to improve the physical and mental health of employees, to increase job satisfaction, and to reduce absenteeism and turnover rates (Kahn 1981). As women become more of a force in the labor market and as men's home responsibilities increase, companies will need to provide creative family support benefit packages to compete successfully in the job market.

Two approaches exist for employers to provide support for the new workforce of parent employees. They can provide supportive programs to enable women to continue to carry the primary responsibility for home and children or they can provide incentives and encouragement for men to assume a more equitable share of family responsibilities. The first option would include (a) providing greater flexibility in work schedules (e.g. flextime plans, part-time employment, job sharing, and work at home options); and (b) developing employer-sponsored child care benefits (e.g. on-site day care, voucher systems, or flexible benefit packages). The second option would focus on providing paternity as well as maternity leave, family leave to stay home with sick children, and company sanction for men to take more time for family responsibilities without harming their perceived attachment to the job.

Human service providers also need to be aware of new American family forms and the corresponding changes in composition of the workforce. A growing area of social work training of vital importance to the family is industrial social work, whether through employer-sponsored employee assistance programs or through contract arrangements with traditional family service agencies. As employers feel the impact of family stress on the members of their workforce, they are seeing the need for offering staff training on work/family issues, support groups for parent employees, and individual and family counseling through employer assistance programs. Social work practitioners must be trained to provide occupational welfare programs for employed families as well as social welfare programs for non-employed, low-income families.

Ethnic and cultural variations

Ethnic and cultural variation among families is a factor that is inadequately addressed in many discussions about the American family.[4] Aggregate poverty rates, for example, or data on incidence of single-parent families in the general population seriously under-represent those issues in the black or Hispanic communities. Similarly, emphasis on the current influx of women into the paid labor force denies the fact that black women, immigrant, and low-income women have always worked outside the home. Management of multiple job and homelife responsibilities is not a new phenomenon for black families (McAdoo 1981). To state that the average woman is having fewer children loses sight of the fact that Hispanic families are growing at a faster rate, are having more children, and therefore are younger on average than the rest of the population (Dieppa and Montiel 1978).

With the large-scale recent immigration of Hispanic and Asian families, in particular, typical American families may be increasingly less likely to speak English as their primary language. They may also be likely to bring customs and traditions from a multiplicity of cultures, many of which may be antithetical to customs and usages in American human service agencies. In working with Vietnamese families, for example, new emphasis may be required on providing family-centered care and including extended family members at all stages of the intervention process (Grosso *et al.* 1981). In assessing child abuse in Vietnamese families, careful attention may need to be paid to cultural health care practices such as coin rubbing which may mimic the manifestations of child abuse and lead to false accusations (Yeatman 1980).

Families from minority ethnic and cultural backgrounds are faced with all of the presures of the changing family which the majority culture is facing. In addition, minority families must cope with the majority's lack of understanding and outright hostility and discrimination against them. Social work curricula which focus on the impact of the changing family must also focus on the way that change intersects with families' ethnic and cultural backgrounds.

Social welfare policy issues

The changing family in its many forms raises numerous policy implications that need to be addressed in a non-sexist social work curriculum. Both federal and state policies have historically provided incentives and protection for the traditional family of a married heterosexual couple with children where the father works outside the home and the mother is a full-time homemaker. Early mothers' aid programs were intended to enable widowed mothers to stay home and care for their children. The Social Security Act mainly provided employment-related benefits to male wage earners in the primary labor force. Since few women earned wages from jobs covered by social security, women and children benefited secondarily as dependents and survivors (Cohen 1985). The original Title IV, Aid to Dependent Children, was considered to be a stop-gap measure until all widows and orphans could be covered under survivor benefits. Divorce and unmarried parenthood were never envisaged as social conditions that needed to be addressed.

Social welfare policy has failed to keep pace with the needs of changing family forms. The traditional family (mother at home) is fast becoming an upper-middle-class luxury. If the purpose of social welfare is to provide protection for vulnerable groups and increased equity among income groups then family policy must be re-examined in social work education to focus on the needs of the new poor, i.e. women and children (particularly non-white women and children), and on the needs of the emerging family forms of single-parent, dual-earner, and non-married families.

Policies affecting single-parent families

Policies which need to be re-examined in the light of the situation of single-parent families include income maintenance, child support, child custody, and child care policy in the public sector along with fringe benefits in the private sector. Income maintenance policy for single parents, primarily AFDC, has placed low-income single mothers in an insoluble double-bind: they are expected to care for their children but are not given adequate income to do so. They are paradoxically expected to earn an income to support their family financially, but cannot as women earn enough in the labor market to be able to afford basic necessities and also pay for the child care which would enable them to participate in the workforce (Dinnerman 1977). At the same time, single fathers have essentially been released from financial responsibility for their families; most fathers are either never ordered to pay child support or, if they are, pay irregularly or not at all (Jones, Gordon, and Sawhill 1976). Child support enforcement is a key policy issue for single parents. Similarly, child custody is a crucial issue. It has only been in this century that women have gained custody of their children after divorce (Mnookin 1978). Previously, children were considered the property of the father. So-called gender-free guidelines in awarding custody take into consideration such factors as the income of the parents and their ability to provide a traditional family form. Since men make more money and remarry sooner after divorce, such guidelines may actually result in denying both custody and accompanying support to single mothers. The guidelines may also be inequitable in disregarding women's disproportionately heavy costs from and high investment in the childbearing process through pregnancy, childbirth, and infant care.

Child care is another crucial policy area for single mothers. The essential issue here is the inability of most employed single mothers to afford child care on their low incomes. Government or employer subsidization is important for their survival unless children are to be abandoned to fend for themselves as latchkey children with little supervision. Finally, single parents in the work setting are faced with major inequities in fringe benefits. For example, single parents are required to pay family rates for health insurance even when they are only a family of two. A male employee with a wife and numerous children pays the same rate. In essence the lower-income single mother is subsidizing the health care of the higher-income male-headed family.

Policies affecting dual-earner families

Current policy has been based on traditional assumptions about women's role in marriage. The result has often been discrimination against women by providing incentives to maintain traditional roles. For example, the tax system taxes employed wives' earnings at the higher rate usually determined by their husbands' income. As a result, the tax rate on employed wives of upper-income men is so high that there is a strong disincentive for them to work outside of the home

(Lloyd and Niemi 1979). There is a strong association between high salaries for men and having a wife who stays home in the traditional role (Burden 1983). Another example of government incentives is the social security system which penalizes employed wives (who are the majority) by providing for non-employed wives of working men without additional contributions. Since wives who do not work outside the home tend to be married to higher-salaried men, the social security subsidy to them is essentially a redistribution of income from lower and middle-income to upper-income groups.

Another crucial area where the assumption of traditional female dependency has resulted in barriers to women's economic advancement is in the development of child care policy. The assumption behind the lack of government-supported child care is that families should care for their own children and that women should stay at home to do that (Friedman 1983). The further assumption is that if a female parent joins the labor market she does so in a secondary and supplemental role to her responsibilities at home. The primary dilemma for government policy-makers is to find ways to support the needs of employed women while at the same time supporting the continued functions of homemaking and child-rearing. To continue simply to rely on women to do both does not seem to be a realistic long-term policy.

These policies illustrate a fundamental conflict in policy between (a) protecting the traditional family by rewarding women's role as child-bearer and men's role as breadwinner, and (b) protecting individual rights and equity by providing equal opportunity to all. Tax and income transfer programs tend to reduce the avantage of market work for married women. Two-earner families pay more taxes and receive lower relative benefits than one-earner families where the wife stays home. The incentive to stay home and care for families does not extend to low-income female heads of household. The option to be a homemaker clearly depends on finding a husband who can benefit from the incentives to have a wife at home. Otherwise a single parent is increasingly expected to work outside the home. Public policy grows less willing to subsidize single women to care for their own children. At the same time, pressure from working women has provided impetus for the enactment of anti-discrimination legislation and the enforcement of affirmative action and equal employment opportunity programs. This policy line emphasizes the equality of all individuals in the workplace. Since there are still large numbers of dependent wives and mothers, however, government programs continue to discriminate against working women and in favor of non-working women.

Issues for non-sexist social service provision

Effective social work intervention increasingly requires work with families that is reflective of changing family forms. Normative assumptions about how a family should be may only serve to stigmatize the majority of current families which do not meet the 'idealized' standard of the traditional family. Such assumptions on the part of social workers may exert pressure on married women in particular to stay in a family form that is physically and emotionally harmful to them. To serve emerging family forms most effectively, the focus of social service should be on providing supportive services for all families in stress. With most adults now in the workforce, families may find it increasingly difficult to seek services in traditional social service agencies. Social workers may need to develop innovative human services which can be provided in the work setting or child care setting. Such services may increasingly focus on devising ways to help families deal with their multiple responsibilities of job, homemaking, and child-rearing. In a society where the growing majority of women work outside the home, questions will continue to arise as to who will care for the children and who will provide the emotional support for the family. Social workers may be called upon more and more frequently to facilitate these roles.

Issues for social work education
A key issue for social work education is whether students are being trained in both knowledge and method areas which reflect and respond to the needs of family structures as they currently exist in the culture. Curriculum and practicum based on theories and practices applicable to traditional families do not relate to the realities of today's world. Traditional social work education has tended to focus primarily on the world of home and on the intrapsychic and interpersonal factors which affect family dynamics. The reality for most families today, however, is that family members spend large portions of their time outside the home in the paid labor force. Policy courses need to examine the implications of the changing family on current policy to assess where policy is causing stress for family members and where it needs to be modified to be made more equitable. Research courses need to explore current research on changing family dynamics and to study social work practice with families to determine whether current practices and outcomes are congruent with the needs of new and diverse family forms. Human behavior and social environment courses must focus not only on human development but equally strongly on the social environment in which individuals and families function in order to examine pressures which may make the traditional family less functional in the modern age. HBSE courses need to focus particularly on multiple family forms to avoid a sexist and heterosexist bias about the desirability of a two-parent traditional family form. Methods courses need to focus on the feasibility of moving services to the work and child care locations where family members can have greater accessibility to care. Traditional individual casework and groupwork may need to focus on more specific educative and supportive models which can help family members cope with the stress of balancing multiple roles and responsibilities.

Conclusion

The American family has been changing in numerous ways. Changing roles of women, economic demands, and technological advancement are major factors compelling that change. Few families conform any longer to the traditional myths of father at work and mother at home with small children. To assume that other family forms are less desirable for children or adults is to condemn the large majority of the population to 'deviancy.' Social work education must take the lead in identifying new functional family forms and in raising the possibility that non-traditional family forms may be equal or even superior to traditional families in providing for the emotional and financial support of family members. Social work education also needs to examine the stresses caused by the changing family particularly on women and children. As women assume new roles and responsibilities outside of the family, strategies must be developed to provide support for her traditional functions inside of the family. To fail to meet this challenge is to abandon women to an inequitable share of responsibility in the society and to exacerbate the emotional and physical stress they experience.

Notes

1. The author wishes to acknowledge the work of Nancy Tavares in developing the section on gay and lesbian couples.
2. Material for the section on heterosexual cohabitation was developed by Diana DeVolk.
3. Material for the section on singlehood was collected by Terry Levin.
4. Contributions to the section on ethnicity and cultural variation were made by Mary Burke, Lisa Mohrwinkel, and Graciela Zisman.

References

Bane, M. J. (1976) *Here to Stay: American Families in the Twentieth Century*. New York: Basic Books.

Bernard, J. (1972) *The Future of Marriage*. New York: Bantam Books.

—— (1979) Policy and Women's Time. In J. Lipman-Blumen and J. Bernard (eds) *Sex Roles and Social Policy*. Beverly Hills: Sage Publications.

Bronfenbrenner, U. (1977) The Calamitous Decline of the American Family. *Washington Post*, 2 January.

Burden, D. (1980) Women as Single Parents: Alternative Services for a Neglected Population. In N. Gottlieb (ed.) *Alternative Social Services for Women*. New York: Columbia University Press.

—— (1983) The Interaction of Job and Homelife Responsibilities: A Comparison of Married and Single Parent Employees. Unpublished doctoral dissertation, Brandeis University, Waltham, MA.

—— (1985) *Preliminary Report on the Managing of Job and Homelife Demands in Corporations Study*. Progress report to USDHHS Office of Human Development Services.

Cargan, L. and Melko, M. (1982) *Singles: Myths and Realities*. Beverly Hills: Sage Publications.

Cohen, W. (1985) The Social Security Act of 1935: Reflections Fifty Years later. In *50th Anniversary Edition, The Report of the Committee on Economic Security of 1985*. National Conference on Social Welfare, Washington, DC.

Condran, J. G. and Bode, J. G. (1982) Rashomon, Working Wives and Middletown, 1980. *Journal of Marriage and the Family* 44: 421–26.

Dieppa, I. and Montiel, M. (1978) Hispanic Families: An Exploration. In M. Montiel (ed.) *Hispanic Families: Critical Issues for Policy and Programs in Human Services*. Washington, DC: COSSMHO.

Dinnerman, M. (1977) Catch 23: Women, Work and Welfare. *Social Work* 22: 472–77.

Fox, K. D. and Nickols, S. Y. (1983) The Time Crunch: Wife's Employment and Family Work. *Journal of Family Issues* 4: 61–82.

Friedman, D. (1983) *Encouraging Employer Support to Working Parents. Community Strategies for Change*. A report of the Working Parents Project. New York: Carnegie Corporation.

Glick, P. C. and Norton, A. (1980) New Lifestyles Change Family Statistics. *American Demographics* 2: 20–3.

Glick, P. C. and Spanier, G. (1980) Married and Unmarried Cohabitation in the United States. *Journal of Marriage and the Family*, February: 19–30.

Grossman, A. S. (1982) More than Half of All Children Have Working Mothers. *Monthly Labor Review* 105(2): 41–3.

Grosso, C., Barden, M., Henry, C., and Vineau, G. (1981) The Vietnamese American Family... And Grandma Makes Three. *American Journal of Maternal Child Nursing* 6: 177–80.

Guttentag, M. and Secord, P. (1983) *Too Many Women? The Sex Ratio Question*. Beverly Hills: Sage Publications.

Hayghe, H. (1981) Husbands and Wives as Earners: An Analysis of Family Data. *Monthly Labor Review* 104: 46–52.

Jones, C. A., Gordon, N. M., and Sawhill, I. V. (1976) Child Support Payments in the U.S. Working paper for the Urban Institute. Washington, DC: Urban Institute, October.

Kahn, R. L. (1981) Work, Stress, and Individual Well-Being. *Monthly Labor Review* 104: 28–30.

Kreps, J. and Clark, R. (1975) *Sex, Age, and Work: The Changing Composition of the Labor Force*. Baltimore: Johns Hopkins University Press.

Lloyd, C. B. and Niemi, B. T. (1979) *The Economics of Sex Differentials*. New York: Columbia University Press.

Macklin, E. (1980) Nonmarital Heterosexual Cohabitation. In *Family in Transition*. Boston: Little, Brown, pp. 285–307.

Macklin, E. and Rubin, R. (1983) *Contemporary Families and Alternative Lifestyles: Handbook on Research and Theory*. Beverly Hills, Sage Publications, Chapter 10.

Masnick, G. and Bane, M. J. (1980) *The Nation's Families: 1960–1990*. Boston: Auburn.

McAdoo, H. (1981) *Black Families*. Beverly Hills: Sage Publications.

—— (1983) *Black Men*. Beverly Hills: Sage Publications.

Mnookin, R. (1978) *Child, Family and State: Problems and Materials on Children and the Law*. Boston: Little, Brown.

Moore, K. A. (1981) Government Policies Related to Teenage Family Formation and Functioning: An Inventory. In T. Ooms (ed.) *Teenage Pregnancy in a Family Context: Implications for Policy*. Philadelphia: Temple University Press.

Nickols, S. Y. and Metzen, E. J. (1982) Impact of Wife's Employment upon Husband's Housework. *Journal of Family Issues* 3: 199–216.

Schottland, C. (1967) Government Economic Programs and Family Life. *Journal of Marriage and the Family* 29: 1.

Shorter, E. (1977) *The Making of the Modern Family*. New York: Basic Books.

Smith, R. E. (ed.) (1979) *The Subtle Revolution: Women at Work*. Washington, DC: Urban Institute.

Spanier, G. (1983) Married and Unmarried Cohabitation in the United States. *Journal of Marriage and the Family*, May: 277–88.

Stein, P. (1983) Singlehood. In E. Macklin and R. Rubin (eds) *Contemporary Families and Alternative Lifestyles*. Beverly Hills: Sage Publications.

Steiner, G. Y. (1981) *The Futility of Family Policy*. Washington, DC: Brookings Institute.

Thornton, A. and Freedman, D. (1983) The Changing American Family. *Population Bulletin* 38(4): 7–10. Washington, DC: Population Reference Bureau.

US Department of Health and Human Services (1980) *The Status of Children, Youth and Families, 1979*. August. Cited in the National Urban League (1984) *The State of Black America 1983*. New York: National Urban League.

Vickery, C. (1979) Women's Economic Contribution to the Family. In R. E. Smith (ed.) *The Subtle Revolution: Women at Work*. Washington, DC: Urban Institute, pp. 159–200.

Walsh, F. (1983) *Normal Family Processes*. New York: Guilford Press.

Yeatman, G. W. (1980) Coin Rubbing: Vietnamese Attitudes towards Health Care. *Journal of American Medical Association* 244: 2748–749.

21 Older women and social work curricula

Nancy R. Hooyman

Introduction

This chapter reviews older women's economic, health, and social status, and emphasizes how a cycle of caring for others throughout their lives shapes many of the problems faced by women in old age. Ways to incorporate social work curriculum content on older women, both as a specialized course and within required policy and practice courses, are also presented.

Older women tended to be invisible in gerontological research and practice as well as in the women's movement until the mid-1970s. For example, women were not added to the Baltimore Longitudinal Study – one of the major studies of older people across the life course – until 1978. The first older women's caucus at the Annual Meetings of the Gerontological Society did not meet until 1975. Research on women's issues, such as menopause, estrogen replacement therapy, and retirement, has been relatively limited. Services for women in the middle and older years have often been based on misconceptions. Some therapists, for example, have viewed older women as unsuitable clients. Divorced or widowed women under the age of sixty who do not qualify for either social security, disability, or aid to mothers with dependent children fall into a social service 'black hole' as displaced homemakers. Until the late 1970s, the women's movement, composed primarily of younger professional women, did not define aging as a feminist issue. Primarily as a result of consciousness-raising by groups such as the Older Women's League, more younger women have become concerned about the economic and social issues affecting older women and have aligned themselves with older women to influence their own aging experiences.

Despite the youth-orientation of many feminist leaders, aging has now emerged as a major feminist issue. The major reason for this change is that older women are the fastest growing segment of our population, making the aging society primarily a female society. In 1980, women represented 59.7 per cent of the United States population aged sixty years and over. For every 100 men over age 65, there are 127 women, increasing to 220 women to every 100 men by age 85 and over (Markson 1983). These disproportionate ratios are due primarily to male–female differences in mortality, with women outliving men by an average of eight years (Verbrugge, 1985). Projections over the next four decades suggest that succeeding cohorts of elderly will continue this pattern, resulting in a large population of old-old women from the so-called baby boom cohort (US Bureau of the Census 1980a). Demography thus shapes the lives of older women.

In addition, the problems of aging are increasingly the problems of women. For example, threats to social security, inadequate health care, and insufficient pensions are issues for women of all ages. Increasingly, older women are not only the recipients of social and health services, but also are cared for by other women, whether as unpaid daughters and daughters-in-law or as staff within public social services, nursing homes, and hospitals. Women's caregiving responsibilities combined with their employment in low status, poorly paid jobs serve to limit their economic and health options in old age. Their status as unpaid caregivers and underpaid employees are interconnected. As a result, women of all ages are interdependent in their shared goals of ensuring women's autonomy in old age and preventing excessive sacrifices among women who provide care to both younger and older generations. Accordingly, the conditions of older women must be central to the consciousness of all women as well as to social work professionals.

An organizing concept for curriculum content on older women is women's role as caregivers throughout their life cycle. Caregiving for dependents – children, spouses, or older relatives – is not a time-limited episode for most women. Their caregiving career and status are played out in their economic, social, and health inequities in old age. Women who devoted their lives to attending to others' needs often face years of living alone on low or poverty level incomes, with inadequate health care, in substandard housing, and with little chance for employment to supplement their limited resources. Frequently outliving their children and husbands, they have no one to care for them and are more likely than their male counterparts to be institutionalized. Tish Sommers (1975), the first President of the Older Women's League, highlighted these inequities: 'Motherhood and apple pie are sacred in our society, but neither guarantees security in old age.'

Older women's economic status

The position of older women in this society and the ways in which they experience aging are largely determined by the segregation of labor that assigns primary family obligation to the woman of the household (Stone and Minkler 1984). Most women in the current cohort of older women were socialized to marry, have children, and respond to others' needs. Caregiving was assumed to be a lifelong and universal role. Even when employed, women's caregiving responsibilities remained central to their identities. The primacy of women's caregiving role has major negative economic repercussions for them. As uncompensated work, it has prevented women from being salaried and from accumulating retirement benefits. The 'in and out' pattern of their paid work has also reduced their opportunities to achieve pension vesting rights as well as having ensured lower wages as a basis for determining retirement income. Older women who attempt to enter the labor force after years devoted to caregiving generally encounter employers who discount their homemaking skills and experiences. Thus women who in young adulthood and middle age followed society's rules by marrying and fulfilling household obligations face structural economic inequality in old age. Gender stratification in youth, based on our society's devaluation of caregiving, produces economic stratification in old age.

Women's institutionalized economic dependency throughout life as wives, mothers, and daughters is played out in their low socioeconomic status in old age. Although women comprise 59 per cent of those over the age of sixty-five, they account for 72 per cent of the elderly poor. With a poverty rate of 19 per cent, older women are among the poorest groups in our society (US Bureau of the Census 1980a). In 1983, older women's median income was $5,999 compared to older men's median income of $9,766. Nearly half of women aged sixty-five and over had incomes below $5,000 in 1983 compared to only 20 per cent of their male peers (Rix 1984). The incidence of poverty increases dramatically for older women living alone, for minority women, and for those aged seventy-five and over. The poverty rate among unmarried older women living alone in 1982 was 28.7 per cent (Rix 1984). Poorest of all are older black women, who in 1980 had a median annual income of approximately $3,500, with 82 per cent classified as poor and 'near poor' (US Bureau of the Census 1980a). For many women, such negative conditions are the last stage in a history of little power or social value. For others, no longer able to derive their status and income from a man, the experience and consequences of poverty are new.

One of the major reasons for older women's low economic status is that most in this current cohort aged sixty-five and over did not work consistently for pay. Their labor force participation rate was 9.7 per cent in 1950, rose slightly in the 1960s and 1970s, and then dropped to 7.8 per cent by 1983. Although black women were more likely to have been employed than white women, their rates of employment throughout their lives were not significantly higher (Rix 1984). Women's lower labor force participation generally made them dependent on men for their income and retirement benefits. Unable to build up their own economic security, most women of previous generations have been 'one man away from poverty' (Friends of the San Francisco Commission on the Status of Women 1980).

Such dependency means that widowed or divorced women lose their primary source of income. Since 85 per cent of wives outlive their husbands, they are then dependent on either their own retirement income, if they have been employed, or their husband's social security or private pension. Most husbands of previous generations covered by private pensions did not select survivors' benefits, which has resulted in only 2 per cent of widows benefiting from their husbands' pensions. Of those eligible for benefits, only 25 per cent receive them in full, primarily because of misinformation (Bernstein 1980). Most women have not been able to count on an adequate income from insurance policies. In one study, for example, the median life insurance claim made by widows whose husbands were at least 65 at their death was only $4,163 (American Council of Life Insurance and Life Insurance Marketing and Research Association 1983 in Rix 1984.) Income level and marital status are thus inextricably linked for the 63 per cent of older women who are currently living without a spouse (O'Rand 1984).

Most women face old age with only social security as their economic mainstay. As 63 per cent of the aged social security beneficiaries, women are three times more likely than men to receive only the minimum social security benefits. In 1982, 66 per cent of women received benefits below the poverty line. The social security lifeline for the majority of older women is thus often stretched thin. The primary reasons for these economic disparities are that women have been more likely to have an interrupted paid work history because of marriage and child-rearing and, when employed, to be low-paid. Even though five years of no or low work benefits can be dropped from the average in computing social security benefits, most women have taken off more than five years from employment to provide care for children. It is not surprising that only 37 per cent of the women applying for social security benefits based on their own earnings in 1980 had a continuous earnings record since 1937. Women who have devoted their lives to family caregiving get no social security benefits and cannot receive disability supports on their own, despite the economic value of their household labor to their families. Since a person must have worked five of the last ten years to qualify for social security disability, women – more likely to have interrupted work for family responsibilities – are less likely to qualify. Social security and disability regulations in effect punish women who have taken time out to perform traditional family caregiving roles. Women who do attempt to balance both employment and family responsibilities often find their benefits based on their husbands' work record to be greater than their own, because of their lower earnings.

Women who cared for husbands and children for years frequently end up alone with only subsistence social security incomes. Widows at age 65 can receive full social security benefits based on their husband's or their own earnings, whichever is larger. Since most women over age 60 are unemployed, they generally opt for immediate income and the lower benefits at age 62, which then remain reduced even after age 65. The average social security benefit for widows was $379 a month in 1982 – an inadequate income, even for women who are no longer caring for other family members (US Department of Health and Human Services 1983).

Older divorced women have even fewer financial resources than widows. Divorced women who were married less than ten years are entitled to no social security benefits from their ex-spouse. Divorced women with inconsistent labor force participation often have little or no social security protection in their own right (US Joint Economic Committee 1980). The dire economic conditions faced by divorced and widowed homemakers have prompted proposals to ensure older homemakers' economic security, such as paying social security or some other income to homemakers, but none of these has received widespread support nor is likely to receive support in the near future.

Even when women of this current cohort aged sixty-five and over were employed, their caregiving roles have generally limited their job and income opportunities. The career pattern of steady work shared by most men is alien to the discontinuities and delayed career entry characteristic of women's lives, placing women at a competitive disadvantage in the job market. Women start full-time work on average five years later than men (O'Rand 1983). In a Census Bureau study, 82 per cent of the women aged 45–64 in the sample experienced at least one work interruption of six months or more, generally for family reasons, as compared to 12 per cent for men. Work interruptions cause married women aged 45–64 to lose an average of 37 per cent of their potential work years (Rix 1984), thereby limiting their earnings and pension opportunities.

Women socially isolated by caregiving responsibilities have often lacked the confidence, academic degrees, and knowledge of resources conducive to securing decent paying jobs. Employers who discount women because of their age, sex, and limited education, have generally been unwilling to credit their past experiences as caregivers and home managers. Because housework has no monetary value and is not regarded as work in our society, women often must settle for low-skilled, low-paying jobs which require little specialized training and afford limited advancement opportunities.

These forces have converged to concentrate women in the secondary labor market characterized by insecurity, low income, few fringe benefits, and no pensions. Service and administrative/clerical support positions claim about half of all middle-aged and older women workers. Eighty per cent of women are employed in approximately twenty-five job categories, most of which involve attending to others' needs and thus are an extension of their familial caregiving roles (Rix 1984). As a result, women at home and in the workplace generally give more support to others than they receive themselves.

Another example of how the deleterious consequences of occupational segregation on the basis of sex persist into old age is that women are less likely than men to be in jobs covered by private pensions. Approximately 44 per cent of men received a private pension in 1982 as compared to less than 20 per cent of women who had been employed, largely because women have shorter paid work careers in low-paying, 'pink collar' occupations. Even when women receive private pensions, their benefit income is approximately half that of men (O'Rand 1984). Pensions plans reward the long-term steady worker with low mobility and high earnings, again penalizing women who have interrupted their paid work to perform family caregiving responsibilities. Although the Employee Retirement Security Act (ERISA) was intended to rectify some of these inequities, it did not address problems emanating from women's diverse work patterns. For example, because of caregiving responsibilities, women are more likely than men to work part-time, but ERISA did not require employers to provide pensions for part-time employees. Ironically, men can perform military service without losing pension credits, but this is not so for women who interrupt their careers to care for children, older parents, or spouses.

These inequities in pensions and social security have converged in women's forming nearly three-fourths of the elder supplemental security income (SSI) recipients. In 1982, the monthly SSI benefit was $284 (O'Rand 1984). As a means-tested program, SSI also carries a stigma of dependency on government support. More likely than men to depend on government assistance, older women are also most likely to be hurt by cuts in income support programs or freezes in social security benefits (Coalition on Women and the Budget 1983).

In summary, women's patterns of discontinuous paid work are related to their child-bearing and child-rearing responsibilities and to their husbands' job-related mobility. Their interrupted work lives combined with lower earnings and limited retirement options produce a double jeopardy for economic status in old age. How this double jeopardy increases their health risks is discussed next.

Older women's health status

Women's prior family caregiving responsibilities and limited economic opportunities adversely affect their physical and mental health in old age. These employment and caregiving patterns also culminate in reduced access to health insurance and quality medical care, particularly for those who lack private health insurance through employment and must depend on Medicaid.

Patterns of childbirth and thus of child-rearing responsibilities also appear to influence women's health. For example, the early scheduling of childbirth seems to be strongly associated with a greater incidence of cancers of the breast and of other reproductive organs. As succeeding cohorts of women delay or forgo child-bearing, the configuration of days of sickness and cause of death among older women may shift, with women perhaps experiencing fewer chronic diseases as a result. The association between earlier caregiving responsibilities and later health status is an area ripe for additional research (Rossi 1980).

Family and work patterns directly affect access to adequate health care, health maintenance information, and dental care. Specifically, the workplace determines such access through opportunities to enroll in group insurance plans. Most insurance systems exclude the occupation of homemaker, except as a dependent. As a result, older women who are never or sporadically employed generally have inadequate health insurance. Low-income divorced or widowed women, unable to rely upon their husands' insurance, are especially disadvantaged. Some uninsured women gamble on staying healthy until qualifying for Medicare coverage at the age of sixty-five. Since the incidence of chronic diseases is higher among older women than men, many women do not win this gamble. Groups such as the Older Women's League advocate conversion laws requiring insurance companies to allow widowed and divorced women to convert their former husbands' insurance policies for themselves. Even with adequate health insurance, older women spend 25 per cent of their median annual income for out-of-pocket health care costs, particularly for medications not covered by Medicaid or Medicare.

Because of their lower socioeconomic status, older women are more likely than men to depend on Medicaid, forming over two-thirds of Medicaid recipients (Coalition on Women and the Budget 1984). An insidious negative effect of this dependency is that health care providers, fearing financial losses, are often unwilling to accept Medicaid patients. Male/female differences in longevity, marital status, and income are central in assessing the impacts of recent increases in Medicaid co-payments and deductibles. Women outnumber men two to one among the frail elderly, where health care use and costs are greatest. This means that as Medicaid costs are shifted to the patient, more low-income frail women will be unable to afford health care. Recent co-payment provisions in Medicaid force some women to choose between prescriptions and groceries or clinic visits and the bus fare to get there.

Their limited insurance options and greater dependence on Medicaid are especially problematic because 85 per cent of older women have some kind of chronic disease or disability. Compared to their male counterparts, they also experience more injuries and days of restricted activity and being confined to bed and consequent higher health care costs. These measures are typically indicators of chronic disorders, although they may also reflect women's greater likelihood of taking curative action when ill. Among people aged seventy-five and over, sex differences in patterns of illness become more dramatic, culminating in sex ratios of three to four females for every male over the age of seventy-five in skilled care facilities (US Department of Health and Human Services 1983).

Older women experience arthritis, diabetes, hypertension, visual impairment, most digestive and urinary disorders, and most orthopedic problems more frequently than do older men. They also face health problems related to their child-bearing functions, including breast, cervical, and uterine cancers, all of which have increased in recent years, as well as high-risk complications from hysterectomies. On the other hand, even though women face more chronic health problems, most of these are not life-threatening. For example, although women generally have higher serum cholesterol levels, they are less likely to suffer from cerebrovascular and coronary heart diseases (until after menopause) than are men (Kerzner 1983). Such differences in types of chronic health problems may be one reason why women live longer than men, even though they are less healthy (Kerzner 1983). Women's problems do, however, interfere with their daily functioning and require frequent physician contacts and hospitalizations.

One especially painful chronic condition disproportionately experienced by women is osteoporosis, or loss of bone mass. Osteoporosis is four times more likely to occur in older women than men. Women begin losing bone mass between 30 to 35 years of age, resulting in a 35 per cent reduction in their bone mineral content by 65 or 70 years of age. This results in an increase in the risk of bone fracture, generally of the hip, as well as of subsequent fractures (Lindsay 1981).

The higher incidence of hip fractures among older women is of concern, because of the approximate 15 per cent mortality rate within three months following a fracture, generally as a result of operative complications (Jensen and Tondevold 1979; Lindsay 1981). The threat of bone fractures can engender numerous fears among older women – of additional falls and fractures, hospitalization, institutionalization, loss of independence, and death. Accordingly, older women's social worlds can become increasingly constrained, resulting in isolation and loneliness.

Menopause is another condition that can be troublesome for some women. Menopause may be perceived as a difficult life transition because of women's roles, not because of the physiological changes themselves. Although menopause is a normal physical process, occurring between 45 and 55 years of age, social and cultural expectations have defined it as a disease. As a result, many women believe that depression, loss of sexual desire, and signs of aging such as wrinkled skin and weight gain are inevitable accompaniments of menopause. Although 80 per cent of menopausal women report uncomfortable symptoms, such as hot flushes and sweats, these changes do not interfere with most women's functioning nor cause psychological distress. Other symptoms reported by middle-aged women, such as headaches, dizziness, palpitations, sleeplessness, depression, and weight increase, show no direct relationship to menopause (Notman 1981). Instead, these symptoms may be associated with other societally defined losses, such as women feeling devalued by the loss of their reproductive functions or no longer considered sexually attractive.

Although the disease model of menopause links depression with endocrine changes, depression among post-menopausal women appears to be more closely associated with psychosocial factors, oftentimes interconnected with caregiving roles, than with physiological variables. Menopausal women experiencing depression tend to have invested heavily in child-rearing responsibilities and to lack supportive family or friends, other satisfying roles, and skills for coping with the loss of family caregiving (Bart 1981; Neugarten *et al.* 1968). Because of the cultural value attached to motherhood, some women experiencing the 'empty nest' can feel superfluous until they achieve other sources of self-esteem. Health care providers have been prone to treat the symptoms of depression with drugs or to assume that post-menopausal women are 'too old' to benefit from therapeutic interventions. More recently, efforts have been made to link women with new ways to exert control over their lives, such as assertiveness training, and to utilize counseling and social supports. Social support groups have been especially effective in helping women identify satisfying roles other than culturally prescribed ones of caregiving.

Alcohol and drug misuse may also be associated with women's loss of mothering roles (Rathbone-McCuan and Roberds 1980). The combined effects of aging and alcohol use decrease the resilience of all body systems, resulting in a decline in both physical resources and emotional stamina as well as problems with the central nervous system, circulation, liver, gastrointestinal tract, kidneys, and sleep. Women who become alcohol-dependent experience more days of sickness and more alcohol-related deaths than do male alcoholics. The physical and mental health problems facing older women – especially depression and substance abuse – are often aggravated by their social status, particularly their greater probability of living alone, which is examined below.

Social status of older women

After a lifetime of caring for others, many older women find themselves alone, without economic security, safe accommodation, or someone to care for them, and thus with reduced abilities to live independently when health problems arise. Another factor that increases the probability of being along among this current cohort of older women is that one in five has either been childless throughout life or has survived her offspring, often because many women of child-bearing age during the Depression limited their family size (Hess and Waring 1983). Widows without children have been found to be more lonely and dissatisfied than widows with grown children (Lipman and Longino 1980). The absence of children and spouse also increases the chance of being institutionalized before the age of seventy-five (Treas 1977). Accordingly, after the age of eighty-five, one in four women, particularly never married and widowed women, are in nursing homes. This pattern suggests that women are more likely to be institutionalized for social rather than medical reasons. Women form 70 per cent of the residents of nursing homes, with close to 90 per cent of them widowed or single, oftentimes dependent on Medicaid and on younger, low-paid women for their care. The nursing home industry is increasingly a women's industry, with low-income women as both residents and attendants.

Although most women in the past were socialized to marry and depend on a man, more than 40 per cent of the current generation live alone for nearly one-third of their adult lives, primarily because of widowhood or divorce. Women living with their husbands represent only one-third of all women aged sixty-five and over, and 20 per cent live with other family members. The percentage of women over the age of seventy-five and living with husbands drops to less than one-fourth while nearly half live alone (Rix 1984; US Senate 1981). In addition to high rates of widowhood, the current cohort of women aged sixty-five and over include a relatively high proportion – 7 to 8 per cent – who have never been married, so that a cohort effect also helps to explain the large numbers of women in their seventies and eighties living without husbands.

The patterns for women to live longer, to marry older men, and, with increasing age, to remain unmarried after the deaths of their husbands makes the status of widowhood a largely female experience. Fifty-two per cent of older women are widowed as compared to 14 per cent of their male peers, with fifty-six as the average age of widowhood. This percentage increases dramatically with age, with 73 per cent of women over eighty years of age widowed. As described earlier, the primary negative consequence of widowhood is poverty, which is experienced by approximately 33 per cent of older widows living alone. Women who adjust best to widowhood have been independent throughout their lives, have higher educations and incomes, and possess coping skills and feelings of personal control – factors that tend to be unrelated, or inversely related, to years devoted to serving others' needs through caregiving (Lopata 1981).

Older women are not immune to the increasing divorce rate; 16 per cent of recent divorces occurred among women aged forty-five and over, a rate that is increasing (Lesnoff-Caravaglia 1984; Warlick 1983). Compared to their married or widowed age peers, divorced older women's financial, health, social, and emotional status is more precarious. An example of the devastating economic impact of divorce is that less than half of currently divorced women receive any property settlement (US Bureau of the Census 1980a). In addition to their lower socioeconomic status, divorced older women have poorer health, higher mortality rates, and lower levels of life satisfaction than divorced men or married and widowed women (Hess and Waring 1983).

Older widowed and divorced women have fewer remarriage options than their male peers. The primary barriers are the disproportionate ratio of women to men aged sixty-five and over and the cultural prejudices against women marrying younger men. At the age of sixty-five and over, remarriage rates are 17 per 1,000 for unmarried men compared to only 2 per 1,000 for unmarried women. Likewise, 70 per cent of men seventy-five years and older are married as compared to only 22 per cent of their female counterparts, with women's chances for remarriage dramatically declining with age (Hess and Waring 1983).

When older women do live with others, they are likely to be caring for their husbands or for frail older parents, typically their mothers. Women, some of whom may be sixty or seventy years old, comprise approximately 80 per cent of the caregivers of elderly relatives (Brody 1985). As invisible laborers, women's work is essential to the health care system and to their relatives' long-term care, but is not supported by social and health policies. Exhausted by round-the-clock caregiving demands, female caregivers are at risk of depression, exhaustion, and physical illness. In fact, their sickness or death often precipitates the institutionalization of the person for whom they cared (Teresi *et al.* 1980). Since they must spend-down their assets to be eligible for Medicaid services, many women end up financially destitute from caring for and institutionalizing their relatives. As the sex segregation of labor continues throughout the life-cycle, the disadvantaged economic position of older women can be compounded.

Fortunately, the number of exceptions to patterns of economic deprivation and social isolation is growing. With their lifelong experiences of caring for others, older women tend to be skilled at forming and sustaining friendships with each other, which provide them with social support and intimacy. Even when their friends die, women generally establish new relationships, exchanging affection and material assistance outside their families (Arling 1980; Powers and Bultena 1980). Support groups for widows and family caregivers build upon such reciprocal exchange relations among peers. In general, older women have fewer economic but more social resources than do older men (Atchley 1982; O'Rand 1983). One function of feminists' affirmation of women's competencies has been to encourage them to support each other rather than depend on men, as evidenced by the growth of shared households, older women's support and advocacy groups, and intergenerational alliances.

With age, some women become comfortable for the first time about being open about their lesbianism and their strong emotional bonds with other women, but may face rejection from their adult children when they do so (Raphael and Robinson 1980). Other lesbians have coped with discrimination all their lives and have developed lifelong friendships equivalent to family bonds in their intensity. Those with families may be bitter if relatives are not supportive during long-term illnesses. In addition, older lesbians face barriers from human service professionals. For example, hospital and nursing home staff may refuse to release medical information or to allow a lesbian partner to visit, while permitting visits from more emotionally distant family members. Social workers must be sensitive to older lesbians' needs for information about their legal options regarding finances, inheritance, funeral arrangements, and medical care. In addition, social workers should not assume heterosexuality when interviewing older women, should discuss homophobia in training their own staff, and should be prepared to address the particular issues faced by older lesbians.

Curriculum implications

The challenge for social work educators is how to incorporate course content regarding the ways women's family caregiving roles are interconnected with their economic, social, and health status. The ideal curriculum format is a separate course on older women, within a gerontology or women's concentration. A specialized course can encompass the changes and problems faced by older women as well as appropriate macro-level and direct practice interventions. Few social work schools or departments, however, have the resources for such a specialized course. In such instances, content on older women can be integrated into courses on social policy and social work practice. This integrative approach has the advantage of exposing all students to older women's life conditions, thereby increasing their awareness of how issues connected to women's family caregiving roles across the life-span may emerge in professional practice. The integrative approach, however, requires faculty development. Faculty knowledgeable about older women and family caregiving dilemmas need to suggest appropriate readings, case materials, and audiovisuals to faculty who teach required courses. This chapter could serve as introductory reading for faculty unfamiliar with aging as a women's issue.

Regardless of the particular course or curriculum format, basic principles for developing course content on older women are:

1. Older women's position in society and the ways in which they experience aging are shaped by their place in the social structure. The concepts of the sex segregation of labor and women's isolation in the labor market are essential to understanding their economic, health, and social status in old age.
2. Women's diversity by age, geographic region, ethnicity, socioeconomic class, and sexual preference must be made explicit when identifying older women's needs and the relevant policy/practice implications.
3. Although facing complex problems, older women possess great strengths, as witnessed by their sheer ability to survive. Course content must present the richness and power of older women's lives, while also recognizing the structural obstacles to their achievement of power.
4. Adequately addressing older women's problems requires structural changes

in the way employment and family caregiving are organized in our society. Therefore, when individual or group treatment interventions are discussed, the need for systemic changes must also be recognized. The interaction between practice and policy must be explicit, both through the types of problems and solutions posed as well as through the models represented by guest speakers, course readings, and audiovisuals.

5. Since most students have probably not interacted extensively with older women, older women should be invited as guest speakers. Women could be selected on the basis of their contrasting lifestyles (e.g. a woman subsisting only on supplemental security income and a career woman with a sizable private pension, or a lesbian and a long-term married woman) as well as their different coping strategies (e.g. a woman who tries to bring about change through organized political activities or a woman who uses her informal networks of friends and neighbors to enable her to remain in her own home). Older women should receive an honorarium for their guest-speaking.

6. Students should also have opportunities to interview older women and to acquire a first-hand view of their daily lives. Older respondents can be conceptualized as the students, partners-in-learning. Prior to such interviews, however, the instructor should develop clear guidelines and obtain the necessary human subjects clearance in respect of older women's rights.

7. The course should include not only didactic presentations, but also experiential opportunities to enhance students' professional sensitivity by modifying their agist, sexist, racist, and homophobic attitudes toward older women. Students need to be aware of their own negative images of older women, and then be presented with positive models for growing old to counter such images. Listing the adjectives they immediately think of regarding older women or sharing examples of older women whom they respect are ways to tap into students' images. Students should also grapple with their own aging, perhaps through time fantasies about their lives at the ages of 65, 75, and 85.

Content on older women should be integrated into required policy courses, since the issues of older women involve major policy dilemmas regarding financial, social, and health care services, as well as how roles are structured in our society. As both the primary users and providers of public services, women of all ages daily confront deficiencies in how services are structured. As noted earlier, younger and older women are increasingly interdependent around policies regarding family caregiving, social security inequities, pension reforms, and access to health care. If unaware of aging issues, social policy instructors may discuss social security, Medicare, or Medicaid without explicitly referring to the differential treatment of men and women. How existing policies hinder women's full access to resources in old age should be examined. When analyzing income maintenance policies, for example, instructors should discuss how social security in old age perpetuates employment and income inequities stemming from caregiving roles at a younger age. The assumptions about marriage, caregiving, and 'deserving' work that underlie social security should be reviewed in terms of benefit inequities for older women, thereby illustrating social security as a critical policy issue for women of all ages. Possible changes in the way social security is structured, such as earnings sharing (e.g. each individual receives half of the total retirement credits earned by a couple during their marriage) or credits for homemaking, can be analyzed in terms of their potential consequences for women. Alternatively, when discussing health care financing, instructors can highlight how women's welfare as family caregivers is not a central goal of most long-term care policies, particularly Medicare and Medicaid which are not oriented to supporting in-home care. The ways in which the lack of policies supporting family caregivers perpetuates gender inequities should also be examined. In their course assignments, students can examine how the gender inequities inherent in various policies and in societal definitions of women's primacy as caregivers are perpetuated throughout the life course.

Content on older women can be incorporated into practice courses on the family, women, and aging as well as into micro methods courses. Practice analyses must begin with recognizing that many practitioners view older women as undesirable clients. The extent to which such perceptions are created by institutionalized sexism and agism must be examined. Students also need to grapple with the question of whether different treatment modalities should be developed specifically for older women. For example, to what extent do techniques for working with younger depressed or alcoholic women need to be modified to account for the different socialization and life experiences of this current generation of older women?

Practice courses should include discussions of the use of informal social networks, such as support groups. These are frequently effective in reducing female caregivers' isolation, giving them 'permission' to meet their own needs, and expanding their awareness of gaps in services to which they are entitled. Raising older women's consciousness and politicizing them is a powerful function of such groups, and one appropriate to addressing the systemic causes of the difficulties experienced individually. Direct service practitioners must avoid suggesting individual responsibility for societally shaped problems. For example, in support groups and educational programs for women caregivers, professionals as presumed experts must not imply that older women simply need to become more efficient at handling their multiple demands.

Whether in policy or practice courses, the central theme is that old age has a double edge for women. Women are the primary users of public policies and family practices that affect how older people are treated and cared for as well as the primary providers of care. How older women and their caregiving roles are influenced by and influence social policy and practice must thus become central to the consciousness of all social workers.

References

Arling, Greg (1980) The Elderly Widow and Her Family, Neighbors, and Friends. In Marie Fuller and Cora Martin (eds) *The Older Woman: Lavender Rose or Gray Panther*. Springfield, IL: Charles C. Thomas.

Atchley, Robert C. (1982) The Process of Retirement: Comparing Men and Women. In M. Szinovacs (ed.) *Women's Retirement*, vol. 6, Sage Yearbooks in Women's Policy Studies. Beverly Hills: Sage, pp. 153–68.

Bart, Pauline (1981) Mental Health Issues: Is the End of the Curse a Blessing? In J. Porcino (ed.) *Health Issues of Older Women*. Stony Brook, NY: State University of New York.

Bernard, Jessie (1979) Policy and Women's Income. In Jean Lipman-Blumen and Jessie Bernard (eds) *Sex Roles and Social Policy*. Beverly Hills: Sage.

Backman, L. and Houser, B. (1982) The Consequences of Childlessness on the Social-Psychological Wellbeing of Older Women. *Journal of Gerontology* 37: 243–50.

Bernstein, M. C. (1980) Forecasting Women's Retirement Income: Cloudy and Colder and 25 Percent Chance of Poverty. In M. Fuller and C. Martin (eds) *The Older Woman*. Springfield, IL: Charles C. Thomas, pp. 243–47.

Brody, E. (1985) Parent Care as a Normative Family Stress. *The Gerontologist* 25(1): 19–30.

Coalition on Women and the Budget (1984) *Inequality of Sacrifice: The Impact of the Reagan Budget on Women*. Washington, DC: National Women's Law Center.

Federal Council on the Aging (1981) *The Need for Long-Term Care: Information and Issues*. DHHS publication No. OHDS81–20709. Washington DC: US Department of Health and Human Services.

Friends of the San Francisco Commission on the Status of Women (1980) *Womennews*, December, p. 1.

Hess, Beth and Waring, Joan (1983) Family Relationships of Older Women: A Women's Issue. In Elizabeth Markson (ed.) *Older Women*. Lexington, MA: Lexington Books.

Jensen, S. and Tondevold, E. (1979) Mortality After Hip Fractures. *Acta Orthopaedica Scandinavica* 50: 161.

Kerzner, Lawrence (1983) Physical Changes After Menopause. In Elizabeth Markson (ed.) *Older Women*. Lexington, MA: Lexington Books, pp. 299–315.

Lesnoff-Caravaglia, G. (ed.) (1984) *The World of the Older Woman*. New York: Human Sciences Press.

Lindsay, Robert (1981) Osteoporosis. In J. Porcino (ed.) *Health Issues of Older Women*. Stony Brook, NY: State University of New York.

Lipman, A. and Longino, C. (1980) The Wife, The Widow and The Old Maid: Support Network Differentials of Older Women. Paper presented at the 33rd Annual Scientific Meeting of the Gerontological Society of America, San Diego, CA, November.

Lopata, H. Z. (1981) Widowhood and Husband Sanctification. *Journal of Marriage in the Family* 43: 439–50.

Markson, Elizabeth (1983) *Older Women*. Lexington, MA: Lexington Books.

Minkler, M. and Stone, R. (1985) The Feminization of Poverty and Older Women. *The Gerontologist* 25: 351–57.

Neugarten, Bernice, Wood, Vivian, Kraines, Ruth, and Loomis, Barbara (1968) Women's Attitudes Toward the Menopause. In B. Neugarten (ed.) *Middle Age and Aging.* Chicago: University of Chicago Press, pp. 195–200.

Notman, M. (1981) Changing Roles for Women at Mid-life. In W. H. Norman and T. J. Scaramella (eds) *Mid-life Developmental and Clinical Issues.* New York: Brunner/ Mazel, pp. 95–109.

O'Rand, Angela M. (1984) Women. In E. Palmore (ed.) *Handbook of the Aged in the United States.* Westport, CT: Greenwood Press.

O'Rand, Angela M. (1983) Loss of Work Role and Subjective Health Assessment in Later Life Among Men and Unmarried Women. In A. C. Kerckhoff (ed.) *Research in Sociology of Education and Socialization,* vol. 5. San Francisco: JAI Press.

O'Rand, A. M. and Henretta, J. C. (1982a) Delayed Work Careers, Industrial Pension Structure and Early Retirement Among Unmarried Women. *American Sociological Review* 47: 365–73.

—— (1982b) Mid-Life Work History and Retirement Income. In M. Szinovacz (ed.) *Women's Retirement.* Sage Yearbooks in Women's Policy Studies, vol. 6. Beverly Hills: Sage.

Powers, Edward and Bultena, Gordon (1980) Sex Differences in Intimate Friendships of Old Age. In Marie Fuller and Cora Ann Martin (eds) *The Older Woman: Lavender Rose or Gray Panther.* Springfield, IL: Charles C. Thomas, pp. 190–204.

Public Health Service Task Force (1985) Report on Women's Health Issues. *Public Health Reports* 100(1): 73–104.

Raphael, Sharon and Robinson, Mina (1980) The Older Lesbian: Love Relationships and Friendship Pattern. *Alternate Lifestyles* 3(2): 207–29.

Rathbone-McCuan, E. and Roberds, L. A. (1980) Treatment of the Older Female Alcoholic. *Focus on Women* 1: 104–29.

Rix, Sara (1984) *Older Women: The Economics of Aging.* Washington, DC: Women's Research and Education Institute.

Rossi, A. S. (1980) Life-Span Theories and Women's Lives. *Signs* 6(1): 4–32.

Scott, Hilda (1984) *Working Your Way to the Bottom: The Feminization of Poverty.* London: Pandora Press.

Shanas, Ethel (1981) Older Parents and Middle-Aged Children. Paper presented at meetings of International Association of Gerontology, Hamburg, Germany, 11–17 July.

Silverman, P., Mackenzie, D., Pettipas, M., and Welson, E. (eds) (1974) *Helping Each Other in Widowhood.* New York: Health Sciences Publishing.

Social Security Administration (1982) Annual Statistical Supplement, 1981. *Social Security Bulletin,* 45.

Sommers, T. (1975) On Growing Older Female (an interview). *Aging,* November–December: 11–12.

Stone, R. and Minkler, M. (1984) The Sociopolitical Significance of Women's Retirement. In M. Minkler and C. L. Estes (eds) *Readings in the Political Economy of Aging.* New York: Baywood Publishers, pp. 225–38.

Taylor, Sue Perkins (1982) Mental Health and Successful Coping Among Aged Black Women. In R. Manuel (ed.) *Minority Aging.* Westport, CT: Greenwood Press, pp. 95–103.

Teresi, J. A., Toner, J. A., Bennett, R. G., and Wilson, D. E. (1980) Factors Related to

Family Attitudes Toward Institutionalizing Older Relatives. Paper presented at the 33rd Annual Scientific Meeting of the Gerontological Society, San Diego, CA, November, pp. 19–22.

Treas, Judith (1977) Family Support Systems for the Aged: Some Social and Demographic Considerations. *The Gerontologist* 17 (December): 486–91.

Tuchman, G. (1978) Introduction. In G. Tuchman, A. K. Daniels, and J. Benet (eds) *Health and Home: Images of Women in the Mass Media*. New York: Oxford University Press.

US Bureau of the Census (1979) Social and Economic Characteristics of the Older Population. *Current Population Reports, Special Studies*. Series P–25, no. 85. Washington, DC: US Government Printing Office.

—— (1980a) A Statistical Portrait of Women in the United States. *Current Population Reports: Special Studies*. Series P–23, no. 100. Washington, DC: US Government Printing Office.

—— (1980b) *Statistical Abstracts of the U.S.* (101st edn). Series P–60, no. 34, Table 17. Washington, DC: US Government Printing Office.

US Department of Health and Human Services (1983) Social Security Administration. *Social Security Bulletin: Annual Statistical Supplement 1982*. Washington, DC: US Government Printing Office.

US Joint Economic Committee (1980) *Special Study on Economic Change, Social Security and Pensions: Programs of Equity and Security*. Washington, DC: US Government Printing Office.

US Senate Special Committee on Aging (1981) *Developments on Aging*. Washington, DC: US Government Printing Office.

Verbrugge, L. (1985) An Epidemiological Profile of Older Women. In M. Haug, A. Ford, and M. Shaefor (eds) *The Physical and Mental Health of Aged Women*. New York: Springer, pp. 41–64.

Von Mering, G. and O'Rand, A. M. (1971) Aging, Illness and the Organization of Health Care: A Sociocultural Perspective. In C. L. Fry (ed.) *Dimensions: Aging, Culture in Health*. New York: Praeger, pp. 255–70.

Warlick, J. (1983) Aged Women in Poverty: A Problem without a Solution? In W. F. Browne and L. K. Olson (eds) *Aging and Public Policy*. Westport, CT: Greenwood Press, pp. 35–66.

22 Conclusion

Naomi Gottlieb and Dianne S. Burden

The utility of this book may derive as much from its perspective and analytic framework as from the content of the chapters per se. Constraints of time and space have limited the book's scope. The material presented reflects scholars' views and empirical findings at a particular point in history – the mid-1980s. Without question, future developments will alter viewpoints as well as enhance knowledge. Space limitations have reduced the depth and breadth of the subject areas covered as well as precluded coverage of many other subject areas of importance to women. These areas include women's sexuality, the physically disabled woman, young female children, and class differences among women. The circumstances of lesbians and women of color have been addressed throughout the book, but the conditions of these women's lives, without doubt, need to be described and analyzed more fully. Thus, though we believe the book's contents can be useful and immediately applied to the education of social workers and other helping professionals, the long-term value of this volume may be tested more realistically by the soundness of its frame of reference.

The book's basic perspective, and the one we maintain will have future utility, has two major aspects. First, the circumstances of women's lives are influenced strongly by social, economic, and political forces. Women's work, both in the home and in the marketplace, has long been devalued. Women are the subjects of discrimination and restrictive stereotyping and are at the lower end of the power imbalance in important areas of their lives. A significant portion of the troubling personal experiences which women bring to helping professionals has its sources in these inequitable conditions. Second, because of these societal forces, women grow up in and live in a world different from men. Only recently have these differences in the male/female experience been seriously studied. The book has attempted to demonstrate the validity of societal explanations of women's problems and to describe the empirical knowledge now available about the distinctive world of women. Whatever a woman client's presenting problem, whether represented in this collection or not, we argue that the application of this analysis is potentially more useful than others which focus primarily on intrapsychic factors and which ignore the impact of gender differences on every aspect of a woman's life.

Projected social and economic developments predict a continuation of changes in women's roles. Those changes will make an analysis of women's condition imperative for developing effective social welfare policies and programs. There is general agreement that women will continue to enter the labor force in unprecedented numbers, that the economic underclass will contain a disproportionate number of women, and that as life expectancy increases, women will be over-represented among the elderly. Women will continue to be expected, as they have in the past, to be this society's caregivers for both young and old. In general, they will be caregivers whether they are in the paid workforce or not and whether there are constructive social programs to assist them or not, though we should not be surprised if increasing numbers of individual women reject this role. Scholars and educators will need to persist in their examination of the separate and combined effects on women of these realities. In the past, social workers and other helping professionals have tended to see women's difficulties within an individual or family orientation. We argue that women are not served well when educators and practitioners focus on women's individual circumstances without addressing chronic gender devaluation and the pressures of social, economic, and political realities.

© *Naomi Gottlieb and Dianne S. Burden*

Name index

Subject index

Note: All references are to women unless otherwise stated.

psychology: adolescence and 228–30; barriers in social work administration 102–03; battering and 210; devaluation of women 94, 95; differences between men and women 42, 43; ego 46; female crime and 178–80; menopause and 139; working women and 200–01
public assistance *see* social welfare

quantitative-qualitative debate in research 54–5

racism *see* color
radical community organization 112, 113
rape 180, 236
rational views of women's place 148
reality, pretence that myths are 17
reciprocal: communication 150–52; determinism 232
regional differences in incarceration rates 187, 188, 190
reinforcement/incentives for traditional roles 26, 33, 42, 45, 48, 49
relapse-prevention model 85
relationship: -building 74–8; interpersonal 3; web of 118; *see also* support
religious beliefs of battered woman 213
reproductive system 35, 36, 100; health care and 134–35, 138–40, 268; impact on lives 43; *see also* abortion; childbirth; menopause
research: adolescence 239–40; alcohol and drugs 171; battering and abuse 219; *see also* dilemmas and strategies
Resource Checklist 83
response set in research 57
responsibilities 149; of perpetrators of violence 48; of women *see* carers
responsivity, emotional, of practitioner 75–6
retirement 60, 199
role/s: models 20, 103, 135, 212; playing 219–20; and status 17; *see also* carers; men
romanticization 61, 148
Roxbury Neighborhood House 114

safe house system 210
sampling 59–60
sandwich generation 249
SASB *see* Structural Analysis

schizophrenia study, women excluded from 60, 61
screening paradigm 50
secrecy: alcohol consumption 162–63; battered woman 214
secretarial work devalued by women's participation 17
Security Employee Retirement Income Act (1974) 199
sedation of women 5
self: -actualization 19; -assessment in job search 202; -awareness, practitioner 76; -blame 48–9, 134, 214; -care 149; -concept 148–52; -confidence, low 103; -development, work as 198; -differentiation 152–53; -directed learning 106; -esteem, low 102, 211, 216; -expression, work as 198; -healing 142; -help 86, 141–42; -modification, practitioner 78, 87; promotion in job search 202; -report surveys of offenders 180; -sacrifice 149; -surveillance, practitioner 76, 78; *see also* identity; personal
settlement houses 29, 112–15
sexism in social work 2–6, 14, 15; *see also* core curriculum; specialization
sex-role behaviors 4, 27; in social work profession 97–101; *see also* carers; gender context; socialization
sexual assault 93, 180, 184, 236
sexual harassment 42, 45, 98–9
sexual identity *see* identity
sexuality: adolescent 233–35; assertive 61; *see also* lesbians; reproductive
shelters for battered women and children 210, 217, 220
sin, poverty equated with 29
single women 25, 196, 252–53; older 266–67, 269, 271–72
single-parents 246; child care 33, 120; common form 30, 248; crime 177, 184; discrimination 99; health 33; increase in 250–51; policy and 257; poverty of 6, 31, 32, 247, 248, 250, 257; working 250, 254
sleep, broken 164
Social Darwinism 28, 29–30
social environment, behavior in 12, 41–52; political power imbalance 42–5, 50; screening paradigm 50; self-blame 48–9; social policy and 26–7;